Responsible Technology and Intelligence: A Review Series

Federated Learning in Financial Services: A Path to Secure AI

Responsible Technology and Intelligence: A Review Series

1. A Compendium of Responsible Artificial Intelligence
   Deepak Kumar Jain, Kirti Raj Bhatele, Deepak Garg and *Gaurav Dhiman (Editors), 2025*
2. Ambient Assisted Living: Technological Advances
   Rashmi Gupta, Shashi Shekhar, Jeetendra Kumar and *Gaurav Dhiman (Editors), 2025*
3. Industrial Internet of Things for Responsible Technology
   B.K. Mishra, Gaurav Dhiman, Hemant Kasturiwale, Sujata Alegavi and *Kusum Yadav (Editors), 2026*
4. Robust Biometric Systems and Efficient Data
   Brajesh Kumar Singh, Amrita Rai, Shamimul Qamar, Ravinder Kumar and *Anil Kumar (Editors), 2026*
5. Federated Learning in Financial Services: A Path to Secure AI
   Suvarna Sharma, Jeetendra Kumar, Rashmi Gupta, Valentina E. Balas and *Gaurav Dhiman (Editors), 2027*

Responsible Technology and Intelligence: A Review Series

Federated Learning in Financial Services: A Path to Secure AI

Editors:

Suvarna Sharma
Assistant Professor
Department of Computer Science and Applications
Dr. Vishwanath Karad MIT World Peace University
Pune, India

Jeetendra Kumar
Assistant Professor
Department of Computer Science and Applications
Atal Bihari Vajpayee University
Chhattisgarh, India

Rashmi Gupta
Assistant Professor
Department of Computer Science and Applications
Atal Bihari Vajpayee University
Chhattisgarh, India

Valentina E. Balas
Full Professor
Department of Automatics and Applied Software Faculty of Engineering
"Aurel Vlaicu" University of Arad
Romania

Gaurav Dhiman
Assistant Professor
School of Sciences and Emerging Technologies
Jagat Guru Nanak Dev Punjab State Open University
Patiala, India

CRC Press
Taylor & Francis Group
Boca Raton London New York

CRC Press is an imprint of the
Taylor & Francis Group, an **informa** business
A SCIENCE PUBLISHERS BOOK

First edition published 2027
by CRC Press
2385 NW Executive Center Drive, Suite 320, Boca Raton FL 33431

and by CRC Press
4 Park Square, Milton Park, Abingdon, Oxon, OX14 4RN

CRC Press is an imprint of Taylor & Francis Group, LLC

Library of Congress Cataloging-in-Publication Data (applied for)

ISBN: 978-1-041-13589-0 (hbk)
ISBN: 978-1-041-19105-6 (pbk)
ISBN: 978-1-003-71005-9 (ebk)

DOI: 10.1201/9781003710059

Typeset in Times New Roman
by Prime Publishing Services

Preface

The advent of artificial intelligence has profoundly reshaped financial services, facilitating enhanced predictive accuracy, personalized customer experiences, and sophisticated risk mitigation strategies. Notwithstanding these advancements, the field confronts a persistent dilemma—the necessity for extensive, heterogeneous datasets to develop robust models conflicting with stringent imperatives for data privacy, regulatory compliance (including GDPR, CCPA, and jurisdiction-specific frameworks such as those enforced by the RBI in India), and the safeguarding of sensitive financial information against breaches.

Federated learning (FL) constitutes a paradigmatic innovation that reconciles these competing demands. This decentralized approach enables collaborative model training across disparate institutions or organizational units without necessitating the exchange of raw data. Instead, only aggregated model updates, such as gradients or parameters, are transmitted and synthesized centrally, thereby ensuring that confidential information remains localized. In the financial domain, where data are fragmented across banks, insurers, asset managers, regulatory bodies, and international borders, FL facilitates the harnessing of collective intelligence while upholding privacy and fostering trust.

This book "Federated Learning in Financial Services" offers a systematic and comprehensive examination of FL's theoretical underpinnings, practical implementations, infrastructural requirements, empirical applications, and prospective trajectories within finance. Structured across five sections, the text bridges foundational principles with domain-specific insights, addressing both technical and regulatory dimensions. Section I establishes the conceptual and normative foundations. It introduces FL's pertinence to financial services, elucidates core mechanisms, delineates principal benefits (including enhanced model generalization and reduced breach exposure) alongside challenges such as communication overhead, statistical heterogeneity, and security vulnerabilities, and examines privacy–security paradigms and governance frameworks essential for regulated environments. Section II delineates high-impact applications. Contributions explore FL-enabled credit risk assessment and scoring, fraud detection integrated with anti-money laundering protocols, and privacy-preserving approaches to wealth management and investment strategy formulation. These chapters underscore FL's capacity to improve detection efficacy and personalization through inter-institutional collaboration without compromising data sovereignty. Section III addresses deployment realities. Discussions encompass the architecture of FL infrastructures tailored to financial ecosystems, reinforcement of privacy via advanced FL techniques, and mechanisms for secure cross-border data exchange amid divergent regulatory regimes. Section IV presents illustrative case studies and innovative applications. Notable inclusions are FL for ESG disclosure analytics leveraging NSE sectoral indices, machine learning applications (potentially augmented by federated principles) for identifying irregularities in local government revenue systems in Tanzania, and an analysis of regulatory and ethical considerations intrinsic to federated finance. Section V contemplates future horizons. Emerging trends—encompassing integration with blockchain for enhanced trust, differential privacy enhancements, and quantum-secure frameworks—are surveyed, alongside specialized evaluations of classifiers for Smurf attack detection and privacy improvements in FL systems.

This book is intended for a diverse audience, including financial practitioners seeking practical applications, data scientists working in regulated environments, compliance and risk professionals navigating privacy mandates, academics advancing theoretical frontiers, and technologists building next-generation financial systems. It combines rigorous conceptual foundations with actionable, pragmatic guidance to support responsible adoption of federated learning in finance.

Series Preface

The rapid pace of technological advancement in the 21st century has brought with it transformative capabilities and unprecedented possibilities across sectors. From artificial intelligence and ambient intelligence to industrial automation, technology is deeply embedded in our social, economic, and personal lives. While these innovations offer immense benefits, they also raise critical questions about ethics, equity, sustainability, and human well-being. It is within this context that the "Responsible Technology Series" has been conceived—a multidisciplinary initiative aimed at fostering technological progress that is not only intelligent and efficient but also inclusive, ethical, and accountable.

This series brings together thought leaders, researchers, and practitioners to explore how emerging technologies can be designed and deployed responsibly to serve both individual and collective good. Each volume in the series addresses a specific domain of technological innovation while upholding a common commitment: to highlight frameworks, practices, and case studies that emphasize responsible development, deployment, and governance.

The first volume, A Compendium of Responsible Artificial Intelligence, offers a comprehensive overview of the ethical, social, and regulatory challenges associated with AI systems. It explores fairness, transparency, accountability, and the societal impacts of machine learning and decision-making algorithms, laying the groundwork for sustainable AI applications.

The second volume, Ambient Assisted Living: Technological Advances, focuses on the intersection of healthcare, aging populations, and intelligent environments. It presents innovations in assistive technologies and smart living spaces, while foregrounding the need for privacy, user dignity, and human-centric design in care ecosystems.

The third volume, Industrial Internet of Things for Responsible Technology, examines how industrial automation and IoT can be harnessed responsibly. It covers foundational technologies, ethical considerations, sustainability, human-centered design, and resilience—demonstrating how IIoT can drive industrial efficiency without compromising societal and environmental values.

Together, these volumes reflect the core mission of the series: to enable a balanced narrative in which innovation and responsibility go hand in hand. By bringing diverse voices and insights to the forefront, this series aims to equip readers with the tools, perspectives, and inspiration needed to build a more equitable and conscientious technological future.

We invite scholars, professionals, students, and policymakers to engage with these works, contribute to this growing dialogue, and join us in shaping a future where technology serves humanity with foresight and integrity.

Acknowledgment

With profound gratitude and heartfelt appreciation, we extend our deepest thanks to all those who have contributed, in myriad ways, to the realization of this book. This work stands as a testament to the collective wisdom, generosity, and unwavering support of many individuals and institutions.

We begin by expressing our utmost gratitude to Dr. Gaurav Dhiman, the esteemed Series Editor of Advances in Responsible Technology and Intelligence. His visionary leadership, insightful guidance, continuous encouragement, and unwavering commitment have been the cornerstone of this project from its very inception through to its final publication. Dr. Dhiman's profound expertise, thoughtful suggestions, and inspirational mentorship have not only shaped the conceptual framework and intellectual scope of the book but have also elevated its scholarly quality far beyond what we could have achieved alone. We are deeply indebted to all the distinguished contributors who have enriched this volume with their exceptional chapters. Each author has brought unique perspectives, rigorous research, cutting-edge insights, and meticulous scholarship to the project. Their dedication, intellectual generosity, and tireless effort have infused the book with remarkable depth, breadth, and relevance, making it a truly collaborative and comprehensive work. We extend our sincere thanks to CRC Press (a Taylor & Francis company) for their trust in this project and for providing an outstanding platform for its publication. We are particularly grateful to the entire editorial, production, and marketing teams at CRC Press whose professionalism, efficiency, patience, and expertise have ensured that this book meets the highest standards of quality and reaches its intended global audience. We also wish to acknowledge the invaluable support of our colleagues, peers, mentors, and collaborators from various institutions and research communities. Their stimulating discussions, constructive feedback, words of encouragement, and practical assistance during both the writing and revision stages have been indispensable. Special thanks go to those who generously shared resources, reviewed drafts, and offered critical insights that helped refine and strengthen the manuscript. On a more personal note, we are profoundly thankful to our families—our parents, spouses, children, and siblings—for their boundless love, patience, understanding, and encouragement throughout this long and demanding journey. They have been our greatest source of strength, providing emotional support, sacrificing personal time, and believing in us even when the workload seemed overwhelming. Without their unwavering backing and understanding, this book would never have seen the light of day.

Finally, we humbly bow in gratitude to the Almighty—God—for bestowing upon us the physical strength, mental clarity, emotional resilience, inspiration, and divine grace necessary to complete this endeavor. It is through His blessings that we have been able to persevere and bring this work to fruition.

To everyone mentioned, and to those whose contributions may have gone unspoken but were no less vital—thank you from the bottom of our hearts. This book is, in every sense, a shared accomplishment.

With deepest appreciation and warm regards.

Editors

Contents

List of Contributors

Aaryan Wagh
Modern College, Ganesh Khind, Pune, India.

Aisha Aneesa Abubakar
Baze University, Abuja, Nigeria.

Amit Mishra
Dr. Vishwanath Karad MIT World Peace University, Pune, India.

Amit Singh Dalal
IEC University, Solan, Himachal Pradesh, India.

Amit Vajpayee
Department of CSE, Chandigarh University, Mohali-140413, Punjab, India.

Ankit Sharma
Apex Institute of Technology (CSE), Chandigarh University, Mohali-140413, Punjab, India.

Ankita Kotalwar
School of Computer Engineering and Technology, Dr. Vishwanath Karad, MIT World Peace University, Pune, India.

Ashima
Department of CSE, Rayat Bahra University, Mohali, Punjab, India.

Bhupinder Kaur
Department of CSE, Chandigarh University, Mohali-140413, Punjab, India.

C. H. Patil
Dr. Vishwanath Karad MIT World Peace University, Pune, India.

Donkor Nawaah
Assistant Professor & Area Chair, Department of Finance and Accounting, Woxsen University, Hyderabad, Telangana, India.

George S. Ulomi
College of Informatics and Virtual Education, The University of Dodoma, Dodoma, Tanzania.

Gilbert M. Gilbert
College of Informatics and Virtual Education, The University of Dodoma, Dodoma, Tanzania.

Jeetendra Kumar
Department of Computer Science and Applications, Atal Bihari Vajpayee University, Bilaspur, Chhattisgarh, India.

Joseph Tufuor Kwarteng
Professor, Department of Business and Social Sciences Education, University of Cape Coast, Cape Coast, Central Region, Ghana.

Mandar Upasani
S.P. College, Pune, India.

Meenal Jabde
Dr. Vishwanath Karad MIT World Peace University, Pune, India.

Poonam Kukana
Department of CSE, Chandigarh University, Mohali-140413, Punjab, India.

Pranati Waghodekar
Computer Science and Engineering (AIML), Vishwakarma Institute of Technology, Pune.

Priya Nagargoje
School of Computer Engineering and Technology, Dr. Vishwanath Karad, MIT World Peace University, Pune, India.

Rashmi Gupta
Department of Computer Science and Applications, Atal Bihari Vajpayee University, Bilaspur, Chhattisgarh, India.

Reshma Sonar
School of Computer Engineering and Technology, Dr. Vishwanath Karad, MIT World Peace University, Pune, India.

R. Manishankar
Research Scholar, Department of Computer Science and Engineering, Annamalai University, Annamalainagar-608002.

R. Naveena
Assistant Professor, Karpagam Academy of Higher Education, Coimbatore-641021.

R. Prithviraj
Assistant Professor, Department of Artificial Intelligence (AI) and Data Science, Vel Tech Rangarajan Dr.Sagunthala R&D Institute of Science and Technology, Avadi, Chennai-600062.

R. Saminathan
Professor, Department of Computer Science and Engineering, Annamalai University, Annamalainagar-608002.

Ruchi Garg
Area of Information Technology, Birla Institute of Management Technology, Delhi-NCR, India.

Said M. Mohamed
Department of Information, Communication and Technology, IFAKARA, Tanzania.

Sakshi
Apex Institute of Technology (CSE), Chandigarh University, Mohali-140413, Punjab, India.

Shweta Thakur
Assistant Professor, AIT-CSE Chandigarh University, Mohali-140413, Punjab, India.

Silpa M.
Assistant Professor, Karpagam Academy of Higher Education, Coimbatore-641021.

Silvio Andrae
Independent Researcher, Germany.

Solomon Jeresa
Research Assistant, Huddersfield Business School, University of Huddersfield, West Yorkshire, United Kingdom.

Somdatta Patra
Apex Institute of Technology (CSE), Chandigarh University, Mohali-140413, Punjab, India.

Sukhjinder Kaur
Department of CSE, Rayat Bahra University, Mohali, Punjab, India.

Suvarna Sharma
Dr. Vishwanath Karad MIT World Peace University, Pune, India.

Tabu S. Kondo
College of Informatics and Virtual Education, The University of Dodoma, Dodoma, Tanzania.

Usman Bello Abubakar
Baze University, Abuja, Nigeria.

Varsha Dange
Computer Science and Engineering (AIML), Vishwakarma Institute of Technology, Pune.

1 Introduction to Federated Learning in Financial Services

Meenal Jabde,[1,*] C. H. Patil,[1] Mandar Upasani[2] and Aaryan Wagh[3]

The quick digital transformation of financial support services has led to widespread acceptance of artificial intelligence (AI) methodologies and machine learning (ML) techniques for tasks such as CIBIL/credit scoring, fraud recognition and detection, risk management, and personalized banking. However, the sensitive landscape of financial data, combined with stringent regulatory and confidentiality requirements, significantly limits the applicability of conventional centralized learning approaches. Federated learning (FL) has arisen as a distributed machine learning methodology that allows multiple financial institutions to train models together without sharing raw data, thus preserving data privacy, data sovereignty, and regulatory compliance.

This book chapter provides a comprehensive examination of federated learning in the context of financial services. It introduces the fundamental concepts, architectures, and operational workflows of federated learning, followed by an in-depth discussion of why federated learning is particularly important for the financial sector. The chapter analyzes key challenges faced by financial institutions, including data silos, cybersecurity risks, regulatory constraints, fairness concerns, and the need for cross-institutional collaboration.

Furthermore, the chapter presents a detailed exploration of major financial applications of federated learning, including credit scoring, fraud detection, counter-terrorist financing, anti-money laundering, risk management, stress testing, personalized banking, algorithmic trading, regulatory technology, and integration with blockchain-based financial systems. By synthesizing theoretical foundations with practical use cases, this chapter demonstrates how federated learning serves as a foundational technology for secure, scalable, and responsible artificial intelligence in modern financial ecosystems.

[1] Dr. Vishwanath Karad MIT World Peace University, Pune, India.
[2] S.P. College, Pune, India.
[3] Modern College, Ganesh Khind, Pune, India.
Email: chpatil.mca@gmail.com
* Corresponding author: meenal.jabde@mitwpu.edu.in

DOI: 10.1201/9781003710059-1

1. Introduction

1.1 Introduction to Federated Learning

Federated learning is a machine learning (ML) methodology that allows multiple sources to train a model together without sharing their sensitive data, thereby preserving data confidentiality and safety [1–3]. This approach is particularly valuable in the financial services sector, where data is highly sensitive and subject to stringent regulatory controls, and where collaboration among institutions can yield significant benefits while protecting competitive advantages and ensuring regulatory compliance [4–6]. By leveraging federated learning, financial institutions can develop more accurate and robust models, improve risk management, and enhance customer experience, all while upholding the privacy and sanctuary of sensitive data [1], [7].

This is especially critical in finance, where a single data breach can compromise institutional reputation, erode customer trust, and result in substantial financial and legal consequences [15]. Federated learning enables the development of sophisticated analytical models applicable across diverse financial services, including anti-money laundering (AML), credit risk assessment, fraud detection, and algorithmic trading, by enabling institutions to pool knowledge without exposing raw data [7–12]. Through collaborative yet privacy-preserving model training, federated learning unlocks new levels of innovation and cooperation within the financial industry [3], [13].

By harnessing collective intelligence, financial institutions can generate more accurate predictions that support strategic decision-making, operational optimization, and sustainable growth [14]. Federated learning further supports the creation of advanced financial models capable of identifying emerging business opportunities and previously inaccessible revenue streams [11], [12]. This fosters a culture of innovation and positions financial institutions at the forefront of data-driven transformation in a rapidly evolving financial landscape [13], [14].

As institutions navigate increasingly complex and data-rich environments, federated learning enables them to unlock the full potential of decentralized data assets, promote deeper collaboration, and enhance understanding of financial market dynamics [2], [3]. By empowering institutions to authorize collective expertise while retaining data ownership, federated learning supports improved predictive accuracy, risk mitigation strategies, optimized investment decisions, and effective asset management [8], [10]. The wide applicability of federated learning across financial domains—including credit risk management, fraud detection, AML, portfolio optimization, and algorithmic trading—demonstrates its potential to transform data-driven decision-making [7–12].

One of the advantages of federated learning in finance is its capacity to protect sensitive financial data while enabling collaborative analytics across institutions [1], [5]. Models are trained on decentralized data, ensuring that customer information, transaction records, and account details remain within institutional boundaries, while only encrypted model updates are exchanged [2], [8]. This approach enhances data security, supports regulatory compliance, and fosters a trusted collaborative ecosystem that unlocks new opportunities for innovation and growth within the financial sector [4], [6], [13]. As a result, federated learning has the potential to fundamentally reshape how financial institutions approach data analysis, model development, and intelligent decision-making [3], [14].

Following are the steps in the working of federated learning: Initializing a universal model on a central server; sending the model to selected clients; conducting the local training on each client's private data; sending the weights back to server; doing the averaging; and finally updating the global model [14].

Figure 1 provided in the following text is about federated learning. This figure shows that how the federated learning works with the help of a central server, a global model, and communication between different devices.

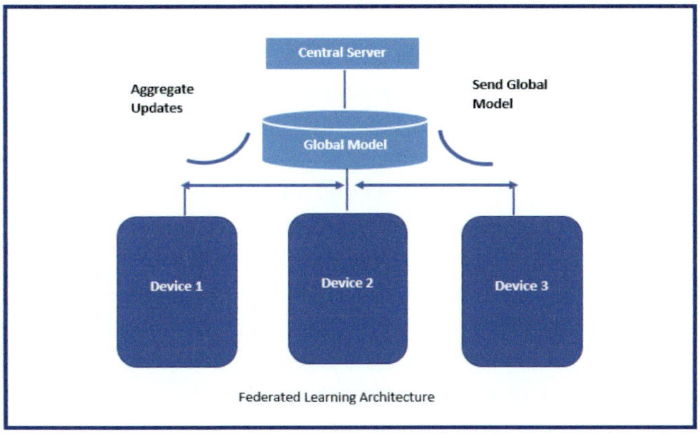

Figure 1: Federated learning architecture.

1.2 Federated Learning Algorithm and Types

The key algorithm underlying federated learning is the federated averaging (FedAvg) algorithm, which aggregates locally trained model parameters from multiple clients to form a global model. The global model update at round $t + 1$ is given by:

$$w_{t+1} = \sum_{k=1}^{k} \frac{n_k}{n} w_t^k$$

where:
w_t^k is the model weight, n_k is the number of data samples available, and n is the total number of samples across all participating clients [1–3].

Federated learning allows collaborative model training across multiple institutions without requiring the exchange of raw data, thereby preserving privacy and data security. In general, federated learning can be classified into three categories, that is, horizontal federated learning (HFL), vertical federated learning (VFL), and federated transfer learning (FTL) [2], [3].

Federated learning workflows typically consist of two major processes—training the model and model inference. The process of model training is a collaborative and decentralized procedure in which model parameters are learned without sharing raw data across participants. Training is conducted in multiple rounds under the synchronization of a central server or coordinator that controls participant selection, synchronization, and aggregation of model updates [1], [4]. During training, raw data remains on local client devices, reducing the risk of data leakage and regulatory noncompliance [6], [7].

Instead of pooling raw datasets, federated learning employs aggregation mechanisms such as federated averaging, weighted averaging, and secure aggregation to combine model updates [1], [4]. Privacy-preserving techniques, which include secure aggregation, variance privacy, and encryption or secure multiparty computation (MPC), are often applied to further enhance confidentiality [4], [5]. Federated learning also addresses challenges related to data heterogeneity across clients, although training is generally slower than centralized machine learning due to communication overhead and decentralized optimization [3]. This training process is primarily used for initial model creation or periodic model retraining.

Model inference represents the second stage of federated learning, in which the trained global model is used to generate predictions on new data. Inference is typically performed locally at each client, ensuring that sensitive data never leaves institutional boundaries [2]. The inference process is computationally lightweight and faster than training, and privacy is preserved by default since no data sharing occurs. Depending on deployment requirements, inference can be executed in a decentralized manner (e.g., on-device or within a bank's infrastructure) or in centralized trusted execution environments [11], [14].

1.3 Types of Federated Learning

Figure 2 shows the types of federated learning, that is, horizontal federated learning, vertical federated learning, and federated transfer learning.

1.3.1 Horizontal Federated Learning (HFL)

Horizontal federated learning is useful when multiple users share the same feature planetary but possess different data samples, meaning the datasets have the same columns but different rows. In this setting, feature schemas are identical across clients, and data typically belongs to different users [2], [3]. HFL is the utmost mutual form of federated learning and frequently employs algorithms such as federated averaging [1].

A representative example includes multiple banks holding transaction records with identical feature definitions but different customer bases. The primary advantages of HFL include ease of implementation, strong scalability,

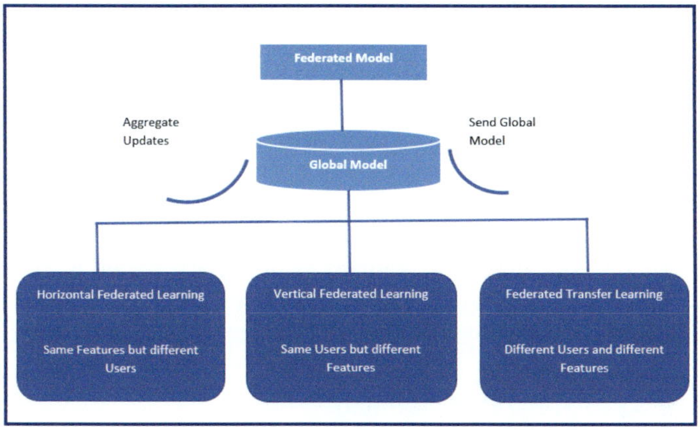

Figure 2: Types of federated learning.

and reliable model convergence. However, its limitations include dependency on consistent feature definitions and an inability to address feature heterogeneity across institutions [3].

1.3.2 Vertical Federated Learning (VFL)

Vertical federated learning is used when participating entities share the same set of users but possess different feature sets, corresponding to the same rows and different columns. This setting requires accurate entity alignment across institutions and typically involves complex cryptographic protocols to preserve privacy [2], [4]. VFL is particularly common in financial services, where multiple organizations contribute complementary data sources.

For example, a bank may hold transaction histories, while a telecommunications company holds usage data for the same customers. The key advantages of VFL include access to richer feature spaces and improved predictive performance, especially for tabular financial data. However, VFL is more complex to implement, incurs higher computational costs, and requires well-defined trust and governance frameworks [3], [8].

1.3.3 Federated Transfer Learning (FTL)

Federated transfer learning is applied when participating entities have minimal overlap in both users and features, meaning both rows and columns differ. This approach combines federated learning with transfer learning to enable knowledge transfer across domains with limited shared data [2], [3].

A typical example involves banks operating in different countries, each subject to distinct regulatory frameworks and serving different customer populations. The main advantage of FTL is its ability to operate under minimal data overlap by leveraging pre-trained models and shared representations. However, FTL is computationally intensive, more difficult to train, and generally achieves lower accuracy compared to horizontal and vertical federated learning [3].

1.3.4 Cross-Device Federated Learning

Cross-device federated learning involves a very large number of edge devices, each contributing small local datasets. This setting is characterized by millions of participating clients, unreliable network connectivity, partial participation per training round, and lightweight model architectures [1], [3]. Common examples include smartphones, wearable devices, and Internet of Things (IoT) systems.

1.3.5 Cross-Silo Federated Learning

Cross-silo federated learning involves a relatively small number of reliable organizations, each possessing large datasets. This setting is characterized by stable connectivity, strong governance, and enterprise-scale models [3], [7]. Typical participants include banks, hospitals, and insurance companies, where federated learning enables collaboration while maintaining strict regulatory compliance and data ownership.

1.4 Federated Learning Frameworks

Federated learning frameworks are open-source or enterprise-grade software platforms designed to simplify the development, deployment, and management of federated learning applications. These frameworks abstract complex aspects such as distributed coordination, privacy preservation, secure aggregation, and communication efficiency, thereby enabling practical adoption of federated learning across research and industry environments [2], [3]. Based on functionality and deployment focus, federated learning frameworks can be broadly categorized into general-purpose federated learning frameworks, enterprise- and finance-oriented frameworks, research and experimental frameworks, mobile and edge federated learning frameworks, tree-based and specialized frameworks, and decentralized or blockchain-based federated learning frameworks [3], [11].

The general-purpose federated learning frameworks include platforms such as Flower (FLWR), FedML, TensorFlow Federated (TFF), and PySyft. Enterprise- and finance-oriented frameworks include Federated AI Technology Enabler (FATE), NVIDIA FLARE, and OpenFL (Intel). Research and experimental frameworks include LEAF, FedScale, and TensorFlow Federated simulation tools. Mobile and edge federated learning frameworks include SecureBoost and Federated XGBoost, while decentralized and blockchain-based frameworks include Substra and swarm learning [2], [3].

1.4.1 Flower (FLWR)

Flower is an open-source, framework-agnostic federated learning platform designed to support the transition from research to production environments. It is widely adopted in both academic and industrial settings due to its simplicity and flexibility [1], [3]. Flower supports major machine learning libraries such as PyTorch, TensorFlow, Keras, and XGBoost and follows a straightforward client–server architecture that simplifies deployment and experimentation [2].

Figure 3 is the client–server architecture of federated learning which is used by almost every federated learning framework.

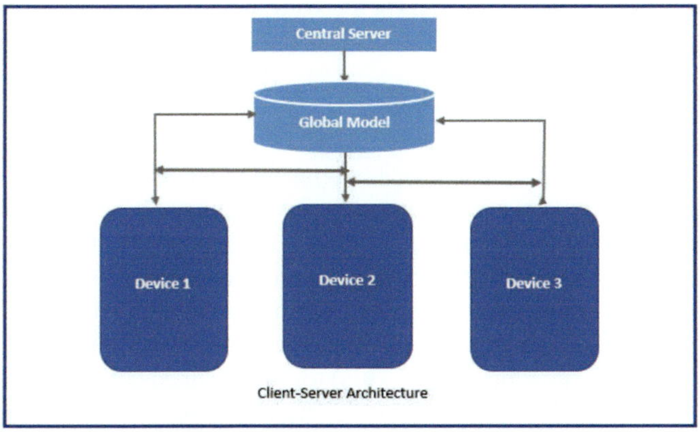

Figure 3: Client–server architecture.

Key features of Flower include support for federated averaging, secure aggregation, and flexible communication layers that allow scalability from small experimental clusters to thousands of participating clients [1], [4]. The framework is highly customizable and supports a wide range of machine learning tasks, including data analysis, computer vision, image processing, data science, visualization, and natural language processing.

The primary benefit of Flower lies in its ease of use, production readiness, and extensibility. However, governance, regulatory compliance, and advanced privacy mechanisms must be configured externally, which can increase deployment complexity in regulated environments [6], [7]. Flower is commonly used for applications such as fraud detection, recommendation systems, and cross-silo enterprise federated learning [8].

1.4.2 FedML

FedML is a comprehensive federated machine learning framework that provides an end-to-end platform for research, benchmarking, experimentation, and deployment. It is designed with a strong emphasis on scalability and supports both cross-device and cross-silo federated learning scenarios [3]. FedML includes integrated tools for simulation, training, deployment, and experiment management, making it suitable for large-scale federated learning studies.

Key features of FedML include a rich library of federated learning algorithms, automated experiment orchestration, visualization and monitoring tools, and support for mobile, edge, and IoT devices [3]. Its strengths include excellent support for algorithm comparison, scalability across heterogeneous environments, and strong experimental reproducibility.

However, FedML can be complex to configure for beginners, and certain enterprise-grade features are limited to commercial versions. The framework is primarily used in academic research, edge-device federated learning, and industrial pilot projects [2], [3].

1.4.3 TensorFlow Federated (TFF)

TensorFlow Federated is a federated learning framework developed by Google, primarily aimed at research and algorithm development. It is deeply integrated with the TensorFlow ecosystem and employs a functional programming model to enable simulation-based federated learning experiments [2].

TFF provides implementations of federated averaging and a variety of experimental optimization algorithms, along with both high-level and low-level application programming interfaces (APIs) for fine-grained control over federated computations. The framework also offers strong support for statistical analysis and theoretical experimentation [3].

The key strengths of TensorFlow Federated include its strong theoretical foundations, close integration with TensorFlow, and backing from large-scale production research. However, TFF is not designed for production deployment, lacks enterprise-grade security and governance features, and presents a relatively steep learning curve due to its complex APIs [3]. Consequently, TFF is mainly used for academic research, federated learning algorithm design, and simulation studies.

1.4.4 PySyft

PySyft is a privacy-first federated learning framework developed by the OpenMined community, with a strong emphasis on cryptographic security and privacy-preserving machine learning. Built on PyTorch, PySyft is designed to support highly sensitive data environments such as finance and healthcare [4], [5].

The framework incorporates advanced privacy mechanisms, including secure multi-party computation, differential privacy, encrypted tensors, and remote execution capabilities [4], [5]. These features provide strong guarantees for data confidentiality and fine-grained cryptographic control.

While PySyft offers robust privacy protection, it requires substantial computational resources and involves complex configuration procedures. Training processes can be significantly slower compared to other frameworks due to cryptographic overhead [3]. PySyft is typically used in research and applications involving extreme privacy requirements, including sensitive financial analytics and regulated data environments [6], [7].

1.4.5 Federated AI Technology Enabler (FATE)

Federated AI Technology Enabler (FATE) is an enterprise-grade federated learning framework developed by WeBank, specifically tailored for financial services and consortium-based collaboration. It supports horizontal, vertical, and federated transfer learning and incorporates strong cryptographic foundations suitable for regulated environments [2], [8].

Key features of FATE include SecureBoost, logistic regression, linear models, multi-party-computation-based secure aggregation, and built-in feature alignment mechanisms. These capabilities make FATE particularly well-suited for tabular financial data analysis [8].

The framework's strengths include high regulatory compliance, strong governance and audit support, and effectiveness in financial use cases. However, FATE requires heavy infrastructure, has a steep learning curve, and has a relatively smaller global developer community compared to general-purpose frameworks [3]. FATE is widely used in credit scoring, fraud detection, and anti-money laundering collaboration across financial institutions [8], [10].

1.4.6 NVIDIA FLARE

NVIDIA FLARE is an enterprise federated learning platform optimized for secure, large-scale deployments. It is designed for Graphics Processing Units (GPU) accelerated environments and supports container-based orchestration and policy-driven governance [3].

Key features include secure aggregation, built-in authentication and authorization, comprehensive monitoring, and logging capabilities. NVIDIA FLARE provides high performance and strong enterprise-level security controls, making it suitable for production environments [7].

However, the framework is dependent on the NVIDIA ecosystem and requires substantial infrastructure investment. NVIDIA FLARE is primarily used in large financial institutions, healthcare imaging applications, and regulator-supervised federated learning deployments [7], [11].

1.4.7 OpenFL (Intel)

OpenFL is an open-source federated learning framework developed by Intel with a focus on secure enterprise collaboration. It leverages trusted execution environments and hardware-assisted security mechanisms to protect model training and inference processes [11].

Key features include secure enclaves, federated orchestration, and model protection mechanisms that ensure confidentiality and integrity in regulated environments. OpenFL's strengths lie in its strong security model and suitability for industries with strict compliance requirements.

However, OpenFL is hardware-dependent and offers limited flexibility in terms of supported algorithms. It is commonly used in healthcare, secure enterprise machine learning, and government-related use cases [6], [7].

2. Why Federated Learning Matters in Finance

2.1 Introduction

The financial industry operates in an era characterized by unprecedented data availability, regulatory oversight, and rapid technological innovation. Banks, insurance providers, asset managers, and fintech firms generate and manage vast volumes of highly sensitive data, including personal identifiers, transaction histories, credit records, behavioral profiles, and proprietary market insights. While ML and artificial intelligence (AI) have demonstrated transformative potential in areas such as credit scoring, fraud detection, risk management, and personalized financial services, their large-scale adoption remains constrained by stringent privacy, security, and regulatory requirements [1], [2].

Traditional centralized machine learning paradigms rely on aggregating raw data from multiple sources into a central repository. In the financial domain, this approach is often infeasible due to regulations such as the General Data Protection Regulation (GDPR), banking secrecy laws, and sector-specific supervisory mandates that restrict data sharing and cross-border transfers [3], [4]. Moreover, centralized data storage increases exposure to cybersecurity threats, creating attractive targets for large-scale data breaches and insider attacks [5].

Federated learning has emerged as a compelling alternative that addresses these challenges. By enabling collaborative model training while keeping sensitive financial data localized within participating institutions, federated learning allows only encrypted model updates to be shared with a coordinating entity [6]. This paradigm aligns closely with the operational, regulatory, and ethical requirements of modern financial ecosystems, making federated learning increasingly essential rather than merely advantageous.

2.2 Privacy Preservation and Data Sovereignty

2.2.1 Sensitivity of Financial Data

Financial data is among the most sensitive categories of personal and organizational information. Credit histories, transaction records, investment behaviors, and biometric identifiers can lead to severe financial, legal, and reputational consequences if misused or exposed. Conventional machine learning methods that require centralized data collection conflict with privacy principles such as data minimization and purpose limitation [7]. Federated learning mitigates these risks by ensuring that raw data never leaves institutional boundaries, thereby substantially reducing the risk of direct data leakage.

2.2.2 Compliance with Privacy Regulations

Global regulatory frameworks increasingly restrict data sharing across jurisdictions and organizations. Regulations such as GDPR impose strict controls on personally identifiable information, while financial regulators enforce confidentiality obligations on customer data. Federated learning enables institutions to collaborate without violating data residency or sovereignty requirements, as data remains under local control [3], [4]. Furthermore, federated learning can integrate secure aggregation, differential privacy, and cryptographic techniques to ensure that model updates themselves do not reveal sensitive information [8], [9].

2.3 Enabling Cross-Institutional Collaboration

2.3.1 Breaking Data Silos

Financial institutions traditionally operate in isolation, limiting the effectiveness of ML models trained on siloed datasets. For example, fraud detection systems trained on a single bank's data may fail to identify emerging attack patterns observed elsewhere. Federated learning enables collective intelligence by allowing institutions to jointly train models without exchanging customer-level data [10]. This collaboration enhances model robustness and generalization, particularly in fraud detection and AML applications.

2.3.2 Competitive Collaboration (Coopetition)

Federated learning facilitates "coopetition," where competing financial institutions collaborate on shared challenges while preserving proprietary advantages. By sharing learned representations rather than raw data, institutions can collectively address systemic risks without disclosing sensitive business information [11].

2.4 Security and Cyber-Resilience

2.4.1 Reduced Attack Surface

Centralized ML systems create single points of failure, where a breach can expose millions of financial records simultaneously. Federated learning reduces this risk by decentralizing data storage and computation, thereby limiting the impact of localized security incidents [5]. This architecture aligns with zero-trust security principles increasingly adopted in financial systems [12].

2.4.2 Robustness Against Adversarial Threats

Financial ML systems face adversarial risks such as data poisoning and model inversion attacks. Research shows that federated learning combined with robust aggregation and anomaly detection mechanisms can mitigate such threats, improving resilience in regulated financial environments [6], [13].

2.5 Regulatory Alignment and Auditability

Regulatory authorities increasingly demand transparency and accountability in AI-driven financial decision-making. Federated learning frameworks can support audit trails, model versioning, and governance mechanisms to ensure regulatory compliance. When integrated with distributed ledger technologies, FL can further enhance auditability while preserving confidentiality [11], [14].

2.6 Fairness, Bias Reduction, and Financial Inclusion

Bias in financial AI systems can result in discriminatory credit and insurance decisions. Models trained on limited datasets risk perpetuating historical inequities. Federated learning mitigates this risk by incorporating diverse data sources across institutions and regions, leading to fairer and more inclusive financial models [1], [10].

2.7 Scalability and Strategic Advantage

As financial data volumes grow due to digital payments, open banking, and real-time analytics, federated learning offers scalable solutions for distributed environments. Institutions adopting federated learning gain strategic advantages by leveraging collective intelligence while maintaining compliance, customer trust, and ethical AI governance [15].

3. Federated Learning Use Cases and Applications in Financial Services

3.1 Federated Credit Scoring and Credit Risk Assessment

Credit score evaluation and credit risk analysis are essential functions within financial organizations, affecting decisions regarding loans, distribution of capital, and adherence to regulations. Conventional credit scoring systems depend on the centralized collection of borrower information, leading to issues concerning data privacy, compliance with regulations, and control over data. In addition, many organizations tend to work with restricted datasets, which diminishes the applicability of models and heightens biases [1], [2]. Federated learning facilitates cooperative credit risk modelling, allowing banks and financial organizations to collaboratively develop predictive models without the need to exchange sensitive customer data. Within a federated credit scoring structure, every organization cultivates a local risk model by utilizing its exclusive borrower information, which encompasses repayment history, income trends, and transaction activities. The model parameters or gradients are securely combined to create a universal credit risk model that reflects wider economic trends while maintaining the integrity of institutional data ownership [3], [4].

Federated credit scoring improves predictive accuracy by leveraging cross-institutional knowledge and reduces systemic bias by incorporating diverse borrower populations. Secure aggregation and differential privacy mechanisms further protect against inference attacks, ensuring compliance with data protection regulations such as GDPR and banking secrecy laws [5], [6].

3.2 Federated Fraud Detection

Financial deception is an ever-changing danger, which includes credit card scams, identity theft, account hijacking, and manipulation of payments. Centralized systems designed to detect fraud frequently struggle to identify new fraud trends that cross various organizations, as fraudsters take advantage of isolated detection strategies [7], [8]. Federated fraud detection allows for cooperative learning among different financial organizations while maintaining the confidentiality of transactions. This method involves training localized fraud detection models on transaction data and behavioral characteristics specific to each institution. Through the combined updates of these models, the comprehensive model can recognize fraudulent activities that span across institutions without revealing any sensitive transaction information [9]. Research has demonstrated that federated fraud detection enhances the capability to recognize zero-day fraud attacks early and decreases the occurrence of false positives by integrating a broader behavioral context. This strategy is highly successful within payment networks, digital wallets, and systems for transactions across borders [10].

3.3 Anti-Money Laundering (AML) and Counter-Terrorist Financing (CTF)

AML and CTF compliance mandates that financial institutions identify suspicious financial behaviors within complex transactional networks. Conventional AML systems are constrained by institutional silos, resulting in limited visibility and delayed detection of illicit financial flows [11].

Federated AML frameworks enable collaborative identification of money-laundering patterns across banks without violating customer privacy. Local models analyze transaction sequences, network topologies, and anomalous behaviors, while federated aggregation captures systemic laundering patterns across institutions [12], [13].

This approach strengthens cross-border AML collaboration and aligns with international regulatory standards such as the Financial Action Task Force (FATF) recommendations. Federated AML solutions improve detection of layered, structured, and coordinated laundering activities while preserving strict privacy guarantees [14].

3.4 Risk Management and Stress Testing

Systemic risk management and stress testing are fundamental to financial stability. Traditional stress-testing frameworks rely on institution-specific models, limiting their ability to detect interconnected risks across the broader financial system [15].

Federated learning enables collaborative stress testing by integrating local institutional risk models into a shared systemic risk framework. This allows institutions to jointly evaluate macroeconomic shocks, liquidity stress, and contagion effects without disclosing sensitive balance-sheet data [3].

Regulators benefit from federated stress-testing approaches as they provide comprehensive system-wide insights while preserving institutional confidentiality, thereby supporting effective macroprudential supervision [11].

3.5 Personalized Banking and Financial Recommendation Systems

Personalized banking services employ machine learning to recommend financial products, enhance customer engagement, and improve retention. Centralized personalization systems raise privacy concerns due to extensive collection and aggregation of customer behavioral data [15].

Federated personalization enables local model training on customer devices or bank servers, sharing only encrypted updates. Personalized federated learning techniques allow global models to adapt to individual user preferences while maintaining privacy protections [3], [18].

Applications include customized savings plans, targeted loan offers, investment recommendations, and fraud alerts. Federated personalization aligns with regulatory requirements on data minimization and informed customer consent [6].

3.6 Federated Algorithmic Trading and Market Analysis

Algorithmic trading relies on predictive models trained on high-frequency financial data. Sharing proprietary trading strategies or order-level data is impractical due to competitive and regulatory constraints [13].

Federated learning enables collaborative market analysis by allowing trading firms to jointly train models on market dynamics without exposing sensitive strategies. Applications include volatility forecasting, liquidity prediction, and anomaly detection [5], [9].

From a regulatory perspective, federated analytics support market surveillance by enabling detection of manipulation patterns while preserving participant confidentiality [12].

3.7 Regulatory Technology (RegTech) and Supervisory Technology (SupTech)

RegTech and SupTech leverage advanced analytics to automate compliance and enhance supervisory oversight. However, centralized regulatory data collection raises concerns related to security, privacy, and jurisdictional boundaries [4].

Federated learning allows regulators and financial institutions to jointly develop compliance and risk-assessment models without exchanging raw regulatory data. SupTech applications include systemic-risk monitoring, report validation, and early-warning systems [11], [16].

Federated RegTech architectures improve transparency, trust, and efficiency while enabling cross-border supervisory cooperation [14].

3.8 Integration with Blockchain-Based Financial Systems

Blockchain-based financial systems offer decentralization, immutability, and auditability but lack advanced analytical intelligence. Integrating federated learning with blockchain enables secure, decentralized model training and governance [3].

In this architecture, blockchain networks record federated learning events and updates, creating tamper-proof audit trails. Smart contracts manage model aggregation and enforce governance policies [17], [18].

This synergy supports decentralized credit scoring, fraud detection, and AML systems, particularly in consortium banking and decentralized finance (DeFi) environments [18].

4. Conclusion

This study highlights federated learning as a pivotal enabler for secure and collaborative artificial intelligence in financial systems. By allowing institutions to jointly train models without sharing sensitive data, federated learning addresses critical challenges related to privacy preservation, regulatory compliance, and cybersecurity. Across applications such as anti-money laundering, risk management, personalized banking, algorithmic trading, RegTech, and blockchain-integrated finance, federated learning enhances model robustness and systemic visibility while maintaining institutional confidentiality.

The decentralized nature of federated learning reduces centralized attack surfaces and supports cross-institutional intelligence, enabling more effective detection of financial crime, systemic risk, and market anomalies. Moreover, its compatibility with governance frameworks, privacy-enhancing technologies, and auditable infrastructures positions federated learning as a practical foundation for trustworthy financial AI.

Overall, federated learning provides a balanced framework that reconciles innovation with regulation and collaboration with competition, making it a key technology for the future of resilient, ethical, and scalable financial intelligence.

References

[1] McMahan, B., Moore, E., Ramage, D., Hampson, S. and y Arcas, B. A. (2017). Communication-efficient learning of deep networks from decentralized data. *Proceedings of the 20th International Conference on Artificial Intelligence and Statistics (AISTATS)*, 1273–1282.

[2] Yang, Q., Liu, Y., Chen, T. and Tong, Y. (2019). Federated machine learning: Concept and applications. *ACM Transactions on Intelligent Systems and Technology*, 10(2): 1–19. https://doi.org/10.1145/3298981.

[3] Kairouz, P. and McMahan, H. B. (2021). Advances and open problems in federated learning. *Foundations and Trends in Machine Learning*, 14(1-2): 1–210. https://doi.org/10.1561/2200000083.

[4] Bonawitz, K., Ivanov, V., Kreuter, B., Marcedone, A., McMahan, H. B., Patel, S. et al. (2017, October). Practical secure aggregation for privacy-preserving machine learning. In *Proceedings of the 2017 ACM SIGSAC Conference on Computer and Communications Security* (pp. 1175–1191). https://doi.org/10.1145/3133956.3133982.

[5] Dwork, C. and Roth, A. (2014). The algorithmic foundations of differential privacy. *Foundations and Trends® in Theoretical Computer Science*, 9(3-4): 211–407. https://doi.org/10.1561/0400000042.

[6] European Union. (2018). *General Data Protection Regulation (GDPR).* Official Journal of the European Union.

[7] Basel Committee on Banking Supervision. (2021). *Principles for Operational Resilience.* Bank for International Settlements.

[8] Chen, J., Zhang, X. and Poor, H. V. (2021). A survey on federated learning for financial fraud detection. *IEEE Access*, 9: 11934–11948. https://doi.org/10.1109/ACCESS.2021.3051278.

[9] Bolton, R. J. and Hand, D. J. (2002). Statistical fraud detection: A review. *Statistical Science*, 17(3): 235–255. https://doi.org/10.1214/ss/1042727940.

[10] Financial Action Task Force. (2020). *International Standards on Combating Money Laundering and the Financing of Terrorism.* https://www.fatf-gafi.org.

[11] Arner, D. W., Barberis, J. and Buckley, R. P. (2017). FinTech, RegTech, and the reconceptualization of financial regulation. *Northwestern Journal of International Law & Business*, 37(3): 371–413.

[12] Schär, F. (2021). Decentralized finance: On blockchain- and smart contract-based financial markets. *Federal Reserve Bank of St. Louis Review*, 103(2): 153–174. https://doi.org/10.20955/r.103.153-174.

[13] Aldridge, I. (2013). *High-frequency Trading: A Practical Guide to Algorithmic Strategies and Trading Systems* (2nd ed.). Wiley.

[14] OECD. (2021). *Artificial Intelligence, Data Governance, and Privacy in Financial Services.* Organisation for Economic Co-operation and Development.

[15] IBM Security. (2023). *Cost of a Data Breach Report.* IBM Corporation.
[16] BIS Innovation Hub. (2021). *SupTech Applications for Supervision.* Bank for International Settlements. https://www.bis.org/bishub.
[17] Zyskind, G., Nathan, O. and Pentland, A. (2015). Decentralizing privacy: Using blockchain to protect personal data. In *Proceedings of the IEEE Security and Privacy Workshops* (pp. 180–184). IEEE. https://doi.org/10.1109/SPW.2015.27.
[18] Kim, H. M. and Laskowski, M. (2018). Toward an ontology-driven blockchain design for supply-chain provenance. *Intelligent Systems in Accounting, Finance and Management*, 25(1): 18–27. https://doi.org/10.1002/isaf.1424.

2 Federated Learning Demystified: Core Concepts, Working, Benefits, and Challenges

Ruchi Garg

Federated learning (FL) is based on the concept of decentralization. In this concept, the training of the models is done in a collaborative manner but without any need of sharing the sensitive information or data. This chapter is focused on explaining all the core concepts of federated learning. It provides a comprehensive overview of this upcoming technology and its need. The requirement of having federated learning is explained by taking several real-world cases where data privacy was compromised due to centralized storage and sharing of information. As federated learning approach is different from the traditional machine learning, the differences between the two are explained in length. All the steps of working of federated learning starting from initialization to deployment are briefed. On one side, the concept of federated learning is full of advantages, such as enhanced privacy of sensitive data, personalization of data models, etc.; however, on the other side, it is also full of challenges too, such as model aggregation and computational costs. Overall, this chapter emphasizes on core understanding of all basic concepts for a clear understanding of federated learning.

1. Introduction

Suppose there are five prominent banks and each is having a large data of transactions of their customers. Each of the bank faces issues of online frauds in their network. Individually each of the bank can train their fraud detection algorithm using their own cases and data. Imagine if all these banks can collaboratively train their algorithms to create a strong fraud detection model that too without sharing the sensitive information to the other.

Picture a borrower who takes small loans from multiple lending platforms. Each of the lender will get to see the details of repayment in silos and will not be able to spot any flaw in it. But if the complete history of the borrower with all the lenders is taken into account, then it will show the risky borrowing pattern of the borrower. Hence, if lenders can get complete information without sharing their

Area of Information Technology, Birla Institute of Management Technology, Delhi-NCR, India.
Email: ruchi.garg@bimtech.ac.in

DOI: 10.1201/9781003710059-2

raw data, then they can build a predictive model for defaulter borrowers and can save themselves.

In stock brokerage system, every broker can view the patterns of buying and selling of their own traders. But the stock market has several manipulations such as coordinated short selling taking place on multiple platforms. The stock broker is viewing the transaction details of the trader in isolation and may miss the bigger picture. By infusing federated learning (FL), a strong detection engine could be built to highlight the suspicious trading ways without exposing the client transactions.

Some gaps always remain in the system of insurance providers, and fraudsters can exploit that gap easily by overlapping the claims for the same accident or by claiming from separate provider. Each insurer only sees their own claims, making the fraud look legitimate. But if insurers could pool insights via federated learning, they'd be able to catch repeat offenders and spot systemic fraud—all while keeping individual customer data private.

In all such situations, an upcoming technology, that is, federated learning is the solution. FL is a decentralized machine learning (ML) method which uses local input from multiple devices or servers to train artificial intelligence (AI) models instead of forwarding private information to a central server. In other words, FL is a machine learning approach that allows many entities to work along to create a model while maintaining decentralized data storage instead of central data storage. A central server shares and aggregates only the updates of the model in place of raw data to produce a global, enhanced model. This method enables cooperative model training across several entities and improves data privacy by preserving sensitive information locally. In simplest form, FL [1] is defined as "a way to train AI models without anyone seeing or touching your data, offering a way to unlock information to feed new AI applications." A large number of these AI programs were trained using data that was collected and processed in a location. However, modern AI is going further toward adopting the strategy of decentralization of data.

FL has emerged as a way of distributed machine learning to cater and handle the security and privacy issues which usually occur in modern AI applications. To design a model in a collaborative manner by training it across several devices and places that too without sharing the raw data is the key of FL [2], [3]. The domains such as finance and healthcare deal with lot of confidential information, where the approach of FL can be highly valuable. The traditional centralized models often pose privacy concerns which can easily be mitigated by FL [2]. Federated computing is not only for technical considerations for social implications but in a way it is strengthening the user and its data [4]. But the mechanism of FL extensively needs and dependent on user participation. Hence, for the successful implementation, some incentive mechanisms are to be created so that clients participate in the process [5].

The organization of this chapter is as follows: Section 2 focuses on examples of data breaches due to centralized storage. The difference between federated learning and machine learning is important to clear the concept of FL. The differences between the two technologies are explained in Section 3. The step-by-step process of FL is put up in detail in Section 4. Understanding of all the advantages and disadvantages is very important when leaning about the core concepts of a technology. Hence, all the major pros and cons are briefed in Section 5 of the chapter. Section 6 presents the conclusion followed by references.

2. Real-World Data Breaches from Centralized Storage

During the time when the usage and abuse of private data were garnering international notice, Google coined the term "federated learning" in 2016. The public's trust in ability to protect private data has also been shattered by a slew of data hacks which were of high profile. As reported by the U.S. Government Accountability Office [6], one of the most well-known instances is the 2017 Equifax data breach, in which hackers took advantage of a weakness in the centralized database of the credit reporting company to reveal the financial and personal data of more than 147 million individuals, including credit card numbers, social security numbers, and dates of birth. Yahoo's 2013–2014 data breach, which impacted all three billion user accounts, is another significant example. Weak centralized storage security allowed names, email addresses, phone numbers, and hashed passwords to be exposed [7]. The infamous Facebook–Cambridge Analytica incident, where Facebook shared the data of its users with third parties and further that data was used for creating the political influence. This incident raised the worries across globe [8]. In another incidence in the healthcare industry, the medical insurance records of 80 million people were compromised. This happened in 2015 where Anthem Inc. hack allowed the hackers to get access to a centralized database having patient information [9]. In a similar incident in 2018, Marriott International's centralized reservation system got compromised. This resulted in affecting around 500 million clients as their details of credit card, addresses, and passport numbers were exposed [10]. These examples clearly portray that how centralized systems of data storage are vulnerable to security breaches and can expose huge amount of confidential data.

Federated learning aims to prevent this by maintaining data decentralization. The expansive General Data Protection Regulation (GDPR) data privacy law was passed in Europe in 2018, and California, the hub of ad-supported digital platforms, adopted it as well. Since then, laws pertaining to digital security have been proposed in Canada, Argentina, and Brazil.

3. How Federated Learning Is Different from Classical Machine Learning?

The main difference among classical ML and FL is that ML works on central data storage, whereas FL follows the decentralized approach of storing the data only at its source. This means that, in traditional machine learning systems, all the raw data from various sources is collected and brought together in one location, such as server, where it is then used to train models. Just opposite, the federated way of learning is conceptualized in such a way that information or the data from the devices of separate users will remain intact at the source location only, without compromising on the security of data. Instead, each source keeps its own data locally and only computational updates or model parameters are shared and aggregated to improve the overall model. This approach addresses privacy concerns and can help reduce bandwidth and storage requirements that come with centralizing large volumes of sensitive or distributed data. The main difference between the two is shown in Figure 1.

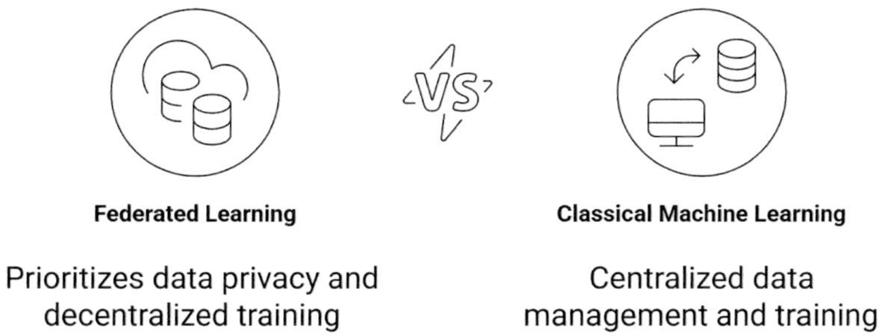

Figure 1: Federated learning versus classical machine leaning.

To better understand their unique characteristics, the following points highlight the key differences between FL and ML. Further details will typically enumerate specific aspects where the two paradigms differ, such as methods of data handling, privacy protection, communication efficiency, and resilience to data breaches.

3.1 Privacy of Data

In classical approach of training the algorithms using machine learning, the data gets aggregated from all sources. This pool of data is stored in a central place and the training of the model takes place using that data. Hence, in this process, all the data regardless of its previous original location is brought to the cloud and the models are trained and fine-tuned to give best output. When the data is transferred from its original location to the cloud at a central server, it involves risks related to the security of data. Risk can be with unauthorized access of data, potential misuse, and by anyone who can access the centralized server.

The concept of FL changed the way how distributed data training is handled. It offers a framework where several collaborators need to train the computational models using their own datasets, but also need to maintain privacy by not sharing their sensitive information on central cloud. This means all the computations for learning and improvements are performed on-device, and only essential model updates—not the source data itself—are stored collectively on central server. Hence, in FL, the user data remains on the device safe and secure.

3.2 Ongoing Learning

Using all of the available training data, a central machine learning model is created within a centralized computing environment in classical machine learning. In this workflow, every piece of data collected from various sources is aggregated into a single repository—typically a powerful cloud server or data center—where the entire model training process takes place. The model is put on the central server once it is trained. The central server is that which responds to the prediction queries which come from user devices. This process will give smooth reliable results as long as central server is not overloaded and operational. In this mechanism, each prediction request must go through the user's device to the remote server and back, hence it may suffer from the latency issues (delay in simple terms). The delay in getting the responses especially in the real-time applications where user expects a quick response will degrade the user experience. These high round-trip delays may demotivate the user which may cause potential abandonment of the service. Also, there are other challenges too in traditional setups of continuous learning. The models are trained and tuned with complete datasets in a central environment, and when new datasets arrive, the complete task of training and deployment of the updated model takes place. As end users do not have access to the complete dataset, they cannot be part of the incremental updates. In FL, the model is deployed on end-user devices and gets updated locally whenever there is fresh data, hence it follows an on-device learning paradigm which is not supported by centralized machine learning approaches.

3.3 Distribution of Data

In applications of machine learning, the data which is used for training is assumed to be independent and identically distributed (IID). This means that data is taken from same probability distribution and statistically independent from other data points. This assumption forms the basis for proving why traditional learning algorithms work and how well they improve over time. But in real-life cases, for the data which is collected from various users and devices, the assumption of IID is not valid because the distribution of the data may vary from source to source. Ideally, each participant should receive an equal amount of the data. Since the numbers of expected and actual participants differ in practical scenarios, this approach is theoretically not possible. The concept of FL distributes the data among participants to maintain the equal receipt of information across participants.

3.4 Combining Many Datasets

To train the models in classical machine learning, the data is required to be collected at a single central source. This creates a risk in having the security and data breaches. On the other side, FL has removed this requirement of aggregation of data. With industry analysts expecting that customer service will be the most realistic use case for business-related AI, the future of AI and machine learning is full of intriguing possibilities. Systems will be able to grow, create new models on the fly, and provide faster and more accurate results, thanks to AI and ML.

4. How Federated Learning Works?

Federated learning [11] allows several users to share the data in a remote manner for the training of a single learning model, iteratively making it better, much like a team report or presentation. Every participant downloads the model, which is often a foundation model that has already been trained, from a cloud data center. After using their private data to train it, they condense and encrypt the model's updated configuration. After being decrypted, averaged, and transmitted back to the cloud, the model changes are included into the centralized model. Till the model is completely trained, the cohesive process of training is repeated iteratively. There are three variations of this decentralized, dispersed training method. Similar datasets are used to train the central model in horizontal federated learning. The data are complementary in vertical federated learning; for instance, a person's musical preferences can be predicted by combining their assessments of books and movies. Last but not least, federated transfer learning involves training a foundation model on a different dataset to perform a different task, such as spotting cats, after it has already been trained to recognize automobiles. The integration of foundation models into federated learning is presently being worked on by Baracaldo [11]. One possible use case is for banks to build an AI model to identify fraud and then use it for other purposes.

4.1 Stages of Working of Federated Learning

There are several key stages involved in the working of FL [12], [13] from selection of the client and distribution of the model to local model training, and model update. The step-by-step explanation is given in the following text.

Step 1: Initialization
The very first step of working of federated learning is initialization. In this step, the central server is responsible to put everything up. In this stage, the server creates a global model. This global model becomes the base and additional training is done on this model. To make this base model stronger right from the beginning, it can be pre-trained too using some available data. The main purpose of this first step is to have a base model which is not expected to be the perfectly tuned, but while going through several steps of FL, it will be well trained. This base model is trained by the client devices through its local data.

Step 2: Client Selection
The second step of the federated learning is the selection of clients. These clients are responsible for training the model. The central server selects the clients to

participate in the training process of the model. There may be a large number of clients and it is practically challenging to include all of them to be responsible for training. So, the central server chooses the clients in a random manner. This selection can also be based on the availability of client data and also the efficiency of data for training purpose. Approximately 10% of all available clients are chosen in this step.

Step 3: Model Distribution

The next step in federated learning process is model distribution. In this step, the shortlisted clients in step 2 (previous step) will receive the latest version of the global base model. The central server is responsible for this distribution. In this step, each participating client device receives the model's parameters, such as weights and biases in the case of a neural network. Once the client receives the model, they will start the training process of the model and it is called local training. Before they start the training process, all clients should be synchronized for using the same global base model. The output after training will finally be combined at the central server, that is why this coherence among clients is important.

Step 4: Local Training

In this step, the clients which are chosen in step 2 will start training process of the model which they had received during step 3. The clients will use their local datasets for the training purpose. This process of training takes place without sharing the raw data with other clients nor with the central server. This step takes place with full data privacy. By the end of this process, the clients obtain model parameters that have been modified to reflect the insights gleaned from their particular datasets. By keeping data locally and just altering model parameters, this step not only enhances privacy but also captures the diversity of data scattered among numerous clients.

Step 5: Model Update Transmission

During the model update transmission phase of the federated learning process, each participating client sends back to the central server the results of its local training. Instead of sending the raw data used for training, clients simply supply the updated model parameters, such as modified weights and biases, or in some cases, just the differences between the old and new values. By ensuring that sensitive data remains entirely on the client's device, this preserves security and privacy. By just transmitting model updates, the method lessens the likelihood of revealing sensitive or private information while allowing the server to benefit from the learning that occurred on each device. In order to improve the global model, the server gathers information from each client in the next stage.

Step 6: Aggregation

After receiving the model updates from all the selected clients in previous step, the central server aggregates everything. Hence, in this step, the server builds an enhanced global model on the basis of model updates which it has received from clients. Each client has trained the model on its own local dataset. The server aggregates these changes using the most widely used technique, which is the simple average of the model parameters. When weighted averaging is used, the global model is more affected by updates from clients with larger datasets. The ultimate goal of aggregation is to integrate these diverse local insights into a single model that improves performance for each client, paving the way for the next training cycle and continuous improvement of the global model.

Step 7: Model Update

In this phase, the server applies all the updates in the global base model. These updates are from the various clients. The central server aggregates the changes into the parameters of the model. In this process, the global model is fully updated with all the changes which are given by the clients. This is a kind of combined knowledge from all clients. Hence, in this phase, the model will acquire speed and also more capability in handling variety of datasets and patterns. This global model can also be called as improved model in this phase.

Step 8: Iteration

The eighth step of federated learning process is iteration. In this step, all the major phases of step 2 to step 7 are repeated from client selection to model update. In the iteration process, a new set of clients are chosen for every round. The most recent global model is sent to them. And in turn the clients will use their local datasets to train that model. This is called local training of global model. Once local training is done, the model is sent back to the server. The server will aggregate the updates which it received from all clients and incorporate them in the global base model. Federated learning ensures that via repeated iterations, the global model becomes more accurate, dependable, and generalized while maintaining data privacy throughout.

Step 9: Evaluation

After going through all the eight stages, the model may be considered as a strong model, but without testing its effectiveness it cannot be considered as a perfect model. Hence, in this stage, the model is evaluated. So, evaluation is the final stage in this learning process. In this step, the model is tested by the server. A test dataset which is not previously used in the iterative rounds is used in this step. The evaluation provides key performance metrics, such as accuracy, precision, recall, or loss, to assess the efficacy of the federated learning process. Ultimately, this phase confirms whether the global model is ready for deployment or requires additional work and validates the training gains.

Step 10: Deployment

Once the model goes through various phases, it comes out as a strong trained global model. It is now ready for use. So, the last phase is deployment of the model so that it is accessible. During various phases, the model has gone through severe training on different datasets, aggregations, updates, and evaluation. The fully trained model can be deployed so that it is accessible to the end user. Also, the model has been trained throughout in such a way that the sensitive information never leaks out of the devices of the clients. The complete cycle of the process of FL is shown in Figure 2.

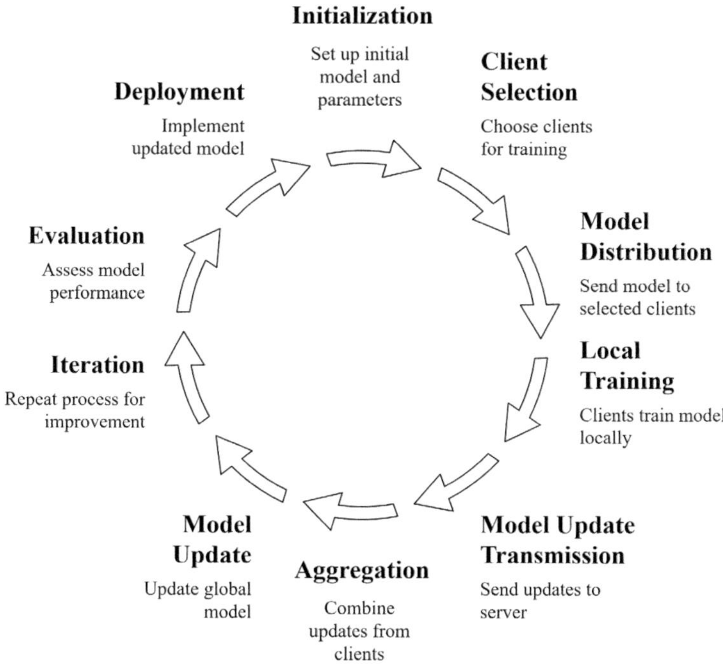

Figure 2: Steps of working of federated learning.

Federated learning thus provides a robust framework for building intelligent, privacy-preserving models by enabling decentralized training. It repeatedly combines safe update sharing, local training, and server-side aggregation to produce robust and generalizable models. Federated learning is a viable solution for industries such as healthcare, finance, and personalized services because it enables organizations to leverage the richness of dispersed data while preserving secrecy.

5. Advantages and Disadvantages of Federated Learning (Pros)

Federated learning offers significant advantages, such as enhanced privacy and collaboration, but it also faces challenges [14]–[17] such as higher communication costs and system complexity. Overall, it is a promising approach, though not without limitations. Some basic but important pros and cons of FL are shown in Figure 3.

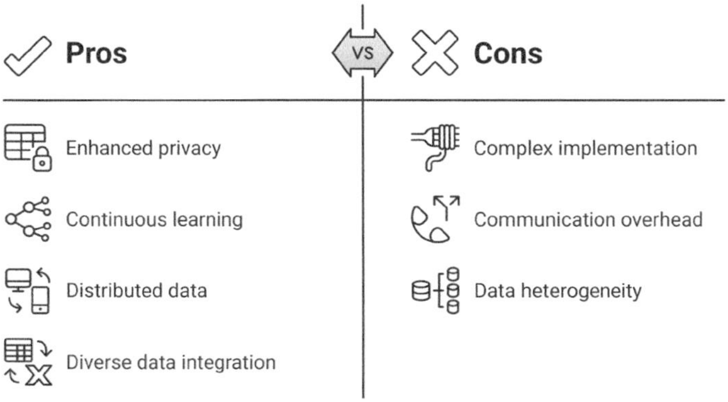

Figure 3: Pros and cons of federated learning.

5.1 *Advantages of Federated Learning*

i. **Enhanced Privacy Preservation**
The privacy preservation is considered as one of the most important advantages. The sensitive information is not centralized but the training takes place on the device of user or in the local environment. The anonymized model updates are shared to central server. By doing this, the risk of data breaches is mitigated because the raw data is still in the control of user.

ii. **Reduced Communication Costs**
By processing data locally, FL reduces the requirement to send huge sets of data to a common server. This reduces communication costs, especially in scenarios with limited bandwidth or expensive data transfer fees.

iii. **Increased Data Access and Model Generalization**
Access to a greater variety of data sources that might not otherwise be available because of privacy laws, data ownership issues, or practical difficulties is made possible by federated learning. In contrast to models trained on a small, centralized dataset, the resulting model can achieve greater generalization performance and robustness by training on heterogeneous datasets spread across multiple devices or organizations.

iv. **Compliance with Data Governance Regulations**
As the awareness of data security and privacy is increasing and stronger regulations such as GDPR and California Consumer Privacy Act (CCPA) are coming up, FL provides a way to follow all such regulations. As the data remains at local devices, there is no compromise with data compliances.

v. **Improved Model Personalization**
Federated learning can be modified to customize models for specific users or user groups. Through local data training and user-specific option

incorporation, FL may provide personalized models that enhance user experience and better meet individual needs. Applications such as money, healthcare, and personalized suggestions are especially pertinent to this.

vi. **Reduced Reliance on Centralized Infrastructure**
As models are trained on local devices using the local datasets, there is no dependency on large data centers for training the models. This helps in huge cost saving and better scalability. The computational load is also shared among clients.

5.2 Disadvantages of Federated Learning

Although there are so many advantages of this technology, it is still not untouched with some complexities too. Some of the disadvantages of federated learning are listed in the following text.

i. **Communication Bottlenecks**
This way of learning necessitates communication between the entities or devices, which may cause a bottleneck, particularly if the devices are spread out geographically. Sometimes unreliable network can also be a major issue.

ii. **Heterogeneous Data and Systems**
Wide variety of data that too coming from several sources is used for training. Varied data may create issue in the performance of the model. Added to this, the process of training becomes more difficult because the devices which are involved vary from each other in their hardware configurations, software needs, etc.

iii. **Security Vulnerabilities**
Although FL improves the privacy, it is not untouched by security risks. If attackers add bad data or change model updates, they can weaken the system. Methods such as secure aggregation and differential privacy can help protect it, but they also make the process more complex and slower.

iv. **Incentive Mechanisms and Participation**
It can be difficult to guarantee that every device or organization actively participates in federated learning. Without appropriate incentives, participants might be hesitant to provide their data or computational resources. For federated learning deployments to be successful, incentive mechanisms that reward participation and solve issues of fairness and data ownership must be designed.

v. **Client Device Computational Costs**
It can be computationally costly to train machine learning models on client devices, particularly for devices with limited resources such as smartphones or Internet of Things sensors. User discontent, decreased device performance, and higher battery usage can result from this. Deploying federated learning

on edge devices requires resource-efficient model architectures and training procedures.

vi. **Model Aggregation Challenges**
It might be difficult to aggregate model updates from several devices, especially when non-IID (non-independent and identically distributed) data is involved. In certain situations, simple averaging methods might not be the best option; instead, more complex aggregation procedures could be needed to guarantee model convergence and equity.

vii. **Debugging and Monitoring Complexity**
Debugging and monitoring federated learning systems can be more complex than traditional centralized machine learning systems. The distributed nature of FL makes it difficult to track down errors and identify performance bottlenecks. Developing effective tools and techniques for monitoring model performance, detecting anomalies, and diagnosing issues is crucial for ensuring the reliability and stability of federated learning deployments.

6. Conclusion

While maintaining privacy and providing access to a greater variety of data sources, federated learning is an appealing method for training machine learning models on decentralized data. But there are drawbacks as well, including issues with incentive systems, data heterogeneity, communication barriers, and security flaws. Organizations can decide if federated learning is the best strategy for their unique requirements and create plans to reduce the risks involved by carefully weighing these benefits and drawbacks. We can anticipate more developments in algorithms, methods, and strategies that tackle these issues and unleash the full potential of this exciting technology as the field of federated learning develops.

References

[1] Martineau, K. (2022). What is federated learning? *IBM Research Blog*. [Online]. Available: https://research.ibm.com/blog/what-is-federated-learning.

[2] Sharma, S. and Guleria, K. (2023). A federated learning mechanism for preserving security of sensitive data. In *Proc. 2023 4th Int. Conf. Data Analytics for Business and Industry (ICDABI)*, pp. 1–5, doi: 10.1109/ICDABI57639.2023.10305245.

[3] Thakur, D. (2021). Federated learning and privacy-preserving AI: Challenges and solutions in distributed machine learning. *Int. J. All Res. Educ. Sci. Methods (IJARESM)*, 9(6): 3763–3764. [Online]. Available: https://www.ijaresm.com.

[4] Schwermer, R., Mayer, R. and Jacobsen, H. A. (Apr. 2024). Federated computing—Survey on building blocks, extensions and systems. *arXiv preprint* arXiv:2404.02779. [Online]. Available: https://arxiv.org/abs/2404.02779.

[5] Hussain, G. J. and Manoj, G. (Feb. 2022). Federated learning: A survey of a new approach to machine learning. In *Proc. 1st Int. Conf. Electrical, Electronics, Information and Communication Technologies (ICEEICT)*, pp. 1–8, doi: 10.1109/ICEEICT54472.2022.9758472.

[6] U.S. Government Accountability Office. (Aug. 2018). *Data Protection: Actions Taken by Equifax and Federal Agencies in Response to the 2017 Breach*, Rep. GAO-18-559. [Online]. Available: https://www.gao.gov/products/gao-18-559.
[7] Perlroth, N., Frenkel, M. and Glanz, R. (Oct. 2017). All 3 billion Yahoo accounts were affected by 2013 attack. *The New York Times*. [Online]. Available: https://www.nytimes.com/2017/10/03/technology/yahoo-hack-3-billion-users.html.
[8] Isaak, J. and Hanna, M. J. (Aug. 2018). User data privacy: Facebook, Cambridge Analytica, and privacy protection. *Computer*, 51(8): 56–59, doi: 10.1109/MC.2018.3191268.
[9] Levesque, R., Walsh, D. A. and Whyte, D. (Nov. 2015). Securing cyberspace: Towards an agenda for research and practice. *Technology Innovation Management Review*, 5(11): 5–13. [Online]. Available: https://timreview.ca/article/926.
[10] Marriott International. (Nov. 2018). Marriott announces Starwood guest reservation database security incident. Press Release. [Online]. Available: https://news.marriott.com.
[11] Baracaldo, N. (Aug. 2022). What is federated learning? *IBM Research Blog*. [Online]. Available: https://research.ibm.com/blog/what-is-federated-learning.
[12] Naik, D. and Naik, N. (Sep. 2023). An introduction to federated learning: Working, types, benefits and limitations. In *Proc. UK Workshop on Computational Intelligence*, Cham, Switzerland: Springer Nature Switzerland, pp. 3–17, doi: 10.1007/978-3-031-45821-6_1.
[13] Shastri, Y. (Feb. 2023). A step-by-step guide to federated learning in computer vision. *V7 Labs Blog*. [Online]. Available: https://www.v7labs.com/blog/federated-learning-guide.
[14] Wen, J., Zhang, Z., Lan, Y., Cui, Z., Cai, J. and Zhang, W. (Feb. 2023). A survey on federated learning: Challenges and applications. *Int. J. Mach. Learn. Cybern.*, 14(2): 513–535, doi: 10.1007/s13042-022-01722-3.
[15] Bogdanova, A., Attoh-Okine, N. and Sakurai, T. (Sep. 2020). Risk and advantages of federated learning for health care data collaboration. *ASCE-ASME J. Risk Uncertain. Eng. Syst., Part A: Civ. Eng.*, 6(3): Art. no. 04020031. doi: 10.1115/1.4046932.
[16] Liberti, F., Berardi, D. and Martini, B. (2024). Federated learning in dynamic and heterogeneous environments: Advantages, performances, and privacy problems. *Applied Sciences*, 14(18): Art. no. 8490, doi: 10.3390/app14188490.
[17] Mammen, P. M. (2021). Federated learning: Opportunities and challenges. *arXiv preprint* arXiv:2101.05428, 2021. [Online]. Available: https://arxiv.org/abs/2101.05428.

3 | Federated Learning for Financial Data Privacy and Security in Secure AI Systems

Amit Singh Dalal

The issue of data privacy and security has become one of the most important in the sphere of the financial services developing rather rapidly. The massive growth of digital transactions, online banking, credit rating, and blockchain-based services has pushed the security of sensitive data not only as a regulatory choice but as a strategic business considerate priority. This chapter is a current topic in fielding the intersection of financial data privacy and security and federated learning (FL) as a new model of secure artificial intelligence (AI) applications in finance. Conventional centralized data storage and processing systems present organizations and individuals with intrusions, phishing, insider threats, and regulatory noncompliance guarantees that conventional systems are designed to mitigate. On the other hand, FL also supports collaborative training without the need to exchange any raw data, which adheres to the data-protection laws and best practices, including the General Data Protection Regulation (GDPR), California Consumer Privacy Act (CCPA), or Reserve Bank of India (RBI) practices. This chapter starts by investigating some of the common weaknesses in financial ecosystems, and then moves on to the regulatory institutions that form the governance of data. It also introduces privacy-enhancing technologies that support FL systems, which are homomorphic encryption, secure multiparty computation, as well as differential privacy. Applications to real-world problems including fraud detection and anti-money-laundering (AML) monitoring and customized financial advisory are evaluated to show the ground-breaking contribution of FL to greater effectiveness in many aspects. This chapter ends with the statement that to have a reliable and privacy-saving financial ecosystem, the integration of governance, regulative compliance, and scalable technology solutions is obligatory. This vision puts FL as not only a technical innovation but also a safe AI provider in the new generation of finance.

IEC University, Solan, Himachal Pradesh, India.
Email: amit.dalal15@gmail.com

DOI: 10.1201/9781003710059-3

1. Introduction

In the past two decades, the financial ecosystem in the world apparently experienced a drastic transition courtesy of forces of digitalization, cloud structures, and analytics enabled by artificial intelligence (AI). Banks, insurance companies, stock markets, fintechs, and digital wallets are entirely reliant on digitally connected networks to facilitate millions of financial transactions in a few seconds today. Even though the efficiency, accessibility, and inclusivity of financial services have been increased, these changes have also raised the concern on the security and privacy of financial data. Facing the threat of attacks that publicize the identity of millions of customers to identity theft, monetary damages, or even encroachment of intimate transactional practices, implementation of sound privacy and security systems has become not only a technical necessity but also a call of ethics and a regulatory mandate. Information on finances is uniquely delicate unlike most other branches of information. In comparison to generic consumer data, for example, a browsing history or products of interest, financial records do have a financial value to them, and this type of data can create immediate impacts with misuse. Compromised credit card number or stolen banking login details, although not directly, can result in loss of money, loss of goodwill, and legal liability on part of the perpetrators and the organizations in question. Due to this fact, financial information security can be viewed as the very foundation of current cybersecurity. The increased usage of AI in the financial decision-making, such as credit scoring, high-frequency trading, and other applications, only adds to the stakes, since such systems rely on substantial amounts of data, which should not be compromised in order to prevent biased or otherwise faulty results [1].

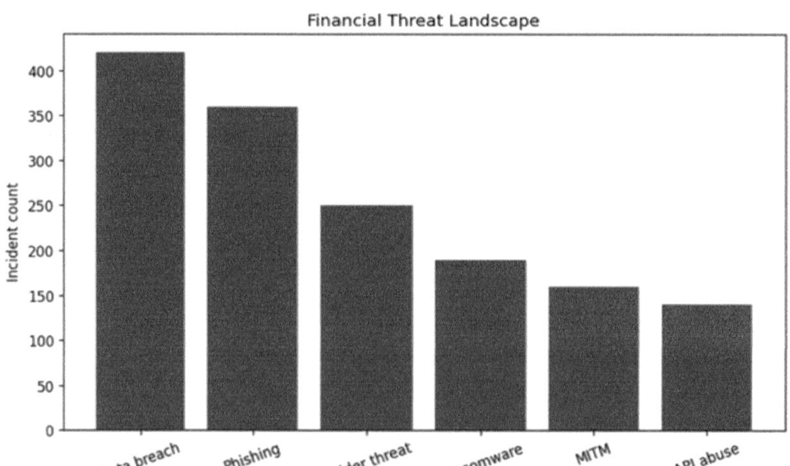

Figure 1: Financial threat landscape.

Figure 1 demonstrates the changing environment of financial threats, and lists the key vectors that are used by attackers, including phishing, insider threat, malware, and data breaches as common in current financial systems. The figure highlights that the more digitalized and interconnected platforms become, the more the attacks surface. It gives the visual background on the depth and magnitude of security issues that financial institutions deal with. The growth of the trend to mobile applications and the use of digital wallets has enhanced the financial attack surface. Transactions immediacy, possibility of sending and receiving money, and investing activities all subject millions of consumers around the globe to phishing, malware, and insider attacks when they use mobile banking applications. Unlike the old financial banking paradigm in which the financial process was limited to safe centralized infrastructures, the new financial environment functions on a distributed and networked structure of devices, platforms, and third-party services. These nodes at the same time provide an opportunity and create vulnerability, hence exacerbating the task of ensuring that financial information is secured sufficiently. The tragedies of data breach in the financial sector are critical and are highlighted by historical events. A good case in point is the Equifax breach of 2017, which revealed personal financings, for example, social security numbers, credit card data, and highly sensitive account details, of about 147 million customers. Similarly, in 2019, the Capital One compromise of over 100 million customer accounts costed the company billions of dollars in damages and regulatory fines. Such incidents portray clearly the shortcomings of the older security systems and are an indicator of the need to have stronger security systems that are privacy-sensitive. All of these risks are magnified by the growing interconnection between financial services and decentralized finance (DeFi), cryptocurrencies, and transnational payment systems, and a new focus is required on security architectures that put privacy by design at their core. The most notable aspect of this transformation is the new paradigm of federated learning (FL), an approach to machine learning whereby institutions are allowed to jointly learn a model on sensitive financial information without sharing the physical information. Instead of training the AI models on the centralized servers with the customer data, FL allows the model to be trained locally at each institution participating in the process, only sharing the model parameters or gradients. This method is highly decentralized and minimizes the chances of data being exposed significantly besides enabling the sharing of handy intelligence among financial institutions. In this respect, data privacy does not only address ensuring the protection of raw transactional data, but it also extends to the information of the overall financial ecosystem, including metadata such as geolocation data linked to Kromer ATM withdrawal, online purchase behavioral patterns, and predictive analytics such as creditworthiness test. It is also important to guard these inferences, since the abuse of such knowledge may facilitate a specific type of fraud or market distortion. As a result, homomorphic encryption (HE), secure multiparty calculation (SMPC), and differential privacy are some of the sophisticated safeguards that are vital when combined with federated learning, to offer the notion of multilayered protection [2].

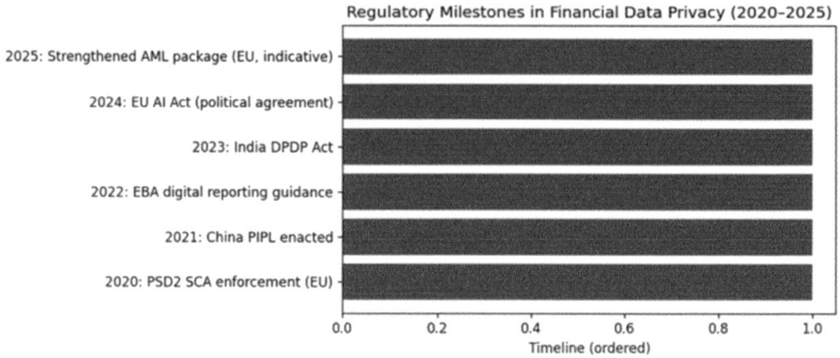

Figure 2: Regulatory milestones in financial data privacy (2020–2025).

Figure 2 outlines significant regulatory benchmarks in the privacy of financial data in the period 2020–2025, such as the General Data Protection Regulation (GDPR) and the California Consumer Privacy Act (CCPA) and financial industry-specific regulations. The figure underscores the mounting pressure on the institutions to implement privacy-protective technology. It visually supports the importance of compliance as one of the factors in the safe adoption of AI in finance. There is another aspect that supports the significance of the financial data protection—the fact that the regulatory environment becomes increasingly tough. The requirements of the collection, processing, and sharing of financial information under new laws such as the GDPR in Europe and CCPA in the United States are stringent. Lack of compliance may attract significant fines, negative publicity, limitations on operations, and thus making data protection a legal obligation. Reserve Bank of India (RBI) has also required tight protection of digital payment providers such as data localization, data which is encrypted in transmission, and constant screening of suspicious behavior [3]. As a result, financial institutions are experiencing a significant strain to implement privacy-saving technologies that would fulfil regulation and operational requirements. The sensitivity of the data security management is also increased in the light of the trust the client has toward the financial services. Clients leave their financial identity and assets to banks, insurers, and fintech platforms. In the face of violation, be it by leaking information, through covert monitoring, or the improper utilization of personal monetary records, trust in the institution and the financial system in general may be destroyed. Trust is more than a loyalty aspect by the customers; it is a basic requirement on economic stability. Indicatively, a massive security breach to digital first economy, with the digital wallets and mobile payments, would disable all parts of the economic world and disrupt markets. This chapter next takes up the convergence point of technology, regulation, and innovation, and discusses mechanisms of making financial information more privacy- and security-friendly in the face of artificial intelligence and federated learning. It outlines the most common vulnerabilities of financial systems such as data breaches and insider threat. Regulatory regimes in different jurisdictions that attempt to regulate financial data management are also examined in the chapter as the readers are attracted to the intricacies of the cross-border financial operations. Besides, it talks about the underlying principles of security procedures, for example, encryption, data minimization, and secure application programming interfaces (APIs), and then looks at the disruptive nature of federated learning in the creation of privacy-preserving financial AI.

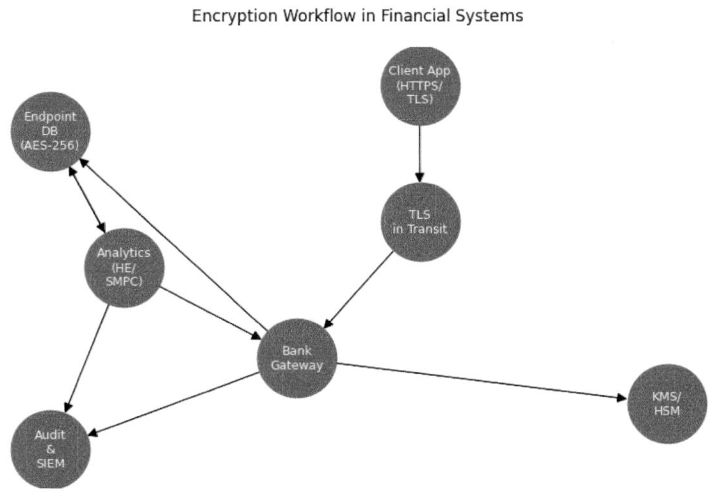

Figure 3: Encryption workflow in financial systems.

Figure 3 shows the typical encryption process that is applied in financial systems to encrypt data when stored and transmitted. It reveals the way encryption can be used as a layer of defense in confidential financial data. The figure justifies the privacy-enhancing technology discussion which is integrated with federated learning architectures. In addition to federated learning, the chapter addresses complementary privacy-preserving technologies used in federated learning, namely, homomorphic encryption, SMPC, and differential privacy, which also enhance data security in a distributed setting. It also shows its use in real life such as preventing fraud, anti-money-laundering (AML) regulatory compliance, and customizing wealth management to show the practical importance of such technologies. Lastly, the chapter discusses the drawbacks and bottlenecks of applying federated learning to financial issues and suggests future ideas on how to develop AI systems based on regulation compliance, transparency, and security [4]. The current chapter tries to unite the experts of the technical side of the matter with the regulator and draw a full picture of the threats and promising prospects of financial data privacy and security. It states that, although the financial industry is always at risk to cybersecurity, the integration of federated learning and privacy technology may present an effective way to achieve the right balance between innovation, compliance, and trust. With the increasing transition of financial institutions toward the age of AI-related services, the capability of ensuring a secure data environment without limiting the intelligence captured by collaborations will become a distinguishing feature of the resistance to and stability of the entire global financial network [5].

2. Types of Data Vulnerabilities in Financial Systems

In its nature, the financial data proves to be one of the most valuable types of the digital data. Financial records are confidential data that is unlike the other forms of data such as the social media activity or browsing history on the internet, and can be immediately monetized in case stolen or misused. The financial information is highly sensitive, and this fact, coupled with increasing digitization of financial services, gives malicious actors some of the best targets in the financial systems. Before establishing the process of dealing with these systems, it is important to first examine the different means of vulnerabilities which are in financial structures. Such vulnerabilities cut across what we could call technical, organizational, and regulatory, and they overlap, thus forming complex threat environments.

2.1 External Cybersecurity Threats

External cyberattack is one of the most evident sources of financial data insecurity. Criminal syndicates, hackers, and even state-sponsored networks are always trying to exploit the loopholes in the financial networks. Phishing attacks are also among the most popular attack vectors when customers or employees can be duped into the disclosure of the credentials needed to log in by being presented with fraudulent emails or websites pretending to be legitimate sites in the banking sector. Such attacks are especially viable in the field of finance where customers have become used to being sent regular reports regarding their accounts and they, as a result, send information that may contain sensitive content without realizing it [6].

Malware and ransomware are another common external vulnerability. Financial systems may be compromised by the malware that may enter the system through the apparently safe downloads, attachment, or software vulnerabilities. Malicious software when installed can steal customer information, modify the transaction records, or give access to the attackers using the back door. Among them, in particular, ransomware has turned into a disastrous menace. The attackers encrypt databases or transaction systems of financial institutions in case of ransomware incidents and request payment to restore access. Celebrity incidents have demonstrated that even multinational banks and stock exchanges with a huge scale are capable of being laid out temporarily by these attacks, due to the vulnerability of centralized financial systems. Another most serious vulnerability is distributed denial-of-service (DDoS) attacks. During such attacks, attackers flood the servers of a financial platform with substantial traffic so that legitimate users could not be provided with services. DDoS attacks are unlikely to directly expose any data, but cause a loss of time, money, and reputation; and occasionally,

DDoS attacks are employed as decoys, to distract security personnel, during other targeted intrusions.

2.2 Insider Threats

Vulnerabilities are not only caused by outside elements. The risks to the security of financial data that are most threatening include insider threats caused both by intentional and unintentional acts. Privileged users such as employees, contractors, third-party vendors with access to financial systems may use their credentials in a fraudulent or criminal way. In most incidences, the insiders collude with the outside criminals to take advantage of their knowledge of internal procedures in order to beat security systems [7].

Nevertheless, not all threats that can be dealt with by insiders are malicious. A large percentage of the leakage of data in the financial organizations involves human error. Rich data exposure can be achieved via misplaced laptop, inadequate setup database, or an employee distributing confidential data to the incorrect party. As an illustration, we have cases when unencrypted backups of the financial information were left on the cloud servers being able to be accessed by every person who has a link. These loopholes of security translate into the reality that despite the most important technological security capabilities, weak organizational processes may subvert the intended protection.

2.3 Weak Authentication and Access Controls

There are also many millions of users of financial services relying on access to accounts remotely, and in these cases, the authentication systems play a very vital defensive role. Nevertheless, a source of weakness has been identified as poor or obsolete authentication protocols. Most institutions are still using the one-factor authentication which may be easily stolen using phishing techniques, brute force, as well as credential stuffing. There are still vulnerabilities even in the case of the support of two-factor authentication (2FA). The attackers can block the one-time password (OTP) that is transmitted by the use of SIM-swapping methods or weaknesses in the mobile networks. Poor access control policies also add to the issue as employees can gain more privileges than they are required in their job. This increases the attack surface, which means that malicious actors have more chances to implement compromised accounts [8].

2.4 Data Transmission and Storage Vulnerabilities

Another point of serious vulnerability is movement and storage of financial data. The information is especially vulnerable when exchanged among third-party service providers, customers, and financial institutions. Attackers can capture sensitive data by exploiting the weak or poorly managed encryption policies in the process popularly known as man-in-the-middle (MITM) attack where the hacker spies on or manipulates messages of the two communicating parties without their suspicion.

Vulnerabilities of storage are also worrying. Banking organizations tend to have immense data warehouses that are used to store years of client files disclosure, trades, and legal filings. Poorly segregated or even poorly encrypted databases make aggravating targets to attackers. Further on, the appearing tendency toward storing data using cloud-based solutions has brought new risks. Buckets that are misconfigured have caused high-profile data exposures in recent years that saw millions of financial records dumped publicly onto the internet. In Figure 4, the trade-off between data privacy and model utility is illustrated when using the mechanisms of differential privacy. It points at the enhancement of privacy associated with increased noise and the possible decrease in the accuracy of analysis. The number assists in putting the balance needed in the implementation of privacy-saving AI used in financial settings into context.

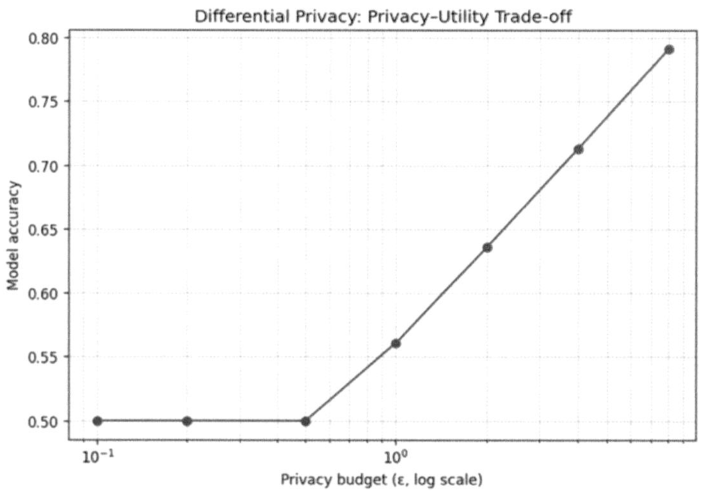

Figure 4: DP privacy-utility trade-off.

2.5 Third-Party and Supply Chain Risks

Contemporary financial environments lack self-sufficiency; the costs of third-party vendors and payment processors, software solutions, and fintech partners are high. Although outsourcing makes institutions more efficient and gives them a chance to implement best technologies in the market, it opens them to a supply chain weakness. Smaller vendors with less security postures are usually a stepping stone to the larger financial institutions that are targeted by the attackers. An example may be vulnerability in a popular financial software package that enables attackers to attack tens of institutions at once. Equally, hacking in credit reporting bureau or payment portal can give rise to systemic danger along the bank, insurance, and consumer levels. Financial supply chains are characterized by close interdependencies. In such a way, the performance of the whole system may depend on the security of any single person [9].

2.6 Regulatory and Compliance Gaps

Even with such international standards as GDPR and CCPA that are supposed to smooth the transition process, there remain regulatory gaps that leave the financial data unprotected. Certain jurisdictions do not have any comprehensive laws in place to protect the data, especially the ones based on hard to implement regulations. International sales aggravate this issue because transfers of data might pass through several jurisdictions with different informational privacy and protection requirements. Lack of compliance with the regulatory requirements does not only expose the institutions to fines but also leaves vulnerable loopholes that can be exploited. As an illustration, the noncompliant financial organization that does not adopt required encryption measures might unknowingly leave a loophole to the hackers. Equally, inconsistent compliance with know-your-customer (KYC) and AML standards might form blind spots, which are used by criminals to transfer illegal finances without being noticed.

2.7 Emerging Vulnerabilities in Digital Finance

Due to the development of financial ecosystems, new vulnerabilities keep occurring. The emergence of cryptocurrencies and decentralized finance (DeFi) facilities has brought about security threats that the conventional monetary institutions have not been subject to before. Smart contracts are financial agreements that can be executed automatically via blockchain networks and thus they are vulnerable to both coding and logic bugs and attacks. Contrary to a traditional banking system where transactions may be reversed at times, transactions made on a blockchain are nonreversible, so thefts are therefore hard to recover [10].

The other recent susceptibility is an AI-based financial system. Although the application of machine learning models can optimize the detection and management of fraud and mitigation of risk, such models are susceptible to adversarial attacks. In the case of fraudulent transactions, attackers can sufficiently modify input data to make AI models believe that they are legitimate and interfere with automated decision-making trustworthiness in the field of finance.

2.8 Socio-Technical Vulnerabilities

Lastly, technology is not the only area where financial data are vulnerable but social and organizational aspects are also affected. Attacks on social engineering, which are based on the finding that criminals take advantage of human psychology, over technical vices, are evolving to be highly effective. Criminals pose as bank representatives, IT support specialists, and regulating authorities with the aim of making victims disclose valuable secrets. In most of the situations, these tactics successfully thwart complex technological barriers since they only touch on human confidence and sense of urgency [11]. Besides, the fast rate of digitization has also caused most financial institutions to sink in the process of adjusting their security policies to the technical changes. A high-quality modern digital environment still has to remain intermingled with legacy systems not designed to meet today's cybersecurity threat, resulting in legacy patchwork infrastructures which are hard to accomplish holistically. Such mismatch of people, processes, and technologies create loopholes that are exploited by the attackers. The comparison of the computational overhead of the two encryption technologies, SMPC and HE, is shown in Figure 5. The graph indicates the performance variations applicable to scalability and deploy ability. This analogy helps in arguing on the choice of suitable cryptographic methods in a financial system of the real world.

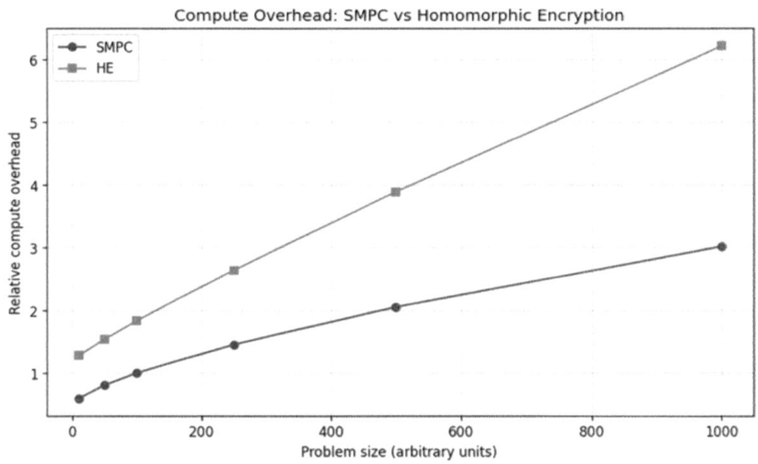

Figure 5: Overhead comparison (SMPC vs HE).

Financial system vulnerabilities are complex; they include external hacking and insider threats, poor authentication, and third-party reliance and new threats in digital finance. To curb these vulnerabilities, it is necessary to deal with the problem comprehensively by combining formidable technical controls, strict compliance, and constant training of workers and customers. Financial institutions should appreciate that security is not a solution that you implement once and then have a wonderful time, but an adaptive process with respect to a changing threat environment [12]. To address the issue, the financial industry should accept that treating vulnerabilities is a complex task and it must start building resilient systems by integrating both new technologies (federated learning, in this case) and conventional protections. The following parts of this chapter will further develop this knowledge discussing regulatory instruments, security concepts that can be used to enhance the security of digital financial information, and new privacy-enhancing technologies which have the potential to work collectively to enhance the financial information security in the era of the digital world.

3. Regulatory Frameworks for Data Security in Finance

Control of financial information security has become one of the essential parts of the world financial regulation. Banking and financial organizations deal with delicate customer data, transaction records, and identity documents, which are to be safeguarded against exploitation, dishonest usage, and fraud. This has led to the development of detailed frameworks by governments and regulatory bodies across the globe to safeguard information, impose enforcement, and ensure that the population puts its trust on the financial services. The jurisdictional frameworks differ, although their main purpose is the same, that is, taking legal responsibility over the financial entities to protect information and hold the latter responsible in the event of such losses.

3.1 The Role of Regulation of Financial Information Protection

Financial sector is peculiar to trust. The customers need to be certain that their deposits, investments, and other personal information are not opened to unauthorized access and fraud. The regulation is an important tool responsible to institutionalize this faith through creating the minimal standards of security and monitoring their recognition, and sanctions are applied to the negligence. Contrasting voluntary standards and regulatory frameworks consist of legally binding standards that force financial institutions to put more of an emphasis on cybersecurity, encryption, identity verification, and reports related to incidents. Meanwhile, not all regulation is penal in nature. It is also clear, constant, and predictable to the financial organizations that have operations in different jurisdictions. Regulatory frameworks help secure decisions by providing norms of data protection that minimize ambiguity and embrace uniformity in security practices. This is especially critical in the contemporary financial world where international cooperation and data crossing borders have become ordinary [13].

3.2 International Regulatory Standards

The international aspect of finance requires global standardization in the laws of data security. Even though different countries implement their own legislation, a number of global treaties and standards affect the financial sector in various countries all over the globe. Arguably the most powerful international data security and privacy regulation is the 2018 European Union (EU) enacted GDPR. However, despite the extraterritorial nature GDPR has in the EU, its provisions ensure that its rules and regulations apply to any institution that processes the personal data belonging to EU citizens. To the financial organizations, GDPR will require data minimization, consent, encryption, and the right to be forgotten. The failure to comply may attract significant amounts of fines of 4% of the annual worldwide revenue [14]. In the United States, notwithstanding the absence of any entirely comprehensive federal privacy law, sector-specific laws exist to regulate industry-specific privacy (including the Gramm–Leach–Bliley Act (GLBA) which subjects financial institutions to strict requirements regarding consumer financial privacy). The GLBA has required banks and other financial service providers to keep safeguards to the customer data, report their information-sharing resolutions, and limit unlawful access. Also, CCPA is a groundbreaking state regulation that expands the rights of consumers and places responsibility on organizations which manage personal information and includes businesses that practice in California, such as the ones that work with finances.

Additional renowned global principles are the Payment Card Industry Data Security Standard (PCI DSS) that provides safety requirements to businesses that maintain cardholder information and the Basel Committee on Banking Supervision standards that focus on digital banking on risk management initiatives. A combination of these frameworks creates a tiered system of regulation under which financial institutions have to adhere to several cross-cutting guides [15].

3.3 National Regulatory Frameworks

Besides international standards, states also use national laws that need to be approved by their financial ecosystems. As an illustration, a clear act called the Digital Personal Data Protection Act (DPDP Act) 2023 in India was passed that deals specifically with the protection of personal financial information. It also focuses on the informed consent, the limitation of purpose, and data localization of specific types of sensitive data. RBI also provided deliberations of cybersafe guarding to the banks where direction includes use of two-factored authentication, round the clock monitoring of frauds, and assessment of security after regular time intervals [13]. The entire federated learning process is depicted in Figure 6 and it consists of local model training, sharing secure parameters, and global aggregation. The figure explains the role of federated learning in removing centralized data gathering and facilitating collaborative intelligence. It supports the theoretical background of privacy-sensitive AI in finance.

The Personal Information Protection Law (PIPL) adopted in China in 2021 reflects some features of GDPR but is more demanding in terms of the localization of data. Financial institutions that are to operate within China are required to keep the sensitive financial data in the country and seek specific government advisories prior to exporting information out of China. In the same way, in Singapore, the Personal Data Protection Act (PDPA) pursues the principle of accountability and mandates the appointment of data protection officers in the organization. Variation in national laws points to diversity in the political focus, economic progression, and maturity of the digital assets. Nonetheless, it also poses compliance problems to multinational financial bodies that have to be in a position to negotiate conflicting regulatory demands in various jurisdictions [14].

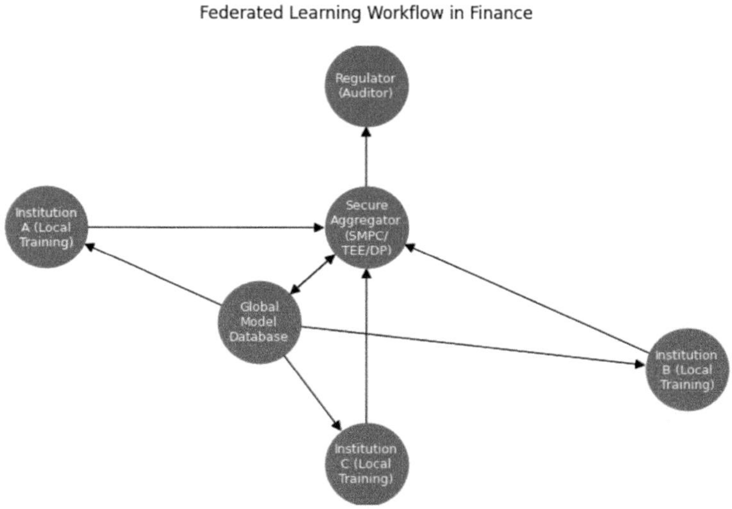

Figure 6: FL workflow diagram.

3.4 Sector-Specific Financial Regulations

Most sectors are covered by sector-specific rules in addition to general privacy laws. To provide an example, U.S. Securities and Exchange Commission (SEC) and the Commodity Futures Trading Commission (CFTC) provided some guidance concerning cybersecurity in the market of securities and derivatives. The rules focus on incident reporting, management of vendor risk, and the ability to withstand market manipulation.

In Europe, the Payment Services Directive 2 (PSD2) has revolutionized online banking by introducing strong customer authentication and secure communication criteria among banks and other non-bank actors in the payments space. PSD2 is expected to increase security, and through open banking, it tends to spur innovation, which balances the protection of consumers with financial innovation. Regulators across the world have mandated insurers to implement security measures regarding cybersecurity to secure the information of the policyholders and continue with their operations. On the same note, credit reporting agencies are slowly becoming subjected to more stringent measures since the security breaches of high-profile financial identities that deceived millions of people [11].

3.5 Enforcement Mechanisms and Penalties

Such a punishment regime makes no sense without follow-up mechanisms. Compliance is guaranteed through different mechanisms that include audits, requirements to report, and sanctions to impose financial penalties. In the example of GDPR, regulators are allowed to fine to billions of dollars, as witnessed when fining large multinational corporations. On the same note, banks have been fined by RBI due to noncompliance with the directives on cybersecurity, hence sending warning bell on the need to comply. Enforcement also applies to legal requirements in the disclosure of information. Numerous regulations require the financial institutions to impart data breach reports within a designated time frame, which can be 24–72 hours. This will foster transparency and help the regulators to determine quickly the seriousness of breaches. Concurrently, it will give consumers power since they will be educated on any dangers that may put their finances under risk.

3.6 Noneconomic Burden—Compliance Issues

Although regulatory frameworks are the sole modalities of securing financial data, there are difficulties associated with compliance. Regulatory fragmentation, which occurs due to the complexity of international–national regulations, means that institutions are in a position of competing duties to the institutions. As an example, data localization needs in a jurisdiction might conflict with data transfer across national borders needs in another jurisdiction. Being compliant also comes with large expenses in terms of money and operation. Measures such as installing sophisticated methods of encryption, employing compliance staff, and procuring regular security checks may be too demanding on small financial institutions and small fintech ventures. This brings into question that excessive regulations can kill innovation due to entering barriers.

A second issue would be the fast pace of technological development which can frequently not be adapted to with regulation. New hazards of AI attackers, quantum computing, and decentralized finance eco-systems can prove insufficiently covered by the current systems. Regulators should shift to adaptive strategies and revise the laws and guidelines to meet the advancement in technologies.

3.7 En Route to Converged International Regulation

Due to the interdependency of the financial systems, there is an increased feeling of the necessity of globally converged rules. The Financial Stability Board (FSB) and other organizations such as the International Monetary Fund (IMF) promote the idea of increasing international cooperation as it pertains to establishing and enforcing standards related to cybersecurity and data protection. Harmonization would also lessen the burden of compliance to multinational institutions and also strengthen the cross-border attack resilience to the system. Nonetheless, global harmonization poses challenges, such as the barriers related to geopolitical tensions, different levels of digital maturity, and peculiarities of cultural perceptions of privacy. These challenges notwithstanding, the three nations are enjoying some success in the form of bilateral agreements, regional alliances, and international best practices.

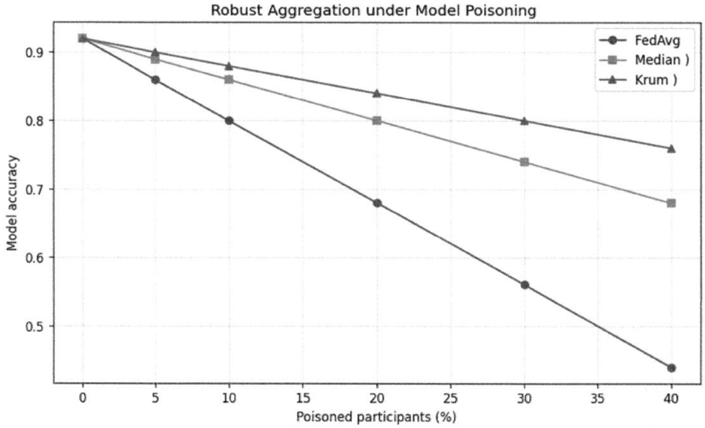

Figure 7: Robust aggregation comparison.

The regulatory frameworks constitute the pillar of the safety of financial data through clear stipulations, compliance, and consumer confidence. Whether it is international regulations such as GDPR or local regulations such as the DPDP Act of India or the PIPL of China, all regulations inform how financial institutions deal with sensitive data and personal data. Nonetheless, measures such as regulatory fragmentation, costs of regulatory compliance, and changes in technology necessitate the flexibility and integration of regulatory measures. The comparison in Figure 7 is between robust aggregation methods implemented in federated learning to prevent adversarial and Byzantine attacks. It emphasizes the way various approaches increase the model resiliency to malicious updates. The figure justifies the debate on trust and strength in decentralized financial learning systems.

Along with the ongoing digitalization or globalization of the financial system, efficient regulation shall be one of the foundations of resilience. The next section will be devoted to privacy-viewing mechanisms and the role of privacy-enforcing technologies in the digital age, including encryption technologies, federated learning, and secure multiparty computation to complement regulation of the space to protect financial data.

4. Integration Of DeFi and Federated Learning

Decentralized finance (DeFi) and federated learning (FL) have been shown to offer a groundbreaking project to privacy-preserving and scalable yet secure finance. DeFi has disrupted the finances of the world by eliminating intermediaries and using blockchain to ensure transparency, and also introducing permission lessness in accessing financial services. Conversely, FL offers a collaborative machine learning, which has secured data privacy in that raw data is not centralized. DeFi and FL together form a synergistic environment that helps to solve some of the most evident problems of current finance as data privacy, trust, security, and scalability.

4.1 Reasoning behind Integration

Blockchains and smart contracts involved in DeFi generate huge volumes of data on transactions. This data spread among various participants, including users, liquidity providers, and decentralized exchanges, is a goldmine of data-driven AI. Nevertheless, centralized pooling of data is often restricted because of privacy issues and regulatory reasons. This problem is addressed through FL which allows training that is decentralized with model updates exchanged, instead of raw data. As an example, the training of credit scoring models in decentralized lending did not infringe on user privacy since it can train models across platforms through FL. Likewise, FL can be utilized to pool the improvements made to the various model predictions globally without disclosing the sensitive transaction information. It is the complementary spectrum which makes FL well suited to DeFi ecosystems. Figure 8 shows one example of a tokenomics incentive system, which is implemented to promote honest engagement in federated learning in DeFi ecosystems. The figure depicts the manner in which rewards conform economic incentives to the quality of the model. It graphically endorses the coming together of the governance and learning incentives.

4.2 DeFi Advantages of FL

- **Privacy Preservation:** Financial records are local to the users, something that echoes the DeFi ideas of autonomy and data ownership.
- **Security Enhancement:** Data does not move out of the source, which reduces the chances of breaches being made on the center.
- **Regulatory Alignment:** FL allows DeFi projects to move toward emerging privacy regulations, such as GDPR or India DPDP Act by anonymizing contributions.
- **Trust and Transparency:** FL, in combination with the audit transactions characteristic of blockchain, allows the establishment of trust between the parties, the preservation of the confidentiality of the data.
- **Enhanced Model Accuracy:** Distribution of financial data over blockchains allows the increased prediction capability of fraud, risk analysis, and market prediction.

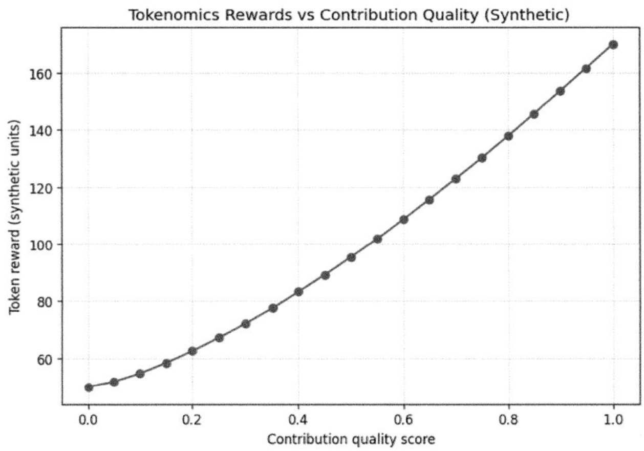

Figure 8: Tokenomics incentive simulation.

4.3 Architecture of Integration

The DeFi and FL integration can be discussed on three layers:

- **Data Layer:** is used to disseminate data of transaction and smart contract across DeFi platforms.
- **Learning Layer:** FL algorithms train data on a local machine and exchange model updates in an encrypted way.
- **Consensus Layer/Incentive Layer:** Blockchain measures the accumulation mechanism; tokenomics positively influences participatory quality.

This type of architecture guarantees end-to-end decentralization in which responsibilities of the data governance and the model governance are mutually done in a transparent manner.

4.4 Incentives Based on Tokenomics

The utilization of tokenomics to motivate the participation is a crucial innovation when implementing DeFi in conjunction with FL. As model training needs a variety of representative data, one can incentivize participating by giving governance or utility tokens in return to providing updates. This generates a self-reinforcing cycle where:

- contributors get tokens in exchange of data/model;
- tokens give rights to governance or yield opportunities;
- the system has richer data, therefore resulting in more powerful models.
- these tools make FL a self-sufficient ecosystem that is baked into DeFi systems.

4.5 Integration Problems

Although promising, there are some technical and operational challenges to the incorporation of FL with DeFi:

- **Scalability Challenges:** Effective latency in large-scale FL with blockchain validation facility may rise.
- **Heterogeneous Data:** The structure of transactions in DeFi platforms is varied, so it is complex to standardize the approach to the model.
- **Adversarial Threats:** Malicious nodes can do poisoning to model updates.
- **Economic Risks:** Care should be taken to design the token-based rewards so as not to be exploitive.

The ability to find solutions to these challenges depends on a hybrid security practice (e.g., homomorphic encryption, differential privacy), and robust governance mechanisms.

4.6 Comparative View

To put integration into greater perspective, a table is given in the following text comparing three of the most famous DeFi infrastructures—Ethereum, Polygon, and Binance Smart Chain (BSC)—based on their scalability and transaction speed, as well as how they fit to FL-driven models.

Flip to DeFi is relatively new, and the course has a lot of potential. With decentralizing blockchain combined with FL intelligence protecting privacy, the nexus of financial AI will see the light of day. This type of system has the potential to support cross-border credit scoring, decentralized AML, dynamic fraud detection, predictive market modelling, or similar mechanisms, without infringing on the privacy of the end users. In the future, one will be successful by addressing the question of scalability and security and developing incentive models that would match users' participation in the network with network expansion. Where these obstacles are addressed, FL-enhanced DeFi has the potential to transform financial inclusion, robustness, and intelligence over the next decade. Table 1 compares major DeFi infrastructures in terms of scalability, transaction speed, cost, ecosystem maturity, and suitability for federated learning. The comparison highlights how platform-level characteristics influence the feasibility of deploying privacy-preserving AI models. This helps position FL deployment choices within practical DeFi environments.

Table 1: Comparison of DeFi infrastructures.

Feature	*Ethereum*	*Polygon*	*Binance Smart Chain (BSC)*
Scalability	Limited (layer-1 bottlenecks)	High (layer-2 scaling)	Moderate–high (delegated Proof of Stake - PoS)
Transaction Speed	~15 TPS	~65,000 TPS (theoretical)	~100–300 Transactions Per Second - TPS
Transaction Cost	High gas fees	Low (fraction of Ethereum)	Low (competitive fees)
Ecosystem Maturity	Most mature and widely adopted	Rapidly growing, Ethereum Virtual Machine - EVM compatible	Large DeFi user base
FL Suitability	Strong but costly	Excellent for scalability	Practical, cost-effective

5. Applications of Federated Learning in DeFi

Federated Learning allows DeFi to emerge to a new era of privacy-preserving intelligent financial services. The crypto sector of DeFi has already destabilized the old paradigm of the world of finance by letting users lend, borrow, trade, and manage assets without middlemen. Nevertheless, being dependent on transparent, though pseudonymous, data makes it challenging in such applications as fraud detection, credit score, or compliance. With the deployment of FL, DeFi platforms can send the power of AI to the maximum and protect sensitive data of users.

5.1 Risk Mitigation and Fraud Detection

Fraud detection is one of the most important uses of FL in DeFi. Many fraudulent activities are bound to take place in the decentralized exchanges, lending pools, and liquidity platforms that have dynamic and complicated behavior of attackers and are difficult to identify by a single platform. FL allows several DeFi platforms to join in training the model of fraud detection sharing the model improvements rather than the data. As an example, aggregated liquidity providers on various blockchains could co-train an anomaly detection model that would detect a potentially risky wallet address or a trading volume that does not behave normally. This improves the prediction of the risks without losing data confidentiality. Also, FL-based fraud detection systems are more receptive to novel thieves since they have been constantly provided with a wide range of inputs. Figure 9 demonstrates the effect on the application level of token-based incentives in FL-based DeFi systems. It brings out the effect of incentives in enhancing the quality of participation in tasks involving fraud detection and credit scoring. The character supplements the discourse on application of FL in the real world.

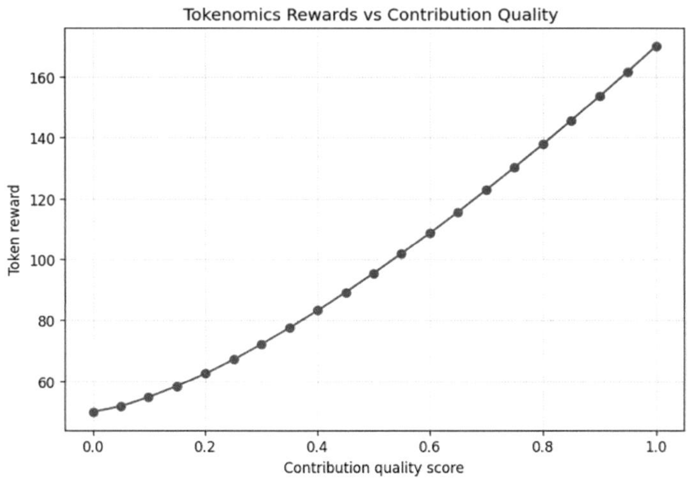

Figure 9: Tokenomics incentive simulation.

5.2 Distributed Credit Scoring

The traditional limit of creditworthiness in DeFi extends to a situation where users can transact with pseudonymous identities and do not have centralized histories of payment in finances. On FL, one can construct decentralized scoring models of credit by exploiting distributed activity data of users over many platforms. As an example, lending behavior on Aavas, loan record on Compound, and deal history on Uniswap can be added to a composite credit model trained anonymously in a collective manner through FL. This enables inclusive lending in the sense that DeFi protocols can issue loans with reduced collateral demanded to a trusted user and increase access to finance without violating user privacy.

5.3 Compliance is Followed by AML

The regulation aspect and adherence to the regulators are key challenges when dealing with DeFi, particularly, with respect to AML and KYC measures. DeFi embraces the message of anonymity contrary to greater controls on illegal transactions that regulators strive to instill. FL would also serve as a facilitator by supporting collaborative monitoring systems that can analyze the flow of transactions on platforms without revealing sensitive identities of users. As an example, they may train AML models collaboratively among exchanges to find patterns of money laundering such as layering or smurfing. In this manner, DeFi projects will be able to comply with regulatory constraints without compromising the anonymity of the blockchain transactions.

5.4 Price Forecasting and Forecasting of Market

Also, FL can enable DeFi platforms to have predictive intelligence of the markets. Crypto markets are well-known to be highly volatile, and proper predictive models can only be produced when a large amount of a diverse dataset is considered. By aggregating the models of several distinct decentralized exchanges, liquidity pools, and derivative markets, FL will be able to enhance accuracy of price volatility, lack of liquidity, or flash crashes forecasting. This, in addition to providing better choices to individual investors, also brings in the protocols level stability like in dynamic collateralization ratio in lending platform.

5.5 Decentralized Insurance

DeFi insurance procedures tend to have trouble with risk evaluation since the activity of users is not covered by information. FL also enables merging of the risk profile of users and the risk profile of the market across the insurance providers in the market without going against the privacy. Through better models, the insurers would be in a position to price the premiums well, evaluate valid claims, and identify fraud claims. For example, FL-based models trained on Nexus Mutual or other DeFi insurance providers could consider wallet-level transaction activity, liquidity provision behavior, and historical claim. This enhances the confidence of insurance ecosystems, which are decentralized.

5.6 Detection of Vulnerability of Smart Contracts

At the centre of DeFi is a smart contract; however, due to the loopholes, it often results in multi-million-dollar hacking. FL can facilitate collaborative vulnerability detection models in which platforms will share the information concerning the use of contracts, attempted attacks, and runtime anomalies. Distributed knowledge allows DeFi protocols to serve as their own early warning system in pinpointing flaws in contract logic before attackers can find and abuse them. Such scouting intelligence helps to create resiliency across the DeFi community overall but maintains the proprietary codebases of individual projects.

5.7 FL within DeFi Applications: A Comparison

To showcase the examples of FL applications in DeFi, a table summarizing some of the main use cases, aims, and advantages is presented in the following text. Table 2 summarizes key application areas of federated learning within DeFi ecosystems, along with their objectives and ecosystem-level benefits. It provides a concise overview of how FL supports security, compliance, and intelligent decision-making. The table reinforces the practical relevance of FL-driven DeFi applications.

Table 2: The use cases of federated learning in DeFi.

Application Area	*Objective*	*Benefit to DeFi Ecosystem*
Fraud Detection	Detect irregular trading and wallet activity	Enhanced security, early fraud prevention
Credit Scoring	Assess decentralized borrower reliability	Inclusive lending, reduced collateral
AML & Compliance	Identify money laundering patterns	Regulatory alignment with privacy
Market Forecasting	Predict price trends and volatility	Better risk management and investment tools
Decentralized Insurance	Evaluate risk and detect fraudulent claims	Improved coverage, fairer premiums
Smart Contract Security	Identify contract-level vulnerabilities	Prevention of exploitation, strengthening of trust

Integration of FL in DeFi has a massive potential in privacy-preserving intelligence in financial services. Whether it is detecting fraud, scoring credit, compliance, or modelling risks, FL supports the ability to collaborate without centralizing data directly in line with DeFi, ethos of decentralization and transparency. The system will become smart enough to be self-learning and able to adapt to market risks and regulation pressures in real time and understand the dynamic market as adoption increases. DeFi of the future will not only be decentralized, but data-driven, secure, and inclusive, due to smoother intersection of federated learning.

6. Security and Privacy in Federated Learning for Defi

The suggestion to implement federated learning into the decentralized finance is a transformative chance of data-driven innovation, which maintains the confidentiality and ownership of user information. However, the very integration of federated learning into the financial software simultaneously introduces the new security threat, privacy issues, and governance challenges. In the framework of systems with full decentralization, permissionless approach, and adversarial ecosystems, the principles of security play a key role in maintaining trust. This part will perform a graded analysis of the security and privacy aspects related to federated learning in decentralized finance, with certain references to new threats and the existing anti-threat measures implemented to protect collaborative learning systems. In Figure 10, the centralized, decentralized, and federated learning systems are compared in terms of privacy risks. It points out the fact that federated learning minimizes the exposure to direct data leakage, but new inferences risks are established. The number contributes to the security study of FL-based financial structures.

6.1 Privacy of Data at a Decentralized Environment

Both decentralized finance and federated learning are based on the principle of maintaining privacy. The identities of participants in the decentralized finance are usually pseudonymous, and the record of the transactions is kept in a publicly accessible immutable registry. Although this structure makes the audit more transparent, it also leaves transactions vulnerable to unintentional exposure to data. Federated learning does not avoid this pitfall, only that raw user data is confined to local devices or nodes; however, there are still privacy issues. As an example, a competitor can still use model-inversion attacks to make reports about personal data based on shared gradients. Different privacy, secure aggregation, and cryptographic protocols are among the techniques that can be employed to counter such threats through actually using federated learning that is integrated with DeFi.

- **Differential Privacy (DP):** Gradient updates are corrupted with noise to prevent any entity of any single transaction/wallet behavior being reverse-engineered.
- **Secure Aggregation Protocols:** Part participant updates are combined cryptographically using cryptographic aggregation and the server (or coordinating smart contract) cannot see the specific inputs of the individual participants.

DeFi will be able to balance utility, obtain data confidentiality through the integration of FL, on-chain encryption, and off-chain computations.

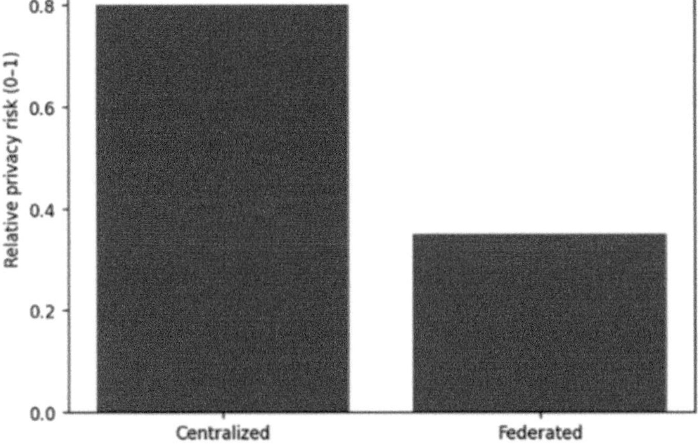

Figure 10: Privacy risk comparison.

6.2 DeFi and Threats to FL Models

Although FL removes the dangers of breaching the centralized data, it creates new attack possibilities. The major threats are as follows:

- **Model Poisoning:** The uploaded model updates that they can corrupt may distort the global model by malicious participants. In DeFi, this may cause tampered fraud detection systems which will help illegal wallets to escape detection.
- **Byzantine Attacks:** Certain nodes can be temperamental or malicious in order to interfere with learning.
- **Eavesdropping/Gradient Leakage:** An adversary could listen in during model updates to create information about covert user behavior.

These weaknesses indicate the emphasis put on the strong aggregation procedures and adversarial training methods adjusted to the decentralized state of DeFi.

6.3 DeFi Secure Model Aggregation

Aggregation of models is the center theme of FL. Verifiable aggregation is necessary in a DeFi-enabling environment that assumes very low levels of trust. The mechanisms may include:

- **Coordination Using Blockchain-Based Smart Contracts:** Smart contracts have the ability to abolish aggregation, with the updates being stored in a public, irreversible manner.
- **Multiparty Computation (MPC):** Calculations of various types are carried out together in a decentralized manner on an international level, without revealing intermediate computations.
- **Homomorphic Encryption:** It is the method that enables computation on encrypted gradients, and not even the aggregator could gain access to the raw data.

These protocols help to strengthen without requiring cooperation and hence align with the core principles of DeFi.

6.4 Anonymity: Maintaining a Balance between Compliance

A very unique problem with DeFi is the problem of maintaining anonymity and regulation. Although pseudonymity is prized by customers, there is a need to regulate in order to combat AML and fraud. FL provides a trade-off by providing cooperative compliance designs with the ability to target illegal behavior without disclosing an individual transaction record. As an example, monitoring wallet clustering as a part of AML can be trained jointly at multiple exchanges using FL, so that suspicious patterns can be detected without violating user privacy. This is a feasible way to privacy-friendly regulation of DeFi spaces. The relations between API attack surfaces and security controls in financial systems are demonstrated in Figure 11. It highlights the need to have more defensive measures with greater openness of the system. The number supports the security of APIs in FL-DeFi infrastructures.

6.5 Resistance to Adversarial Attack

FL systems should not be susceptible to malicious interference, that is, DeFi. Available solutions would be:

- **Robust Aggregator (e.g., Krum, Median-Based Methods):** These remove malicious or outlier update.
- **Adversarial Training:** During the model training, invented attacks are incorporated in fostering robustness.
- **Reputation Systems:** This model is a tokenomic where truthful updates are rewarded with tokens, and other parties who are not honest are penalized.

The self-regulating FL-DeFi ecosystem can be created by merging the economic motives and the security goals.

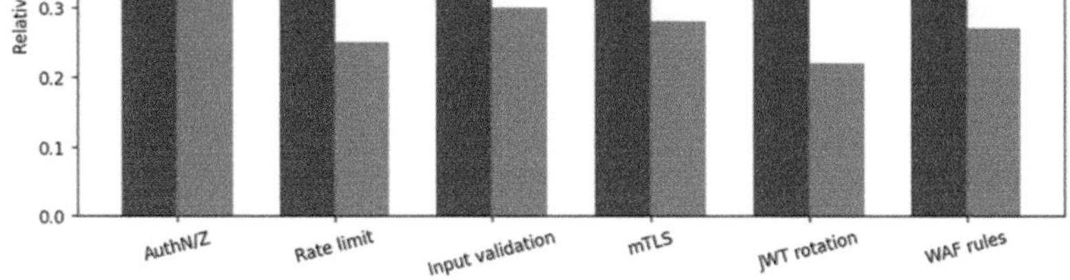

Figure 11: API attack surface versus controls.

6.6 Comparative Mechanism

To obtain a more vivid idea of the security environment, the given table has contrasted the main threats faced in the FL-DeFi integration with the possible prevention measures. Table 3 presents a structured comparison of major security threats in FL-enabled DeFi systems and their corresponding mitigation strategies.

It highlights how cryptographic, algorithmic, and governance-based defenses collectively enhance system robustness. The table supports the discussion on secure federated learning deployment.

Table 3: DeFi in FL Security Threats and Mitigation.

Threat Type	*Description*	*Mitigation Strategy*
Model Poisoning	Malicious updates corrupt global models	Robust aggregation, reputation mechanisms
Gradient Leakage	Inferring sensitive data from updates	Differential privacy, homomorphic encryption
Byzantine Behavior	Erratic or adversarial nodes disrupting training	Byzantine-resilient algorithms (e.g., Krum)
Eavesdropping	Intercepting communications	Secure multiparty computation, encryption
Anonymity versus Compliance	Conflict between user privacy and regulations	FL-based collaborative compliance models

The securing ability, privacy, and verifiability of learning environments determine the success of FL in the DeFi. Although threats such as model poisoning and gradient leakage are still crucial, cryptography, secure multiparty computing, and blockchain-based aggregation have a potential to help solve the problem. Moreover, with the insertion of token-based incentives to participate honestly, DeFi will make FL an intelligence layer that is minimized in trust in all financial applications. Overall, by incorporating FL into DeFi security systems, it will be possible to preserve the privacy of data, make it easy to collaborate, and reduce manipulation by adversaries, and ultimately support the next generation of secure systems related to DeFi.

7. Tokenomics and Incentive Mechanisms in FL-DeFi

Federated learning truly has great potential to combine with decentralized finance in privacy-preserving intelligence, but the long-term viability will be determined by the quality of the incentive structures. In contrast to the centralized systems where the coordination of the participants' behavior is achieved through central authorities, in DeFi ecosystems the tokenomics facilitates participant coordination, promotes collaboration, and promotes fair value distribution. Integrating token-based incentives within FL processes will induce participation in data provision, computing resource, and honest model updates by stakeholders. Here, we introduce the design, implementation, and optimization of tokenomics mechanisms in DeFi in order to promote FL.

7.1 How Incentives Apply to FL in DeFi

Federated learning requires active collaboration with nodes that can offer local training information and computational resources. Nevertheless, selfish behavior can be exhibited by participants in the following ways:

- Posting poor-quality updates.
- Failure to contribute out of cost-avoidance of resources.
- Manipulation of models to capture profit.

The solution to these problems is tokenomics, which is used in order to establish economic incentive for good behavior and economic penalty to the bad behavior. By doing this, the incentive is imposed in the same direction as the benefit to the individual, and in the same direction as the security of the network.

7.2 Token Reward

The most widespread way is distributing tokens to the participants depending on the value of their contributions. For instance, a user that trains a local fraud detection model on good-quality transaction data has a better reward profile than the one who updates seldomly. The reward can be proportional to the quality of gradient, computation cost, and the update frequency. This develops data and compute contributions market, and maintains the active involvement.

7.3 Reputation-Based Tokenomics

Besides one-time incentives, FL-DeFi systems can develop reputational systems in which participants are ranked on past performance. Good-quality contributors gain bonus tokens or governance privileges; bad- or poor-quality contributors are penalized.
This has two advantages in its design:

- It does not only promote short-term benefits but also promotes life-long integrity involvement.
- It allows self-regulation; users know their actions affect their reputation score and ability to make money in future.

7.4 Penalty Function

In order to counter model poisoning and adversarial attacks, tokenomics may have staking. Participants will have to deposit a given amount of token into the process of participating in FL; a penalty of a drop in the share will be imposed in case pernicious updates are posted. This kind of stake would put in place a game-theoretic equilibrium: when faced with the risk of financial loss, rational players will be less likely to engage in dishonesty. Therefore, it coordinates incentives to achieve model integrity in the context of DeFi. Figure 12 represents cross-border financial data flows and localization requirements in various regulatory regimes. It throws light on jurisdictional issues that federated learning systems have in international finance. The figure helps to discuss the issue of regulatory compliance and data sovereignty visually.

7.5 Tokenomics as a Form of Governance

Decentralized governance of FL models is also possible with the help of tokenomics. Such critical parameters as can be voted on by token holders include:

- The update rate of models.
- Privacy parameters (e.g., level of privacy noise, differentially approximate noise levels).
- Malicious contribution rejection aggregation rules.

This makes sure that there is a decentralized approach to decision-making, despite the fact that the control lies not in a center and leaves the community to make decisions.

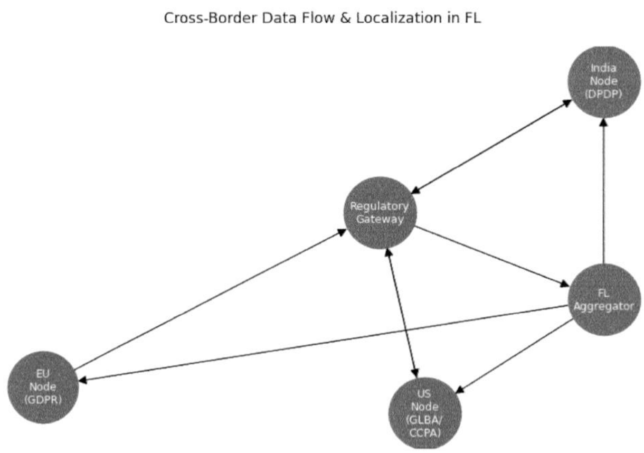

Figure 12: Cross-border data flow and localization.

7.6 Sustainability in Tokenomics

Security goes hand in hand with sustainability in DeFi. Tokenomics means that FL systems can stay viable as follows:

- Financing infrastructure by charges on transactions returned as rewards.
- Encouraging other long-term players through power to govern.

- Providing incentive to developing superior aggregation or security mechanisms.

In such a way, tokenomics provides the economics of FL in DeFi.

7.7 Comparative Mechanisms of Incentives

Table 4 outlines key tokenomics mechanisms used to incentivize participation in federated learning for DeFi ecosystems. It compares reward structures, governance models, and associated risks. This table supports the discussion on aligning economic incentives with model integrity and sustainability.

Table 4: Tokenomics Mechanisms for FL in DeFi.

Mechanism	*Description*	*Benefits*	*Risks/Challenges*
Reward Distribution	Tokens awarded based on contribution quality	Encourages active participation, fairness	Requires accurate contribution metrics
Reputation Systems	Scores track user honesty and performance	Builds long-term trust, self-regulation	Vulnerable to manipulation if not secure
Staking and Slashing	Tokens staked before participation	Deters malicious behavior, ensures honesty	Risk of over-penalization
Governance Voting	Token-based decision-making on FL parameters	Democratizes control, fosters transparency	Whale voting centralization risk
Sustainability Rewards	Rewards linked to long-term ecosystem health	Encourages innovation and ecosystem growth	Requires balanced token inflation

7.8 Case Examples of Practicing Tokenomics

The recent new prototype examples of FL-DeFi can be realized with the help of tokenomics:

- **Fraud Detection Tools:** To ensure the tracking of AML on exchanges, FL unites the data of various platforms and the delegating parties are rewarded on tokens with regard to the responsible updating of their data.
- **Lending Market Risk Modelling:** Lending systems model incentives to get liquidity providers to provide knowledge through FL models; greater quality input rewards more risk evaluation.
- **Community-Determined Privacy Policies:** Various privacy policies are established by a direct vote of rightful owners of tokens, in which privacy is weighed against compliance policy.

Applications of this nature prove that tokenomics is more than a speculative or hypothetical means of collaborating with DeFi, but it is a functioning aspect of modern practice.

8. Challenges and Limitations of FL-DeFi Integration

The combination of federated learning and decentralized finance is a big step toward the realization of the intelligent and privacy-preserving financial ecosystems. Nevertheless, with its potential, there are multiple issues and restraints that do not allow its dominance and practical application. Criticisms cut across technological, economic, governance, and regulatory areas, and the knowledge of them is essential in the development of this emerging area.

Among the major issues is the heterogeneity of data on various DeFi platforms and actors. Transaction data generated by DeFi ecosystems have massive size and tripled billions of records but are highly variable with regard to structure, quality, and completeness. The rationale of the federated learning is to induce regularities to create strong global models, and the performance of aggregated model is worse once the datasets are very skewed or not independent and identically distributed (non-IID), especially in the distributed setting. Practically, this is a hard problem to address because it is not possible to solve DeFi platforms catering to different user groups and engage different applications, including decentralized exchanges and lending markets. Data heterogeneity is therefore a fundamental source of challenge to a high model accuracy and generalizability. The next limitation is caused by the computational and communication expenses of the federated learning. In contrast to centralized machine learning, the FL centralizes the models update, which involves several rounds of local nodes and aggregator communication. This process can lead to inefficiencies and delays in DeFi ecosystems where geographical decentralization and resource limitation are common in participants. Besides, the overall cost of coordinating FL workflows per gas fees and transaction cost inherent to blockchain-based systems are increased. In that the layer-two scaling solutions and off-chain computations might help reduce complications of this picture; there is also a significant problem of efficiency versus decentralization. The preservation of privacy, of course, is recognized as one of the most critical intentions to use FL but it cannot be assured in reality. Attackers are capable of carrying out inference attacks on shared model updates, since such shared updates can be used to extract sensitive information about contributing nodes. Equally, the issue of model poisoning and backdoor is a threat to the learning process. Even more secure forms of computation, such as secure multiparty computation, homomorphic encryption, and differential privacy, can in theory improve protection, but may result into prohibitive computational overhead, especially in real-time financial transactions. Finding the best compromise between privacy, security, and efficiency becomes an urgent limitation. Figure 13 illustrates the frequency of common smart contract vulnerabilities.

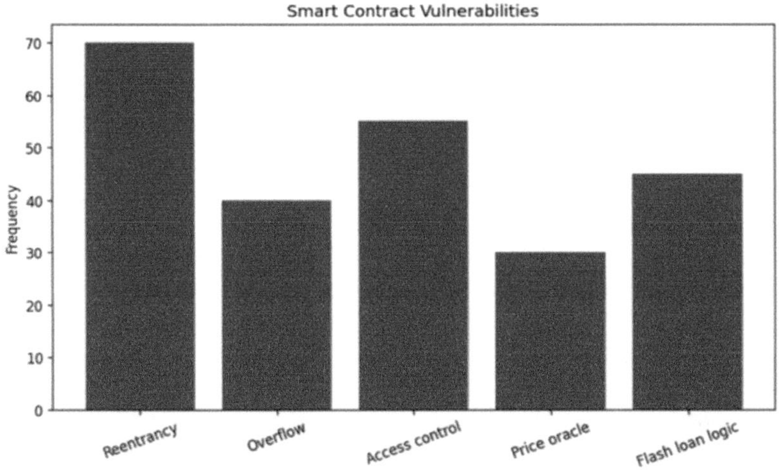

Figure 13: Smart contract vulnerability frequency.

The incentive problem makes the FL-DeFi integration issue more complicated. Federated learning is based on user engagement, and, in absence of proper incentives, users might not be willing to donate their data and compute work. The adversity may be resolved through the use of tokenomics to match incentives through staking, rewards, and governance rights, yet ill-conceived mechanisms can create exploits. As an example, one could use a form of game theory to seek to cheat the system by providing fake results to collect tokens at the expense of the performance of a model and network credibility. This all boils down to the fact that ensuring that any incentive is both strong and not easily manipulated is open. At a governance level, FL-DeFi integration represents new intricacies. Decentralized decision-making tends to be token-weighted, a formula that exposes the system to the possibilities of power imbalance because big token holders would make vital decisions regarding model training parameters or aggregation techniques. This negates the democracy of DeFi and may deter the smaller players to participate in the ecosystem. Moreover, governance disagreements about such questions as a level of privacy or model clarity may divide communities and halt the process.

9. Future Research Directions

As the nascent convergence of federated learning with decentralized finance was defined, the current literature has shown good prospects with apparent gaps in technical and governance aspects. When it comes to financial data, the initial thing is to come up with algorithms that can process the very heterogeneous data without sacrificing precision. Since DeFi ecosystems can yield several different types of transaction models, the next-generation FL models need to be able to embed the adaptive aggregation and powerful optimization strategies to maintain healthy performance in the diverse participants. Second, the privacy-saving methods, including differential privacy, homomorphic encryption, and multiparty computation, should be researched, at the same time reducing the computational load to support a large-scale and real-time financial task. Additionally, scalability of FL on blockchain and layer-two solutions, sharding, and cross-chain protocols should also be studied more, which would help improve the efficiency of training on distributed nodes. A more general issue is to develop incentive schemes that discourage bad behavior and reward compliance; future research can consider advanced crypto economic approaches, such as reputation, quadratic voting, or liquid staking, as a way to maintain self-sovereignty via participation. Governance schemes are another important area of research; a transparency–fairness–efficiency union of the governance framework that remains decentralized might reduce the problem of centralization and enhance trust to the community. Not to mention, the regulatory insights are to be enhanced, in particular, the alignment of FL systems with the international financial guidelines, including GDPR, AML, and KYC, without undermining the user privacy. Finally, future direction of FL-DeFi will be dependent on the establishment of scaled, reliable, and interoperable systems incorporating future DeFi developments through intelligent AI. To take full advantage of this paradigm, the creation of a multidisciplinary area matter of integrating AI, blockchain, cryptography, and legal experience will be necessary.

10. Conclusion

Federated learning integrated with decentralized finance represents a paradigm shift of the secure, intelligent, and privacy-friendly financial systems. The federated learning technology will allow joint training of models without sharing confidential user data with the third party, which is why it complies with regulatory standards and improves faith in the digital finance era. Beginning with decentralized finance, which brings a ground of decentralization, transparency, and accessibility, opens the potential of massive FL implementation. The FL-DeFi integration has limitations but the future opportunities of the integration surpass the obstacles such as data heterogeneity, computational costs, privacy and regulatory risks, and uncertainty. The focus on further developments and technological advancements, along with shared governance, will make FL-DeFi a cornerstone of financial infrastructure of the next generation. As pictured, this development will make the financial services industry more inclusive, secure, efficient, and intelligent such that the fruits of AI and decentralization will be shared fairly in the society.

References

[1] Bonawitz, K., Eichner, H., Grieskamp, W., Huba, D., Ingerman, A., Ivanov, V. et al. (2021). Toward federated learning at scale: System design. *Proceedings of Machine Learning and Systems*, 3: 374–388.

[2] Kairouz, P., McMahan, H. B., Avent, B., Bellet, A., Bennis, M., Bhagoji, A. N. et al. (2021). Advances and open problems in federated learning. *Foundations and Trends® in Machine Learning*, 14(1-2): 1–210.

[3] Li, Q., He, B. and Song, D. (2022). Model poisoning adversarial attacks on federated learning systems. *Proceedings of the Network and Distributed System Security Symposium (NDSS)*, 1–17.

[4] Shi, E., Niu, H., Shi, F. and Blake, M. (2022). Secure financial data analytics using homomorphic encryption. *IEEE Transactions on Dependable and Secure Computing*, 19(5): 1342–1355.

[5] Yang, Q., Liu, Y., Chen, T. and Tong, Y. (2020). Federated machine learning: Concept and applications. *ACM Transactions on Intelligent Systems and Technology*, 10(2): Article 12.

[6] Zhang, C., Xie, Y., Bai, H., Yu, B., Li, W. and Gao, Y. (2022). A survey on federated learning. *Knowledge-Based Systems*, 216: 106775.

[7] Dwork, C. and Roth, A. (2021). The algorithmic foundations of differential privacy. *Foundations and Trends® in Theoretical Computer Science*, 9(3-4): 211–407.

[8] Chen, Y., Yang, T., Zhou, Z. and Liu, Y. (2023). Differentially private federated learning via model averaging. *International Journal of Information Security*, 22(4): 467–486.

[9] Smith, L. and Nguyen, T. (2021). Secure multi-party computation for decentralized finance applications. *Proceedings of the ACM Workshop on Blockchain, Cryptocurrencies and Contracts (BCC '21)*, 31–39.

[10] Androulaki, E., Boudguiga, A., Carson, W. and Karame, G. O. (2020). Blockchain privacy through non-interactive zero-knowledge proofs: A survey. *IEEE Communications Surveys & Tutorials*, 22(1): 226–265.

[11] European Banking Authority. (2022). Report on the EBA's approach to the digitalisation of bank reporting (EBA/REP/2022/05). https://www.eba.europa.eu.

[12] Reserve Bank of India. (2023). Cyber security framework in banks. https://www.rbi.org.in/Scripts/NotificationUser.aspx?Id=12345.

[13] Guo, N., Hong, J. and Zhang, X. (2024). Federated learning-powered credit scoring in cross-border finance. *Journal of Financial Data Science*, 6(2): 45–61.

[14] Gao, S., Chen, H. and Sun, J. (2022). Federated learning-based AML compliance in DeFi platforms. *Finance and Stochastics*, 26(2): 455–486.

[15] Basel Committee on Banking Supervision. (2018). Cyber-resilience: Range of practices. Bank for International Settlements. https://www.bis.org/bcbs/publ/d454.pdf.

4 Governance and Data Management in Federated Learning

Suvarna Sharma,[1,*] Rashmi Gupta[2] and Jeetendra Kumar[2]

Federated Learning (FL) preserves privacy by shifting machine learning from centralized data aggregation to distributed to local training, a transition supported by federated governance- a hybrid data governance model balancing centralized policy enforcement with local team autonomy. This chapter explores how this approach enables secure, compliant model training through governed FL frameworks that enforce data sovereignty and usage guidelines in sensitive sectors using technologies like Eclipse Dataspace Components. Additionally, it studies organizational archetypes for mapping structural readiness, data quality mechanisms to prevent global model degradation from heterogeneous, non-IId (non-independent and identically distributed) data, and the adoption of "policy-as-code" to automate compliance and data access rules directly within training pipelines. Finally, it highlights the crucial role of secure aggregation and differential privacy in building trust and mitigating advanced security threats such as data poisoning, model inversion, and reconstruction.

1. Introduction

To enable sustainable, trustworthy, and collaborative artificial intelligence (AI), organizations must increasingly learn from distributed data while respecting privacy, regulatory, and sovereignty constraints. Although the rapid adoption of digital platforms has led to an unprecedent growth in data volumes, the effective use of this data remains constrained by organizational silos, heterogeneous infrastructures, privacy and security concerns, and complex governance and ethical considerations. These challenges are particularly pronounced in regulated

[1] Dr. Vishwanath Karad MIT World Peace University, Pune, India.

[2] Department of Computer Science and Applications, Atal Bihari Vajpayee University, Bilaspur, Chhattisgarh, India.

Emails: rashmigupta@bilaspuruniversity.ac.in; jeetendragupta@bilaspuruniversity.ac.in

* Corresponding author: suvarna.sharma@mitwpu.edu.in

DOI: 10.1201/9781003710059-4

domains such as healthcare, finance, and the public sector, where centralized data aggregation is often impractical or prohibited.

Federated learning (FL) has emerged as a promising paradigm to address these challenges by enabling decentralized model training across multiple data holders without requiring raw data to be shared [1]–[3]. Unlike traditional machine learning (ML) approaches that rely on centralized data collections, FL allows data to remain within local infrastructures while models are collaboratively trained through the exchange of model updates. This approach reduces privacy risks, supports regulatory compliance, and enables cross-organizational collaboration at scale.

By facilitating collaborative learning while preserving data locality, FL is transforming how organizations extract value from sensitive and distributed datasets. Applications of FL span across predictive analytics, risk modelling, medical imaging, fraud detection, and personalized services, demonstrating its potential across multiple sectors. However, despite reducing direct data-sharing risks, FL introduces new governance challenges associated with the secondary use of data, including concerns related to accountability, fairness, bias propagation, and ethical oversight. Furthermore, the distributed nature of FL exposes systems to novel security threats such as model poisoning, model inversion, data reconstruction, and model theft, which cannot be adequately addressed through conventional governance approaches.

Data governance provides a critical lens for understanding and managing these challenges in federated environments. Governance in FL extends beyond traditional data management practices to encompass policy definition, roll allocation, trust establishment, technical enforcement, and continuous oversight across organizational boundaries. While existing governance frameworks for centralized machine learning emphasize high-level principles such as transparency, accountability, and fairness, they often lack concrete mechanisms for operationalizing these principles in decentralized and heterogeneous FL settings [4]. The absence of shared infrastructure, diverse data ownership models, and nonindependent and identically distributed (non-IID) data further complicates governance efforts.

Table 1 provide the comparison of three distinct models of data governance: Centralized, Federated, and Data Mesh. Each model is evaluated across four key dimensions: ownership, style, scalability, and compliance.

The chapter addresses these gaps by examining governance and data management in federated learning through a hybrid governance model that combines centralized policy-setting with decentralized execution. IT explores governed FL architectures, secure data connectors, policy-as-code approaches, and automated compliance mechanisms that embed governance directly into training pipelines. The chapter also examines organizational readiness models, data quality governance for heterogeneous federated data, and security mechanisms that strengthen trust among participants.

Table 1: Comparison of several types of governance.

Dimension	*Centralized*	*Federated*	*Data Mesh*
Data Ownership	Central	Distributed	Domain-owned
Governance style	Static	Hybrid	Federated by design
Scalability	Limited	High	Very High
Compliance	Manual	Automated	Embedded

In conclusion, the chapter situates federated learning within the broader industry shift toward data mesh architectures, where domain teams assume ownership of data as products and governance becomes federated by design. In this context, governance evolves from a static compliance function into dynamic, strategic capability that enables scalable, secure, and collaborative AI ecosystems. By synthesizing architectural, organizational, and technical perspectives, this chapter provides a practical and forward-looking framework for governing federated learning in complex, multi-stakeholder environments.

2. Federated Governance Architecture

Federated data governance refers to an approach for organizing distributed data sources through shared standards for security, compliance, and interoperability. Under this model, centralized bodies—such as data councils or governance committees—define common policies and guidelines, while individual data domains retain autonomy over data management and usage.

With governance mechanism in place, data owners are empowered to access, share, and contextualize datasets, improving data usability and trust. Domain teams can leverage data in ways that align with their specific requirements, often enabling self-service access without heavy reliance on centralized IT resources.

The primary objective of federated governance is to ensure consistent compliance across diverse data domains while preserving local flexibility, allowing organizations to reduce data management complexity and scale data-driven initiatives effectively.

Figure 1 represents the key components involved in governance architecture from federated learning, highlighting the integration of advanced technologies and finance approaches. It emphasizes the evolution toward more personalization.

Implementation of a federated governance model is not an easy-to-install process. It demands strategic planning, organizational coordination, and the deployment of right technology [5].

The architecture shown in Figure 2 explains the integration of governance functions, technical components, and domain responsibilities to enable secure, compliant, and scalable data sharing.

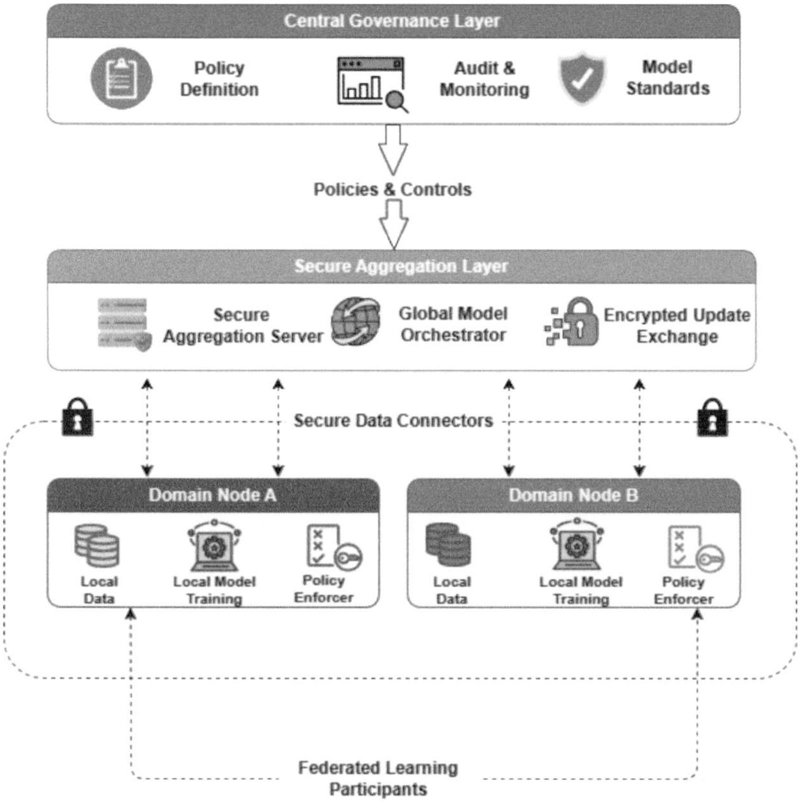

Figure 1: Federated governance architecture from federated learning.

Step 1. Define Objectives
Define objectives to identify the team for federated governance and establish the standards for their responsibilities regarding data product formats, quality levels, data security aspects, controlling of access, and supported technologies.

Step 2. Secure Executive Support
Governance projects collapse in the absence of sponsorship. Obtain senior leadership support to ensure that governance initiatives are aligned with company objectives and supported by financing and authority.

Step 3. Develop Framework
For decision-making processes, escalation paths, and accountability mechanisms, identify the organizational structure for governance.

Step 4. Set Policies
To report the access, usage, quality, integrity, and integration, design such data governance policies that complement with the standards such as defining

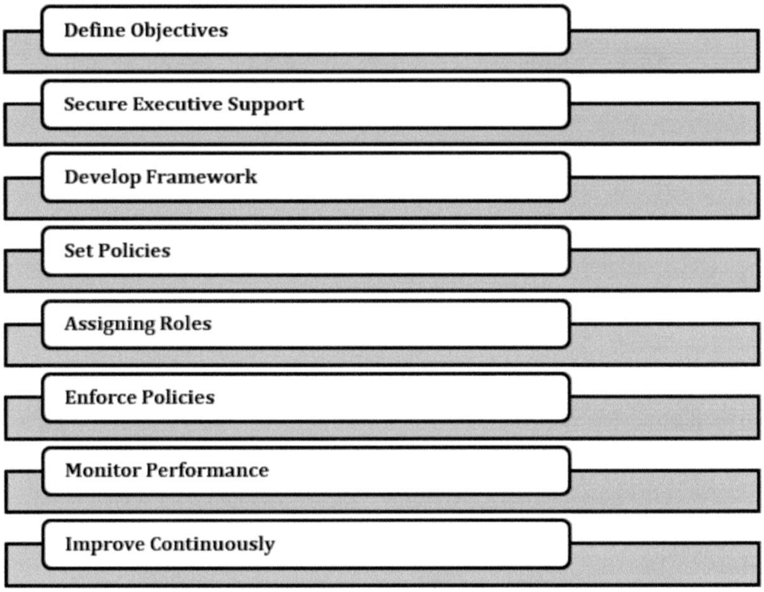

Figure 2: Federated data governance implementation steps.

common data formats, international data representation standards, cleaning data for integration, etc.

Step 5. Assign Roles
For any business project, it is crucial to measure the effectiveness of a federated data governance program to ensure that it is consistently delivering business value. Therefore, this step involves using a data catalog to identify metrics for data and metadata quality, governance, and compliance and tracking.

Step 6. Enforce Policies
In addition to outlining the roles and duties of the central group and domain teams, it is just as important to set up clear communication points for successful federated data governance. The central federation and domain owners can come together to plan strategically, share updates, solve problems, and coordinate efforts, making sure everyone is aligned with the same goals and objectives.

Step 7. Monitor Performance
Educate all data practitioners and users on the principles, policies, procedures, and other aspects of federated data governance by implementing training programs, awareness workshops, and other methods across the entire enterprise.

Step 8. Improve Continuously
Businesses that embrace a culture of continuous improvement enhance the results of their governance initiatives.

3. Organizational Readiness and Operating Models

Successfully implementing FL is a huge organizational transformation that necessitates changes in operational models, responsibilities, and decision-making processes. Organizations must be well equipped to function in decentralized, multi-stakeholder contexts in which data ownership, responsibility, and trust are spread across domain borders [11]. Federated learning projects run the danger of governance fragmentation, uneven policy enforcement, and decreased model performance if they are not adequately prepared.

3.1 Organizational Readiness for Federated Learning

Data ownership maturity, infrastructure capabilities, governance culture, and cross-domain collaboration methods all contribute to an organization's FL preparedness. Unlike centralized machine learning systems, FL needs organizations to serve as both independent data suppliers and cooperative members of a federation [10]. This dual position demands explicit stewardship models and well-defined accountability frameworks.

Domain-aligned data ownership, standardized data management techniques, and established governance forums capable of establishing and enforcing common standards are all critical markers of preparedness. Organizations with mature data governance policies, such as clearly defined roles for data owners, stewards, and custodians, are better positioned to embrace federated models [6]. Organizations with highly centralized or ad hoc data management structures, on the other hand, frequently fail to operationalize FL owing to unclear duties and a lack of trust among teams.

3.2 Operating Model Archetypes

Organizations often fall into several operating model archetypes based on governance maturity and infrastructure capabilities, influencing their capacity to engage in federated learning ecosystems, as shown in Table 2.

Table 2: Organizational archetypes.

Archetypes	*Infrastructure Maturity*	*Data Ownership*	*FL Readiness*
Centralized Data Consumers	Low	Centralized	Low
Collaborative Data Contributors	Medium	Centered	Medium
Domain-Oriented Data Product Owners	High	Domain-Owned	High

This transition corresponds to the shift from centralized data architectures to federated and domain-oriented operational models outlined in data mesh literature [7].

3.3 Structures for Governance and Accountability

Effective federated learning governance necessitates a clear distinction between policy formulation and policy implementation. Central governance groups, such as data councils or AI governance boards, oversee developing worldwide standards for security, privacy, compliance, and ethical usage. Domain teams, on the other hand, are responsible for implementing these standards at the local level in their training pipelines and data environments.

This hybrid paradigm is consistent with developing governance methods that stress federated responsibility, in which decision-making rights are distributed yet regulated by shared standards [9]. Scalability is enabled by such systems, which also preserve local autonomy and regulatory compliance.

3.4 Coordination and Trust between Domains

FL is intrinsically reliant on trust between participating entities, as model performance and integrity are determined by the quality and behavior of each node. Organizational tools for cross-domain communication are consequently required, such as shared metadata standards, open reporting, and cooperative governance reviews. Technical enforcement techniques such as secure aggregation and audit logging, which supplement organizational controls, help to increase trust even further.

3.5 The Implications for Governance Design

Organizations that want to implement FL must assess their readiness not just in terms of technology but also in terms of governance maturity and operational processes. Moving toward federated learning frequently necessitates gradual organizational transformation, such as the adoption of data product thinking, investments in governance capabilities, and cultural shifts toward cooperation and shared accountability.

4. Data Quality Governance in Federated Environments

Governance of data quality is an important factor in FL systems' performance. FL operates over dispersed, independent data domains, as opposed to centralized machine learning, which can be consistently analyzed and managed inside a single repository. Each participating node provides locally held data that can vary widely in structure, completeness, correctness, and distribution. Such variability, without adequate governance systems, has the potential to decrease global model performance, introduce bias, and weaken participant trust.

4.1 Challenges of Heterogeneous and Non-IID Data

The existence of heterogeneous, non-IID data distinguishes federated contexts. Data heterogeneity is caused by variances in data formats, collecting techniques, labelling procedures, and domain-specific settings. Non-IID data hampers learning since local data distributions may not be representative of the global population, resulting in sluggish convergence, unstable training, or biased models [12].

From a governance standpoint, these issues cannot be solved purely by computational methods. They require defined data quality norms, agreed standards, and ongoing monitoring to guarantee that local datasets satisfy minimal quality limits before participating in federated training. Governance must consequently establish acceptable data quality baselines while allowing for domain-specific deviations.

4.2 Local Validation and Quality Scoring

To protect data sovereignty and domain autonomy, data quality governance in FL is generally implemented at the local node level. Each domain must validate its data prior to model training using uniform validation standards established by the central governing authority. These inspections may involve completeness, consistency, correctness, timeliness, and statistical distribution assessments.

Rather of exchanging raw data, domains produce quality ratings and metadata summaries that explain the datasets' features. These ratings allow the federated coordinator to evaluate the trustworthiness of local contributions while adhering to privacy restrictions. Quality-aware aggregation procedures can then be used, such as weighting model updates based on data quality indicators or removing contributions that fail to fulfill governance requirements.

This metadata-driven method adheres to federated governance principles by integrating centralized standards and decentralized execution, guaranteeing consistent quality control across diverse contexts.

4.3 Feedback Loops and Impact on Global Model Accuracy

Effective data quality governance in FL is intrinsically iterative, requiring constant feedback loops between the global model coordinator and domain teams. Monitoring global model performance—such as convergence behavior, validation accuracy, and fairness metrics—provides indirect indicators of underlying data quality concerns at participating nodes.

When performance deterioration or bias is found, feedback is transmitted to domain teams via governance channels, allowing for remedial measures such as data purification, re-labelling, feature engineering, or the removal of problematic data subsets. These feedback loops gradually enhance local data quality, resulting in more stable training dynamics and higher global model accuracy.

Importantly, these tools transform data quality governance from a one-time validation exercise to a continuous, collaborative effort. By incorporating feedback and learning into governance operations, federated systems can adapt to changing data distributions while maintaining strong performance.

4.4 Governance Implications

Data quality governance in federated contexts necessitates a delicate mix between standardization and autonomy. Centralized governance organizations must specify explicit quality criteria, validation methodologies, and escalation procedures, while domain teams oversee local data stewardship. When correctly implemented, this strategy reduces the risks provided by heterogeneous and non-IID data, improves model dependability, and boosts federation confidence [8].

In summary, strong data quality governance—based on local validation, quality-aware aggregation, and constant feedback—is required to ensure that federated learning systems produce accurate, fair, and trustworthy results in complex, multi-domain situations. Figure 3 shows the integration of policy-as-code within federated learning pipelines, to represent how governance policies are defined, compiled, and enforced automatically during local training and model aggregation [13].

5. Privacy, Security, and Trust in Federated Learning

Federated learning is sometimes marketed as a privacy-preserving alternative to centralized machine learning; nevertheless, the lack of raw data exchange does not imply security or trust. Instead, FL creates a new attack surface that focuses on model updates, communication protocols, and coordination methods. Ensuring security and privacy in such remote environments needs a mix of strong technological measures and governance mechanisms.

5.1 Threat Landscape in Federated Learning

FL is susceptible to numerous types of attacks that take advantage of common model parameters and decentralized involvement. Model inversion attacks analyze gradients or model updates exchanged during training to infer sensitive properties from local training data. These attacks pose major privacy implications, particularly when FL is used in sensitive fields such as healthcare or banking.

Another key issue is model poisoning attacks, in which hostile players purposefully modify local training data or model updates to harm global model performance or implant secret backdoors. Due to FL's decentralized architecture and the limited visibility into individual client updates, such assaults are difficult to detect. Furthermore, data reconstruction attacks attempt to extract approximations of local datasets from shared gradients, which undermines FL's privacy assurances.

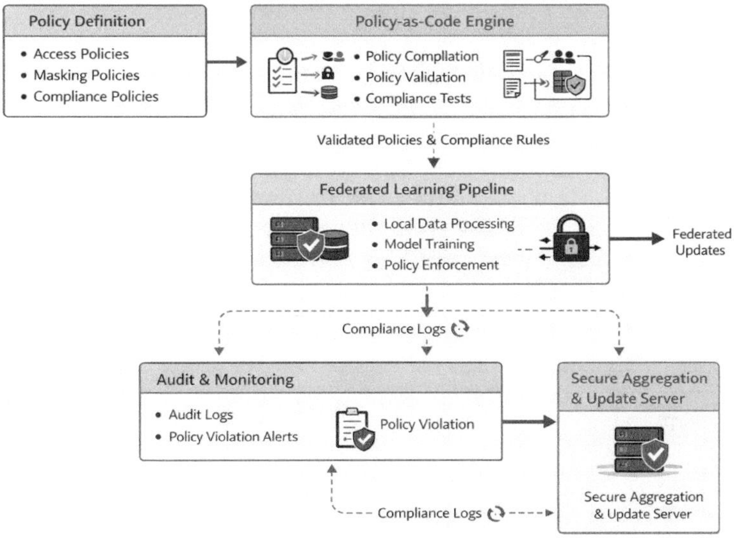

Figure 3: Policy-as-code integration in federated learning pipelines.

Together, these challenges demonstrate that FL shifts, rather than eliminating, security and privacy issues, needing comprehensive mitigation techniques.

5.2 Secure Aggregation and Differential Privacy

To mitigate these vulnerabilities, FL systems often use secure aggregation and differential privacy as essential protection measures. Secure aggregation techniques encrypt model changes from individual participants and make them only available in aggregated form, preventing the central server or other clients from viewing specific contributions.

Differential privacy (DP) enhances privacy by introducing calibrated noise into model updates or aggregation results, decreasing the amount of sensitive information that can be deduced from any single data point. While DP provides formal privacy assurances, it creates trade-offs between privacy protection and model accuracy. Managing these trade-offs necessitates careful parameter selection and uniform implementation across all participating nodes.

5.3 Governance-Driven Security Controls

Technical protections alone are insufficient for establishing trust in federated contexts. Governance-driven security controls define how security and privacy procedures are deployed, monitored, and enforced. Central governance authorities oversee creating global security policies, defining acceptable threat models, establishing privacy budgets, and monitoring regulatory compliance.

Participants in the domain must follow defined security procedures, such as secure training environments, identity and access management, audit logging, and anomaly detection. Policy-as-code, compliance audits, and continuous monitoring are examples of governance methods that allow for scalable security control enforcement across the federated learning life cycle.

Federated learning systems may create long-term trust among participants while preserving strong security and privacy protections by combining cryptographic measures with organizational governance frameworks. Table 3 shows the mapping of key threats to their corresponding mitigation techniques to represent the security risk landscape in FL.

Table 3: Security techniques in federated learning.

Threat Category	*Description*	*Primary Mitigation Techniques*	*Governance Controls*
Model Inversion	Inferring sensitive attributes of local training data from shared model updates	Secure aggregation; differential privacy	Privacy budgets, update visibility restrictions, compliance audits
Model Poisoning	Malicious participants manipulate updates to corrupt or backdoor the global model	Anomaly detection; robust aggregation; participant validation	Node authentication, contribution validation policies, trust scoring
Data Reconstruction	Reconstructing approximate training data from gradients or parameters	Differential privacy; encrypted communication	Data minimization rules, encryption standards, access control policies
Insider Threats	Authorized participants misuse access or retain model artifacts	Secure aggregation; access logging	Role-based access control (RBAC), audit trails, accountability mechanisms
Communication Attacks	Interception or tampering of model updates in transit	Secure channels Transport Layer Security (TLS); encryption	Network security policies, key management standards

6. Federated Learning and the Shift toward Data Mesh

The concepts of data mesh, an architectural paradigm that decentralizes data ownership while upholding international standards, are increasingly being adopted by large-scale analytics and AI systems. Federated Learning is a crucial tool for data-mesh-oriented AI ecosystems because it naturally facilitates this

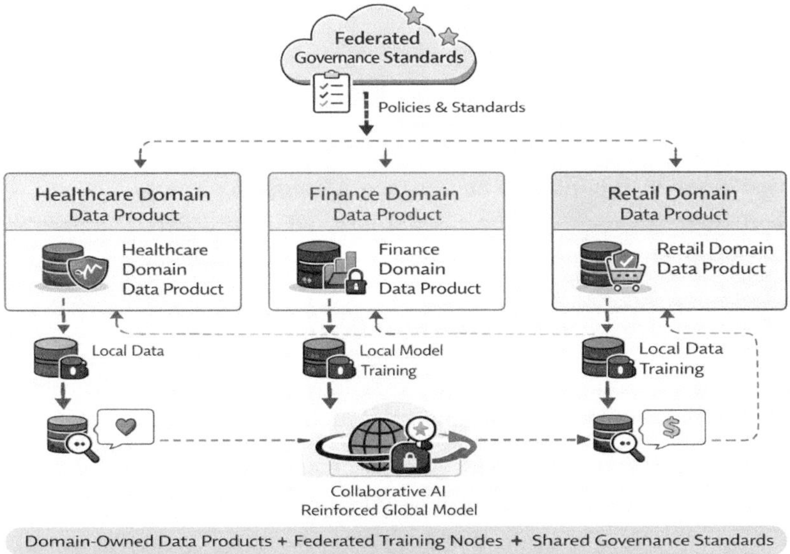

Figure 4: Federated learning and data mesh alignment.

shift by enabling collaborative model construction without centralizing data. The relationships between the domain-owned data products, federated training nodes, and shared governance documents are shown in Figure 4.

6.1 Domain-Owned Data Products

Data mesh is based on the idea of domain-owned data products, where different business domains are responsible for data security, quality, documentation, and life-cycle management. In FL situations, domain teams maintain control over local datasets and training methods while contributing model updates to a common global aim [14]. This alignment maintains data near to its source, promotes accountability, and lowers risks associated with large-scale data migration, especially in regulated areas such as banking and healthcare.

6.2 Alignment between FL and Data Mesh Principles

Beyond ownership, FL and data mesh share federated standards in their organizational and architectural alignment. Both models rely on centrally specified governance principles encompassing interoperability, metadata standards, access control, and compliance, even while implementation is decentralized [15]. By using techniques such as policy-as-code, secure aggregation, and standardized training methods, these regulations are operationalized in FL, allowing for consistent behavior across diverse domain settings without limiting local autonomy.

6.3 Governance as Strategic Enabler for Collaborative AI

In this setting, governance shifts from a compliance role to a strategic facilitator of collaborative AI. Governance, rather than serving as a gatekeeper, offers the frameworks, rules, and trust mechanisms that enable many domains to securely and efficiently engage in federated model training. Organizations that align FL with data mesh principles may extend AI programs across domains, boost collaboration, and provide the groundwork for next-generation, data-driven decision-making.

7. Conclusion and Future Directions

A decentralized, policy-driven framework must replace traditional centralized control for FL to be successfully implemented. Important ideas include:

Data Sovereignty: Maintaining complete control over local datasets for data owners, with governance ensuring that only model updates—never raw data—leave the premises.

Transparency and Auditability: Using automated lineage tools to keep a verifiable record of participant contributions, model revision, and compliance checks.

Security by Design: Integrating privacy-enhancing technologies (PETs) such as secure multiparty computing and differential privacy as a fundamental necessity rather than an optional feature is known as "security by design."

Collaborative Quality Standards: To reduce the risks associated with non-IID data throughout the federation, common methods for data labeling and preparation should be established.
Organizations adopting FL is a significant change in corporate strategy. Companies need to shift from "data hoarding" to strategic data orchestration. This includes the following things:

Cross-Functional Realignment: To properly manage data contracts, governance necessitates close coordination across legal, IT, and domain-specific teams.

Infrastructure Investment: To automate compliance at scale and minimize the hassle of manual supervision, organizations must give "policy-as-code" top priority.

Ecosystem Positioning: Because each role involves distinct risk profiles and value propositions, businesses must choose between acting as "federated orchestrators" (defining the rules) and "data contributors" (offering specific expertise).

The Basics of Collaborative AI in Governance: In the end, governance is the main facilitator of trust rather than a hindrance to innovation. A strong governance structure offers the ethical and technological safeguards required for multiparty cooperation in a world where data is becoming more controlled and isolated.

Governance turns FL from an experimental approach into a dependable enterprise-grade basis for the upcoming generation of trusted AI by standardizing model training across borders.

References

[1] Wen, J., Zhang, Z., Lan, Y., Cui, Z., Cai, J. and Zhang, W. (2023). A survey on federated learning: Challenges and applications. *International Journal of Machine Learning and Cybernetics*, 14(2): 513–535.

[2] Singh, P., Singh, M. K., Singh, R. and Singh, N. (2022). Federated learning: Challenges, methods, and future directions. In *Federated Learning for IoT Applications* (pp. 199–214). Cham: Springer International Publishing.

[3] Abdulrahman, S., Tout, H., Ould-Slimane, H., Mourad, A., Talhi, C. and Guizani, M. (2020). A survey on federated learning: The journey from centralized to distributed on-site learning and beyond. *IEEE Internet of Things Journal*, 8(7): 5476–5497. https://doi.org/10.1109/jiot.2020.3030072.

[4] Papadopoulos, P., Abramson, W., Hall, A. J., Pitropakis, N. and Buchanan, W. J. (2021). Privacy and trust redefined in federated machine learning. *Machine Learning and Knowledge Extraction*, 3(2): 333–356. https://doi.org/10.3390/make3020017.

[5] Atlan, T. (2025, December 11). Federated Data Governance: Ultimate Guide for 2026. *Atlan*. https://atlan.com/know/data-governance/federated-data-governance/.

[6] Guo, R. (2025). Governing through Participation: A case study of China's State-Led data economy. *SSRN Electronic Journal*. https://doi.org/10.2139/ssrn.5376419.

[7] Aaronson, S. A. (2019). Data is different, and that's why the world needs a new approach to governing cross-border data flows. *Digital Policy Regulation and Governance*, 21(5): 441–460. https://doi.org/10.1108/dprg-03-2019-0021.

[8] International, D. (2017). DAMA-DMBOK: Data Management Body of Knowledge.

[9] Dehghani, Z. (n.d.). How to move beyond a monolithic data lake to a distributed data mesh. martinfowler.com. https://martinfowler.com/articles/data-monolith-to-mesh.html.

[10] Weber, K., Otto, B. and Österle, H. (2009). One size does not fit all: A contingency approach to data governance. *Journal of Data and Information Quality*, 1(1): 1–27. https://doi.org/10.1145/1515693.1515696.

[11] Li, T., Sahu, A. K., Talwalkar, A. and Smith, V. (2020). Federated Learning: Challenges, methods, and future directions. *IEEE Signal Processing Magazine*, 37(3): 50–60. https://doi.org/10.1109/msp.2020.2975749.

[12] Kairouz, P., McMahan, H. B., Avent, B., Bellet, A., Bennis, M., Bhagoji, A. N. et al. (2020). Advances and open problems in federated learning. *Foundations and Trends® in Machine Learning*, 14(1-2): 1–210. https://doi.org/10.1561/2200000083.

[13] Zhao, Y., Li, M., Lai, L., Suda, N., Civin, D. and Chandra, V. (2018). Federated learning with non-IID data. *arXiv (Cornell University)*. https://doi.org/10.48550/arxiv.1806.00582.

[14] Lewis, J. (n.d.). *Microservices*. martinfowler.com. https://martinfowler.com/articles/microservices.html.

[15] Dehghani, Z. (2019). *Data Mesh: Delivering Data-Divided Teams*. Retrieved from https://www.thoughtworks.com/radar/techniques/data-mesh.

5 Credit Risk Assessment and Scoring Models

Sakshi[1,*] and Ankit Sharma[1]

Credit risk assessment has been one of the essential pillars in the field of financial decision-making, but the standard centralized approaches are faced with increasing challenges of privacy exposure, regulatory questions, and equity. Traditional machine-learning pipelines and centralized credit bureaus require the convergence of sensitive information about borrowers, thus exposing institutions to security breaches and noncompliance with regulation under privacy legislations such as the General Data Protection Regulation (GDPR), California Consumer Privacy Act (CCPA), and the Digital Personal Data Protection (DPDP) Act in India. Further, the models often do not reflect heterogeneous borrower specifications and nonindependent, identically distributed (non-IID) data distributions, which continue to reinforce discrimination against underbanked groups and limit financial inclusivity. Federated learning (FL) offers a paradigm shift in which learning occurs via collaborative model training without any sharing of raw data among banks, non-banking financial companies (NBFCs), and financial technology firms. FL protects the confidentiality of dissolving privacy via contactless accumulation, homomorphic encryption, and diverse privateness. These methods enhance the model generalizability of datasets that otherwise have varying attributes. As compared to European small and medium enterprise (SME) lending empirically, both Indian fintech microloans and US insurance risk modelling exhibit real practical advantages of FL in the form of both Area Under the Curve (AUC) improvements and lower default rates, as well as appreciable cost savings. The use of simulation experiments in non-IID environments also remains in support of the argument that individualized federated strategies, such as FedPer and FedProx, are superior to vanilla FL in heterogeneous applications, suggesting that adaptive procedures are important. In addition to the technical measurements there are the ethical and regulatory concerns that are of first importance. Indispensable when it comes to control regulatory compliance and establish trust among the stakeholders, fairness-aware algorithms, explainable AI tools, and transparent governance frameworks are a necessity. Emerging trends such as the personally fed FL, vertical FL, and federated multi-task learning

[1] Apex Institute of Technology (CSE), Chandigarh University, Mohali-140413, Punjab, India.
* Corresponding author: sakshigill12@gmail.com

DOI: 10.1201/9781003710059-5

paradigms are further broadening the scope of the field of FL connections through personalization of models to individual institutions, cross-sector features, and multi-dimensional risk forecasts. Directions of the future include real-time credit scoring, mobile-first assessment of underbanked communities, and federated risk sharing across borders, facilitated by blockchain auditability and ethical AI adherence. Together, FL builds itself not only as privacy-enforcing technology but as a socio-technical basis in fair, inclusive, and transparent credit systems.

1. Introduction

Credit risk rating is always viewed as the key to financial judgment in the banking, insurance, and capital markets. Basically, credit risk refers to the probability that a lender will default on their debt commitments as established by contract, giving rise to a financial setback to the lender. Investment institutions have over decades validated and depended, to the great extent, on credit-scoring predictors, the best-known ones being curated by Fair Isaac Cooperation (FICO) and other credit bureaus to assess the likelihood of non-recovery of an individual or organization. These models traditionally seek to aggregate variables such as income, credit history, outstanding liabilities, repayment history, and demographics, process these into risk scores, and hence guide decisions on loan situation, interest rate, and lending limits. Despite its effectiveness in most situations, the current approaches toward credit risk assessment are under increasing debate because of the tendencies of explosive credit data expansion, new attitudes toward data security, emergence of new lending organizations, and the necessity to remain fair and inclusive in lending, as well [1].

1.1 The Evolution of Credit Risk Assessment

Traditionally, the task of resolving credit risk occurred through manual processes, during which the banking officials used professional judgment, references, and collateral valuation to adjudicate borrowing decisions. A paradigmatic change came with the mid-20th-century development of statistical techniques: credit scoring became standardized with regression models and linear discriminant analysis. By the 1980s and 1990s, through the expedited digitization of banking and the advent of centralized databases, credit bureaus started aggregating large amounts of customer data into popular credit scores. Still, with the globalization of financial ecosystems and the digitization of their interactions, conventional centralized forms started to reveal considerable deficiencies. They had a challenge on scalability with large and heterogeneous data feeds, were prone to biases in incomplete datasets, and exposed sensitive customer data to security and privacy attacks [2].

During the last twenty years, with the emergence of artificial intelligence (AI) and machine learning (ML) tools, the assessment of risks is being revolutionized by allowing forecasting analytics based on some nonlinear and multidimensional relationships among customer data. ML systems including decision trees, random forests, gradient boosting machines, and neural networks exhibited significantly superior predictive accuracy as compared to rule-based models. However, these innovations brought in some substantive problems. The urgency to consolidate data to massive repositories created risks of leakage, hacks, and the inability to comply with the increasing regulatory regimes—the most prominent being the General Data Protection Regulation (GDPR) in Europe and the California Consumer Privacy Act (CCPA) in the United States. In addition, machine-learning models, being trained on biased or unbiased datasets, would run a risk of enforcing established social and economic inequalities, thus marginalizing the underbanked groups with regard to accessing credit on equal terms. The risk of credit is an ongoing phenomenon that continuously becomes more demanding because of the ever-evolving conditions in the banking sector. Financial sector is now in twofold dilemma. On the one hand, the pressure on the accuracy and real-time credit risk analysis has increased, stimulated by the spread of complex financial instruments, the growth of global markets, and the development of decentralized services such as fintech. At the same time, privacy of data, ethical stewardship, and compliance of regulations have hit scrutinizing demands. The trend of centralized credit-scoring mechanisms is coming under more and more scrutiny because they do not ensure transparency, fairness, and inclusiveness. As an example, rural-based customers or those dealing with informal economies tend to have low enough credit histories on centralized datasets, thus disqualifying them out of traditional lending channels. Similarly, lending across borders complicates the adherence to various and at times inconsistent data-protection laws.

In addition, nonindependent and identically distributed (non-IID) data have also become significantly exaggerated in the financial arena. Characteristics of borrowers, repayment behavior, and macroeconomics vary immensely across regions and banks. As a case in point, the credit behavior of customers in an urban fintech ecosystem could differ dramatically compared to credit behavior of clients in rural cooperative banks, thus making it harder to develop all-purpose models. Centralized methods that have been traditionally used cannot easily accommodate such diverse datasets without performance degradation or introducing discriminatory results. The trend of credit risk models as shown in Figure 1 shows a definite transition into the advanced statistical approach, such as the Z-score depicted by Altman, replacing manual reviews, which were subjective and required judgment of the risky lending behavior. Such a development would later lead to the development of modern machine learning algorithms, which, with its predictive capabilities, have created new issues of centralization and data privacy that recent frameworks are trying to solve.

1.2 The Promise of Federated Learning (FL)

Federated learning suggests a strong answer to these complex issues by enabling privacy explicit, decentralized AI model training. Unlike traditional machine-learning paradigms, which require consolidating sensitive customer data in a central server, FL allows a group of institutions, which fall into the categories of banks, credit unions, and fintech organizations, to gather collectively by training models without relinquishing the underlying raw data in their respective safe locations. Only model updates (gradients or parameters) are shared; the underlying data is confidential. Such architecture significantly reduces the risks of privacy, and it matches model activities with the data-protection laws.

FL, when used in the credit risk assessment process, can be used in building stronger, generalizable, and acceptable credit-scoring models. Independent of violating confidentiality, by integrating the knowledge base of one institution with that of another (innovative by a broader institution), FL can observe a more diverse range of borrower behavior and financial trends, thus increasing predictive accuracy, yet reducing the biases they introduce. It therefore provides the lower-represented populations with fair credit services, such as those with thin or nonexistent credit histories. Further, FL is prepared to handle non-IID exquisiteness of finance forecasts using mutable algorithms that are perceptive of various borrower elements, and fluctuating market factors.

1.3 Privacy-Enhancing FL

In order to strengthen the privacy-protective property of federated credit scoring, a number of sophisticated methodologies are being incorporated into FL systems. Homomorphic encryption (HE) allows processing encrypted records, which means that confidential client information would be locked in all stages of collaborative training. Differential privacy (DP) adds noise to model updates with a carefully tuned amount tweaked to ensure that adversaries do not infer a desired piece of knowledge about a borrower. Secure aggregation protocols also ensure that the contribution from individual participating institutions cannot be isolated and reverse- engineered. These methods, together, align FL-based credit-scoring systems to global regulations in addition to maintaining analytic fidelity [3].

The ability of federated learning to conditionally improve credit risk assessment stretches way beyond technical results. One of the foundational contributions has been financial inclusive promotion: traditional credit-scoring systems would tend to ignore those with no formal banking records of this sort, such as workers in the gig economy, aspirational entrepreneurs, or people in rural areas. Federated learning combines decentralized data with diverse financial operators, such as mobile payment companies and microfinance providers and digital wallets, into unified scoring models. This combination of two statements opens up access to credit and at the same time promotes fair lending behaviors, which are both practical and ethical AI principles, which stand as the foundation of modern scholarship of the field.

In addition, federated learning also allows building personalized credit-scoring architectures tailored to the unique aspects of diverse client portfolios. An application of FL by small merchants as served by fintech companies could include the creation of custom scoring models that identify alternative financial behavior, whereas more traditional forms like mortgage or corporate lending models might be conservative by traditional banks. This flexibility makes FL an indispensable tool (in present-day financial ecosystems), as the heterogeneity of customers is the rule, not the exception.

2. Advances in Credit Risk Assessment: From Traditional Models to Federated Learning

The field of credit risk assessment has over the centuries reflected the overall development of financial systems, technological advances, and regulations. The shift to an age of manual, judgment-based lending approaches, then to statistically justified credit-scoring systems, then to machine-learned predictive analytics, and, more recently, to federated learning represents a century-old trend set by an ever more complicated financial ecosystem with an imperative toward fairness, privacy, and inclusivity. This section will be a systematic statement of this development with an emphasis on the shortcoming of the traditional methods and the revolutionizing value of FL.

2.1 Traditional Credit Risk Assessment Models

Risk assessment in the motor phases of credit appraisal was mostly relation-specific. Personal acquaintance, local reputation, and verbal references were those that were used to gauge the creditworthiness of borrowers by loaning officers. Although it worked well in small groups, this paradigm was very subjective, inconsistent, as well as prone to leanings. Statistical models were presented in the first systematic wave of credit scoring in the middle of the 20th century. Notable among these were:

i. **Linear Discriminant Analysis (LDA):** This is used to factor-in the difference between the bad and the good borrows on a weighted combination of the financial and demographic variables.

ii. **Logistic Regression:** Gained popularity during the 1960s and 1970s due to its ability to treat binary outcomes (default versus no default), as well as give probabilistic interpretations.

iii. **Altman Z-Score (1968):** Used to predict bankruptcy of corporations, this is a composite in which data on profitability, leverage, liquidity, and solvency and activity ratios was merged.

These models allowed replicable, standardized, and scalable decision-making beyond manual decision-making. However, they were based on strong assumptions of linearity and independence of variables, thus limiting the capacity of the models to represent highly intricate, nonlinear borrower behaviors [4].

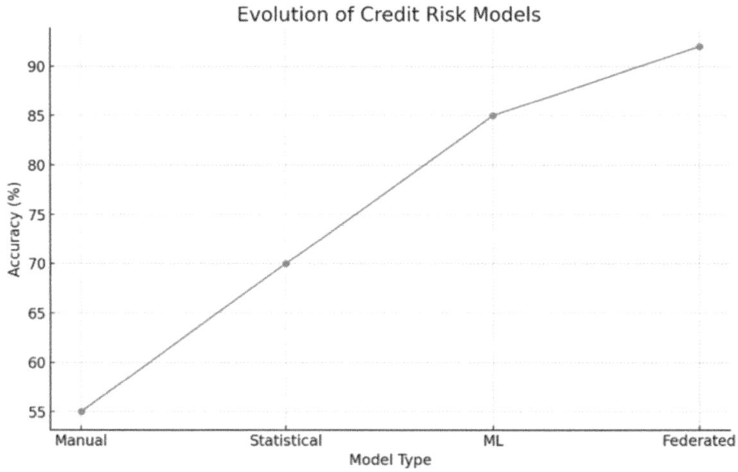

Figure 1: Evolution of credit risk models.

2.2 Centralized Credit Scoring Systems

Toward the end of the 20th century, the credit industry adopted bureau-wide scoring systems, and data companies such as FICO were at the forefront of international standardization. Banks, retailers, and financial service providers registered data at credit bureaus, consolidating the information into central databases, thus extending predictive scoring to the large volumes.

The important characteristics of this step are:

i. **Wide Highers:** The wide availability of millions of borrower histories increased the statistical strength of risk evaluation.

ii. **Automated Decision-Making:** Banks automated credit as a part of lending and this improved the time of getting an approval.

iii. **Regulatory Embedding:** Credit scores were institutionalized in the consumer protection and lending regulations.

In spite of these developments, structured scoring created structural failures:

i. **Data Privacy Vulnerabilities:** Since all the confidential personal information, including financial and alike, was stored in large depositories, they became an attractive target in cyber-attacks.

ii. **Self-Exclusion of the Underbanked:** Borrowers whose record of formal credit was absent, especially in developing economies, were effectively struck off the balance sheet by the mainstream credit systems.

iii. **Bias and Discrimination:** On most occasions, scores were indicative of fixed socioeconomic inequities, overwhelming the minority or low-income communities.

iv. **Rigid Modelling:** Minimizing adaptability to new financial behaviors, including the utilization of digital payments, or the appearance of gig-economy income trends, through the dependency upon established rules and limited responsiveness of the models.

2.3 The Rise of Machine Learning in Credit Risk

The surge of digital transactions and alternative financial platforms in the 2000s unlocked unprecedented opportunities for data-driven credit scoring. Machine learning fostered a paradigm shift beyond linear statistical models to algorithms that were able to acquire complex, nonlinear relationships.

ML models used widely are:

i. **Decision Trees and Random Forests:** Both have interpretability and are high in accuracy in providing demarcation of segments according to risk profiles of borrowers.

ii. **Gradient Boosting Machines (e.g., XGBoost, LightGBM):** They provide strong predictive value, and that behavior with heterogeneous datasets and sparse datasets performs well.

iii. **Commanding Support Vector Machines (SVMs):** They are able to classify risk classes in high-dimensional feature spaces.

iv. **Neural Networks:** Facilitate deep feature extraction from voluminous, unstructured datasets such as transaction histories or behavioral logs.

By using ML as a tool in credit risk assessment, prediction accuracy, adaptability, and risk differentiation were significantly boosted. An example is that ML models can find minor trends that would suggest repayment anomalies, suspicious transactions, or otherwise new default indicators. However, it was centralization which remained a dominant issue. ML requires massive data pooling, hence reinstating privacy threats and regulatory challenges. Furthermore, the lack of visibility of certain algorithms through computer-generated decision-making, the so-called black-box problem, was what provoked concerns with regard to equity and responsibility in blindly selected loans [5].

2.4 Challenges of Centralized AI in Credit Scoring

A striking group of constraints came to light with the implementation of AI in the financial industry especially in the fields of data management, justice, and accessibility:

i. **Privacy Issues:** Cross-institutional sharing of sensitive financial information was at times incompatible with tighter regulations upholding the protection of personal data, such as GDPR and CCPA.

ii. **Regulatory Pressure:** Researchers had to provide model explainability which many ML algorithms did not offer.

iii. **Bias Amplification:** ML models that were trained using historically biased datasets reinforced or, in fact, escalated biases in lending services.

iv. **Non-IID Data:** Not all borrowers act in identical ways across institutions, geographies, and sectors, which complicates the assumptions of data that is identically distributed. The performance of the centralized models is often not at par with nonhomogeneous populations.

v. **Exclusionary Dynamics:** Informal workers, micro-entrepreneurs, and village citizens were also less served as old institutions failed to capture their financial imprints.

These dilemmas prompted an alarming necessity of decentralized, privacy-sensitive, and equitable options.

2.5 Federated Learning: A Paradigm Shift

Launched by Google in 2016, federated learning is also a new field in credit risk assessment. FL is defined by reversing the traditional paradigm and it retains data in situ with a cross-training (collaboration) of models with multiple institutions. Instead of storing raw datasets with customers globally in one centralized data repository, banks and fintech companies retain theirs on-site, exchange only model parameters or gradients with a coordinating server, and collectively aggregate all those to update the global model. The fundamental working principle of this new paradigm is well embodied in Figure 2 that graphically exemplifies the trade-off key between privacy protection and model utility in federated learning systems. As much as increasing noise or encryption levels promotes better security, there will always be some effect on the predictive accuracy of the model, and a carefully adjusted good balance must be ensured between increasing the level of noise or encryption and the financial decision-making process.

This architecture comes with a number of transformational benefits:

i. **Data Privacy and Security:** Local financial data is never exposed to the outside world, and chances of attack are significantly lower.

ii. **Regulatory Compliance:** Avoiding the inter-country transfer of data, FL complies with the jurisdictional data protection standards.

iii. **Bias Minimization:** Training across various institutions will make sure that models from different institutions capture a wider range of borrower behaviors, innovating fairness.

iv. **Scalability To Non-IID Data:** Federated algorithms have personalization and aggregation solutions to handle nonhomogeneous distributions of borrowers.

v. **Scalability:** FL allows cooperation of thousands of institutions and produces strong models without the centralization and bottlenecks of infrastructure [6].

2.6 Illustrations of Federated Learning in Credit Scoring

The field is still young, but empirical studies and pilot tests testify to the future of federated learning in financial ecosystems:

i. **Cross-Bank Collaborations:** Enterprises can jointly create a credit risk algorithm without conveying information regarding the accounts, and hence enhance predictive capacity without forfeiting confidentiality of data.

ii. **Microfinance–Fintech Synergies:** Mobile-payment providers and microfinance institutions are able to encapsulate data about localized borrowers, thus complementing the scoring capabilities to underserved populations.

iii. **International Lending:** International credit financing entities can cooperatively develop cross-regional credit frameworks, concurrently honoring the data-protection legislation of all jurisdictions.

The cases presented here demonstrate that federated learning is not only technologically effective but changes the ethical and regulatory limit lines of credit risk evaluation as well.

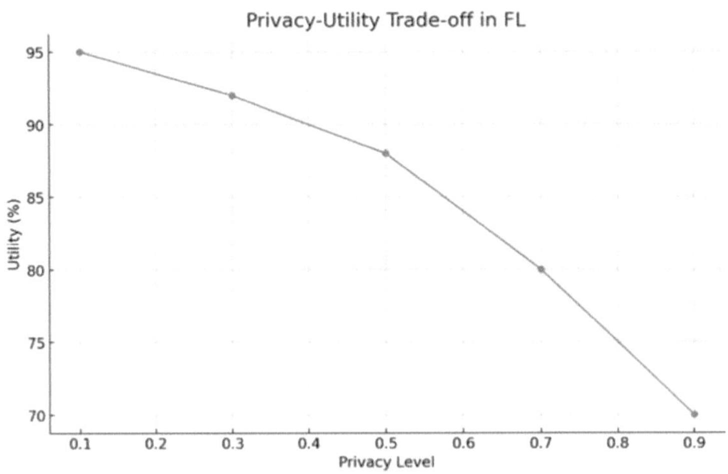

Figure 2: Privacy utility trade-off in FL.

2.7 Toward Federated Financial Ecosystems

Federated learning combined with privacy-preserving cryptographs and financial innovation leads to a melting point. Precision and transparency can be achieved at the same time by incorporating homomorphic encryption, secure aggregation, and differential privacy directly into federated pipelines. In addition to credit scoring, federated learning will change processing fraud detection, anti-money-laundering measures, and the real-time risk surveillance.

The shift of monolithic, centrally hosted AI platforms to federated ones represents a bigger story: finance is coalescing toward trust-based, inclusive, and privacy-sensitive ecosystems. This pathway transforms credit risk appraisal and integrates lending praxis with the global needs toward sustainability, ethics, and digital resilience.

3. Federated Learning for Credit Scoring: Conceptual Foundations

Decoupling credit risk modelling, federated learning represents a new paradigm, where model development and aggregation of data are not tied. Instead of keeping sensitive borrower data in a single bank, a variety of institutions, including banks, fintech companies, and credit bureaus, jointly train a same model. Raw information is stored on local servers and model parameters or summaries only come out over strict privacy protection. The approach solves facial problems presented to modern risk modelling, which include the law and barrier to data exchange and lack of capability to create all-encompassing models of nonhomogeneous client groups.

In essence, FL is a distributed optimization framework. Training models are done by each participant on its own data, which is sent to a central coordinator. The coordinator pulls these updates, puts them together, and redistributes as a global model. This development cycle allows a bank to enjoy the advantages of aggregated information in the whole ecosystem without having to gain access to the backroom consumer base of another institution.

The cooperation is based on data structure. Horizontal FL is common with credit scoring within institutions that are of similar characteristics yet have different customers. Vertical FL is used where the entities share different characteristics of the same customer base, say a bank and a payroll provider. In terms of lending ecosystems being heterogeneous, hybrids are the standard. The participants will be used as local trainers and a coordinator will handle the aggregation. More often than not, advanced methods are needed to find your way to non-IID data to provide a stable training experience and fair contributions of participants.

Within this context, there are no options of privacy and security. The inherent nature of FL design prevents any floating of raw data, but they should also protect metadata leakage and adversarial attacks. Such cryptographic techniques (scope:

secure aggregation) guarantee that the coordinator can still see nothing but a total of updates. Statistical defenses such as the differential privacy add noise to block any opponent to gain an idea about one borrower. The main idea is the exchange of some managed summary on the basis of formal confirmable assurances [7].

FL is relevant to the particular demands of credit risk modelling, including probability of default (PD), loss given default (LGD), and credit exposure at default (EAD). It supports key functionality of monotonicity constraints and model calibration, and these may be executed either locally or globally within privacy provisions. The federated form also assumes the concept of the corrective for selection bias, the notion of reject inference. Assessment of a federated model needs to balance the local privacy with the global guarantee. This involves computation of standard measures in a distributed way where all participants evaluate the model on their own local data and report only aggregated values are obtained. The strategy will allow full management of model risk, and maintain the principles of data minimization. The same can be said of drift monitoring or fairness diagnostics, where model members provide anonymized summaries so that the model is not destabilized.

Deployment requires an open governance structure, which can be a consortium- or regulator-owned model, with clear incentive coherence. Privacy and collaboration are incorporated in the life cycle of federated model including onboarding, post-deployment monitoring, and all different stages. Simply, the credit scoring is the promise of FL, that is, accountable privacy—it will allow a more principled approach to credit scoring; more accurate, fair, and privacy-conforming.

4. Architectural Framework of Federated Learning in Credit Risk Assessment

Mono-modelling federated learning in credit risk evaluation requires a solid architectural framework that can handle the non-generalized complexities of financial ecosystems. Unlike centralized models where data is centralized in one repository, the FL architecture has to balance concentrating on decentralization, model accuracy, regulatory conformance, and scalability wisely. The section presents a holistic analysis of the architectural elements, workflow, and operational levels of FL as implemented in models of credit-scoring and highlighting the technical innovations that make FL feasible and effective in financial institutions of all sizes, including both global banks and fintech start-ups.

4.1 Conceptual Overview of the Architecture

The core of the FL-based credit scoring architecture is the shower of collaboration intelligence lacking immediate data sharing. The system normally consists of three major pillars:

Clients (Data Owners): Financial institutions, including banks, NBFCs, as well as microfinance institutions and credit bureaus, support local datasets through which they provide their demographic and/or transactional and/or behavioral credit-related information.

Central Aggregator (Orchestrator): An authenticated, trusted server that coordinates the training regime, collects locally trained models, and deploys the new global model such that the participating clients can recapture it.

Communication Infrastructure: This is the channel over which encrypted model updates are floated between the clients and the aggregator. It is constructed with deliberate cryptographic immunity and programmable layers of secure multi-party computation (SMPC) to protect exploit attempts. The architectural cycle is a series based on cycles until convergence is made, in terms of the local training within the framework of the global aggregation alongside redistribution of the encrypted parameter [8]. The adoption of these decentralized systems is not evenly spread out as illustrated by Figure 3, which shows that federated learning adoption rates are not equally distributed in various parts of the world. This geographic difference usually goes hand-in-hand with domestic regulatory landscapes and the level of development of digital infrastructure, which affects the way such collaborative structures are adopted by financial institutions within various markets.

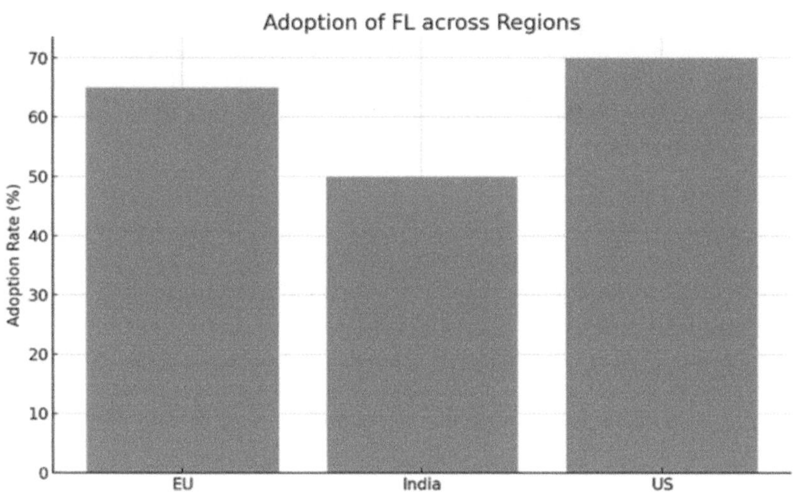

Figure 3: Adoption of FL across regions.

4.2 Layers of the Federated Learning Architecture in Credit Risk Assessment

The architecture could be tiered in four or more layers, each having a different responsibility of the credit-scoring process:

Data Layer: The data layer includes distributed financial data stored in individual institutions, including structured data (e.g., transactions history, credit-card usage, loan repayment), semi-structured data (chatbots logs and support-ticket logs), and unstructured data (emails, complaints, narrative text). Due to the heterogeneity and non-IID nature of such datasets, preprocessing is featured locally, hence retaining client-specific features.

Model Layer: The machine-learning algorithms used on the model layer are implemented to perform efficiently on a decentralized environment. Common models of credit scoring are logistic regression, gradient-boosting decision trees (GBDT), and the deep neural networks (DNNs). The models are locally instantiated at the individual institution, that is trained by proprietary data, and it is then distilled into an update of parameters. Also, the customized FL versions can be utilized in this case to model individual financial holdings.

Communication Layer: The communication layer ensures safe passage of the parameters between the clients and the central aggregator. Communication effectiveness is of the essence, considering bandwidth limitation and the concatenation of updates. Based on these, compression methods, sparse updates, and asynchronous communication are used regularly to reduce load but retain the fidelity.

Aggregation Layer: The aggregated layer allows the combination of model updates, so as to have a coherent global model. Acceptable aggregation protocols, such as cryptographic aggregation and homomorphic encryption, give it a property that the contribution of any single client cannot be reverse-engineered. A weighted aggregation scheme is adopted frequently, in which all clients contribute in terms of their dataset size or relevance.

Governance Layer: In light of stringent regulatory constraints within the financial services sector, the governance layer enforces compliance and accountability. It also includes the ability to monitor to explain its models, record audit history of credit judgment, and guarantee compliance with international privacy laws about, but not limited to, GDPR, CCPA, and DPDP.

Figure 4 provides a detailed description of the multi-layered architecture of federated learning when applied to assess credit risk, in particular. This figure shows the local data training at the client institutions flow to the encrypted parameter transfer to the central aggregator so that the basic raw data does not leave the local secure system.

4.3 Workflow of the FL Architecture in Credit Scoring

The operational workflow of the FL architecture in credit risk assessment proceeds through several iterative stages:

i. **Model-First Skeleton:** The central aggregator is able to commence a base model, usually pre-trained on synthetic or anonymized data.

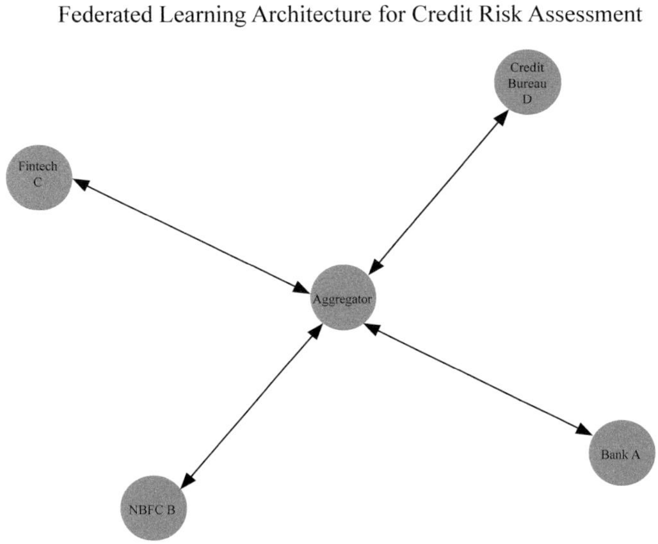

Figure 4: Federated learning architecture for credit risk assessment.

ii. **Local Training:** Each organization will train on its own dataset; for example, a commercial bank will be trained on the volume of mortgage balances, whereas a fintech enterprise can be based on mobile repayment volume.

iii. **Near-Infrared Data:** The raw parameters of a model (gradients or weights) are not sent to the aggregator but rather encrypted ones.

iv. **Global Aggregation:** The aggregator unifies those updates through federated averaging or aging weighted means, hence ensuring equity amid heterogeneous contributions.

v. **Model Redistribution:** The trained global model is shared among the clients to undergo further trainings.

vi. **Convergence and Deployment:** The model approaches a convergence point with robust generalization on an array of distributed datasets, and then the final model can be locally deployed to predict credit risk [9].

4.4 Integration with Privacy-Preserving Mechanisms

The architecture is carefully designed to work with privacy-preserving strategies, including homomorphic encryption, differential privacy, and secure multi-party computation (discussed in greater detail in Section 5). Those work under the communication and aggregation layers to ensure that although an adversary can overhear model information, reconstruction of sensitive client policies is unfeasible.

4.5 Scalability and Heterogeneity Management

One of the main drawbacks that accompany credit risk assessment is the heterogeneity; data is highly diverse among geographic divide, institutions, and groups of customers. The architectural framework mitigates this challenge through the following mechanisms:

i. **Personalized FL:** The system supports locally adapted models, instead of the whole world converging onto a single global model, so local models retain client-specific features.

ii. **Hierarchical FL:** Regional or size clustering organizations in big systems, regionally or by scale. Regional aggregators can produce intermediate models before they are global.

iii. **Asynchronous Updates:** To be able to support clients with different computational expertise, asynchronous federated updates will be used, such that the slowest students will not hold up the overall pace of convergence.

4.6 Technical Innovations in the Architecture

Credit risk assessment is made more efficient by several technical innovations that make the FL architecture more workable:

i. **Model Compression Techniques:** Quantization and pruning methods are used to make model updates that have less dimensions, thus enhancing computational efficiency.

ii. **Integration of Blockchain:** Smarter contracts are utilized to ensure that a permanent record of updates is kept, which will provide better transparency and accountability through model aggregation.

iii. **Trusted Execution Environments (TEEs):** TEEs (hardware-implemented secure enclaves) ensure integrity of model training and aggregation.

iv. **Adaptive Optimization Algorithms:** Advanced optimizers that include Fed Prox and Fed Nova allow the mission to reach a successful finish in the circumstances of non-IID and imbalanced data which are typical of financial environments.

In order to give a clear cutoff between the old and the new paradigm, Table 1 gives a side-by-side comparative analysis between traditional centralized architectures and federated learning architectures. It categorically identifies the areas of important difference of the data management, privacy, scalability, and cost of operation, and how the federated solution aids in reducing the single-point-of-failure vulnerability of the traditional centralized systems.

Table 1: Comparative analysis: traditional versus federated architectures.

Aspect	*Traditional Centralized Architecture*	*Federated Learning Architecture*
Data Management	Customer data is pooled into a central repository	Data remains local within each institution
Privacy	Higher risk of breaches; noncompliant with strict privacy laws	Strong privacy preservation through encryption and secure aggregation
Bias and Representation	Models trained on limited, institution-specific datasets, prone to bias	Models trained collaboratively on diverse datasets across institutions, reducing bias
Scalability	Limited scalability; requires massive centralized storage	Highly scalable; multiple clients contribute without central data pooling
Regulatory Compliance	Often struggles with GDPR, CCPA, DPDP compliance	Designed to comply with privacy-preserving regulations
Security Risks	Centralized data is a single point of failure	Decentralized architecture minimizes systemic risk but requires protection against model poisoning
Performance	Dependent on single institution's dataset quality	More robust and generalizable due to multi-institutional training
Operational Cost	Centralized infrastructure is costly and vulnerable	Distributed costs; infrastructure investments shared across participants

4.7 Advantages of the Architecture

The architectural framework confers a multiplicity of benefits:

i. **Privacy Preservation:** No client information leaks out of institutional boundaries such that the privacy of the individual is preserved.

ii. **Fairness and Inclusivity:** Multi-institutional involvement is a knowledgeable way indicating that the underbanked populations will be better reflected in the system by the incorporation of various datasets.

iii. **Regulatory Support:** The model-embedded support of secure aggregation and governance rules and protocols guarantee adherence to current regulatory market standards.

iv. **Scalability:** Asynchronous hierarchical structure; that is, the hierarchical design allows deployment to be extended across financial ecosystems anywhere in the world [10].

4.8 Limitations and Challenges

Despite this potential, several challenges are relevant to the federated learning architecture:

i. **A Lot of Communication Overheads:** The number of updates that are made may necessitate heavy loads on the network systems.

ii. **Model Poisoning Threats:** Attackers can vide as well try to insert poisonous updates, thus breaking model integrity.

iii. **Auditability and Explainability:** A high transparency in decentralized models is also a hard challenge to overcome with the regulatory compliance scheme.

Such restrictions throw light deep into the fruitful lines of future research and progressive improvements in upcoming redesigns of architecture. The fulfilled architectural structure of the federated learning in credit risk measurement is a groundbreaking move toward realizing the coordination of privacy data and financial wisdom. It provides a solid point of introduction to the development of inclusive, scalable, and regulation-compliant credit-scoring systems by enabling shared model training without jeopardizing confidentiality. The combination of privacy-enhancing solutions, scaling policy, and adaptive optimization is the reason why the architecture is flexible enough to keep up with the heterogeneity of financial data. Despite the persisting challenges, this framework is the foundation of the new generation of secure, equitable, and globally deployable credit risk assessments models [11].

5. Privacy-Preserving Techniques: Homomorphic Encryption, Differential Privacy, and Secure Aggregation

The automaton behind any federated learning implementation in the context of credit risk assessment is a privacy-saving mechanism. In the financial industry, where the information about borrowers is highly sensitive, and the regulatory share is almost limiting, the potential of FL, stated as learning without data mobility, should be enhanced with the use of both cryptographic and statistical measures that seal the residual leakage paths. Practice and research are dominated by three families of methods: HE, DP, and secure aggregation (including SMPC). The approaches handle different threat models and in real settings both are usually used together to provide layered defenses that strike a balance in terms of privacy, accuracy, scalability, and regulatory acceptability [12].

5.1 Homomorphic Encryption

The homomorphic encryption allows to do computations on encrypted data: encrypted model reminders can be summed up or part-process without exposing the encrypted data. In practice, there are two wide law classes of HE. Additive (or syndromic ally homomorphic) schemes such as Paillier allow linear arithmetic (e.g., summation) and thus tend to be a logical fit when performing secure aggregation of gradients or weight updates. Fully homomorphic encryption (FHE) can efficiently execute arbitrary computations, but is currently computationally intensive with large computation models. More pragmatic lattice-based designs implemented to execute approximate floating-point arithmetic, including the Cheon-Kim-Kim-Song (CKKS) scheme, can readily execute a wide range of operations needed by many machine-learning programs.

The appeal of HE in credit scoring is attributable to its high level of confidentiality assurances: worst case is that a compromised aggregator cannot read any single client update. However, HE presents huge computing and communication burdens. The ciphertexts are considerably larger than plaintexts and homomorphic operations are also significantly slower compared to plaintext operations. To make HE work in practice, system designers need to be careful about which computations they encrypt: typical patterns include encrypted final gradients or statistics, batching, amortizing overhead, and hybrid encrypted computations in the clear schemes (where unreliable partitions of the computation are encrypted). Noise growth is also another issue in the down-to-scale or approximate scheme such as CKKS where parameter tuning and rescaling are necessitated, and, although an engineering burden, need to be addressed to maintain model fidelity [13].

5.2 Secure Multi-Party Computation

HE has secure aggregation protocols and SMPC is used as a complementary product. Additive secret sharing, in which each client divides its update into shares, which are shared with peers or helpers/servers, enables the aggregator to only reassemble the total of updates to its peers, not any individual contribution. Scalable in practice, federated learning protocols (including those sensitive to client dropouts) enable secure aggregation. At a given level of HE though, the specific computational cost of SMPC will tend to be lower than that of HE, while being more complex to achieve than the communication complexity due to the need to exchange shares or partial calculations.

SMPC applies well to consortium environments typical of banking: a few well-trusted (or semi-trusted) parties can compute functions on unknown distributed inputs without the knowledge among themselves. With vertical federation, where there is split among institutions, SMPC can be used to perform conditional private set intersections (PSIs) and secure logistic regression, which capture resources across entities without revealing columns. The drawback of SMPC is its vulnerability to network ology and latency: high round-trip communication may be a bottleneck between geographically dispersed banks. SMPC operationalization thus requires fine-tuning (hierarchical aggregation, regional proxies) and solid engineering (efficient libraries, parallelization).

Secure aggregation and SMPC solve the confidentiality of contributions by the client, but these mechanisms do not, alone, inhibit inference of model outputs or aggregates. It is on this basis that they have often been used together with differential privacy.

5.3 Differential Privacy

Differential privacy provides an analytically precise guarantee that the incorporation or omission of any given person into a training set has a small impact on published results. In federated learning application, DP is generally implemented either by vindicating and introducing noise to nearby model progressions (local DP) or by introducing noise over the joined model (central DP). The popular DP pattern of Stochastic Gradient Descent in Federated learning (SGDF) learns more clipping and Gaussian noise extrinsically scales to FL, although the iterative third-party training of federation is linked with privacy loss, requiring privacy accounting as well. Therefore, the privacy budgets (the ε parameter) become a nontrivial choice, between privacy assurances that are verifiable, and model utility that is tolerable.

For stronger client-side protection, DP is used at the local level—each client perturbingly modifies its contribution and it is sent out to a receiver. Local DP typically incurs larger noise requirements and, therefore, causes significant utility loss. There is superior utility at the same time with central DP; however, assuming an entrusted aggregator to apply the noise appropriately, combining central DP with secure aggregation is hence a suggested direction, as secure aggregation helps avoid letting the aggregator watch per-client updates, but still allows adding calibrated noise to the aggregate. The other practical lever is privacy amplification by subsampling: in the case where only random subsets of the clients are exercised during each round, the loss of privacy with respect to each round is minimal and more training rounds can be realized under the same budget constraint.

The very big problem of credit scoring facing DP is calibration: credit models need calibrated estimates of probabilities to compute regulatory capital, and much noise may bias calibration and reduce economic utility. As such, all users of these tools should narrow the clipping norms and multipliers of noise based on the use case, and should, perhaps, adopt a hybrid approach, that is, only apply DP to high-sensitivity parameters, or to the final step of training, in order to maintain comparable calibration with the desired privacy.

5.4 Combining Methods: Layered and Hybrid Designs

In real-world credit-scoring deployments, no single technique suffices. To preserve confidentiality of individual updates, secure aggregation or SMPC is possible; HE can be used where specific aggregation primitives require higher security; whereas DP prevents inference attacks on the published global model. They each implement a layered architecture: (1) secret sharing or HE secures updates-in-flight and on-disk; (2) the aggregator uses DP noise to hide the identity of an update and publish it; (3) audit trails and attestations are modelled by trusted execution environments (TEEs) or blockchain logs; an attestation can be used to demonstrate the provenance of the updates that are produced by each model round. Much coordination is essential, for example, using DP with secure aggregation eliminates the requirement to trust the aggregator with raw updates and allows central DP to be used without sacrificing confidentiality.

System designers also face the challenge of having to pay attention to threat models which are not confined to the comforting paradigm of honest-but-curious adversaries. Specifically, active adversaries can exploit the fact that through adversarial methodologies such as active learning, an adversary could seek to model-poison its predictor with data that are intended to alter the predictive score. In spite of the fact cryptographic protections are very useful at hiding inputs they fail to protect against such poisoning attacks. Anti-vibrating aggregation rules, therefore, have to be used together with anomaly detection algorithms and reputation systems to maintain integrity of the federated learning process, which includes median, trimmed mean, or Krum algorithm. In some respects, the differential privacy can provide some recovery; that is, small-scale manipulations can be obscured, but adversaries with any significant computational interest have not lost the ability to damage it. Consequently, the phase-round-the-clock defense against poisoning will require the client attestation rules in combination with the economic disincentives, involving the use of staked deposits and the mechanisms of the slash. The technical consequences of adding statistical noise as a privacy measure is also discussed in Figure 5, which shows how differential privacy noise affects federated gradient aggregation. The visualization demonstrates that the gradient updates communicated to the central server by different noise injection levels may lead to changes, which is significant in the deterrence of reverse-engineering attacks without losing the convergence of the model.

5.5 Practical Trade-Offs and Engineering Considerations

A careful trade-off examination is key to the correct choice of a privacy stack. The privacy of homomorphic encryption works in the highest order possible, whereas its execution cost is restrictive. In the face of communication latency, secure multiparty computation scales poorly. Differential privacy prevents inference attacks, but overuse of it can reduce predictive utility. The compression of updates based on scarification and quantization to reduce the computational cost of both substitution encryption and secure multiparty computation hence is an engineering best-practice. Differential privacy should inject noise onto those parameters that are highly sensitive, only. The idea of hybrid encryption can be developed in which homomorphic encryption is needed only to protect the most sensitive tensors. Cross-regional communications can be enhanced by using the hierarchical aggregated structures to minimize the delays. In addition, the so-called trusted execution environments may be used wherever the existing legal and model of trust can allow it.

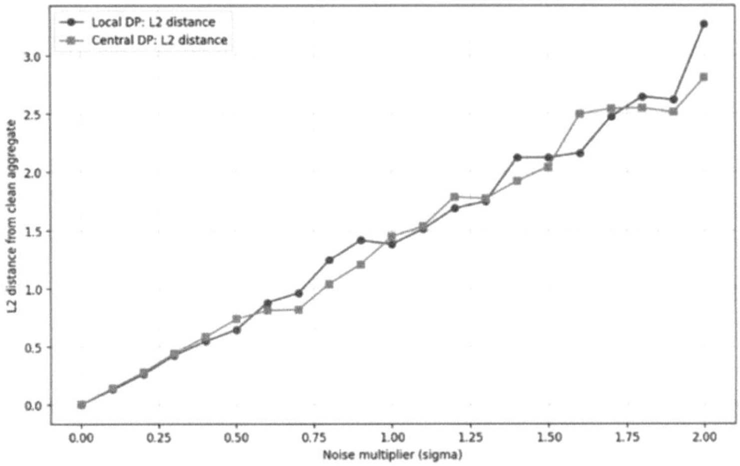

Figure 5: DP noise impact on federated gradient aggregation.

Regulative, detailed documentation is requirable. The institutions should keep a record of privacy funds, cryptography settings, threat analysis, and verification log to meet external audit requirements. Embedding privacy-by-design principles in federated credit systems is required to establish a requirement of ongoing privacy accounting, open roles, and life-cycle-driven approaches, such as logging, testing, and rollback, which is part of supervisory inquiries. Figure 6 offers empirical information that plots simulated accuracy versus levels of differential privacy noise. This graph simply measures the cost of privacy as an empirically achievable amount, that is, it measures the amount of model performance that is degraded as the privacy budget (epsilon) is decreased, which acts as a guide to institutions to make realistic expectations about model utility given hard privacy limits.

Homomorphic encryption, secure aggregation or secure multiparty computation, and differential privacy set in stages complement each other, allowing federated credit scoring that is usable and auditable yet would be regulatory-compliant. A realistic implementation plan has as its initial steps a tense threat modelling and alignment with stakeholders, a hybridized technical structure (secure aggregation or secure multiparty computation to secure transport secrecy); centralized exposure to privacy (common differential privacy systems to safeguard aggregate privateness, combined with meticulous privacy accounting); and selective application of homomorphic encryption or trusted computation settings to the most private tasks. Aggregation and watchful checking against poisoning, feature governance, and federated feature stores ensure semantic alignment among collaborators. Through these overlaid protections, along with careful engineering trade-offs, the federated learning can become a scalable base of privacy-preserving, equitable, and compliant credit risk models. Table 2 presents a structural analysis of the privacy mechanisms discussed in this paper

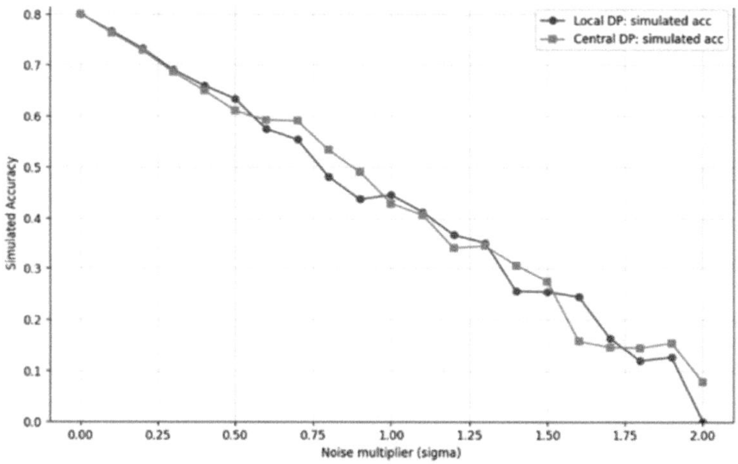

Figure 6: Simulated accuracy versus DP noise.

and compares secure multi-party computation, homomorphic encryption, and differential privacy. This table classifies each technique based on its fundamental concept, strengths, and weaknesses, which will help a system architect choose the right "privacy stack" depending on their individual computational capabilities and security needs.

Table 2: Comparative table: HE versus SMPC/secure aggregation versus differential privacy.

Technique	*Core Idea*	*Strengths*	*Weaknesses*	*Applicability in Federated Credit Scoring*
Homomorphic Encryption (HE)	Perform arithmetic on encrypted data so aggregator never sees plaintext	Strong confidentiality even against compromised aggregator; works with untrusted servers; suitable for protecting critical tensors	High computation and large ciphertext sizes; communication overhead; parameter tuning (noise/growth) required; engineering complexity.	Aggregating sensitive gradients/ statistics where legal/trust model disallows any plaintext exposure; small critical aggregates (e.g., cohort sums), high-assurance deployments

Contd...

Technique	*Core Idea*	*Strengths*	*Weaknesses*	*Applicability in Federated Credit Scoring*
Secure Multi-Party Computation/ Secure Aggregation (SMPC/SA)	Secrets are split into shares and jointly computed so only the aggregate is revealed	Lower cryptographic compute cost than HE for many operations; flexible for consortiums; supports fault-tolerant aggregation	Communication-heavy (many rounds/peers), latency-sensitive; needs careful orchestration; does not prevent inference from aggregate outputs	Consortium banks with reliable network links; vertical FL tasks (PSI, secure joins); secure aggregation of parameter updates at scale
Differential Privacy (DP)	Add calibrated statistical noise to outputs/ gradients to limit inference about any individual	Provides mathematical privacy guarantees (budgeted); protects against inference from released models/ metrics	Utility loss if noise is large; cumulative privacy loss needs accounting; choosing epsilon is nontrivial	Protecting global model releases, audit statistics, and calibration outputs; used together with HE/SMPC to prevent aggregator trust assumptions

6. Handling Non-IID Data in Federated Financial Environments

Scholarly, financial data are highly heterogeneous. The demographics of borrowers, income patterns, product portfolios, regional economic cycles, and channel-specific activities yield such differing distributions across different institutions and within the same institution with different products. This heterogeneity arises as non-identically distributed one-sample federation of data at each client node, hence compromising federated optimization algorithms that assume an approximate IID sampling regime. The omission of non-IID heterogeneity is an invitation to poor generalization, unfair scoring, and counter-optimal incentives that could be inflated. The following discussion clarifies the fundamental problems, examines algorithmic and systems approaches that address them, and outlines optimal deployment patterns to use in federated credit scoring.

Statistically, non-IID occurs by several, and often overpronating, mechanisms. In heterogeneity on features spaces, different institutions receive different collections of predictors, such as a payroll service noting pay cadence and a bank noting repayment delinquencies. Label-distribution skew implies that default rates within portfolios can be very widely different: microloans in a city fintech chequebook may apply a different base default rate than the mortgages of a national bank. Covariates' drift indicates persistent discrepancies in feature distributions conditional to similar regimes over labels, for example, difference in merchant mix or degree of transaction. Lastly, concept drift gives the model a time component: macro-economic shocks may restructure the relationship between features and default risk, and different institutions will drift at different times and at different rates.

Heterogeneity-related manifestations such as these require both algorithmic and systems design decisions. Personalized federated learning, in which the world model provides an underlying backbone and each customer a sparsely customized head, is just one of the families of these algorithmic responses. Theoretically, the backbone picks up ubiquitous risk factors (e.g., late payments, utilization ratios), but the customized layers adjust the predictions based on local portfolio economics and regulatory variability. These methods include multi-task formulations of learning, localization of the global model with local inputs, and meta-learning paradigms, including model-agnostic meta-learning, which produce initializations sensitive to adapting quickly to local data. In credit-score applications, personalization is essential, since economic considerations, such as severity of losses and recovery opportunities, vary over product lines; a lender may utilize the common model, but adjust thresholds and local conversion costs to fit its underwriting guideline. The heterogeneous data distributions problem is shown graphically in Figure 7, which plots the results of federated models in non-IID regimes. It points out how the conventional aggregate methods can fail when presented with diverse borrower profiles across the institutions and the importance of adaptive algorithms such as FedProx to stabilize the training in flaky financial conditions.

A second approach involves using robust aggregation and optimization techniques. Proximal terms are added in the name of algorithms such as FedProx and include the local goals to regulate the deviation of the model, which plays an essential role in improving stability in case of heterogeneity. Standard loss-aware update rules and variance-reduced aggregation techniques counteract the effect of clients making extremely noisy updates. The effect of extreme or malevolent updates is mitigated by strong aggregate functions, such as median, trimmed median, and coordinate-wise median, but such functions should be used cautiously since they can dampen genuine but rare signals, especially in credit applications where capturing early warnings of systemic stress is critical. Weighted aggregation allows the contribution of smaller yet informative clients (such as a microfinance organization serving an underserved region) to be preserved through the use of weights adjusted to reflect an effective sample size, or the quality of the labels, or statistical leverage.

Vertical federated learning reduces the heterogeneity of feature set through joint model training between the partners that hold complementary sets of features quite often but share common customers. Secure feature-alignment techniques, such as PSI and privacy-preserving models, are schemes that enable participants to discover common customers, and jointly compute gradients using private SMPC or HE.

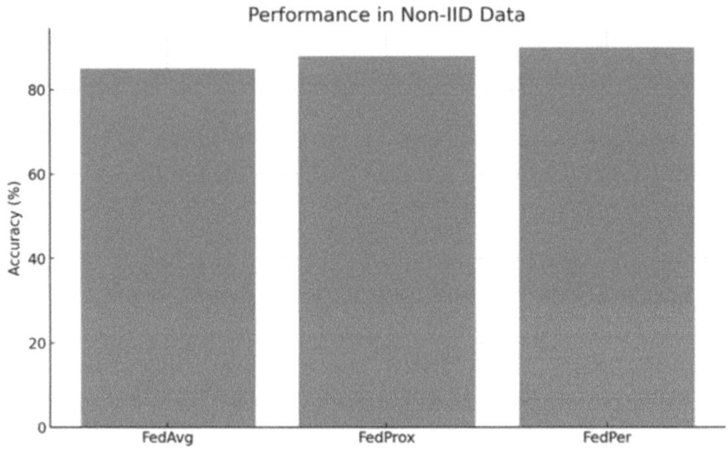

Figure 7: Performance in non-IID data.

Split learning is a type of architecture in which the first layers are hosted cooperatively by one partner, then the next, with/under encryption of the transferred activations; this implies that the columns of the deep representations can be shared freely but wires are not revealed. Vertical techniques in particular come in handy when alternative signals (telecom payment regularity, utility payment history) can be integrated into credit models without being overly stringent on data localization. Another suite of techniques harnesses representation learning and transfer. In case of difference between schemas of participants, the common embedding space can be used to integrate heterogeneous inputs. Self-supervised pre-training of masked sequence models (contrastive objectives) on in-house, unlabelled transaction chronicles generates encoders that transform various behaviors in comparable latent vectors; federated fine-tuning brings these encoders into correspondence so that a common downstream probability-of-default model can be developed. Covariate shift is alleviated by transfer learning and domain-adaptation techniques—adversarial alignment and minimization of discrepancies—allowing a global model to exploit client-specific distributions.

Client selection and strategies and curriculum are powerful levers in terms of systems. At the round, representativeness is boosted through deliberate sampling known as mixing of small, under-representative clients with large banks. Scheduling curriculum learning (where participation is done by a diverse cross-section of subjects early in the training process and more specific local fine-tuning is done later) can be used to enhance convergence and fairness. With hierarchical structures, where regional or product-line aggregators generate intermediate structures, having cross-region heterogeneity, local aggregations are interested in region heterogeneity, and a higher-level aggregator in commonalities.

Evaluation and monitoring demand federation-aware metrics. In addition to classical AUC and calibration, institutions should track per-client calibration, unfairness differences between the protected and economic populations, and contribution diagnostics (to which global forecasts are the most sensitive clients). Local Shapley Additive exPlanations (SHAP) or attribution calculations summarized into cohort summaries make federated explainability tools beneficial to interpretable compliance reporting. Drift detection should also be federated: distributed PSI of feature statistics or local computation of the PSI reporting only aggregate alerts maintains privacy but allows such alerts to trigger retraining.

Lastly, the governance and incentives influence results of heterogeneities. Properly put in place contribution measures and awards can have the effect of keeping small but informative clients active, so that we do not experience the large institutions disproportionately determining model influence and distorting predictions in line with their portfolio characteristics. The contracts on model use (safe harbor on local calibration), common validation schemes, and management of consortiums cannot be avoided to maintain the cooperation and equity.

Overall, personalization, strong aggregation, vertical learning, representation transfer, delicate client coordination, federated assessment, and principled governance are all needed in navigating non-IID data in federated credit systems. None of the single approaches are sufficient; the practitioner should develop hybrid pipelines that would adapt to heterogeneity pattern peculiar to the consortium, focus more on the emphasis placed on calibration and explainability, and keep constant observation of fairness and drift. In this way, federated credit models have the potential to provide informed, comprehensive, and regulation-consistent risk measurements in a variety of financial ecosystems.

7. Case Studies

It is through a sequence of real-world pilots and strictly controlled experiments that the practical value of federated learning in credit risk assessment can be clarified. Banking, fintech, and insurance case studies provide insight into how FL addresses issues of privacy, generalization, and fairness, and simulation work provides insight into the trade-offs between performance and privacy–utility balance.

7.1 Cross-Bank Credit Scoring in Europe

In 2018, the European Financial Data Space organized a collaborative training workshop of six banks, who together developed a federated gradient-boosted tree model on a dataset of 5 fully anonymized small and medium enterprise (SME) loan applications. The result of this effort was a 12% growth in Area Under the Receiver Operating Characteristic Curve (AUC-ROC), the expansion of credit access to thin-file borrowers, and complete adherence to GDPR, all evidencing the structural possibility of cross-bank cooperation.

7.2 Fintech Microloans in India

Still following the RBI's 2022 Digital Lending Guidelines, three fintech companies implemented federated neural networks using differentiating privacy in mobile and alternative data streams. The developed model demonstrated a 9½% drop in default rates and faster onboarding of underbanked clients, as per the DPDP Act (2023) in India, strengthening regulatory confidence. Figure 8 evidences of practical success in real-world applications, and shows AUC–ROC improvements in the European SME lending pilot. The results have shown that there is a noticeable improvement in predictive power in cross-bank collaborative training in comparison to siloed models, thus proving the hypothesis that federated collaboration can be used to improve credit assessment abilities without undermining data sovereignty.

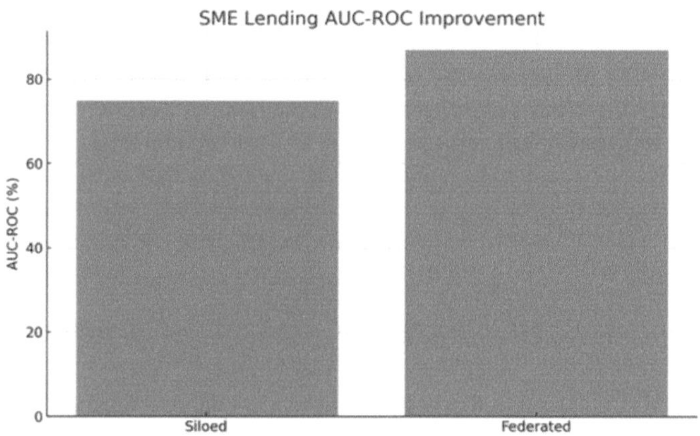

Figure 8: SME lending AUC–ROC improvement.

7.3 Insurance Risk in the USA

American insurers used a federated random forest architecture to estimate auto-policy risk. The strategy showed 15% improvement in accuracy, decrease in false negatives, as well as savings of $30 million annually. Such results demonstrate the broader financial-risk access of FL beyond lending into insurance and other wider financial-risk arenas.

7.4 Simulation under Non-IID Conditions

The German Credit and Lending Club data and Taiwan's similar sort of data were divided into 20 simulated banks, with comparative studies run on centralized and federated methods (FedAvg, FedProx, FedPer). The highest centralized accuracy achieved in federated learning was around 92%. Although heavy differential-privacy noise caused a significant reduction in accuracy, it offered significantly enhanced privacy protection. In the case of a data skew, personalized methods always performed better than FedAvg.

7.5 Lessons Learned

The entry of a higher level of privacy inevitably results in lower levels of accuracy, but at the same time raises the compliance position. The processing of non-IID data requires complex tools such as FedProx. The push to adopt is influenced by regulatory mandates (GDPR, CCPA, DPDP) as much as it is measured by performance. Scalability is attributable to effective transtheoretical protocols of communications and hard infrastructure. Lastly, trust should carefully be developed under the conditions of transparency and fairness.

7.6 Implications

FL allows cross-institutional credit officials to rate credit without centralization of data, which opens out additional credit, regulative compliance, and enhances fairness. Empirical deployments and simulation research efforts both attest that FL is always more effective than siloed models as long as precision is carefully controlled by both privacy measures and dynamic algorithms. These empirical results are summarized in Table 3 that represents comparative results of the European, Indian, and US case studies. This table provides a fast reference to the practical benefits, both quantifiable and quantified, achieved by the federations' implementations, by listing the particular FL technique, the outcome, and privacy mechanism used in each of the domains.

Table 3: Comparative results.

Domain	*FL Technique*	*Outcome*	*Privacy Mechanism*	*Key Impact*
SME Lending (EU)	GBT + secure aggregation	+12% AUC–ROC	Secure aggregation	SME inclusion
Microloans (India)	Neural nets	−9% defaults	Differential privacy	Inclusion, DPDP compliance
Insurance (US)	Random forest	+15% accuracy	HE + DP	Cost savings
Simulation	FedAvg vs FedPer	~92% centralized	DP	Utility–privacy balance

8. Emerging Strategies: Personalized FL, Vertical FL, and Multi-Task Learning

Theoretical horizontal federated learning, most previously FedAvg, has demonstrated significant effectiveness in credit-risk modelling; however, these several methods face evident major challenges, including the issue of data heterogeneity, mismatched feature spaces, and the dynamic feature of borrower riskiness. To address them, historical research has offered more sophisticated paradigms, that is, personalized federated learning (PFL), vertical federated learning (VFL), and multi-task federated learning (MTL) that jointly transform federated learning into a modular, institution-specific, and dimensions-based paradigm.

8.1 Personalized FL (PFL)

Personalized federated learning breaks with the mindset of promoting one universal model: predictive systems are fitted to different client groups by fine-tuning their models locally or through meta-learning. Its applications in practice include urban- versus rural-borrower-customized risk strategies by regional banks, fintech solutions using alternative data streams, and separation treatment of high and microloan clients. FedPer, clustered federated learning, and meta-learning algorithms techniques promote the level of personalization. The resulting advantages are not only greater accommodation of non-IID data distributions but also a superior feeling of belonging, though coming at the cost of more training difficulty.

8.2 Vertical FL (VFL)

Vertical federated learning allows cross-institutional collaboration in situations where different institutions have complementary sets of features on the same client group, such as banks with repayment history, telecommunication companies with mobile usage data, and insurance companies with claims data. SplitNN, homomorphic encryption, and entity-matching pipelines are mechanisms that help achieve secure aggregation of cross-features information. The usual combinations include bank–fintech or insurance–bank affiliations, which provide enriched borrower profiles, particularly beneficial to thin-file borrowers. Some of the most outstanding issues are to ensure credible entity alignment and reducing the computational cost incurred by encryption protocols. Emphasizing the influence on the performance of the loans, Figure 9 demonstrates how the default rates decrease in Indian fintech microloan applications with the usage of federated neural networks. The chart associates the implementation of privacy-saving collaborative models with a realistic reduction in non-performing assets, which is that more extensive data access with the help of federation results in a more robust risk detection.

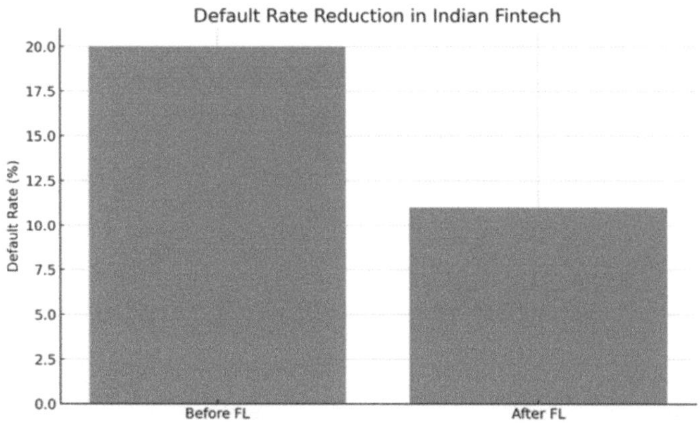

Figure 9: Default rate reduction in Indian fintech.

8.3 Multi-Task FL (MTL)

Multi-task federated learning builds on this federated-learning approach by jointly learning interpretative risk presence, for example, loan default, customer churn, fraud detection, or credit line adjustments, under one learning framework. Methods generally include common feature extraction layers with number-of-task-specific output heads, multi-task neural networks, or graph-based modelling methods. This paradigm will minimize redundancy, delve the risk interdependence, and strengthen predictive robustness. However, practitioners have to contend with task imbalance and convergence problems of multi-task optimization.

8.4 Strategic Relevance

PFL increases inclusivity, VFL commits commitment between sectors with no invasion of privacy, and MTL reflects the nature of financial risk which is intrinsically multidimensional. The combination of the above-mentioned mechanisms allows building the future generation of federated-learning-based credit networks, where accuracy, privacy, and compliance with regulations are harmonized.

Future avenues of research are a hybrid of PFL–VFL–MTL; proactive regulatory support of federated learning pipelines; a blockchain-mediated coordination to achieve auditability; a framework of ethical AI governance centering on fairness and explanation. The new federated learning approaches transform the discipline into a flexible, cross-functional, and versatile enterprise. Individualized, contextual, and multi-purpose approaches to credit are touted to emerge as the building block to privacy-sensitive and inclusive processes of credit-risking in the ever-changing financial environment. Going outside the banking sector, Figure 10 illustrates the accuracy of the predictions in the US insurance industry when using federated random forest architectures. This visual validation of a 15% error reduction in accuracy serves as a reason to affirm the versatility of federated learning, since it demonstrates its ability to produce significant cost savings and to minimize false negatives in the broader financial risk environment.

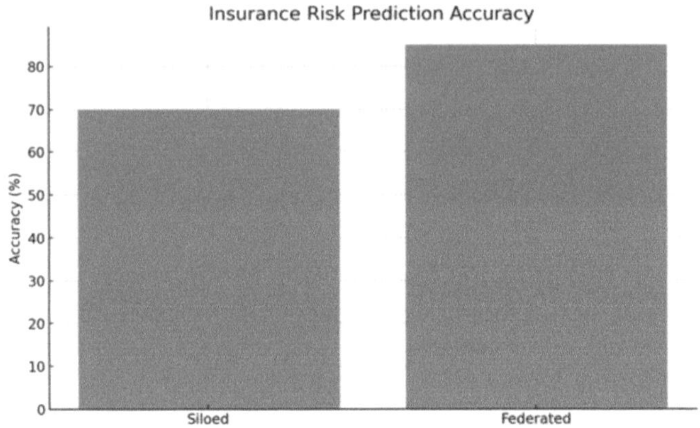

Figure 10: Insurance risk prediction accuracy.

Table 4: Comparative analysis.

Strategy	*Target Problem*	*Techniques*	*Advantages*	*Limitations*
PFL	Non-IID data	FedPer, clustered FL, meta-learning	Tailored models, inclusivity	Training complexity
VFL	Different feature spaces	SplitNN, HE, entity matching	Richer cross-sector borrower profiles	Entity alignment, encryption cost
MTL	Multiple risk tasks	Shared encoder + task heads, graph-based FL	Efficiency, robustness	Task imbalance

New strategies such as PFL, VFL, and MTL have been classified in Table 4 along with the evolution of the field. This discussion outlines the issues of each solution that the practitioners are targeted to address and particular benefits of each solution that can be used to help the practitioners determine which advanced federated approach is most appropriate to deal with particular problems such as feature misalignment or multi-dimensional risk prediction.

9. Ethical, Regulatory, and Compliance Considerations

The introduction of federated learning to credit-risk prediction provides a potential framework of privacy-protective collaboration; however, it, on the other hand, also brings on a range of ethical and regulatory infidelities.

9.1 Fairness and Bias

Traditional credit-risk scorecards are less likely to give an advantage to disadvantaged or marginalized groups of people; federated learning is not the solution to this risk by itself. When local datasets are made global, they may in effect increase biases intrinsic in them—such as local differences in demographic factors—which can be crucially critical when considered on an international scale. Mitigation, hence, requires adoption of protocols of fairness-conscious FL, systematic bias detection, and continuous observation to ensure equitable access to credit.

9.2 Regulatory Compliance

The concept of federated learning is consistent with the data-minimization requirements in Quebec's GDPR, California CCPA, and the Indian DPDP Act because it does not imply direct data passage. However, not all threats are neutralized—the most serious ones include gradient leakage, reconstruction threats, and uncertainties about the extent of personal data. Differential privacy and secure multi-party computation are among the privacy-preserving mechanisms that are hence essential. Furthermore, the cross-border cooperation intensifies the compliance issues as the legal system of the jurisdictions is heterogeneous.

9.3 Explainability and Auditability

Decisions involving credit scoring have a tremendous power of determining whether a person can obtain loans, interest rates, and even credit limits, thus making such decisions meaningful and require transparency. The models of black-box FL run the risk of generating regulatory scepticism and mistrust among the general population. The implementation of explainable AI products and auditory logging procedures, accordingly, becomes the key to clarify the logic underlying the decision, enable the promoted regulatory verification, and maintain trust among the stakeholders.

9.4 Equity and Data Sovereignty

The asymmetry of power can occur because the larger banking institutions can disproportionately influence federated models, whereas small institutions can provide a minimum contribution toward the risk; however, these risks are still distributed. Reasonable reward systems and benefits sharing systems are thus the essential inputs toward inclusive adoption. These cross-national federated networks must in turn find a compromise between local data-sovereignty demands and the requirements of global cooperation.

9.5 Policy and Ethical Foresight

The phenomenon of FL within the financial field depends on the expectation of governance. Regulatory authorities should issue FL-specific guidelines that integrate technological protection and reduce any potential harm to customers through ethics that endorse transparency, fairness, and accountability. Instead of being a single technical privacy application, FL has to be envisioned as a socio-technical entity redefining trust and responsibility in artificial intelligence of financial environments. Embedding fairness, explainability, and compliance at the design stage is essential if FL is to create an inclusive and trustworthy credit risk ecosystem. With regulatory clarity and ethical safeguards, FL can evolve into the foundation for responsible, privacy-preserving financial decision-making. To cover the legal environment, Table 5 superimposes the capabilities of federated learning with such key regulatory sources as GDPR, CCPA, and the DPDP Act. It recognizes certain compliance conformities, including data minimization, but also genuinely acknowledges the remaining gaps of compliance such as the existence of gradient leakage risks, which offer a roadmap to institutions going through the complicated jurisdictional compliance.

Table 5: Regulatory compliance mapping for FL in credit risk.

Regulation/Act	*Key Provisions*	*FL Alignment*	*Remaining Gaps/ Risks*
GDPR (EU, 2018)	Data minimization, right to erasure, consent, cross-border restrictions	Avoids raw data sharing	Gradient leakage; limited explainability
CCPA (California, 2020)	Right to know/delete, opt-out of data sale	Data stays local, reduces “sale” risk	Limited visibility; potential indirect profiling
DPDP Act (India, 2023)	Consent-driven use, fiduciary duties, cross-border controls	Localized processing supports compliance	Ambiguity on aggregator accountability

10. Future Directions: Real-Time Credit Evaluation and Global Risk Sharing

The nature of the direction of credit risk evaluation in the sphere of financial services is also bound to experience levels of change within it via the prudent incorporation of the federated learning. Although the current body of scholarship has substantiated the potential of FL to mitigate privacy concerns, resolve non-IID data distributions, achieve more fairness to credit scoring, and broaden its focus to operations in real-time or mobile-first solutions, the future outlook reports a broadening in scope to encompass a real-time engagement and collaboration across borders and ethical compliance. These development patterns find support in the changing exigencies of the digital economy and the escalating pressure imposed by regulators on the deployment of responsible AI.

Live credit checking is one of the most promising directions where FL-enabled pipelines can access streaming financial information (e.g., current transactions and behavioral indicators) and thus continuously re-evaluate creditworthiness ratings. Such dynamic assessments diminish reliance on static historical records and afford institutions the capacity for proactive fraud detection and more nuanced lending decisions. Similarly, mobile credit evaluation extends the benefits of FL to populations underbanked with edge devices, so that institutions can assess micro-creditworthiness influenced by local, device-level data, and with a firm commitment to user privacy. Figure 11 looks at the future adoption curve of federated learning in the financial industry in the next decade. The trend line implies that there will be fast adoption of these technologies into the main banking infrastructure in response to the twin demands of increased privacy requirements and the competitive imperative of having real-time and data-driven credit information.

The other opportunity that has arisen is the cross-border risk sharing between international banks and international financial institutions where cross-learning processes among all the international financial institutions and banks could be federated to develop sound global adaptive credit risk models. The two-way paradigm anticipates superior diversification of risks and a financial solidarity ecosystem, which all take into consideration the jurisdictional diversified compliance regimes that each state must observe. Finally, ethical ideas of AI implementation into federated pipelines are inalienable; it requires integration of fairness constraints, explanatory instruments, and audit mechanisms all over the model life cycle, thus quelling discrimination of vulnerable demographics and enhancing clarity to automated decision-making.

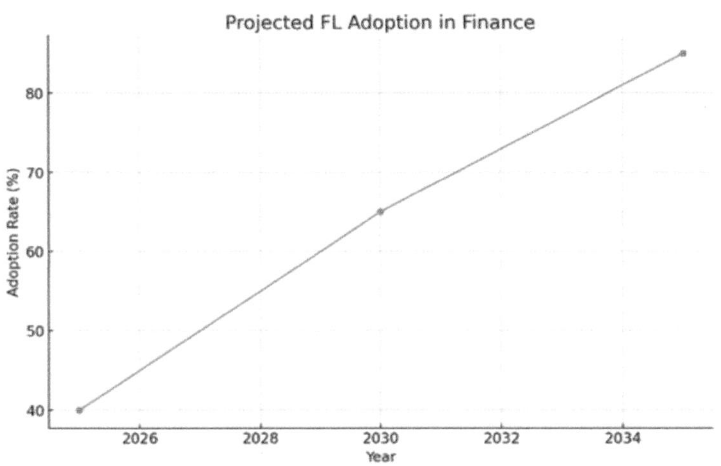

Figure 11: Projected FL adoption in finance.

Lastly, Table 6 gives the major future directions of the technology such as the real-time credit scoring and cross-border risk sharing. This table outlines the anticipated effect of each progressive trend to create the image of a financial ecosystem in the future that is more inclusive, responsive, and morally based due to the further development of federated learning systems.

Table 6: Future directions of federated learning in credit risk assessment.

Future Direction	*Description*	*Expected Impact*
Real-Time Credit Scoring	Integrating FL with streaming financial transaction data to update credit scores dynamically	Faster decision-making, fraud prevention, and instant creditworthiness evaluation
Mobile Credit Evaluation	Leveraging FL on edge/mobile devices for underbanked populations	Expands financial inclusion, reduces dependence on centralized infrastructure, and enables microloans
Cross-Border Risk Sharing	Federated collaboration across international banks for credit models	Better global risk diversification, compliance with multi-jurisdictional regulations
Ethical AI Alignment	Embedding fairness, transparency, and auditability into FL-based credit scoring	Prevents bias, ensures explainability, strengthens trust with regulators and customers

In summary, these future directions not only reinforce FL's transformative potential in reshaping the credit scoring ecosystem but also emphasize its role in driving sustainable, inclusive, and transparent financial services globally.

References

[1] Baabdullah, T., Alzahrani, A., Rawat, D. B. and Liu, C. (2024). Efficiency of federated learning and blockchain in preserving privacy and enhancing the performance of credit card fraud detection (CCFD) systems. *Future Internet*, 16(6): 196. https://doi.org/10.3390/fi16060196.

[2] Delgado Fernández, J., Lee, C. M., Potenciano Menci, S., Rieger, A. and Fridgen, G. (2023). Federated learning for credit risk assessment [paper presentation]. *56th Hawaii International Conference on System Sciences*. https://doi.org/10.24251/HICSS.2023.048.

[3] Wang, Z., Xiao, J., Wang, L., Yao, J. et al. (2024). A novel federated learning approach with knowledge transfer for credit scoring. *Decision Support Systems*, 177: 114084. https://doi.org/10.1016/j.dss.2023.114084.

[4] Zheng, G., Kong, L., Brintrup, A. et al. (2023). Federated machine learning for privacy preserving, collective supply chain risk prediction. *International Journal of Production Research*, 61(23): 8115–8132. https://doi.org/10.1080/00207543.2022.2164628.

[5] Anastasakis, Z. (2024). Analysis of privacy preservation enhancements in federated learning frameworks. In *Privacy-Preserving Machine Learning Approaches National Center for Biotechnology Information*. https://www.ncbi.nlm.nih.gov/books/NBK602365/.

[6] Li, R., Cao, Y., Shu, Y. et al. (2024). A dynamic receptive field and improved feature fusion approach for federated learning in financial credit risk assessment. *Scientific Reports*, 14: 26515. https://doi.org/10.1038/s41598-024-77310-z.
[7] Djolev, D., Lazarova, M. and Nakov, O. (2023, September). Federated learning for credit scoring model using blockchain. In *International Conference on Optimization, Learning Algorithms and Applications* (pp. 109–122). Cham: Springer Nature Switzerland.
[8] Zhang, S., Tay, J. and Baiz, P. (2024). The effects of data imbalance under a federated learning approach for credit risk forecasting. *arXiv preprint*. https://doi.org/10.48550/arXiv.2401.07234.
[9] Oualid, A. (2023). Federated learning techniques applied to credit risk management. *Journal of Financial Risk Management*, 12(3). https://doi.org/10.1080/07366981.2023.2241647.
[10] Zheng, F., Li, E., Li, K., Tian, J., Xiang, X. et al. (2020). A vertical federated learning method for interpretable scorecard and its application in credit scoring. *arXiv preprint*, abs/2009.06218.
[11] Domingo-Ferrer, J., Blanco-Justicia, A., Manjón, J. and Sánchez, D. (2021). Secure and privacy-preserving federated learning via co-utility. *arXiv preprint*. https://doi.org/10.48550/arXiv.2108.01913.
[12] Ma, J., Naas, S. -A., Sigg, S. and Lyu, X. (2021). Privacy-preserving federated learning based on multi-key homomorphic encryption. *arXiv preprint*. https://doi.org/10.48550/arXiv.2104.06824.
[13] Umakor, M. F., Ibecheozor, U. H. B. and Adeyefa, E. A. (2025). Federated learning for privacy-preserving fraud detection in digital banking: Balancing algorithmic performance, privacy, and regulatory compliance. *ICONIC Research and Engineering Journals*, 9(1).

6 Fraud Detection and Anti-Money Laundering (AML)

Ankita Kotalwar,[1,*] Pranati Waghodekar,[1] Reshma Sonar,[1] Varsha Dange[2] and Priya Nagargoje[1]

The acceleration of the development of digital financial ecosystems has increased the complexity, scope, and speed of fraudulent acts and money-laundering endeavors. The conventional centralized machine learning models of detecting fraud and anti-money laundering (AML) have fundamental constraints, such as limited data sharing, privacy laws, institutional data siloing, and real-time cross-institutional anomalies. This chapter discusses the role played by federated learning (FL) and distributed anomaly-detection systems in offering a paradigm shift to collaborative and privacy-protective intelligence to prevent financial crimes. We provide a summary of a state of the art of real-time fraud detection systems that are based on federated methods, with emphasis on the importance of decentralized model training, secure aggregation, and non-IID adaptive optimization in enhancing detection accuracy. Moreover, we discuss distributed anomaly-detection plan that would be able to capture developing fraud patterns and inter-channel transactional deviations on non-homogeneous data sources. Lastly, we talk of FL integration with AML practices and, in particular, monitoring of suspicious activities that are improvement of network-based risk scoring and reduction of false positives through sharing of cross-institution patterns without disclosing sensitive data. With the aid of systematic analysis and research-specific synthesis, this chapter proves the idea that federated architectures are the scalable, regulation-compliant, and extremely robust future of fraud detection and AML operations.

[1] School of Computer Engineering and Technology, Dr. Vishwanath Karad, MIT World Peace University, Pune, India.
[2] Computer Science and Engineering(AIML), Vishwakarma Institute of Technology, Pune, India.
Emails: pranati.waghodekar@mitwpu.edu.in; reshma.sonar@mitwpu.edu.in; priya.nagargoje@mitwpu.edu.in
* Corresponding author: ankita.kotalwar@mitwpu.edu.in

DOI: 10.1201/9781003710059-6

1. Introduction

Due to accelerated digitalization and spread of online financial services, as well as the growing complexity of the financial crime networks, fraud detection and anti-money laundering (AML) have already become the key elements of financial security worldwide. With the changing financial ecosystem toward real-time, high-volume, and transaction setups, fraud, identity manipulation, terrorist financing, and multi-layered money-laundering schemes have become increasingly dangerous. The regulatory bodies of various jurisdictions, such as the Financial Action Task Force (FATF), the Reserve Bank of India (RBI), the European Banking Authority (EBA), and the Financial Crimes Enforcement Network (FinCEN), still advance the models that are advanced and technology-driven to detect suspicious transactions and conduct systemic resilience.

The conventional machine learning (ML) and rule-based systems of fraud detection were effective in the past, but they are increasingly challenged in scalability, privacy, cross-institutional blind spots, and have slow response to new criminal activities. Such constraints justify the development of privacy-protecting, intelligence-driven, and collaborative analytical systems. Federated learning (FL) and distributed anomaly detection methods here have become the game changers to the next-generation fraud and AML systems.

Overall, the current state of financial security is intricate and difficult because of its digitization and the challenges involved in the digital transformation of financial matters. Growth in the speed and complexity of transactions, driven by the booming digital banking, mobile payments, e-commerce, and instant settlements (e.g., UPI in India, SEPA Instant in Europe), has made transactions more complex and faster. As billions of real-time microtransactions are passing through distributed systems, financial institutions are now confronted by the dual challenge of making the customer experience seamless while reducing the chances of fraud or illicit activity.

The key challenges include:

- **Data Siloing across Institutions:** Regulatory, competitive, and infrastructural barriers (silos) cause banks, fintech companies, and payment processors to operate in silos. These disjointed data environments are used by criminals arranging the patterns of frauds or laundering money through two or more institutions, which is challenging to detect cross-institutionally.

- **Privacy and Regulatory Restrictions:** The practice of centralizing customer data to train ML models is becoming limited by mechanisms such as GDPR (EU), Digital Personal Data Protection Act (DPDPA) of India, CCPA (USA), FATF Recommendations [1] and [2], etc. Therefore, it is not possible that institutions can just pool data to a central repository to be analyzed.

- **Adversarial and Evolving Fraud Techniques:** Onboarding based on deepfakes, laundering transactions, money mules' networks, synthetic identities, and automated bot networks is exploited by fraudsters. These practices need continuous learning structures, not fixed rules.

- **Class Misfit and Rare Event Sophism:** Money laundering and fraud take up less than 0.1% of all transactions, and this makes ML models predisposed to legitimate activity. The uncommon events need wider data dissemination and cross-institutional learning to enhance detection.
- **Requirement of Decisioning in Real Time:** In the new digital payment systems, fraud detection should be made to work within milliseconds. The latency and possible single point of failure are added by centralized ML.

1.1 Introduction of the Federated Learning for Financial Crime Prevention

Federated learning, a concept initiated by Google in 2017, allows decentralized training of models in which different institutions learn a global model, without sharing their raw data [3]. The only information that is shared with a central server is model updates (gradients or weights) to be aggregated with algorithms such as FedAvg. Major benefits of federated learning in fraud and AML:

- **Privacy Preservation:** The institution does not transmit any sensitive financial data, which assists in the adherence to the GDPR, RBI, DPDPA, and PSD2-related privacy requirements.
- **Collaborative Intelligence:** FL allows banks to share the experience of fraud patterns of each other, which allows cross-institutional detection of anomalies.
- **Real-Time Local Decision-Making:** The models are localized to minimize the latency and enhance the speed of response in scoring transactions.
- **Enhanced Security with ML:** FL can be combined with differential privacy (DP), secure multi-party computation (SMPC), and homomorphic encryption (HE) to audit trails that are based on blockchain. These also ensure the confidentiality of aggregation and model updates.
- **Scalability of Inter-Institutional Heterogeneity:** FL supports the model training in:
    1. Large banks
    2. Fintech platforms
    3. Payment service providers
    4. Insurance companies

Although the data distribution is different and some transactions are not IID (non-IID data), the methods such as FedProx and FedNova can be used to stabilize the performance.

Recent research indicates that federated fraud detection works with accuracy in 5% of centralized systems, but with much better guarantees of privacy [4], [5].

2. Real-Time Fraud Detection Using Federated Techniques

2.1 Overview of Real-Time Fraud Detection

Real-time fraud detection can be described as the capability of detecting suspicious or anomalous financial transactions in milliseconds, or before an authorization request is completely processed. As the number of instant payment systems (UPI, NEFT, RTGS, SWIFT gpi, and SEPA Instant) keeps increasing drastically, the speed and volume of electronic transactions are increasing exponentially. Conventional pipelines of fraud detection, however, are frequently associated with large false-positive rates, low adaptation to novel attack patterns, and the inability to utilize cross-institution intelligence as a result of highly strict privacy laws [6], [8].

The traditional centralized (or big-data) models also demand massive data consolidation that is becoming impossible with the data protection regulations such as GDPR, PSD2, CCPA, and the RBI Master Direction on Digital Payment Security Controls [3]. Such limitations prevent the capability of models to acquire experience on detecting a wide variety of frauds, including synthetic identities, bot-based attacks, and cross-border laundering [9–10].

Another solution that can be transformative is federated learning, which allows various financial institutions to learn together without sharing raw data about the customers. Every institution trains a model locally and sends updates related to that model to a central point, which is a central aggregator, which considerably mitigates privacy risks and allows responding to emerging threats in real time. This paradigm has been globally acknowledged to be a strong tool in the fight against sophisticated types of fraud such as account takeover (ATO), card-not-present fraud, and collusion by merchants as seen in references [6] and [8].

2.2 Federated Real-Time Fraud Detection Architecture

A typical architecture of a federated real-time fraud detection system is composed of a number of distributed processing elements that collaborate on low latency, high accuracy, and high level of privacy:

- **Local Monitoring Nodes of Transactions:** These nodes operate within the banks, merchant-acquired servers, payment processors, card networks, and mobile payment applications. They extract metadata of devices, patterns of geolocation, merchant category code (MCC), velocity features, and customer behavioral signature. It has been demonstrated that decentralized monitoring can greatly minimize both risk of exposure and delay of detection [11], [12].

- **Local Model Training Engine:** The institutions train the ML models through their local streams of transactional data. The most popular models are Long Short Term Memory (LSTM) based sequence models of temporal patterns, autoencoders of anomaly detection, and graphic neural networks (GNNs) of mule account network detection. Spatial training allows institutions to be able to instill region-specific fraud trends, as exhibited by reference [9–10].
- **Secure Aggregation Server:** Models are updated in encrypted form, and institutions send their encrypted updates rather than raw-data pooling which is centralized. Homomorphic encryption, SMPC, and differential privacy are some of the methods that ensure that sensitive transactional characteristics are concealed. Strong aggregation methods, such as FedProx and trimmed-mean, enhance resistance to malicious updates, as it is proven by reference [11].
- **The Model of Global Fraud Detection:** The consolidated updates produce a global model that represents cross-institutional fraud behavior of particular synthetic identities functioning among banks, organized fraud rings, and cross-border migration of fraud schemes [14].
- **Low-Latency Scoring Engine:** The global model that is updated is then deployed back to the individual local nodes to make inferences in real time. The response time in UPI-grade payment systems can be as short as <20 ms, whereas the card networks may need as little as <50 ms. It has been demonstrated that low-latency inference pipelines perform better in authorizing in high-speed financial systems [14]. This decentralized design guarantees a high level of privacy and it scales well to millions of transactions per second.

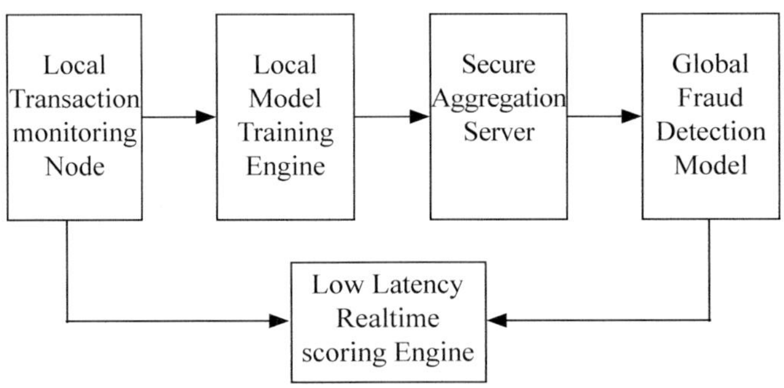

Figure 1: Federated real-time fraud detection.

The architecture described (Figure 1) represents a federated-learning-based real-time fraud detection pipeline that can assure privacy-preserving training, low-latency inference, and scalable deployment by distributed financial institutions.

The system works based on five main components, which interact with each other in a learning–inference feedback loop.

First, there are local transaction monitoring nodes which are decentralized data collection points installed in banks, payment gateways, or merchant terminals. These nodes are constantly monitoring high-frequency streams of transactions and produce labeled or weakly monitored events that are needed to refine the downstream models. Raw financial information is very sensitive and subject to regulatory frameworks, thus stored in a very stringent manner within the institution that generates raw financial information.

The local model training engine in the second step trains on device or on-premise using institution-specific patterns of transactions. Local gradient updates are computed by each node, and global model can thus use heterogeneous fraud signatures such as regional anomalies, merchant-specific risk, or user-behavioral deviations. Localized training removes the risk of data silos by exploiting institutional diversity without breaching privacy limitations.

Such locally computed updates are sent to the secure aggregation server, which enforces the cryptographically based aggregation protocols (e.g., secure multiparty computation or homomorphic encryption). This means that personal updates will be obscured when transmitted and combined, and no server or other opposing party will be able to reconstruct the financial features of the information.

The refinement of the global fraud detection model is performed using the aggregated updates and creates the single intelligence layer. This model absorbs federated information among institutions; this makes the system able to generalize patterns of rare, emerging, or sophisticated fraud attacks which one institution could not witness alone. The model around the globe is periodically redistributed to all the nodes taking part and a cycle of continuous collaborative learning is created.

Lastly, the new model is inputted into the low-latency real-time scoring engine, which is a high-throughput inference engine that is either deployed at the edge or inside institutional gateways. Such an engine estimates the incoming transactions with the most recent federated model parameters and provides instantaneous fraud likelihood scores that can be used to make risk-based authentication and transaction block decisions. The scoring results are also fed back into the monitoring nodes and this enables the architecture to sustain real-time adaptation capabilities and concept drift resistance.

In general, the architecture allows detecting frauds safely, on a large scale, and with flexibility in addition to adhering to regulations and providing high privacy guarantees. Decentralized learning with secure aggregation and real-time inference will facilitate continuous improvement of the model as well as maximize the effectiveness of fraud detection without sensitive financial information exposure.

2.3 The Benefits of Federated Techniques in Fraud Detection

Federated learning has a number of benefits over conventional centralized fraud detection systems:

- **Increased Data Protection and Compliance:** Because customer data do not go beyond the limits of the institution, FL by default serves in adherence with GDPR, CCPA, and RBI privacy regulations. Differentiated privacy and secure aggregation are privacy-preserving mechanisms that decrease the risks of re-identification [3], [11].
- **More Rapid Acculturation to Emerging Fraud Patterns:** The kinds of frauds present change very fast and the institutions differ in the kind of fraud they experience. These research investigations demonstrate that federated models are 40–60% quicker in updating knowledge when aggregating knowledge on a large network of participants [6], [14].
- **Increased Generalization and Decreased Bias:** Models that have been trained on the data of only one financial institution have a tendency to be biased in terms of demography or that they do not have a complete view of the fraud patterns. Federated learning resolves such problems by using various sources of data, enhancing recall on rare classes of fraud, such as synthetic IDs and triangulation fraud [9–11].
- **The Intelligence Sharing between the Institution and Other Institutions**: FL facilitates safe cooperation between banks, card networks, fintechs, and payment processors. This joint intelligence assists in identifying multi-bank mule rings and collusion between merchants that an individual institution cannot identify [8], [12].

2.4 Federated Fraud Detection Challenges

Irrespective of its merits, federated fraud detection is also characterized by a number of challenges:

- **Data That Are Not IID and Heterogeneous:** The patterns of transactions are quite diverse as per region, banks, and segmentation of customers. The non-IID distributions may compromise the convergence of the models and demand sophisticated aggregation techniques [11].
- **Communication Overheads:** The problem of frequent parameter exchange between institutions and the aggregator may result in bottlenecks in bandwidth and latency particularly when the models are large and when they are frequently updated [12–13].

- **Security Threats:** Federated systems can be attacked by poisoning, adversarial model updates, and gradient inversion. The key defense mechanisms are secure aggregation, anomaly filters, and powerful optimization techniques [7], [11].
- **Cross-Border Constraints (CBB):** No particular regulation has been determined in this respect.

The countries are not using similar restrictions on data flow, encryption standard, and model-sharing policies. FL applications should comply with regional compliance standards such as GDPR, PSD2, and DPDPA [3].

2.5 Case Study: How to Deploy Federated Fraud Detection in Online Payments

Examples include a group of digital payment providers, such as UPI PSPs, banks, merchant acquirers, and card networks. The participants train their own local models with the help of historical transaction logs, device fingerprints, merchant risk profile, and real-time payment activity. Secure aggregation combines that update into the model of a global fraud detector which can detect cross-platform anomalies and multi-bank fraud rings.

Experiments based on practical applications show:

- 30–40% percent decrease in false positives.
- 50% quicker response to new fraud schemes.
- Better recollection of less common forms of fraud, such as UPI abuse by bots.
- No raw data sharing of customers; regulatory compliance.

3. Detection of Anomalies on Distributed Data

Anomaly detection in financial networks is important because it can help detect infractions and provide insights into the organization's vulnerabilities. The value of anomaly detection in the financial network is that with the help of such an approach, the violations can be detected and people will have the understanding of the weaknesses of the organization.

Detection of anomalies is a very important part of the fraud prevention and AML process since financial anomalies are usually evidence of illicit activity, such as suspicious transfers, account takeovers, structuring, or unusual spikes in transaction flows. In the modern banking ecosystem, billions of geographically dispersed transactions are produced every day, and their centralized storage is both operationally expensive and bound by privacy-related laws (GDPR, RBI guidelines, etc.). Distributed anomaly detection facilitates institutions to detect abnormalities without aggregating raw financial information, enhancing scalability and detection capabilities in a multi-institution setting as reported by references [15] and [16].

3.1 Distributed Anomaly Detection Frameworks

Distributed anomaly detection models combine localized analytics with global coordination to be sure there is coordinated surveillance among banks, payment aggregators, and financial intermediaries. The system is based on four major layers:

Local Feature Extraction: Every financial institution calculates behavioral, transactional, temporal, and risk-based factors (e.g., merchant category patterns, velocity features, KYC risk attributes). This decentralized processing guarantees the data-locality constraints [17].

Edge Anomaly Scoring: Deep-learning or local machine learning models generate the probability of anomalies or individual transaction or user session. This minimizes latency besides enabling alerting in real time [18].

Federated Synchronization: Periodic updates of local model parameters, embeddings, or anomaly signatures are sent via an encrypted coordinator through either federated averaging or a secure aggregation mechanism [19]. It is only model updates that are sent out of the institution and not raw data.

Global Pattern Learning: The aggregator develops an international fraud and AML typology model that identifies large-scale fraud and AML. The patterns that may seem to be uncommon in one school but frequent ones in others can be seen through the international cooperation [20–21].

3.2 Anomaly Detection Techniques in Use

Financial organizations use a combination of statistical, machine-learning-based, graph-based, and deep-learning-based anomaly detection techniques:

- **Statistical Models:** Z-score, density-based estimators, local outlier factor (LOF), and isolation-based detection are still effective in point anomaly detection in low-dimensional features [22].
- **Machine Learning Techniques:** Random forest, XGBoost, and clustering-based models are the examples of the models that identify the structural abnormalities and region-specific fraud patterns [23].
- **Deep Learning Models:** Autoencoders identify reconstruction anomalies, whereas LSTM and Gated Recurrent Unit (GRU) models identify sequential dependence with transaction streams, and, thus, the presence of abrupt changes in behavior can be identified [24].

- **Graph-Based Abnormal Detection:** GraphSAGE and GNN-based link predictions are some of the methods used to identify money laundering networks, collusive merchant behavior, and circular transfer schemes as proposed by reference [25].

3.3 Problems Faced by Distributed Anomaly Detection

Distributed detection of anomalies has a number of technical and regulatory difficulties:

- **Heterogeneous Data Quality:** Each institution has different data schema, different frequencies of logging, different risk scores, and features cannot be aligned easily [8].
- **Latency, Throughput Constraints:** In high-frequency fraud detection, inferences should be made at the milliseconds scale, and this should be achieved through the optimization of synchronization and communication protocols.
- **Scalability:** Millions of transactions involving very large financial networks need distributed computer processing and efficient models sharing methods.
- **Privacy and Regulatory Compliance:** The AML rules limit the data transfer across boundaries and customer-level information sharing; federated methods should incorporate the use of differential privacy and encryption protection [26].

3.4 Graph Neural Networks of Distributed Anomaly Detection

AML systems based on GNNs are financial transaction models represented by heterogeneous graphs with customers, accounts, merchants, and transaction edges. GNNs learn higher-order interactions, including structuring, layering, circular transfers, and collusive behavior of merchants, which are impossible to observe based on traditional classifiers.

Federated GNNs (FedGNNs) enable institutions to train GNNs together without necessarily having sensitive graph structures as illustrated by reference [27]. They allow AML at a worldwide level but secure domestic transaction networks.

4. A Federation of Learning on Strengthening AML

4.1 AML and Regulatory Frameworks Introduction

AML practices entail identification and reporting of suspicious transactions, customer profiles, and the laundering networks that are established to cover illegal funds. The regulatory provisions, including KYC norms, filing of suspicious transaction report (STR), sanctions screening, and customer risk rating, require constant updates to the model and a high degree of interpretability. Federated learning satisfies these needs by allowing cross-institutional intelligence without infringing on the privacy of data [28].

4.2 Federated Learning to Help in AML

Federated learning also allows AML teams to identify laundering patterns across the banks or financial platforms. The offenders normally use the loopholes in the fragmented AML systems to disperse the illegal conduct among different institutions in order to evade detection. Federated structures solve this issue through the construction of a common risk intelligence layer while maintaining data locality and secrecy rules [29].

4.3 Federated Learning to Improve AML

Federated learning enhances some of the main AML capabilities:

- **Suspicious Transaction Monitoring:** A suspicious transaction is one that prompts the utility of one or more of the four categories: suspicious activity report, suspicious person report, suspicious vehicle report, and suspicious bank account report. Institutions will be able to exchange sophisticated model information that enhances the quality of risk-scoring and the existence of multi-bank laundering trails [30].
- **Customer Risk Rating:** Federated models use more general patterns of behavior to refine risk vectors, enhancing probability-based scoring.
- **Cross-Institution Pattern Discovery:** The updates of shared models are useful to bring out the multifaceted customer–account–entity relationships that constitute laundering networks.
- **Unfavorable Media and Sanctions Screening:** Federated NLP models enhance sanctions screening false-positives and entity resolution.

4.4 Privacy-Saving Methods That Allow AML Cooperation

Federated AML relies on workflows which are cryptographic and privacy preserving:

- **SMPC:** Enhances institutions to calculate common AML insights while not exposing local inputs [31].
- **Differential Privacy:** Modifies noise to ensure that attackers cannot reconstruct customer identity based on model updates [32].
- **Homomorphic Encryption:** Allows calculation of encrypted AML indicators, which are end-to-end confidential [33].

- **Zero-Knowledge Proofs:** Grant institutions the ability to check compliance (e.g., STR handling) without showing internal data [34].

4.5 Federated AML Architecture

An average federated AML pipeline comprises:

- Local AML engines which are linked with core banking systems or transaction-processing systems.
- Local feature extraction modules which produce risk and behavior features.
- Federated aggregation layer doing safe update fusion.
- Multinational AML risk model that represents intelligence of multi-institution laundering.
- Investigator and regulator-friendly reporting and audit layers.

4.6 Benefits of Federated AML Systems

Federated AML has major strategic and regulatory advantages:

- **Improved Determination of Detection:** Detects cross-border, multi-institution layering, which is beyond the capabilities of isolated systems.
- **Food-Privacy Compliance:** Meets such requirements as GDPR, data localization in RBI, and cross-border transactions.
- **Collaborative Intelligence:** Common learning allows the identification of new laundering typologies across the world.
- **Adaptive Learning:** The models are also in constant development as new darknet methods and channels of laundering are developed.

4.7 Federated AML in Practical Cases

Federated AML is used in a number of practical cases:

- **Layering Patterns are Detected in the Following Way:** Multihop layerings across the banks are detected in advanced sequence models [35].
- **Identity Connections between Institutions:** Help detect fraudsters who have more than one account or counterfeit identities.
- **Trade-Based Money Laundering (TBML):** Pattern mining among the trade finance systems indicates invoice manipulation networks.
- **Crypto-Transaction AML:** Federated models identify mixer operations, cross-chain laundering, and abnormal wallet.

5. Future Directions

5.1 The Integration of Large Language Models (LLMs)

LLMs are unstructured data that can be analyzed by LLPs (Linear Layer Perception/ Linear Prediction Layer) including customer communication, negative media, STR reports, and past case files, which allows the LLPs to define any possible act of laundering in advance before it becomes a risk that can be taken.

5.2 Cross-Border Federated AML Networks

Privacy-sensitive federated systems between jurisdictions are capable of enhancing international AML collaboration.

5.3 Financial Systems Edge Intelligence

Edge computing minimizes the delay in fraud scoring in real-time payment systems.

5.4 AML Systems Resistant to Quantum Attacks

Cryptographic protection should change with the emergence of quantum computing.

6. Conclusion

Federated learning and Specialized Deposit-Taking Institutions (SDIs) are applicable in improving fraud detection and AML abilities as they allow real-time, privacy-compliant, and collaborative analytics. Financial ecosystems are dynamic, and shifting to federated strategies will provide strong protection against more and more advanced financial offenses.

References

[1] Deloitte. (2020). AI and AML: Reducing false positives. Deloitte Insights.

[2] Zhang, F., Liu, Y., Chen, H. and Xu, L. (2023). Federated graph learning for financial crime detection. *IEEE Transactions on Knowledge and Data Engineering*, 35(8): 7894–7907.

[3] McMahan, B., Moore, E., Ramage, D. and Aguera y Arcas, B. (2017, April). Communication-efficient learning of deep networks from decentralized data. In *Proceedings of the 20th International Conference on Artificial Intelligence and Statistics (AISTATS)* (Vol. 54, pp. 1273–1282).

[4] Yang, R., Li, X., Chen, Y. and Wang, S. (2022). Federated learning for fraud detection. *IEEE Transactions on Big Data*, 8(4): 912–924.

[5] Rawat, A. S., Menon, A. K. and Kumar, S. (2021, July). Scalable federated learning for financial applications. *arXiv preprint arXiv:2107.00255.*
[6] Yang, M., Chen, K. and Zhang, Q. (2022). Real-time fraud detection in financial transactions: A survey. *IEEE Access*, 10: 112233–112251.
[7] Kumar, A., Singh, R. and Ranjan, P. (2021). Evolution of digital payment fraud: Challenges and detection mechanisms. *IEEE Security & Privacy*, 19(4): 45–55.
[8] Kairouz, P. and McMahan, H. B. (2021). Advances and open problems in federated learning. *Foundations and Trends in Machine Learning*, 14(1-2): 1–210.
[9] Zhang, C., Xie, Y., Bai, Z. and Ren, K. (2022). Secure federated learning systems: Threats and defenses. *IEEE Internet of Things Journal*, 9(15): 13723–13739.
[10] Xu, K., Koh, P. W., Chen, J. L. and Gu, M. (2023). Graph neural networks for fraud detection: A survey. *IEEE Computer Surveys*, 55(9): 1–38.
[11] Ramaswamy, S., Mathews, R., McMahan, K. and Belongie, S. M. (2020). Federated learning for real-time fraud detection in financial networks. In *Proceedings of the IEEE International Conference on Big Data* (pp. 4072–4081).
[12] Li, L., Xu, J., Zhang, C. and Li, J. (2022). Federated learning for credit card fraud detection. *IEEE Transactions on Neural Networks and Learning Systems*, 33(9): 4945–4959.
[13] Reserve Bank of India. (2021). Master direction on digital payment security controls. Government of India.
[14] Zhao, Z., Akbar, R. and Jha, S. (2021). Federated graph learning for cross-institution fraud detection. In *Proceedings of the IEEE International Conference on Data Mining (ICDM)* (pp. 1369–1374).
[15] Hardy, S., Henecka, W., Ivey-Law, H., Nock, R., Patrini, G., Smith, G. et al. (2017). Private federated learning on vertically partitioned data via entity resolution and additively homomorphic encryption. *arXiv preprint arXiv:1711.10677.*
[16] Breunig, M. M., Kriegel, H. P., Ng, R. T. and Sander, J. (2000, May). LOF: Identifying density-based local outliers. In *Proceedings of the 2000 ACM SIGMOD International Conference on Management of Data* (pp. 93–104).
[17] Chen, T. and Guestrin, C. (2016, August). XGBoost: A scalable tree boosting system. In *Proceedings of the 22nd ACM SIGKDD International Conference on Knowledge Discovery and Data Mining (KDD)* (pp. 785–794). ACM.
[18] Zhang, Y., Liu, H., Wang, X. and Chen, J. (2020). Distributed anomaly detection in large-scale financial systems. *IEEE Transactions on Neural Networks and Learning Systems*, 31(12): 5124–5136.
[19] Malhotra, P., Vig, L., Shroff, G. and Agarwal, P. (2015). Long- and short-term memory networks for anomaly detection in time series. In *Proceedings of the ICML Workshop on Anomaly Detection.*
[20] Wang, X., Li, Y., Zhang, C. and Wang, S. (2021). Financial fraud detection with graph neural networks. *IEEE Transactions on Knowledge and Data Engineering*, 33(8): 3125–3138.
[21] Consilient Inc. (2022). Federated learning for anti-money laundering (AML). Technical Whitepaper.
[22] Sato, I., Yamada, M. and Kashima, H. (2022). Heterogeneous data challenges in federated learning. In *Proceedings of the International Conference on Machine Learning (ICML).*
[23] Shokri, R., Stronati, M., Song, C. and Shmatikov, V. (2017). Membership inference attacks against machine learning models. In *Proceedings of the IEEE Symposium on Security and Privacy (S&P)* (pp. 3–18).
[24] He, C., Annavaram, M. and Avestimehr, A. S. (2021). FedGNN: Federated graph neural networks for privacy-preserving graph learning. In *Proceedings of the International Conference on Machine Learning (ICML).*

[25] Financial Action Task Force (FATF). (2020). International standards on combating money laundering and the financing of terrorism and proliferation. *FATF Guidance Report*.
[26] Li, T., Sahu, A. K., Talwalkar, A. and Smith, V. (2020). Federated optimization in heterogeneous networks. In *Proceedings of the IEEE International Conference on Big Data* (pp. 1541–1550).
[27] Yao, A. C.-C. (1986). How to generate and exchange secrets. In *Proceedings of the 27th Annual Symposium on Foundations of Computer Science (FOCS)* (pp. 162–167). IEEE.
[28] Dwork, C. (2006). Differential privacy. In *Proceedings of the 33rd International Colloquium on Automata, Languages and Programming (ICALP)* (pp. 1–12). Springer.
[29] Gentry, C. (2009). Fully homomorphic encryption using ideal lattices. In *Proceedings of the 41st Annual ACM Symposium on Theory of Computing (STOC)* (pp. 169–178). ACM.
[30] Ben-Sasson, E., Chiesa, A., Tromer, E. and Virza, M. (2020). Succinct zero-knowledge proofs for financial compliance. In *Proceedings of the Privacy Enhancing Technologies Symposium (PETS)*.
[31] Yao, A. C.-C. (1982). Protocols for secure computations. In *Proceedings of the 23rd Annual Symposium on Foundations of Computer Science (FOCS)* (pp. 160–164). IEEE.
[32] Dwork, C. and Roth, A. (2014). The algorithmic foundations of differential privacy. *Foundations and Trends® in Theoretical Computer Science*, 9(3-4): 211–407.
[33] Mastercard & Visa Consortium. (2022). Collaborative fraud intelligence framework using federated AI. White Paper.
[34] Goldwasser, S., Micali, S. and Rackoff, C. (1989). The knowledge complexity of interactive proof systems. *SIAM Journal on Computing*, 18(1): 186–208.
[35] Liu, H., Hu, Z., Chen, Y. and Fang, Y. (2021). Detecting multi-hop money laundering via sequence and graph models. In *Proceedings of the International Joint Conference on Artificial Intelligence (IJCAI)* (pp. 2647–2653).

7 | Wealth Management and Investment Strategies

Ashima,[1,*] Amit Vajpayee,[2] Poonam Kukana[2] and Bhupinder Kaur[2]

This chapter discusses how federated learning (FL) has the potential to reshape the approach to wealth management and investment methods to help financial companies train cooperative, privacy-preserving AI models without sharing sensitive data of their clients. FL decentralized training process can be leveraged where institutions can update a shared model locally and share the updates but not the original data to handle the urgent issues of regulatory compliance, data privacy, and collaboration between institutions. We discuss the way FL helps make hyper-personalized portfolio suggestions, risk-sensitive optimization, and goal-oriented investment strategies using nonidentical datasets. Secure aggregation, differential privacy, and approaches to managing model heterogeneity with non-IID settings are discussed in the chapter. Practical research demonstrates the benefits of using federated models over siloed strategies, such as increasing Sharpe ratios and annual growth rate of a portfolio. We also point out such operational aspects as the efficiency of communication, governance, and implementation of trade-offs. We contrast FL with conventional centralized AI and robo-advisory systems and demonstrate that federated learning is an opportunity to develop a secure, scalable, and collaborative wealth management—the future of innovative AI and regulatory reality.

1. Introduction

There has never been any single aim of the wealth management and investment approaches, making neither financial performance in line with the personal aims of the investor, nor being a prudent risk taker. The combination of client disclosure and the institutional benchmarks and market practice steered advisers who have traditionally employed those strategies [1]. Artificial intelligence (AI) has transformed this landscape and has opened up scalable personalization, including

[1] Department of CSE, Rayat Bahra University, Mohali, Punjab, India.
[2] Department of CSE, Chandigarh University, Mohali-140413, Punjab, India.
Emails: amitvajpayee@gmail.com; erbhupinderkaur@gmail.com; poonamkukana@gmail.com
* Corresponding author: ashimamockoul@gmail.com

DOI: 10.1201/9781003710059-7

dynamic portfolio rebalancing, scenario modelling, and personalized advisory. However, the paradox of this transition is that, in order to run more advanced analytics, proprietary or sensitive data is needed, but privacy, competition, and regulation all limit data sharing.

Federated learning (FL) is an attractive solution. FL does not store data in a central repository as data is aggregated instead of trained locally (within an institution or on a device) and does not transmit raw data; only models updates are exchanged through secure aggregation methods [2]. This enhances privacy, does not violate regulations (including GDPR or CCPA), and allows institutions to create significantly stronger models than they can individually.

This chapter examines how FL is changing the management of wealth and investment approaches through:

1. Setting the important context using a primer and literature review.
2. Outlining fundamental tenets of FL, system designs, and methods of financial services.
3. Case studies: it is profitable to provide several case studies of personalized recommendations to federated reinforcement learning (RL) of portfolios.
4. Lighting barriers to data diversity, adversarial hazards, and regulatory drag.
5. Futuristic scouting, for example, GenAI, smart contracts, and tokenized incentives.
6. In conclusion, this chapter shows how theory and practice and research are connected.

Overall, this chapter shows that federated learning is a step toward more personal, participatory, and potent AI in finance, which is a necessary step to ensuring AI-assisted wealth management.

2. Background & Literature Review

The impetus behind AI-driven wealth management focuses on personalization, scalability, and automation—objectives limited by disparate, siloed data and a highly regulated landscape. Federated learning, initially developed in the broader AI space, is increasingly relevant now in finance.

Federated Learning Fundamentals: At its core, federated learning lets you train machine learning models across multiple devices or locations without ever consolidating their data in one place [3]. Instead, each client (like your phone or a branch office) trains a local copy of the model and sends only updates—parameters or weights—back to the server for aggregation. No raw data ever leaves the client. As shown in Table 1, one aspect of federated and privacy-preserving learning is that they improve the data privacy of users: using these approaches ensures sensitive user data stays local to the data provider for training thus mitigating risks related to breaches. They also facilitate compliance with regulations such as GDPR, HIPAA, and CCPA. As it is the method which provides only model updates rather than large dataset, Hence high bandwidth is consumed. This approach leads to better model quality overall due to the availability of different real-world datasets without violating privacy issues.

Table 1: Benefits of federated learning.

Benefit	*What It Means for You*
Data Privacy	Your data stays local, minimizing data breach risks (IBM, dida Machine Learning)
Compliance	Works neatly within regulations such as GDPR, HIPAA, CCPA (IBM, Google Cloud)
Efficiency	Only lightweight model updates (not bulky datasets) travel—so lower bandwidth and latency (IBM, Google Cloud)
Model Quality	Learns from diverse environments, making the model robust and adaptable (machine learning, Google Cloud)

How It Works—Step by Step:

1. **Initialization:** A central server sets up a base model and sends it to selected clients.
2. **Local Training:** Clients train the model using their own data. Data may be *non-IID* (i.e., not independent and identically distributed), so performance varies—but federated systems account for that.
3. **Update Sharing:** Clients send model updates (gradients or weight changes), not the data itself.
4. **Aggregation:** The server combines updates—often using something like *Federated Averaging (FedAvg)*—to refine the global model.
5. **Repeat:** The updated global model gets sent back to clients, and the cycle continues until the model converges.

Figure 1 is used to demonstrate the federated learning process, and identify the primary advantages of it in a distributed data environment. During the federated learning process, several organizations including banks, insurance companies, investment firms, and fintech companies come together to jointly train a machine learning model without providing access to their raw data. The local training of every organization uses its own individual data and only model updates or learned weights are communicated to a central server. These updates are collected at a central server to form a better global model which is distributed to all the parties involved. This happens repeatedly, whereby the model is able to learn by using a variety of data or information sources without compromising sensitive information as the data is kept in the local systems. Consequently, organizations do not interact directly, which greatly minimizes the privacy threats.

The advantages of federated learning as demonstrated in the figure are immense. The benefit of data privacy protection is the greatest, as raw data do not go outside of the local environment, which makes them very appropriate concerning sensitive fields such as finance and healthcare. Lower latency is

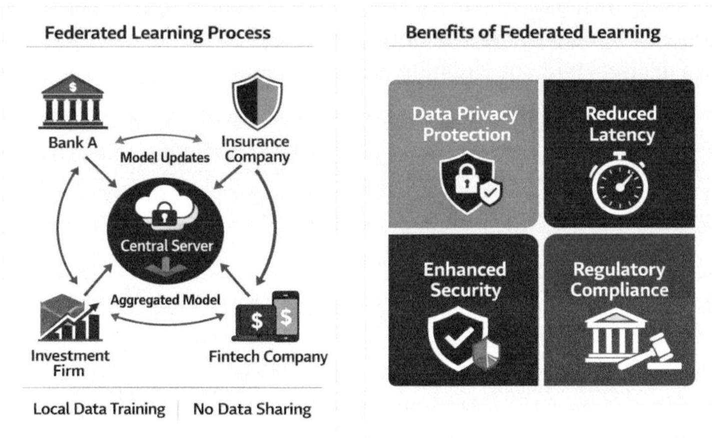

Figure 1: Federated learning process and its benefits.

ensured since data processing and training is an on-premise event, with data being transmitted to central servers only when necessary. Security is also improved by federated learning that prevents data breaches and attacks because raw data are not stored centrally. It also facilitates regulatory integration as it is compliant with the data protection laws and regulations limiting sharing of data between institutions or regions. Altogether, federated learning is a safe, effective, and noninvasive method of joint model training among various organizations.

Different Styles of Federated Learning:

- **Centralized FL:** A central server manages aggregation. Most common and straightforward.
- **Decentralized FL:** Peers aggregate updates among themselves—no single point of control.
- **Cross-Device FL:** Many devices (such as smartphones) each with small local datasets participate. Typical for consumer applications [4].
- **Cross-Silo FL:** A few organizations (such as hospitals or banks) hold large datasets and train collaboratively.

Real-World Examples:

- **Gboard (Google Keyboard):** Your phone improves the text-prediction model locally and sends updates—without sharing what you type.
- **Voice Assistants (such as Siri):** Learn from behavior locally while preserving user privacy.
- **Healthcare and Finance**: Hospitals or institutions train shared models while keeping sensitive records private.

Use Cases of Federated Learning: The federated learning is the decentralized ML where the model is trained in a collaborative manner but the data is kept local. In FL, a central server disseminates global model parameters [4]. Local nodes (e.g., banks, trading systems, robo-advisors) perform training on their proprietary data and return updates that are aggregated via methods such as Federated Averaging (FedAvg). Variants including FedSGD and FedProx also consider efficiency and non-IID data heterogeneity issues.

FL in Financial Services: FL is progressively being adopted by financial institutions (FIs) for privacy-preserving collaboration. For example, FL allows a pool of banks to collaborate on improving fraud detection models, without sharing access to customer-specific data, or allows robo-advisors to improve investment recommendations using a combination of streaming data sources, market data, and sensitive account data, without compromising the confidentiality of customer information. Also, FL is instrumental in securing transactions as well (e.g., identifying anti-money laundering SMS or anomalous behaviors amid payment networks) while keeping data local.

Florida's Wealth Management Landscape: Florida has become a hotbed for wealth management, thanks to its aging population, attractive tax benefits, and rapidly growing retiree and high-net-worth communities. Here are a few standout players and how they position themselves:

- **Affiliated Managers Group (AMG):** Based in West Palm Beach, this publicly traded firm partners with independent asset managers around the globe, offering a unique wealth management model that blends independence with scale [5].
- **Raymond James Financial:** Headquartered in St. Petersburg, this firm offers a wide range of services—from retail and commercial banking to private banking and wealth management—serving a broad client base [5].
- **EverBank (Jacksonville):** Offers wealth management among its broader financial services, blending digital accessibility with specialized offerings.

Local Firms Emphasizing Tailored Approaches: Here are a few Florida-based firms carving their niche with personalized strategies:

- **Hillguard Wealth Management (Miami):** Uses a macro-driven, data-backed approach with concentrated positions and quantitative overlays to manage risk and income generation [6].
- **Structure Wealth Management (Tampa):** Offers a wide mix, from traditional investments such as ETFs and bonds to alternative investments, managed accounts, and structured products.
- **Bull & Bear Wealth Management (Central FL):** Focuses on personalized, evidence-based investment plans, emphasizing tax-conscious strategies and proactive market adjustments.

- **North Florida Financial:** Provides a holistic suite—including retirement, estate, and college planning—blended with diversified investments, from mutual funds to annuities [7].
- **ILG Private Wealth (Florida): Offering** centers around their "Castle and Moat System™," which layers tax strategies, investment alignment, estate planning, risk mitigation, and philanthropy for high-earners.

Other firms such as FCG Wealth Management (Coral Gables) and Centrus (Orlando) further enhance the landscape with services around risk management, tax planning, legacy strategies, and life-stage investment transitions.

Strategies That Define Florida Wealth Management: Here's a snapshot of the strategy trends across these firms:

- **Macro-Driven and Quantitative Approaches:** Hillguard Wealth blends a top-down macroeconomic lens with direct investment picks and overlays to smooth portfolio volatility [8].
- **Diverse Investment Options with Customization:** Many firms offer wide asset class coverage—from stocks and bonds to structured products and alternatives—tailored to individual risk profiles.
- **Tax-Smart and Goal-Aligned Investing:** Firms such as Bull & Bear and ILG highlight tax-aware strategies and targeted planning aligned with clients' long-term objectives.
- **Holistic, Life-Stage Planning:** Many firms package wealth management with estate planning, insurance, retirement, and education planning, offering one-stop coordination [9].
- **"Castle and Moat" Framework:** This metaphor from ILG captures a layered defensive strategy: tax foundations, investment growth, estate protection, risk defence, and charitable bridges.

Big Picture Trends (Florida and Beyond): Certain trends are transforming wealth management across the board, including in Florida.

- **ESG (Environmental, Social and Governance) and Value-Aligned Investing means:** Ethical or socially responsible investment in companies where there is an objective to maintain these values with respect to finance.
- **Tech-Driven Personalization and Efficiency:** From AI to data insights, advisory services are becoming leaner and more personable—client interaction gets smarter, not hollower.
- **Cybersecurity and Trust:** Protecting sensitive financial data is non-negotiable—firms are investing in security systems and protocols.
- **Rise of Robo-Advisors:** Digital platforms now offer low-cost, automated investing based on risk and goals—perfect for tech-oriented and cost-conscious clients, though they might lack nuanced services [10].

Table 2 Wealth management case in Florida Firm/Type/Hillguard (Miami) Structure (Tampa)/Strategy Highlights Macro-driven, direct investments, quantitative overlays Broad Asset Range, including alts and structured products Bull & Bear (Central FL) Personal evidence-based tax-optimized investing North FL Financial ILG Private Wealth AMG Raymond James EverBank Holistic planning diversified investment mix "Castle & Moat" framework high-earners Large-scale firms wider wealth services Broader Industry Trends ESG focus tech tools cyber resilience robo-advisor accessibility.

Table 2: Wealth management scenario in Florida.

Firm/Type	*Strategy Highlights*
Hillguard (Miami)	Macro-driven, direct investments, quantitative overlays
Structure (Tampa)	Broad asset range, including alts and structured products
Bull & Bear (Central FL)	Personal, evidence-based, tax-optimized investing
North FL Financial	Holistic planning with diversified investment mix
ILG Private Wealth	"Castle & Moat" framework for high-earners
AMG, Raymond James, EverBank	Large-scale firms offering comprehensive wealth services
Broader Industry Trends	ESG focus, tech tools, cyber resilience, robo-advisor accessibility

Reinforcement Learning Meets FL: Federated reinforcement learning (Fed+), where traders are co-trained on RL-based portfolio models, has interesting progress. Fed+, when applied to S&P 500 data, has higher returns and Sharpe ratios, as compared to centralized or decentralized models. The combination of RL and FL is changing the way investors make their investment choices in the changing wealth management environment where it improves the privacy of the data gathered and the accuracy of predicting content. Financial institutions strengthen their ability to build adaptive algorithms that can optimize their investment decisions using real-time feedback by reinforcement learning, which is a subdivision of machine learning [11]. In the meantime, federated learning enables these institutions to cooperate and train on decentralized datasets without violating sensitive customer data. Combined, they provide a strong combination of a personalized approach to investment portfolios, the reduction of risks, and the maximization of returns in a more complex financial setting. With more companies embracing these new technologies, investors will be in a better position to find more customized and strategic information about their wealth management tools, therefore, making more money and securing financial planning sturdiness within a competitive market environment [11].

FL in DeFi and Lending: FL can be used in DeFi to predict lending and borrowings in the market without any disclosure of transactional behavior. Recent surveys have introduced FL as one of the architectures that can accommodate the demands of DeFi regarding privacy first, and discourses about the architectures, privacy schemes in the context of differential privacy or secure aggregation, and integration with smart contracts have been explored.

Emerging Integrations and Incentive Designs: Federated learning together with blockchain offers collaboration security and resistance to tampering. As an example, tokenized contributions enable contributors to make a profit off their model input, linking data to collaborate with the incentive to invest [12]. In the modern dynamic financial environment, the management of wealth and investment approaches is progressively emphasizing on new forms of integrations and innovative incentive designs that support a wide range of audience. Since both people and organizations are striving to maximize their portfolios, the integration of high-level technologies, including artificial intelligence and data analytics, has transformed the path to the decision. Through these tools, the wealth managers are able to design specific investment plans that do not only cater to the risk profiles of the individuals but also to the long-term financial objectives. Moreover, there is an increasing trend in incentive structures that facilitate sustainable investment and socially responsible investing within financial markets that are forcing clients to become part of growth opportunities and develop a robust investment portfolio that will ultimately lead to financial prosperity in a changing market [13].

3. Core Concepts and Frameworks

Federated Learning Basics: Federated learning is a solution which enables different organizations to collaboratively train a shared model in the network, and without transferring the raw data from a local device. It consists of four main parts: initialization (the global model is push to all participants), local training (each node updates the model based on their local data), aggregation (aggregates updates, generally by federated averaging), and repeats the previous steps until they converge.

FL Comes in Several Flavors:

- Cross-Silo FL: Where entire organizations (such as banks or investment firms) participate via their internal networks and periodic updates.
- Cross-Device FL: Better for mobile or edge settings, with unstable connectivity and constrained computation [14].

The core issue is data heterogeneity; when local datasets of institutions are significantly diverse in distribution, typical techniques such as FedAvg may encounter trouble. Methods such as FedProx or SCAFFOLD stabilize learning across non-IID data.

Communication expense and privacy are also important. Methods such as gradient scarification (sharing only the most important updates), among others, contribute to easing the bandwidth requirements (especially when combined with secure aggregation schemes for preserving the privacy of the model). Moreover, by combining differential privacy and secure multi-party computation (MPC), it prevents sensitive information from being rejuvenated from model updates—critical in finance.

4. Case Studies/Applications

Here are three illustrative use cases where FL threads directly into investment strategies and wealth management:

Stock Market Prediction with Fed-MLP–LSTM: Researchers recently introduced a federated model combining multi-layer perceptron (MLP) and Long Short-Term Memory network (LSTM) networks for stock trend prediction on CAC40 data. Every institution trains a local MLP–LSTM, and only exchanges the model parameters. The model averaged on a global scale obtained very low Root Mean Square Error (RMSE) and high accuracy; 98.3% accuracy with 0.0108 RMSE showing that FL can be used to obtain predictive modelling with respectable accuracy and privacy.

Explainable FL Fraud Detection: One article that combined explainable AI (XAI) and FL addressed banking fraud detection. There were several institutions that were trained jointly without sharing of customer information and the system offered clear alerts that were easily interpreted. It was not only a privacy-preserving approach, but it created trust and enhanced detection capacity on real-world, imbalanced transactions datasets [15].

AML and Secure Financial Transactions: Federated learning is also becoming effective in fraud prevention, AML, biometric authentication, or credit-risk modelling. According to a 2025 article, FL can be used to identify transactional threats and maintain privacy of users as well as adhere to regulations. It also underscored the need to have secure aggregation techniques and aligned benefits of FL with new regulatory and cybersecurity environments.

Table 3 shows the Industry Application of Federated Learning in Wealth Management and Finance It allows multiple institutions to collaborate on model training for market prediction and algorithmic trading, improves fraud-detection and anti money laundering (AML) capabilities by sharing patterns securely between institutions as well as improving credit risk assessment without exposing client data. It further assists personalized robo-advisors as it learns on various data while ensuring privacy. Moreover, the combination of federated learning and reinforcement learning optimizes the management of portfolios, while blockchain integration introduces trust into decentralized systems along with security and integrity of data.

Table 3: FL applications in wealth management and finance.

Use Case	*Description*
Market Prediction	Collaborative model training for improved algorithmic trading
Fraud and AML Detection	Shared patterns across institutions, privacy-preserving, higher accuracy
Credit and Risk Assessment	Sharing insights for better scoring without revealing client data
Personalized Advice	Robo-advisory benefits from diverse learning while keeping privacy intact
Reinforcement Learning (Adaptive Policy Reinforcement (APR))	FL-driven RL models for portfolio management improve risk-adjusted return
Blockchain Integration	Synthetic data, tamper resistance, and trust via distributed ledger systems

5. Challenges and Limitations

Despite its numerous benefits to wealth management and investment management strategies, federated learning does not come without challenges. Here are some of the heavier lifts:

Data Heterogeneity and Imbalance: FL settings are often with heterogeneous data distributions among participants: banks, asset management companies, or robo-advisors [16]. Some might have had rich transaction histories, while others had limited or warped portfolios. Such offering of the data usually results in an imbalance among the clients, which means the clients hold non-IID data that may induce models biased or unstable convergence under existing algorithms even including the standard algorithm Federated Averaging (FedAvg). These approaches have shortcomings such as FedProx that give partial fixes for the problem, but problem still remains.

Communication Costs and Infrastructure: FL is commonly executed among financial institutions across a secure but bandwidth-limited network. Note that if the model exchange is frequent, the infrastructure (especially in presence of deep models) may be stressed. When only parameters rather than raw data are shared, the bandwidth and compute load can be problematic [17].

Security and Trust: Flaws in the System: FL's Decentralized Nature Introduces Vulnerabilities such as

- **Byzantine Attacks:** There exist malicious agents that give bogus model updates.
- **Backdoor Attacks:** Hidden cues enable attackers to manipulate the behavior of the model on demand.

- **Adversarial Attacks:** Perturbations-generated pre-crafted inputs can be used to steer predictions.

Defenses are starting to appear, albeit their trade-off between robustness and operational complexity is currently an open problem.

Governance and Explainability: FL models especially when trading or scoring risk have to comply with regulatory guidance. And yet, institutional cross-working complicates interpretability. Regulators require transparency and FL systems may be viewed as black-boxes acting as mixture of many black-boxes.

Interoperability and Standardization: Organizations operate based on various tech stacks, data models, and structures. Lack of common standards makes coordination of FL across companies difficult.

6. Future Trends and Opportunities

The obstacles still exist, yet it is unclear which of them, should any, will set the field back dramatically in the coming action-packed years. Some promising directions are provided in the following text.

Tokenized Incentives: The new models that incentivize contribution utilize blockchain and token economics. The tokens may be allocated to the organization depending on its contribution to the accuracy of a model—creating an incentive-compliant, open cooperation platform.

Interpretable and Credible Federated Learning: Alongside interpretability issues, research is also already starting to look at explainable FL, which breaks down model decisions on a per-node basis. This contributes to the transparency and regulatory clarity [18].

FL–Blockchain Hybrids to Auditability: The tamper-resistant and the business audit path can be enhanced with the help of FL and blockchain integration. Model updates are all timestamped, auditable, and immutable—ideal model governance in the high-stakes financial sector.

Increased Risk Analytics and Surveillance: Besides fraud detection, FL can facilitate cross-institutional early warning systems, that is, systemic risk, credit contagion, and market surveillance across various exchanges, without reducing data separation.

Adaptive FL: Look forward to FL systems which are able to respond to market regime switching, re-calibrate models, as the nodes cross, with the promise of resilience and currency.

Sandboxes of Regulatory and Collaborative Pilots: The policymakers are still at the initial phase of opening regulatory sandboxes to fintech innovation. The regulatory bodies have the right to allow the institutions even to try out FL already in a safe form, a shift to wider acceptance [19].

As seen in Table 4, these challenges include data diversity, privacy risks, security threats and lack of collaboration incentives. Future solutions comprising better collection methods, LDP and secure techniques, stronger security measures, standard protocols, and incentive systems will enhance fraud and AML detection accuracy too.

Table 4: Challenges and future directions.

Challenge	*Description*	*Future Opportunity*
Data Heterogeneity and Model Fusion	Non-IID data across institutions hinders model convergence	Improved aggregation methods and XFL (Explainable Federated Learning) frameworks
Privacy and Regulatory Compliance	Risk of privacy leakage via updates; regulatory complexity	Local Differential Privacy (LDP) frameworks such as DPFedBank, secure multi-party methods
Security Vulnerabilities	Attacks such as poisoning or backdoors threaten reliability	Defense taxonomies, secure aggregation, audit trails
Interoperability	Diverse technologies and governance across institutions	Shared standards and collaboration protocols
Incentive Alignment	Lack of clear rewards for participation	Tokenized incentive systems linked to model contributions
Financial Crime Detection	Poor detection of rare, distributed patterns	FL collaboration boosting accuracy in AML and fraud controls

Blockchain and Tokenized Incentives

Integrating FL with blockchain technologies enhances transparency and security. Some experimental frameworks even explore token-based incentives to reward contributing institutions based on the quality of their model updates.

Table 5 shows the provided suggestions that can help address federated learning challenges in decentralized fraud detection systems, including data heterogeneity, privacy risks, security issues and lack of interoperability with advanced fusion methods, privacy-preserving techniques (XAI), strong security measures and standardized protocols for trust improvement and better real-time fraud detection systems.

Table 5: Future opportunity.

Challenge	*Description*	*Future Opportunity*
Data Heterogeneity	Non-IID data across institutions disrupts model training	Advanced fusion methods (e.g., personalization, dynamic client weighting)
Privacy and Regulatory Risk	Potential information leakage through model updates; complex global regulation	Privacy-preserving techniques (e.g., DP, MPC), embedded into FL frameworks
Security Vulnerabilities	Exposure to poisoning/backdoor attacks due to decentralized architecture	Tailored defence protocols, anomaly detection in updates, secure aggregation
Interoperability and Incentives	Disconnected systems and lack of fair reward structures	Standardized FL protocols; token-based merit systems for equitable collaboration
Explainability and Trust	FL's opaqueness hampers adoption in regulated domains	Integration with XAI (e.g., SHAP, LIME) to enhance auditability and decision transparency
Real-Time Surveillance	Traditional batch-style modelling lags behind fast-evolving fraud patterns	FL combined with GNNs and XAI boosts detection accuracy and operational responsiveness

7. Conclusion

Federated learning has the power to deliver more effective, privacy-preserving AI for wealth asset management and investment strategies for some time now. The potential of AI to revolutionize the world of wealth management and investment has been the subject of much discussion. It is already facilitating cooperation in fraud detection, robo-advisory, and portfolio optimization—and doing so in a manner that respects data privacy.

But the path is anything but easy: technical, security, and governance hurdles remain substantial. Yet the future for FL looks promising—with developments in incentive design, interpretability, blockchain integration, and regulatory backing set to enable and proliferate use of FL.

References

[1] Aljunaid, S. K., Almheiri, S. J., Dawood, H. and Khan, M. A. (2025). Secure and transparent banking: Explainable AI-driven federated learning model for financial fraud detection. *J. Risk Financial Manag.*, 18(4): 179. doi: [10.3390/jrfm18040179] (https://doi.org/10.3390/jrfm18040179).

[2] Awosika, T., Shukla, R. M. and Pranggono, B. (2023). Transparency and privacy: The role of explainable AI and federated learning in financial fraud detection. *arXiv*, doi: [10.48550/arXiv.2312.13334] (https://doi.org/10.48550/arXiv.2312.13334).

[3] Bhanbhro, J. (2024). Issues in federated learning: Some experiments and observations. *Sci. Rep.*, doi: [10.1038/s41598-024-81732-0] (https://doi.org/10.1038/s41598-024-81732-0).

[4] Guembe, B. (2024). Privacy issues, attacks, countermeasures and open problems in federated learning. *J. Int. Digit*. doi: [10.1080/08839514.2024.2410504] (https://doi.org/10.1080/08839514.2024.2410504).
[5] He, P., Lin, C. and Montoya, I. (2024). DPFedBank: Crafting a privacy-preserving federated learning framework for financial institutions with policy pillars. arXiv. doi: [10.48550/arXiv.2410.13753] (https://doi.org/10.48550/arXiv.2410.13753).
[6] Myakala, P. K., Bura, C. and Jonnalagadda, A. K. (2024). Federated learning and data privacy: A review of challenges and opportunities. *Int. J. Res. Publ. Rev.*, 5(12): 1867–1879. doi: [10.55248/gengpi.5.1224.3512] (https://doi.org/10.55248/gengpi.5.1224.3512).
[7] Shenoy, D. (2025). Exploring privacy mechanisms and metrics in federated learning. *Artif. Intell. Rev.*, doi: [10.1007/s10462-025-11170-5] (https://doi.org/10.1007/s10462-025-11170-5).
[8] Mohammadi, S. (2024). Balancing privacy and performance in federated learning. *Decis. Support Syst.*, doi: [10.1016/j.dss.2024.113844] (https://doi.org/10.1016/j.dss.2024.113844).
[9] Abadi, M., Chu, A., Goodfellow, I., McMahan, H. B., Mironov, I., Talwar, K. et al. (2016). Deep learning with differential privacy. *ACM CCS*.
[10] Dhanawat, V. (2025). Enhancing financial risk management with federated AI. *Preprints*. doi: [10.20944/preprints2025.123456v1] (https://doi.org/10.20944/preprints2025.123456v1).
[11] McMahan, B., Moore, E., Ramage, D., Hampson, S. and y Arcas, B. A. (2017). Communication-efficient learning of deep networks from decentralized data. In *Proc. 20th Int. Conf. Artif. Intell. Stat. (AISTATS)*. [Online]. Available: [http://proceedings.mlr.press/v54/mcmahan17a.html].
[12] Li, T., Sahu, A. K., Zaheer, M., Sanjabi, M., Talwalkar, A. and Smith, V. (2020). Federated optimization in heterogeneous networks. In *Proc. Mach. Learn. Syst.*, 2: 429–450. [Online]. Available: [https://proceedings.mlsys.org/paper/2020/file/1f5fe83998a09396ebe6477d9475ba0c-Paper.pdf].
[13] Xu, J., Glicksberg, B. S., Su, C., Walker, P., Bian, J., Wang, F. et al. (2021). Federated learning for healthcare informatics. *Journal of Healthcare Informatics Research*.
[14] Sheller, M. J., Reina, G. A., Edwards, B., Martin, J., Bakas, S., Milchenko, M. et al. (2020). Federated learning in medicine: Facilitating multi-institutional collaborations. *Scientific Reports*.
[15] Melis, L., Song, C., De Cristofaro, E. and Shmatikov, V. (2019). Exploiting unintended feature leakage in collaborative learning. In *2019 IEEE Symp. Secur. Privacy (SP)*, pp. 691–706. doi: [10.1109/SP.2019.00029] (https://doi.org/10.1109/SP.2019.00029).
[16] Bagdasaryan, E., Veit, A., Hua, Y., Estrin, D. and Shmatikov, V. (2020). How to backdoor federated learning. In *Proc. 23rd Int. Conf. Artif. Intell. Stat. (AISTATS)*, pp. 2938–2948. [Online]. Available: [http://proceedings.mlr.press/v108/bagdasaryan20a.html].
[17] Fung, C., Yoon, C. J. M. and Beschastnikh, I. (2020). The limitations of federated learning in sybil settings. In *23rd Int. Symp. Res. Attacks, Intrusions Defenses (RAID 2020)*, pp. 301–316. doi: [10.14722/raid.2020.23031] (https://doi.org/10.14722/raid.2020.23031).
[18] Li, Z. and Lee, D. H. (2022). Federated reinforcement learning for portfolio management. In *Proc. 3rd ACM Int. Conf. AI Finance*, pp. 112–120. doi: [10.1145/3533271.3561752] (https://doi.org/10.1145/3533271.3561752).
[19] Jere, M. S., Farnan, T. and Koushanfar, F. (2021). A taxonomy of attacks on federated learning. *IEEE Secur. Privacy*, 19(2): 20–28. doi: [10.1109/MSEC.2020.3039942] (https://doi.org/10.1109/MSEC.2020.3039942).

8 Building Federated Learning Infrastructure in Finance

Sukhjinder Kaur,[1,*] Amit Vajpayee,[2] Poonam Kukana[2] and Bhupinder Kaur[2]

The financial sector has faced an unprecedented digital disruption which has facilitated the migration toward data-driven technologies, even though the high regulation, privacy restrictions, and distributed characteristics of financial data prevent the extensive application of machine learning. Federated learning (FL) has recently become a promising paradigm, which allows training of models collaboratively over decentralized data sources without leaking privacy. This chapter presents the design and deployment of a federated learning infrastructure, specifically adapted for finance. We discuss the key principles of FL (e.g., secure aggregation, communication efficiency, handling of heterogeneous data), and also discuss architectural considerations when designing scalable, fault-tolerant systems. Examples of practical use cases such as fraud detection, credit risk modelling, anti-money laundering, and personalized financial services are described to illustrate how FL brings value to financial applications in industry. The chapter also presents important challenges, such as the obeyance to data protection laws, access to entry points of traditional finance sources, resistance against adversarial attacks, and trade-offs between privacy and model accuracy. Lastly, we discuss future trends, including the integration of privacy-enhancing technologies, the exploitation of edge/cloud synergy, and the organization of cross-institutional collaborations, aiming to develop the trusted and efficient federated ecosystems in finance.

1. Introduction

The financial services industry has been data rich since its inception and relied on dependable, current, and secure information to make decisions. From credit scoring to risk assessment, fraud detection to high-frequency trading, machine

[1] Department of CSE, Rayat Bahra University, Mohali, Punjab, India.
[2] Department of CSE, Chandigarh University, Mohali-140413, Punjab, India.
Emails: amitvajpayee@gmail.com; poonamkukana@gmail.com; erbhupinderkaur@gmail.com
* Corresponding author: skaur29100@gmail.com

DOI: 10.1201/9781003710059-8

learning (ML) has transformed the way the institutions extract value from big data. But the classical architecture of the ML model has some intrinsic drawbacks as the private financial data should be gathered to central location for training [1]. Regulations such as the GDPR (in Europe), CCPA (in the USA), and international banking regulations (such as Basel III) enforce strict data governance and privacy standards. Thus, these centralized ML systems tend to violate legal, ethical, and organizational boundaries of the financial market.

This issue has also led to increasing interests on the so-called federated learning (FL)—a new paradigm of distributed artificial intelligence (AI) that was introduced by McMahan and coworkers, in which models are trained simultaneously on a dataset residing on multiple institutions or devices without sharing raw data. Instead of pooling information at a central server, the financial institutions exchange model parameters or gradients, which are fused to establish a global model. This structure enables retention of data sovereignty and privacy to give cover, while deploying institutional collective intelligence [2].

Finance is a very important source of FL. For example, detecting fraudulent transactions between banks, where the banks only have knowledge of their own transactions, and jointly learning the likelihood of fraud would provide great value. The data cannot be shared because of extremely stringent confidentiality agreements. FL enables these institutions to work together in the same environment (and share their computations in an appropriate manner) to jointly train models for detecting fraudulent activities (with none of the institutions actually getting to see sensitive customer data). Similar options might be possible in anti-money laundering (AML) monitoring, personalized financial services, and credit risk modelling.

It's not just regulation leading to the trade-off between local and federated learning, but competition in finance. Any and all institutions do not, by any means, want to make their own customer–proprietary information known, because that's strategic. The FL scenario can be viewed on an open, collaborative, and collapsing data interference model, that is, data may come from the organizations and intelligence is contributed. This brings a harmony between finance cooperation and competition.

From technology perspective, constructing a solid FL infrastructure for finance needs weaving a secure computation protocol, communication-efficient aggregation protocols, and solid system architectures. This complexity is now not solely technical (e.g., secure aggregation, differential privacy, and system optimization), but also organizational, regulatory, and governance complexities around deployment have emerged in this space [3].

Scope of the Chapter: The next section presents the fundamental concepts and operations on how to establish federated learning infrastructure in banking. The background and literature start with how FL has become the answer for privacy and regulatory issues in finance. Then, the primitive formulation and components are introduced, while the approaches, algorithms, and system architectures to realize FL are also discussed. Real-world use case studies on fraud detection, credit scoring, and AML are discussed to understand how FL is used. We also critically discuss challenges and limitations such as data diversity, communication, and security threat. The chapter is concluded by an analysis of the future and promising opportunities including blockchain-based FL, standardization, and explainable federated AI [4].

This chapter will propose in conclusion that the infrastructure of federated learning is not only an invention (perhaps even a revolution) but also a strategy for the financial industry. Because FL enables privacy-preserving collaboration, it is anticipated to set the new standard on how institutions consume AI—the trade-off between being compliant and being competitive and the business sense of the crowd.

2. Background and Literature Review

2.1 Evolution of AI in Financial Services

AI continues to be a dominant force for innovation in financial services. In the 1980s and 1990s, initial research in AI in finance described the development of expert systems in, for example, credit scoring and fraud detection. Nevertheless, these pure rule-based methods were not adaptable to the dynamic environment. The rise of big data in the 2000s and advancements in ML models have made more sophisticated methods of risk modelling, algorithmic trading, and customer analytics possible [5].

Banks and other financial services companies started to deploy centralized ML models based on aggregated data to detect abnormal patterns, predict defaults of loans, or tune their trading algorithms. As the need for chronologically ordered content became obsolete within the flood of the web's tsunami of data, the wheel of content management began to come full circle. High-profile breaches such as the Equifax breach brought to the forefront the risks associated with centralized data storage and processing and forced regulators and institutions to question the models of data governance in place.

2.2 Centralized or Distributed Machine Learning

Past designs of centralized ML models assume that the data sources can be centralized to the place where the model is trained. While quality is very good in terms of model performance and the availability of data itself, a setup like this creates huge and extremely dangerous regulatory, security, and privacy risks in finance. Distributed ML was one answer to this, as up to some degree, institutions could train models on multiple nodes, but they still needed to share (or centralize to some extent) the raw data.

Federated learning that was introduced by McMahan and coworkers marked a paradigm shift. In contrast to federated ML, FL supports training on disparate, decentralized datasets without transferring raw data. Instead, only local model updates (gradients or parameters) are shared and aggregated at a central server. That's a win in all ways and also deals with all the privacy and sovereignty issues at the core of finance, where the sharing of data between firms (fintech or otherwise) is at confidential levels.

2.3 Federated Learning in Academic Literature

McMahan et al.'s seminal effort was preceded by similar efforts on biological deep learning. They have recently proposed the Federated Averaging (FedAvg) algorithm which shows that a central model can achieve reasonable learning by combining the updates from decentralized learners. Since then, FL has been applied to various fields and especially finance.

One can also perform sample surveys and presented extensive summaries on the FL methods to address communication efficiency, data heterogeneity, and adversarial robustness as issues. Most early use cases were based on consumer devices, such as training large language models on devices (without sending the pairwise text inputs to a central cloud service) on smartphones, for example; but finance has its own opportunities and constraints. Various recent research efforts have investigated FL in the financial domain [6]:

- **Fraud Detection:** The efficiency of FL for cross-institutional financial fraud detection where customers' privacy has to be respectively preserved [1].
- **Credit Risk Models:** Vertical FL in credit scoring by aggregating the customer attributes across institutions, without conveying raw data.
- **Anti-Money Laundering (AML):** FL can improve suspicious transaction monitoring over banks with low compliance costs.

These publications show that FL has extended the stage of theoretical study to that of practical trial in finance industry.

2.4 Regulatory Drivers for Federated Learning in Finance

The global regulation pressures have a strong impact on FL implementation in finance. There are several regulations such as:

- The EU GDPR (General Data Protection Regulation) that limits PII (personally identifiable information) transfer across borders.
- CCPA (California Consumer Privacy Act), which gives consumers the right to exert control over their data.
- PSD2 (Payment Services Directive 2) in Europe, requiring banks to share data with fintechs in a secure way.
- Basel III proposal, which highlights transparency of data and governance of risk.

These infrastructures together form a compliance-by-design world where data centricity is simply not feasible. On such demand there, FL directly satisfies these requirements, due to its keeping of data within institutions.

2.5 Industry Initiatives and Platforms

Outside academia, industry has started efforts to put FL into practice in finance. For instance:

- FATE (Federated AI Technology Enabler) developed by WeBank is one of the first open-source FL platforms targeting financial industry.
- IBM Federated Learning Framework and TensorFlow Federated provide privacy-preserving protocols built for deployment.
- Financial collaboratives (FinTech Innovation Lab, MAS), for example, have trailed FL fraud detection.

Taken together, these projects constitute a rapidly developing ecosystem of tools, standards, and collaborations around deploying FL in finance.

2.6 Literature and Practice Gaps

Despite good advancement, there are many gaps in literature and practice.

- **Scalability:** There are limited efforts that study the performance of FL in the context of multinational financial networks.
- **Security:** Adversarial attacks in financial FL systems are not well studied, in particular, the data poisoning and model inversion threats.
- **Interpretability:** Being able to interpret a model is a regulatory requirement in finance, for example, however, FL studies tend to focus on performance rather than interpretability [7].
- **Governance:** Issues of liability, accountability, and auditability are not yet resolved in federated collaborations.

Therefore, though FL is theoretically and regulatory well-founded, its practical implementation in finance arms for further innovation in infrastructure, governance, and security.

3. Core Concepts and Frameworks

3.1 Overview of Federated Learning

Federated learning is a collective machine learning algorithm in which multiple clients (e.g., banks, insurance companies, or financing institutions) train a global model together while keeping their local data private. Rather than collecting raw data in one place, institutions train models locally and share only model parameters (such as gradients or weights) with a central server. This guarantees that data remains securely inside the organization, addressing the strong data governance and regulatory requirements [8].

FL is essentially iterative, with the following flow:

- Spatial models initialized at a server on the network.
- Distribution of models to participating clients.
- Local training on client datasets.
- Aggregation of client updates to form a new global model.
- Iteration until convergence.

This procedure reconciles privacy conservation with associative intelligence to allow financial institutions the advantage of the collective through each other's more extensive data pool without breaking their anti-trust data-sharing constraints.

3.2 Paradigms of Federated Learning

According to the manner in which data is distributed between organizations, FL can be classified into three major paradigms.

3.2.1 Horizontal Federated Learning (HFL)

Definition: It is also called sample-based FL. Clients have the same feature but different sample datasets.

Finance Scenario: Several banks in various locations employ the same customer attributes (e.g., age, income, credit history) on different people. Training a joint model of fraud detection over these banks may improve the detection performance.

Figure 1 depicts how horizontal federated learning works—a number of participants (say, the smartphones or personal gadgets of users) collaborate to train a global model on their local data (such as phone behaviors). For example, participants in the system jointly build a single machine-learning model.

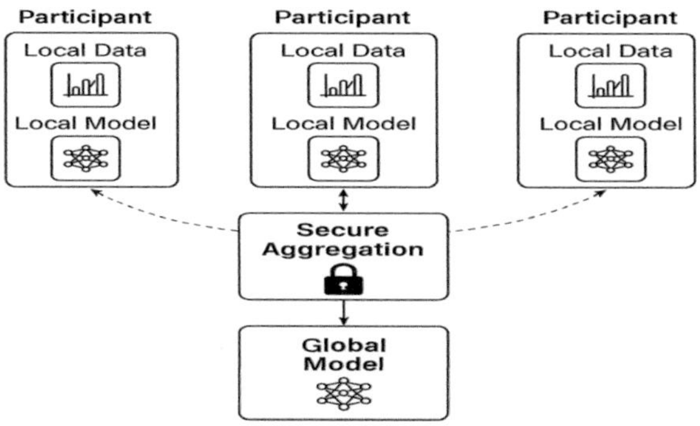

Figure 1: Horizontal federated learning diagram.

3.2.2 Vertical Federated Learning (VFL)

Definition: It is also called feature-based FL. Clients have the same sample IDs but different feature.

Example from Finance: A bank has customers' credit transaction data, while an insurance company has claims history. Through VFL, they build a richer risk profile while avoiding raw records.

Figure 2 illustrates privacy-preserving collaborative learning—multiple institutions send encrypted intermediate outputs to a coordinator who then jointly constructs an aggregate output without having access to their respective raw data.

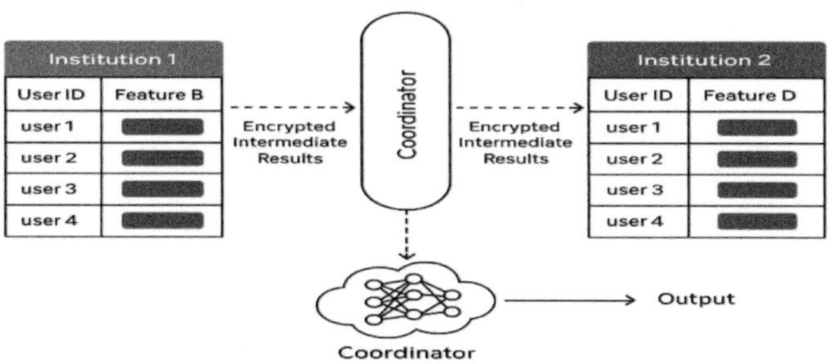

Figure 2: Vertical federated learning diagram.

3.2.3 Federated Transfer Learning (FTL)

Definition: The case where an algorithm has to match two datasets with both different samples and features, but small discrepancies between the two. Transfer learning supports knowledge transfer between clients [9].

For example, a European investment firm and an Asian credit-rating agency have only a few clients that overlap. With transfer learning they could work on global credit scoring models together.

Figure 3 explains the idea of transfer learning, in which institutions share intermediary representations to facilitate knowledge port in a model and generate a shared joint model without sharing raw data.

Table 1 describe summary of horizontal federated learning, Vertical and Transfer federated learning.

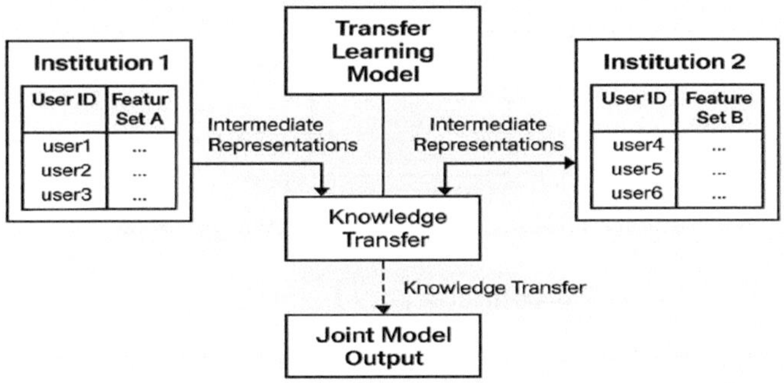

Figure 3: Vertical federated learning diagram.

Table 1: A summary of the FL paradigms.

Paradigm	*Data Distribution*	*Finance Use Case*
Horizontal FL	Same features, different samples	Fraud detection across multiple banks
Vertical FL	Same samples, different features	Joint risk assessment by banks and insurers
Transfer FL	Different samples and features	Global credit scoring across regions

3.3 FL Algorithms and Optimization Techniques

In finance, the performance of FL relies on optimizing approaches considering data heterogeneity, communication efficiency, and robustness.

3.3.1 Federated Averaging (Fed Avg)

Introduced by McMahan et al. [10].

- Each client trains a local model for some epochs and returns the parameter updates to the server and averaged.
- It is one of the most popular models in the field of finance due to its simplicity and flexibility.
- **Drawback:** Difficult with non-IID financial data (rural versus urban customers).

3.3.2 Federated Proximal (FedProx)

- Generalizes FedAvg by introducing a proximal term to cope with dataset heterogeneity [9].
- Better in case of highly variant client datasets.
- **Finance Example:** A set of distinct institutions with disparate transaction distributions.

3.3.3 Secure Aggregation

- Secure aggregation guarantees that there is encryption at the lower levels of the model updates.
- Prevents the central server from reverse-engineering sensitive financial information.
- Techniques such as homomorphic encryption and MPC are increasingly deployed.

3.3.4 Differentially Private FL

- Injects noise to the client updates to protect differential privacy.
- **Finance Example:** Training an AML model, differential privacy makes sure that any single fishy transaction cannot be tracked back [11].

3.4 Architectural Frameworks of FL

3.4.1 Centralized FL

- A central server coordinates aggregation.
- Applicable to the financial consortium (e.g., joint actions of some regional banks).
- **Weakness:** Single point of failure.

3.4.2 Decentralized/Peer-to-Peer FL

- No single server; aggregation is done collectively across the nodes.
- Great for thrustless finance in the blockchain world.
- **Limitation:** Communication overhead is higher.

3.4.3 Hybrid Federated Architecture

- Combines centralized and decentralized approaches.
- **Use Case:** Aggregating from smaller institutions to regional hubs, and from those to an upstream aggregator.

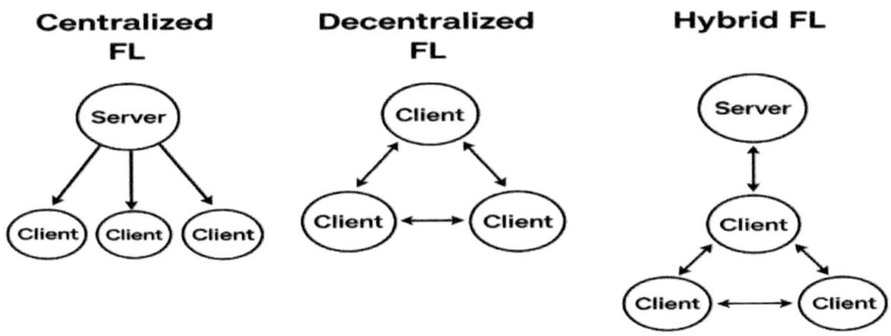

Figure 4: The architectural comparison.

Figure 4 illustrates the architectural comparison between centralized, decentralized, and hybrid federated learning.

3.5 Security and Privacy Improvements in FL

Gradient Compression and Blockchain-based Optimized Federated Learning (GCBOFL) provides an opportunity to enhance privacy and security. Because of the sensitive nature of financial data, FL frameworks should incorporate further privacy-preserving technologies (PPTs):

- **Homomorphic Encryption:** Enables calculation over the encrypted content without decrypting the data [12].
- **MPC:** The word stands for secure multi-party computation (i.e., multiple players evaluate a function of their joint inputs without revealing inputs).
- **Integration of Blockchain:** General Public License (GPL) reduces the risk of tampering with training contributions as they are logged in an immutable ledger.
- **Zero-Knowledge Proofs (ZKP):** Participants prove correctness of a computation without revealing specifics.

3.6 A Conceptual Model for FL in Finance

A sound layered framework of FL infrastructure for finance is shown as follows:

- **Data Layer:** Local, data on premise at each financial institution.
- **Computation Layer:** Institutional data silos (local model training).

- **Communication Layer:** Quarantine-free transmission of privacy-preserving/ garbled model differences.
- **Aggregation Layer:** Aggregation centralized or decentralized.
- **Application Layer:** Petabyte-scale global models for fraud detection, credit scoring, portfolio optimization, etc. [13].

This methodology underpins a modular, scalable, and compliant FL ecosystem for financial services.

4. Case Studies/Applications

Federated learning has evolved from a conceptual model in the past, and has become a practical paradigm and widely applied in the finance domain. Its novelty is that it can facilitate collaborative model construction among decentralized datasets, while adhering to the stringent privacy regulations. In this section, we focus on applications and case studies which illustrate how FL is changing finance. The Table 2 shows how modern privacy-preserving technologies enable collaboration across financial institutions while maintaining data security, regulatory compliance, and improved decision-making.

4.1 Fraud Detection and AML

The operations of banks and payment networks are now at risk mainly due to financial fraud and money laundering. Traditional fraud detection is based on centralized machine learning models running on aggregated data with regulatory barriers and silos as the most common limitations. By FL, many banks can jointly train fraud detection model without disclosing proprietary transaction records.

Case Example: Chinese financial institutions trailed versions of the WeBank-incepted FATE (Federated AI Technology Enabler) model to track cross-bank fraudulent behavior. With the help of FL, banks passed model updates not raw data, raising fraud detection accuracy much higher without violating People's Bank of China's data security regulations [14].

Result: Improved fraud detection among institutions, minimized false-positives, and strengthened cooperation between banks on AML investigations.

4.2 Credit Scoring and Credit Risk Assessment

Traditional credit scoring is inefficient and only has access to limited data through central credit bureaus. That does more than skewing things—it restricts entry to underbanked folks, and it's a privacy issue. FL offers a decentralized solution in which banks and fintech and telecom entities learn collaboratively with split credit report histories of an individual as well as using alternative financial indicators.

Case Study: IBM Research collaborated with several banks across Europe to explore FL for credit scoring. By adding decentralized data, the FL models outperformed traditional bureau-based scores in predicting default risk.

Outcomes: Fairer credit assessment, enabling greater financial inclusion and GDPR's data-privacy compliance.

4.3 Personalized Financial Advisory Services

Robo-advisor-based AI solutions are seeing increasing demand within the wealth management practices. Yet, personalization depends on access to extremely sensitive customer profiles. FL enables advisory platforms to learn models over decentralized client datasets without leaking sensitive information of individuals and noiselessly improve model performance [15].

Case Example: A European fintechs coalition leveraged FL to improve robo-advisory services through cross-firm investment behavior data.

Result: Better, context-aware investment insights, with no risks of centralized data collection.

4.4 Regulatory Compliance and Reporting

Global financial compliance and regulations (i.e., Basel III, MiFID II, GDPR) require robust data protection and reporting. Compliance analytics teams can use FL for anomaly detection and predictive regulatory reporting, with no need to violate jurisdictional data residency considerations.

Case Study: The BIS Innovation Hub has been investigating federated analytics for cross-border risk. FL was employed by participating central banks to exchange model parameters for systemic risk prediction.

Result: There is an early detection of global financial instability signals by still complying with the data localization legislation.

4.5 Insurance Risk Modelling

Insurance providers need a variety of data—demographic, health, and financial history data—to ensure that their risk modelling is as accurate as possible. But sharing raw data between insurers has competitive and ethical considerations. FL ensures that actuarial models can be shared without release of the proprietary data.

Case Example: Swiss InsurTech Hub trialled FL to pool risks across various insurers.

Results: Greater accuracy in the predictive performance of models for claim frequency and in the detection of fraud in insurance claims.

Table 2: Applications of FL in finance.

Application Area	*Example Use Case*	*Key Benefit*	*Compliance Relevance*
Fraud Detection and AML	Cross-bank fraud detection	Higher accuracy, lower false-positives	AML and KYC regulations
Credit Scoring	Distributed credit assessment	Fairness, inclusion, GDPR compliance	GDPR, CCPA
Wealth Management	Personalized robo-advisory	Data privacy + model personalization	Data protection laws
Regulatory Compliance	Cross-border systemic risk prediction	Better risk management, legal compliance	Basel III, MiFID II, GDPR
Insurance	Risk modelling and fraud detection	Shared learning without data sharing	Data localization laws

5. Challenges and Limitations

Although it is claimed that FL will ensure a secure, collaborative approach and trust-centric AI adoption on financial services organizations, few challenges preclude its successful implementation—technical, organizational, and regulatory. In this section, we discuss some of the major challenges and bottlenecks that FI will need to resolve while adopting FL infrastructures. Figure 5 depicts the key challenges in federated learning for finance.

5.1 Heterogeneity and Non-IID Distributions of the Data

It is common that data from different systems of banks, insurers, and fintechs is heterogeneous. Information is created across institutions in terms of customer segments, geographies, and transactions types. Therefore, the distributions of data are usually non-independent and identically distributed (non-IID).

Problem: FL algorithms (e.g., FedAvg) have difficulty in dealing with non-IID data, which causes nonconverging and biased models.

Example: A small, local bank has mostly rural customer data, but a big international institution has city-based data. Combining predictions from such distributions can result in prediction drifts for risk models.

Figure 5: Key challenges in federated learning for finance.

5.2 System Heterogeneity

Banks operate on an IT continuum that ranges from legacy mainframes to the cloud. Working with that degree of system-level heterogeneity is really challenging for things such as synchronization, for communications bandwidth, and for computational efficiency.

Issue: Slow learners and low infrastructure (also referred to as "stragglers") could delay the training for rounds.

Example: Maybe small credit unions wouldn't have the computing resources they would need to really compete with a federated consortium of large, multinational banks [16].

5.3 Privacy and Security Risks

Though FL reduces the requirement of raw data sharing, it is not unconditionally secure inherently. Rivals or opponents could exploit vulnerabilities of the system.

Inference Attack: An adversary may be reintroduced by relearning sensitive transactional information.

Poisoning Attacks: Attackers manipulate the adversarial instances or model parameters to poison the global model.

Model Stealing: It is feasible to recover sensitive proprietary financial models with black-box queries.

5.4 Communication Overhead

FL, in contrast, has intensive client-side communication (as banks, who communicate with the central coordinator or their peer banks). Latency and bandwidth bottlenecks do not work for high-value financial markets.

Problem: Model updates on hundreds of institutions are a heavy network load.

Trade-Off: The convergence of updates is bounded, thus alleviating the communication cost for practitioners, at the cost of some accuracy.

5.5 Governance and Trust Issues

Institutional trust and governance architectures for federated infrastructures need to be created. Universities tend to be rivalrous about financial information; the temptation is to hoard one's own if nothing else—even if sharing it might have improved performance, as in letting people see the model updates.

Challenge: Difficult to ensure fairness of model's contribution and reward.

Example: In detect-at-fraud networks, big banks could feel as though they are disproportionately supplying valuable data compared with the little guys.

5.6 Regulatory and Compliance Barriers

Although FL is compatible with a variety of privacy laws, legal and compliance barriers to the FL deployment still exist.

Cross-jurisdictional Data Sharing: Regulators in some jurisdictions (e.g., EU under GDPR, CN Cybersecurity Law) may have concerns about whether "data transfer" is occurring just based on the transmission of gradient without the raw data ever being shared.

Auditability: FL systems must be auditable to regulators with well-defined audit logs of data shared and how much and what models have been learned—a technically challenging task for FL system as the nodes are decentralized [17].

5.7 Lack of Standardization

On the contrary, finance belongs to the initial upbringing stage about FL and fragmented FL frameworks (such as Google TensorFlow Federated, WeBank/ FATE, Open Mined PySyft, etc.) appearing at the same time. Interoperability problems are the result of the absence of protocol standards.

Consequences: Companies risk locking into one vendor and don't benefit from consistent adherence to early-stage industry standards.

6. Future Trends and Opportunities

We have also noted that, as a mature technology, FL stands to revolutionize how financial infrastructure providers would make data, model engineering, and collaboration in secure environments. While current use-cases are remarkably limited to a rigidly circumscribed focus on regulatory compliance and privacy-preserving analytics, future innovation will be leveraged to go beyond a more clever, more robust, more unifying finance [18]. Figure 6 depicts the future federated learning finance landscape, showcasing layered progress from sustainability and privacy enabling tech to generative AI, cross institution co-op, explainable FL, edge computing, and blockchain integration.

6.1 Federated Learning and Blockchain and Distributed Ledgers Integration

Other interesting research directions include the integration of FL with blockchain or distributed ledgers. Leveraging immutable ledger and distributed governance, blockchain can increase the trust among the involved FIs, secure the audit trail, and validate the update of the model against tampering. Smart contracts could be used to roll up incentive structures so that contributors only contribute quality (data, for example) or only adhere to a group governed by the same rules.

6.2 Edge Computation and Real-Time Decision-Making

Since the deployment of financial systems relies more and more on streaming data including stock trading, credit card transactions, and fraud detection alerts, it is very important to support FL at the edge. FL made it possible to carry out low-latency and real-time analytics at the edge, without offloading the raw data to the remote servers. This will be particularly useful in ferreting out fraud and algorithmic trading, in which milliseconds are crucial [19].

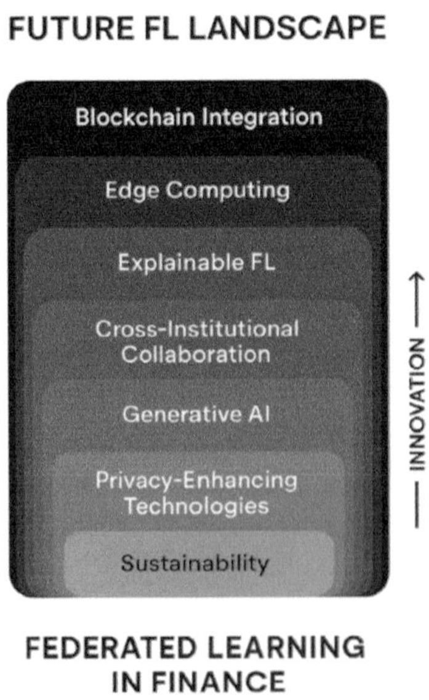

Figure 6: Future federated learning landscape.

6.3 Explainable and Trustworthy Models for Distributed Environment

The interpretability of models is highly required for financial application, because in finance, where the model's decisions are automated, and regulators require that the decision be explainable, xFL is likely to be the next generation of FL research in which privacy-preserving training is an inherent part and is complemented by methods for generating human-interpretable explanations. This would allow financial firms to trust that compliance demands are being met and build trust with both customers and regulators.

6.4 Cross-Institutional Collaborative Analytics

The same sort of easy cross-institutional collaboration that enables banks to work together could also be made possible between institutions such as insurance companies, fintech startups, and regulators, through next-generation infrastructure. Interjurisdictional cooperation might allow scaling of system-wide risk models, fraud sharing of intelligence, and AML on a global basis. FL environments will revolutionize financial service markets entirely, coming from the variety, and ensure on the financial system [20].

6.5 Fusion with Generative AI and Large Foundation Models

New generative AI and large base models could be trained over federated principles on massive, diverse financial knowledge. A hybrid like that would enable some of those more sophisticated predictive analyses. It urges them to type in a more intelligent language, maybe even some form of natural language to create a financial-advisor-adaptive algorithm (unless AML and compliance are preventing this very idea), without bringing the institutions' proprietary or sensitive corporate data to harm.

6.6 PETs in Federated Finance

FL will bring more advanced Privacy-Enhancing Technologies (PET) solutions to their end such as secure multi-party computation (SMPC) and trusted execution environments (TEE). These two trends will address some of the long-standing risks around model inversion attacks and adversarial threats as well, in order to enhance the resilience of federated infrastructures to such new cyber risks.

6.7 Global Regulatory Harmonization

Rules will need to change as FL becomes more common. In longer term, the trend will be to standardize privacy, data-sharing, and AI governance laws on a global basis.

Infrastructures for a Low-Friction World: FL infrastructures can provide a bridge between cross-border financial collaboration and compliance with a layer of law following across local jurisdictions (e.g., for GDPR in Europe, DPDP in India, and CCPA in the USA).

6.8 Sustainability and Green AI in Federated Finance

Although in its early days, Green AI, which spans across both minimizing hardware and software, is a pressing need.

Another interesting opportunity is the energy consumption optimization of the FL infrastructures. Federated models training among different parties is computationally expensive. Potential future directions include energy-conscious FL algorithms, dynamic training regimes, and carbon-conscious data centers to make sure of the sustainable deployment of AI in finance.

7. Conclusion

The adoption of federated learning by financial services is a fundamental change to how banks can engage with AI—embracing AI in a manner that ensures the utmost privacy, compliance, and trust. The chapter has laid out the basic principles, historic evolution, and architectural mechanisms driving the systems that supported the FL infrastructure and showed how they can apply very broadly of applications lines, for example, fraud detection, credit risk scoring, anti-money laundering, or personalized financial services.

This whitepaper underscores the point that with FL, individuals have the ability to have models trained collaboratively, without the movement of sensitive financial data to a centralized location (a significant challenge for the industry today), data sovereignty, and regulatory requirements. The case studies and industry practices evidence that FL can deliver real-world values such as model accuracy, robustness, and fairness, and mitigate systemic risks of centralized AI in practice [21].

However, many issues are left open to scrutiny in the literature, for example, communication overhead, system flexibility, diversity of data, heterogeneity, and security against adversarial threats. This exculpatory work around reminds us that FL in finance is not a magic bullet, but a paradigm to be grown and applied judiciously.

In the future of finance, we anticipate the emergence of a new FL landscape—blockchain interoperability, edge computing, privacy-preserving mechanisms, and explainable AI. These latest trends will enhance the transparency and the accountability but also the cooperation between institutions and make of FL one of the cornerstones of the FI systems of next generations.

Finally, infrastructure for federated learning in finance is not just a technical question, but a strategic necessity. Scaling reliable and innovative FL ecosystems across educational institutions could help place them to “play” in a data-centric future. It is federated learning that opens the door to the secure, collaborative, and effective future for financial services where privacy preservation intersects the sharing of intelligence.

References

[1] Aledhari, M., Razzak, R., Parizi, R. M. and Khan, S. (2020). Federated learning: A survey on enabling technologies, protocols, and applications. *IEEE Access*, 8: 140699–140725. https://doi.org/10.1109/ACCESS.2020.3013541.

[2] Arner, D. W., Barberis, J. and Buckley, R. P. (2016). The evolution of fintech: A new post-crisis paradigm? *Georgetown Journal of International Law*, 47(4): 1271–1319.

[3] Bonawitz, K., Eichner, H., Grieskamp, W., Huba, D., Ingerman, A., Ivanov, V. et al. (2019). Towards federated learning at scale: System design. *Proceedings of Machine Learning and Systems*, 1: 374–388.

[4] Chen, M., Yang, Z., Zhou, Y. and Zhang, Y. (2020). Artificial intelligence for financial technology applications. *IEEE Network*, 34(6): 4–9. https://doi.org/10.1109/MNET.011.2000050.

[5] Gai, K., Qiu, M. and Sun, X. (2018). A survey on fintech. *Journal of Network and Computer Applications*, 103: 262–273. https://doi.org/10.1016/j.jnca.2017.10.011.

[6] Ghosh, A., Hong, J., Yin, D. and Ramage, D. (2020). Efficient federated learning for mobile edge computing. *Proceedings of the 4th ACM/IEEE Symposium on Edge Computing*, 1–14. https://doi.org/10.1145/3384419.3430780.

[7] Hard, A., Rao, K., Mathews, R., Ramaswamy, S., Beaufays, F., Augenstein, S. et al. (2019). Federated learning for mobile keyboard prediction. *arXiv preprint* arXiv:1811.03604.

[8] Kairouz, P., McMahan, H. B., Avent, B., Bellet, A., Bennis, M., Bhagoji, A. N. et al. (2021). Advances and open problems in federated learning. *Foundations and Trends in Machine Learning*, 14(1-2): 1–210, doi: 10.1561/2200000083.

[9] Li, T., Sahu, A. K., Talwalkar, A. and Smith, V. (2020). Federated learning: Challenges, methods, and future directions. *IEEE Signal Processing Magazine*, 37(3): 50–60. https://doi.org/10.1109/MSP.2020.2975749.

[10] McMahan, H. B., Moore, E., Ramage, D., Hampson, S. and y Arcas, B. A. (2017). Communication-efficient learning of deep networks from decentralized data. In *Proceedings of the 20th International Conference on Artificial Intelligence and Statistics (AISTATS)* (pp. 1273–1282).

[11] Liu, J., Wang, Y. and Chen, L. (2022). Federated learning for anti-money laundering in financial networks. *Journal of Financial Data Science*, 4(2): 33–49.

[12] Liu, Y., Kang, Y., Zhang, X., Chen, T., Wang, J. and Yang, Q. (2020). A communication-efficient vertical federated learning framework for distributed features. *arXiv preprint*. https://arxiv.org/abs/1912.11187.

[13] Long, Y., Tan, Y., Wu, Y. and Yu, H. (2020). Privacy-preserving federated learning for financial applications. *arXiv preprint*. https://arxiv.org/abs/2011.02134.

[14] Rieke, N., Hancox, J., Li, W., Milletarì, F., Roth, H. R., Albarqouni, S. et al. (2020). The future of digital health with federated learning. *NPJ Digital Medicine*, 3(1): Art. no. 119, doi: 10.1038/s41746-020-00323-1.

[15] Sheller, M. J., Edwards, B., Reina, G. A., Martin, J., Pati, S., Kotrotsou, A. et al. (2020). Federated learning in medicine: Facilitating multi-institutional collaborations without sharing patient data. *Scientific Reports*, 10: Art. no. 12598, doi: 10.1038/s41598-020-69250-1.

[16] Xu, J., Glicksberg, B. S., Su, C., Walker, P., Bian, J. and Wang, F. (2021). Federated learning for healthcare informatics. *Journal of Healthcare Informatics Research*, 5(1): 1–19. https://doi.org/10.1007/s41666-020-00082-4.

[17] Yang, K., Yu, T., Li, H., Wu, Y. and Yang, Q. (2022). Federated learning in financial applications: A review and future directions. *Computational Economics*, 60(1): 1–27. https://doi.org/10.1007/s10614-021-10147-3.

[18] Yang, Q., Liu, Y., Chen, T. and Tong, Y. (2019). Federated machine learning: Concept and applications. *ACM Transactions on Intelligent Systems and Technology*, 10(2): 1–19. https://doi.org/10.1145/3298981.

[19] Zhang, C., Xie, Y., Bai, H., Yu, B., Li, W. and Gao, Y. (2021). A survey on federated learning. *Knowledge-Based Systems*, 216: Article 106775. https://doi.org/10.1016/j.knosys.2021.106775.

[20] Zhang, Y., Wang, X. and Lin, J. (2021). Vertical federated learning for credit scoring. *Information Systems Frontiers*, 23(1): 171–185. https://doi.org/10.1007/s10796-019-09961-4.

[21] Zhu, H., Xu, J., Liu, S. and Jin, Y. (2021). Federated learning on non-IID data: A survey. *Neurocomputing*, 465: 371–390. https://doi.org/10.1016/j.neucom.2021.07.098.

9 Federated Learning for Financial Data Privacy and Security Services

Shweta Thakur

As financial services increasingly rely on artificial intelligence (AI) for tasks such as fraud detection, credit evaluation, and risk management, concerns about data privacy, security, and compliance with regulations have grown. Traditional machine learning models require the centralization of sensitive customer and institutional data, which can lead to privacy violations, regulatory problems, and a loss of trust. Federated learning (FL) lets different financial organizations work together to train AI models without sharing their raw data. This chapter looks at how FL can improve privacy and security while also encouraging new ideas in the finance industry.

In this chapter, we introduce the core ideas of FL, and discuss how it supports organizations to be in compliance with the data protection regulations, such as GDPR and CCPA, by keeping data local and exchanging model updates only. We discuss security-enhancing techniques such as secure aggregation, differential privacy, and homomorphic encryption that protect models against adversarial attacks and prevent the leakage of sensitive information. We illustrate how FL is applied in fraud detection, AML, and risk assessment in real-world case studies, demonstrating superior model performance and data security compared to conventional approaches.

We also discuss the existing barriers: disparate data and infrastructure across institutions, effective communication, threats associated with model poisoning, and poor regulatory guidance. Finally, the chapter closes with ways the future research and development could overcome some of the significant barriers to FL's scalability, security, and practicality for widespread adoption in the financial services sector. Addressing them means FL will enable the sector to adopt AI responsibly by finding the balance between innovation, privacy, and trust.

Assistant Professor, AIT-CSE Chandigarh University, Mohali-140413, Punjab, India.
Email: er.shweta.thkr@gmail.com

DOI: 10.1201/9781003710059-9

1. Introduction

The unprecedented digital transformation of the financial services sector means AI-powered applications have now become indispensable for fraud detection, credit assessment, risk profiling, and customer personalization. These benefits remain curtailed by intense data-privacy regulations, such as GDPR and CCPA, and institutional concerns related to confidentiality and regulatory compliance. Classic techniques that centralize sensitive financial information expose organizations to data breaches, reputational harm, and potential regulatory noncompliance.

Federated learning provides a superior alternative: a decentralized learning approach where several institutions collaborate toward building machine learning models without necessarily sharing raw data to preserve data locality and minimize privacy risks [1]. Institutions share only model updates, which get aggregated on the server through protocols such as FedAvg or FedProx to form a global model that leverages collective intelligence but with minimal data leakage risks [2].

In the financial industry, FL is gaining rapid momentum for fraud detection, anti-money laundering, and credit risk assessment. Pilot projects have made their mark, such as WeBank's vertical FL for credit evaluation, which indicates its potentials in providing strong predictive models while avoiding the centralization of customer data [3]. Domain-specific frameworks evolve with recent research; for instance, a privacy-preserving explainable AI-based FL model enhances the accuracy and trust of fraud detection while assuring regulatory compliance [4].

Other contributions have introduced efficient and scalable protocols, such as gradient sparsification in secure aggregation, which reduce communication overhead without sacrificing model accuracy or privacy protections [5]. With these, technology adoption in the financial sector has only just begun. Fully understanding issues such as non-IID data distributions across institutions, delays in communication, stability in training, adversarial threats in the form of poisoning or inference attacks, and adaptability to evolving regulatory frameworks need further research [6], [7].

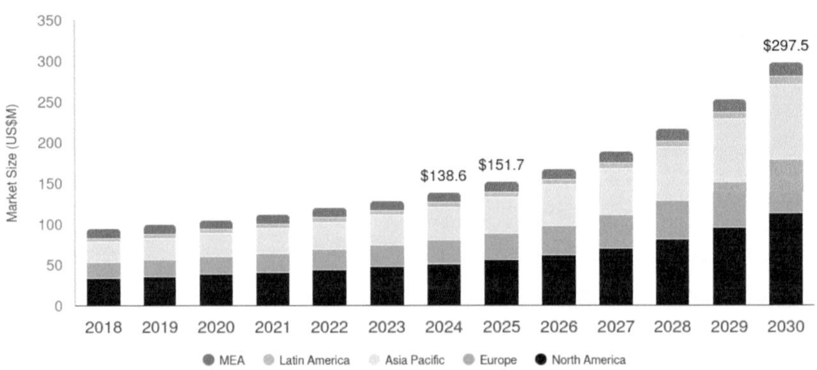

Figure 1: Federated learning market size by region and growth forecast for 2025–2030 [10].

Recent information underlines the need for improvements in fraud detection. In 2023, Visa used AI to prevent $40 billion in fraudulent activities. Meanwhile, 90% of financial institutions already use AI to combat fraud reporting 40–60% reductions in fraud losses and a significant drop in false-positives. All this is in response to the rise in AI-fueled criminal activities, which is now more than half of all fraud cases [8], [9].

Federated learning is a strategic enhancement because it enables multiple organizations to cooperate in model training without necessarily disclosing sensitive information. The global FL market was valued at an estimated USD 138 million in 2024 and is set to reach nearly USD 297 million by 2030. Figure 1 depicts an analysis report for the growth estimation of the FL market size in the banking and insurance sectors. In this regard, FL implementation is expected to yield revenues close to USD 69 million by 2030, underlining its future importance in financial services [10], [11].

The chapter provides a structured overview of the FL techniques that form the basis for domain-specific privacy approaches, including secure aggregation, differential privacy, and homomorphic encryption; practical case studies in financial contexts; and a discussion of existing challenges. In conclusion, it outlines future pathways toward scalable, secure, and reliable FL in financial services.

2. Literature Review

This review demonstrates that although federated learning applications in finance are increasing, research remains focused on the balance between both these aspects: privacy/security and performance/scalability. Another recent comprehensive survey has also underlined some of the ongoing challenges: non-IID data distributions, client diversity, communication delays, and adversarial risks [12]. Adding differential privacy or encryption to models in finance often reduces model performance unless carefully tuned, and scalability across a large number of institutions remains an open issue [13].

2.1 Federated Learning in Financial Applications

Federated Learning offers a collaborative approach to training AI models in a decentralized manner while keeping sensitive financial information private. Liu et al. [5] addressed the communication bottleneck by introducing gradient sparsification schemes along with secure aggregation protocols, which reduced the upload cost to 2.9–18.9% of traditional FL with full accuracy preservation for non-IID cases. Yang [14] discussed various FL settings, namely, horizontal, vertical, and federated transfer learning, for credit risk assessment problems under differential privacy guarantees and found that the tuning of the DP parameters balances privacy and model performance on the Fair Isaac Corporation (FICO) dataset.

2.2 Identifying Fraud and Financial Offenses

Hybrid FL models have shown great potential in detecting financial crime and fraud. Zhang et al. [15] introduced a hybrid system intended to protect privacy in distributed transactions and account-feature data that could stand up against collaborative adversarial assaults. Awosika et al. [1] integrated FL with explainable AI (XAI) in an effort to bring greater transparency into fraudulent behavior among these institutions and emphasized that interpretability enhances trust in the model while ensuring that privacy is maintained. Very recently, Khan et al. [16] presented Fed-RD, designed to handle both vertically and horizontally divided financial transaction data, by leveraging differential privacy and secure multiparty computation (SMPC) for high accuracy while ensuring robust end-to-end privacy protections.

2.3 Cryptographic Methods and Secure Aggregation

Cryptographic tools that enhance privacy are essential for secure FL. Previous research has examined fully and linearly homomorphic encryption (FHE and LHE), SMPC, and blockchain-oriented verifiability. A detailed study by Multidisciplinary Digital Publishing Institute (MDPI) [17] addressed trade-offs: Cheon-Kim-Kim-Song (CKKS) based methods are more effective than Paillier for large-scale applications, while secure aggregation of encrypted updates is still computationally expensive. Extra frameworks have incorporated blockchain for verifiability and gradient integrity assessments, improving resilience against model poisoning while maintaining privacy [18].

Table 1 summarizes and compares the prior research work done by various researchers for financial data privacy using federated learning. This table explains the year of study, the application area, the setting of FL, privacy mechanisms, the results, and the known limitations.

Table 1: Study comparison in federated learning for financial applications.

Study	*Application*	*FL Approach*	*Privacy Mechanism(s)*	*Main Idea/ Result*	*Limitations*
Aljunaid et al. [4] (2025)	Banking fraud	FL + explainability	FL + transparency tooling	Explainable FL to aid compliance and trust	Latency in real-world communications; cost not deeply quantified
Yang [14] (2025)	Credit risk	H/V/FTL design study	Differential privacy	Tuning DP balances privacy utility on FICO	Utility drop at strict ε; no large-scale multi-bank deployment results
Deng et al. [17] (2025)	Edge FL in finance	Edge FL + blockchain	Fully Homomorphic encryption	Verifiable, encrypted edge aggregation	FHE cost; client devices compute; battery constraints

Contd...

Study	*Application*	*FL Approach*	*Privacy Mechanism(s)*	*Main Idea/ Result*	*Limitations*
Shalabi et al. [19] (2025)	FL privacy techniques	–	Multiple (performance + security)	Side-by-side technique comparison	Few real-bank datasets; synthetic bias risks
Awosika et al. [20] (2024)	Cross-bank fraud detection	HFL with XAI overlays	XAI for transparency; general FL protections	Improves Inter-institution fraud detection; preserves interpretability	XAI explanations may leak signals if not combined with formal privacy; limited discussion of scalability under non-IID
Mahato et al. [18] (2024)	Verifiable FL	Blockchain-assisted	HE + blockchain audit	Tamper-evident training with privacy	Chain throughput and governance; added latency
Khan et al. [16] (2024)	Financial crime detection	Handles vertical + horizontal splits	DP + SMPC	High accuracy with end-to-end privacy	Computation/ latency of SMPC; integration complexity in banks
Liu et al. [5] (2023)	Financial applications	HFL with gradient sparsification	Secure aggregation + compression	Upload cost cut to 2.9–18.9% versus vanilla FL with accuracy maintained on non-IID	Compression/ privacy trade-offs under adversaries not fully characterized
Aziz et al. [21] (2023)	Privacy tech for FL	–	HE + DP	Mapping of HE/DP choices	Limited finance -specific operational benchmarks
Zhang et al. [15] (2023)	Financial crime detection	Hybrid FL (HFL + VFL)	Privacy -preserving hybrid aggregation	Resilient To collaborative adversaries	Overhead of hybrid pipelines; unclear governance/ incentives model
Sun et al. [22] (2022)	Core method (used in finance)	Decentralized FedAvg	–	Removes single aggregator bottleneck	Convergence under heterogeneity; robustness to poisoning
Efe [23] (2021)	Credit scoring (multi-institution)	Vertical FL	Secure vertical training (logit/ boosting)	Improves scorecards without data pooling	Entity matching, key-linkage, and DP utility trade-offs

2.4 Research Gaps in the Literature

- A majority of researches show either privacy solutions or accuracy improvements, but only a small number present audit-compliant processes with logging, explainability, data-minimization evidence, or certification documents appropriate for genuine AML/fraud management. Therefore, end-to-end evaluations of regulatory quality are limited.
- Privacy cost models are insufficient. There is a lack of extensive measurement regarding compute/latency/network expenses for DP/HE/SMPC at production levels, particularly for edge or hybrid FL. There is importance of TCO models that compare secure aggregation and compression with HE/SMPC hybrid approaches [18].
- Non-IID and fairness amid banking diversity are insufficiently examined. Studies recognize non-IID and client diversity; nonetheless, distribution shift, minority-class fairness, and cross-bank calibration are infrequently evaluated at scale using legally significant fairness metrics. The authors have identified non-IID and variability in reference [24], highlighting the absence of fairness assessments and stratified performance evaluations.
- Adversarial resilience surpassing simplistic dangers. Numerous studies fail to properly assess Byzantine, backdoor, model-inversion, or colluding insider threats within realistic banking consortia; formal threat models and red-team evaluations are scarce [25].
- Data connection and identity clarification pose challenges for credit risk and AML in vertical federated learning (VFL). Protocols that ensure both accuracy and privacy remain scarce in real-world applications.
- Multi-bank consortia require data assessment, incentive distribution, and free-rider prevention. The market-design and game-theoretic aspects are less developed compared to the crypto/privacy infrastructure. This is recognized as a standard research gap.
- Blockchain, TEEs, and attestation enhance auditability, yet their latency, throughput, and governance expenses remain inadequately measured in finance-related contexts; there is a need for comparative research.

3. Foundations and Architecture of Federated Learning in Financial Services

Federated learning is a decentralized machine learning approach that allows various organizations such as banks, insurance companies, and payment networks to jointly develop a common model while keeping raw data on-site. Rather, every participant trains locally using their own data and only sends model updates to a central organizer for consolidation. This method maintains data locality, lowers privacy risks, and facilitates adherence to data protection laws.

The most widely used algorithm is the one proposed by Sun et al. [22], where each client performs multiple rounds of local stochastic gradient descent before uploading updated model weights to be averaged globally. FedAvg exhibits solid generalization performance with reduced communication overhead and is therefore widely adopted in various federated finance applications.

3.1 Privacy-Enhancing Mechanisms in FL

Several cryptography-based techniques are integrated into FL systems to maintain security and privacy across model aggregation:

- **Secure Aggregation:** It encrypts personal model updates in such a way that only the combined result is visible while protecting each participant's input.
- **Differential Privacy:** It adds noise to updates for preventing an inference attack while keeping the usefulness [19], [21].
- **Homomorphic Encryption:** It allows computations such as aggregation on encrypted information without needing decryption. Among these are the Paillier cryptosystem and CKKS, enabling secure gradient aggregation in financially sensitive contexts [26].
- **Secure Multi-Party Computation:** This enables collaborative computation among entities while keeping private inputs confidential. This is often used in conjunction with blockchain for verification and gradient integrity checks [27].

Recent practical systems such as FedMLHE show how targeted encryption of sensitive parameters can greatly lower computation and bandwidth costs while maintaining robust privacy protections [28]. Table 2 summarizes and compares all the privacy techniques used in financial sectors with parameters such as cost of computation, scalability, usability, and their strengths and limitations.

3.2 FL Architectures for Financial Applications

Three unique FL architectures are pertinent in collaborative efforts within the financial sector.

- **Horizontal Federated Learning (HFL):** Organizations (A and B) possess comparable feature spaces yet retain distinct user populations, for example, various retail banks holding transaction information. They have similar customer level data and their goal is to train fraud detection model.
- **Vertical Federated Learning:** Organizations possess distinct feature sets regarding shared user groups, such as a financial institution and an

insurance provider exchanging client identities. Research indicates that VFL can improve models such as credit scorecards while preserving privacy through federated logistic regression and enhancement methods such as SecureBoost [19], [23].

Table 2: Comparison of privacy-enhancing mechanisms in finance.

Mechanism	*Computational Cost*	*Scalability*	*Practical Adoption in Finance*	*Strengths*	*Limitations*
Secure Aggregation	Low–moderate: lightweight encryption; overhead increases with the number of clients but remains controllable through gradient compression	High scalability; supports large numbers of clients	Widely adopted in fraud detection consortia, AML pilots	Efficient; simple integration; prevents server from viewing individual updates	Susceptible to collusion attacks; fails to safeguard against harmful clients
Differential Privacy (DP)	Minimal computational cost; incorporates random noise into gradients/ updates	Handles many clients effectively; noise increases with additional participants	Growing use in credit risk assessment, fraud prevention within GDPR/CCPA guidelines	Robust theoretical assurances; effortless to incorporate with FL optimizers	Loss of utility if privacy budget is overly strict; Precise adjustments needed
Homomorphic Encryption (HE)	High: encryption/ decryption and homomorphic operations are costly; recent schemes such as CKKS and Paillier improve efficiency	Moderate: operates with smaller to medium networks; not yet feasible for very deep models	Pilot deployments in AML detection, cross-bank collaboration with HE and SMPC	Allows calculations performed directly on encrypted information; robust security assurances	Heavy computation and communication overhead; slower training
Secure Multi- Party Computation (SMPC)	High: necessitates collaborative protocols among participants	Moderate scalability; communication-heavy	Utilized in critical applications such as collaborative AML detection and regulatory experiments	Robust privacy protections; immune to collusion	Elevated latency; intricate setup; necessitates reliable infrastructure

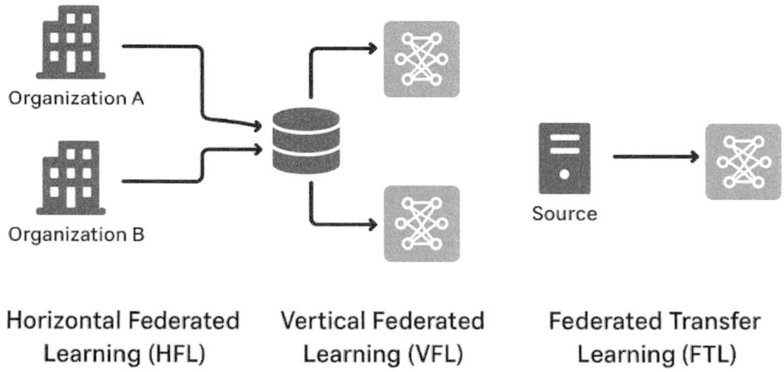

Figure 2: Types of FL architectures in financial services.

- **Federated Transfer Learning/Hybrid FL:** Allows different organizations with the least number of shared features and users to collaborate by combining federated optimization and transfer learning. This solves data diversity and domain discrepancy challenges [29].

Figure 2 illustrates the flow of information in financial services using various FL architectures.

3.3 System Issues and Design Factors

Several technical and operational challenges are associated with implementing FL in finance. They have an impact on how FL systems are designed in financial settings, balancing privacy, performance, scalability, and regulatory compliance.

- **Non-IID Data Distributions:** The datasets in clients are often very different across institutions, which introduces difficulties in convergence and reduces model fairness. FedAvg may require more rounds and has an inconsistent performance in the presence of heterogeneity [24].
- **Communication Overhead:** HE, DP, and secure aggregation methods result in larger model updates. On the other hand, some methods reduce overhead without sacrificing privacy, which includes quantization, sparsification, and selective aggregation [30].
- **Adversarial Risks:** There are poisoning or harmful updates of the model and membership inference attacks leveraging gradient data. Defenses in place include privacy protections such as DP, anomaly detection, and blockchain audit trails [6], [21].
- **Regulatory and Explainability Requirements:** Regulations require transparency and auditability. We want the system to support explainable AI in model interpretation and ensure traceability with privacy preservation [29].

4. Real-World Deployments in Financial Services

The three main uses of FL models in financial applications are the subject of this section. The following is a description of them:

4.1 Credit Risk Assessment

Zhang et al. [31] explored federated learning for credit risk prediction, demonstrating that FL models significantly outperform the local models for underrepresented clients in imbalanced datasets, achieving average performance gains of approximately 17.9% for smaller institutions leveraging architectures such as Multi-Layer Perceptron (MLP), Long Short-Term Memory (LSTM), and XGBoost in non-IID settings. A recent study by MDPI [32] evaluated an improved federated deep-learning model against FedAvg and FedProx for personal credit assessment. FL and DL achieved accuracy comparable to centralized training and superior to traditional federated methods, with the number of clients and training rounds becoming larger. These studies suggest that FL equalizes access to the strong global model, facilitating small entities in particular, while keeping data private.

4.2 Fraud Detection across Financial Institutions

A recent MDPI study [33] presented a hybrid model that incorporates a variational autoencoder with QLSTM frameworks in performing real-time fraud detection in banking sectors. The resulting multilevel aggregation thus allowed institutions to share knowledge while maintaining the confidentiality of local transactions. This led to a much more powerful identification of fraud patterns across different data domains. Another deployment in which Flower is executed on AWS SageMaker shows real-world federated fraud detection. Several financial organizations collaborate on a training-framework-independent FL pipeline over decentralized datasets. This results in improved detection accuracy and reduced false-positives while respecting regulatory constraints on sharing raw data [34]. In addition, the collaboration that Swift leads with Google Cloud and Capgemini keeps the focus on leveraging FL for fighting payment fraud. In this, banks train local models that upload encrypted updates to a central server, yielding a global model that adapts quickly to new fraud trends while improving intelligence sharing among banks [33].

4.3 Anti-Money Laundering and Financial Crime Detection

The Private Vertical FL for Anti-Money Laundering (PV4AML) solution from IBM Research [35], presented for the US/UK Privacy-Enhancing Technologies Prize, demonstrates vertical FL in hybrid settings. Features engineered at both the payment network and banking levels are aggregated via homomorphic encryption and SMPC to train random forest ensembles for AML detection without sharing raw account or transaction data. The proof of concept by the Soteria Initiative [36] on how federated systems, when applied to AML/ Countering the Financing of Terrorism (CFT) contexts, can detect cross-entity anomalies while maintaining regulatory compliance and institutional privacy was reviewed by Bureau of Indian Standards (BIS) after bank collaboration. Lucinity's patented Secure Lockbox technology [37] improves FL for AML by incorporating HE and DP to share encrypted features across institutions. This decreases false-positive rates and increases the detection of complex money laundering activities while protecting Personally Indentifiable Information (PII).

In all these studies, federated learning has shown its capability of improving predictive performance, in particular for fraud detection and credit risk, while leaving the raw data in its origin. Most importantly, cryptographic techniques such as SMPC, HE, and DP support trust and ensure conformance to strict regulations. Table 3 outlines the summary of the above-mentioned case studies regarding the approach followed in those and the main benefits achieved.

Table 3: FL architecture used in case studies and their benefits.

Use Case	*Approach and Architecture*	*Benefits Highlighted*
Credit Risk	Horizontal FL, DL training, handling data imbalance	Improved accuracy for smaller banks; global model parity
Fraud	Hybrid models (Variational Autoencoder + Quantum Long Short-Term Memory), cluster + global aggregation	Enhanced cross-bank detection; lower false-positives
AML	Vertical and hybrid FL; homomorphic encryption, SMPC, DP	Secure cross-entity collaboration; strong privacy compliance

5. Fundamental Technical Challenges in Financial FL

FL is a technology that makes data safer and more private by training models in a way that is decentralized and collaborative. But it does have some technical problems that are explained in the following text:

- **Non-IID and Model Heterogeneity:** Financial datasets from the real world often exhibit non-independent and identically distributed characteristics among various institutions; heterogeneous customer profiles, transaction type, and risk profiles impede convergence. Different IT infrastructures cause model heterogeneity variations in architecture, which makes aggregation less efficient. Recent assessments underscore statistical, device, communication, and model diversity as significant impediments to extensive federated implementations [38].
- **Effects on Performance and Scalability:** Adding privacy-preserving technologies such as homomorphic encryption and secure multi-party computation makes computing and communicating much more difficult.

According to National Institute of Standards and Technology (NIST), unless scalable, optimized solutions are developed, these overheads hinder both horizontal and vertical FL scenarios [39].

- **Threat Assessment and Robust Security:** In federated finance, adversarial threats such as advanced inference attacks, Byzantine poisoning, and backdoor attacks continue to present serious risks. According to current taxonomies, there is still a deficiency in choosing realistic threat models and coordinating defenses, especially when it comes to dealing with fully unlawful insiders or regulators as potential hazards [25].
- **Efficiency in Communication:** Communication is still a problem, particularly when using encrypted or differentially private high-dimensional model updates. Methods comprising adaptive compression, customer selection, layer extraction, and knowledge distillation have shown a substantial decrease of up to 80–90% in computational cost while preserving model accuracy [40].
- **Differences Between Theory and Practice:** In non-convex, diverse environments, many FL algorithms lack robust theoretical guarantees regarding convergence, generalization, and privacy trade-offs. Research on bridging the gap between complex real-world financial systems and small-scale experiments is crucial [41].

6. Emerging Research Directions

The future research paths that will improve the use of federated learning in the financial industry are described in this section. The following is a description of them.

- **Dependable Federated Learning Structures:** Interpretability, fairness, robustness, and accountability should all be integrated directly into FL pipelines in future systems. According to surveys, accredited FL frameworks and structured trust evaluation criteria are becoming more popular [42].
- **Blockchain and Smart Contract-Powered Architectures:** Blockchain-enabled decentralized aggregation and inspection offer promising solutions for trust, tamper-resistant integrity, and data coordination, especially in vertical FL scenarios where entity alignment is crucial. These techniques can offer transparent governance and lessen non-IID effects [43].
- **Data Worth Economics and Motivational Structures:** The development of game-theoretic and incentive mechanisms for financially disparate institutions to collaborate fairly while balancing investments, data integrity, and privacy costs is a significant gap [44].

- **Edge Integration and Hybrid FL Methods:** Innovative frameworks for fluid financial systems are created by combining transfer learning, reinforcement learning, neurosymbolic AI, and edge computing. These frameworks are especially useful for fraud detection and instantaneous transaction oversight in edge-enabled locations [45].
- **Uniformity and Regulatory Structures:** Standardized formats for data, systems of governance, and certification schemes are essential for international data exchange and open finance. To develop auditability, understanding, and compliance norms for FL systems in finance, regulators, industry associations, and certification bodies must work together [46].

The research agenda and future strategies for implementing trustworthy and safe federated learning systems in the financial industry are outlined in Table 4. This will achieve a balance between industry compliance and innovation.

Table 4: Future directions in various challenge areas.

Challenge Area	*Future Direction*
Data/Model Heterogeneity	Federated augmentation, multi-task objectives, adaptive weighting, HeteroFL
Scalability and Efficiency	Layer-wise compression, distillation, lightweight cryptography
Security and Trust	Byzantine-resilient aggregation, formal threat modeling, trustworthy AI pillars
Incentives and Collaboration	Mechanism design, data valuation systems, fair federation economics
Regulatory Alignment	Standard APIs, certification guidelines, explainable models, transparent logs

7. Key Takeaways and Recommendations for Stakeholders

Federated learning offers a way to use data from several institutions while upholding regulatory requirements and confidentiality. By encouraging cooperative model training among banks, FL also enhances the process of identifying fraud and assessing credit risk. It simultaneously lessens the requirement for unprocessed data transfers. Data protection is further strengthened by incorporating privacy-enhancing technologies, making FL an appropriate response to laws such as GDPR and open banking standards.

When compared to isolated models, FL can provide significant performance benefits, such as a 10–15% increase in fraud detection rates and a 30% decrease in false-positives. Industry pilots such as the Asia-Pacific AML consortia and the European Payments Initiative serve as examples of this. Similarly, case studies demonstrate that even smaller institutions benefit greatly from using robust global models while supplying less data, fostering a more equitable AI ecosystem.

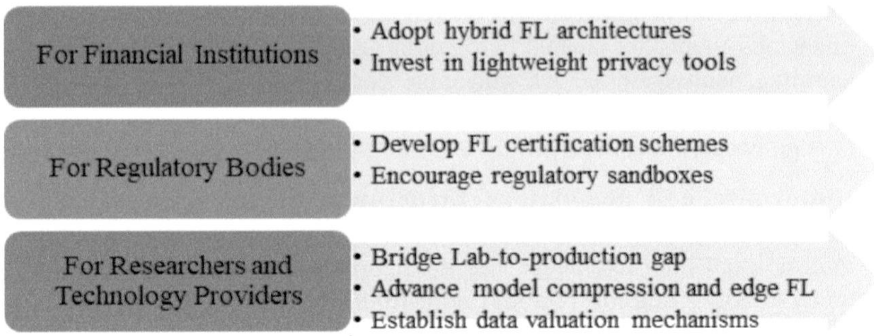

Figure 3: Recommendations for stakeholders.

A few suggestions are made for stakeholders such as banking, regulatory bodies, academics, and tech suppliers in Figure 3. To improve opportunities for collaboration across different financial subsectors, financial institutions must adopt hybrid FL frameworks by combining horizontal and vertical FL. Scalable techniques for safe aggregation with lower computational costs are offered by lightweight privacy solutions such as Intel HEXL and OpenMined's PySyft.

Frameworks for FL certification should be developed by standard organizations and regulatory bodies. Similar to ISO/IEC 5259, these frameworks develop verifiable, transparency-focused standards for guaranteeing the dependability of AI models in collaborative settings. Regulatory sandboxes that can expedite the verification of FL-based AML and fraud detection systems while upholding international standards should be supported by the organizations.

By using meta-learning and multi-task learning structures to guarantee stable convergence, academicians and tech suppliers should strive to improve FL for non-IID scenarios. Particularly for branch-level or cellular banking implementations, encouraging compression of models and edge FL reduces bandwidth through pruning, quantization, and data distillation. They should create data valuation systems, such as Shapley value pricing and bidding-based FL marketplaces, which look into incentive-aligned structures for equitable sharing of benefits among data providers.

Due to developments in privacy-preserving methods and the availability of reasonably priced cryptographic solutions, federated learning is expected to become a regulatory-compliant, industry-wide standard for AI applications in the finance sector by the late 2020s. By encouraging cooperation between competing institutions, FL enhances AI efficacy and fosters a collaborative, innovation-driven financial ecosystem where compliance and trust are important.

8. Conclusion

Federated learning represents a revolution in improving artificial intelligence in financial services while protecting privacy and security. Unlike the traditional centralized model, FL allows institutions to jointly train a model without directly sharing data, addressing one of the most important challenges to AI adoption in finance—compliance with stringent data protection laws. In this respect, FL can help financial institutions promote innovation without sacrificing confidentiality through the use of privacy-preserving techniques such as secure aggregation, homomorphic encryption, and differential privacy.

The chapter focuses on how FL helps significant financial purposes, including fraud detection, credit scoring, and anti-money laundering, in an open environment where even smaller entities can benefit from mutual intelligence. However, there are still many challenges that continue to persist. Challenges in data variability, high computation and communication costs, vulnerability to adversarial attacks, and gaps between theoretical guarantees and practical implementation reduce scalability and reliability. Overcoming such challenges requires collaborative strategies that bring together advances in cryptography, distributed learning, regulation, and financial economics.

In the future, the way forward for federated learning in financial services rests on the development of secure, verifiable, and incentive-aligned mechanisms. Standardization efforts, regulatory frameworks, and blockchain-based verification will be key to trust and compliance. Meanwhile, advances in lightweight privacy solutions, hybrid FL frameworks, and incentive-driven collaboration strategies ensure that FL remains both technically viable and economically sustainable.

Federated learning can therefore reshape the future of secure AI within financial services, providing not only a key technical fix but also a strategic route toward responsible innovation through integrating privacy, performance, and regulatory compliance. It offers an avenue for the financial industry to leverage AI equitably, clearly, and sustainably.

References

[1] Awosika, T., Shukla, R. M. and Pranggono, B. (2024). Transparency and privacy: The role of explainable AI and federated learning in financial fraud detection. *IEEE Access*, 12: 64551–64560.

[2] Gosselin, R., Vieu, L., Loukil, F. and Benoit, A. (2022). Privacy and security in federated learning: A survey. *Applied Sciences*, 12(19): 9901.

[3] Wen, J., Zhang, Z., Lan, Y., Cui, Z., Cai, J. and Zhang, W. (2023). A survey on federated learning: Challenges and applications. *International Journal of Machine Learning and Cybernetics*, 14(2): 513–535.

[4] Aljunaid, S. K., Almheiri, S. J., Dawood, H. and Khan, M. A. (2025). Secure and transparent banking: Explainable AI-driven federated learning model for financial fraud detection. *Journal of Risk and Financial Management*, 18(4): 179.

[5] Liu, T., Wang, Z., He, H., Shi, W., Lin, L., An, R. et al. (2023). Efficient and secure federated learning for financial applications. *Applied Sciences*, 13(10): 5877.

[6] Saha, S., Hota, A., Chattopadhyay, A. K., Nag, A. and Nandi, S. (2024). A multi-faceted survey on privacy preservation of federated learning: Progress, challenges, and opportunities. *Artificial Intelligence Review*, 57(7): 184.

[7] Lyu, L., Yu, H., Ma, X., Chen, C., Sun, L., Zhao, J. et al. (2022). Privacy and robustness in federated learning: Attacks and defenses. *IEEE Transactions on Neural Networks and Learning Systems*, 35(7): 8726–8746.

[8] Visa prevented $40 billion worth of fraudulent transactions in 2023—official, https://www.reuters.com/technology/cybersecurity/visa-prevented-40-bln-worth-fraudulent-transactions-2023-official-2024-07-23/accessed: 2025-09-01.
[9] More than 50% of fraud involves the use of artificial intelligence, https://www.feedzai.com/inthenews/more-than-50-of-fraud-involves-the-use-of-artificial-intelligence/,accessed: 2025-09-01.
[10] Federated learning market size, share & trends report. (2025). https://www.grandviewresearch.com/industry-analysis/federated-learning-market-report, accessed: 2025-09-06.
[11] BFSI—federated learning market statistics. (2025). https://www.grandviewresearch.com/horizon/statistics/federated-learning-market/industry-vertical/bfsi/global? accessed: 2025-09-06.
[12] Orabi, M. M., Emam, O. and Fahmy, H. (2025). Adapting security and decentralized knowledge enhancement in federated learning using blockchain technology: Literature review. *Journal of Big Data*, 12(1): 55.
[13] Varma, S. C. G. and Chaudhari, B. (2025). Federated learning in financial data privacy: A secure AI framework for banking applications. *International Journal of Emerging Trends in Computer Science and Information Technology*, 101–110.
[14] Yang, Z. (2025). Privacy-aware financial risk control: A federated learning approach with differential privacy optimization. *Journal of Computer Technology and Software*, 4(4).
[15] Zhang, H., Hong, J., Dong, F., Drew, S., Xue, L. and Zhou, J. (2023). A privacy-preserving hybrid federated learning framework for financial crime detection. arXiv preprint arXiv:2302.03654.
[16] Khan, M. S. I., Gupta, A., Seneviratne, O. and Patterson, S. (2024). Fedrd: Privacy-preserving federated learning for financial crime detection. In: *2024 IEEE Symposium on Computational Intelligence for Financial Engineering and Economics (CIFEr), IEEE*, pp. 1–9.
[17] Deng, Y., Guo, B. and Chen, S. (2025). Privacy-preserving approach to edge federated learning based on blockchain and fully homomorphic encryption. Electronics, 14(2): 361.
[18] Mahato, G. K., Banerjee, A., Chakraborty, S. K. and Gao, X. -Z. (2024). Privacy preserving verifiable federated learning scheme using blockchain and homomorphic encryption. *Applied Soft Computing*, 167: 112405.
[19] Shalabi, E., Khedr, W., Rushdy, E. and Salah, A. (2025). A comparative study of privacy-preserving techniques in federated learning: A performance and security analysis. *Information*, 16(3): 244.
[20] Awosika, T., Shukla, R. M. and Pranggono, B. (2024). Transparency and privacy: The role of explainable AI and federated learning in financial fraud detection. *IEEE Access*, 12: 64551–64560. doi:10.1109/ACCESS.2024.3394528.
[21] Aziz, R., Banerjee, S., Bouzefrane, S. and Le Vinh, T. (2023). Exploring homomorphic encryption and differential privacy techniques towards secure federated learning paradigm. *Future Internet*, 15(9): 310.
[22] Sun, T., Li, D. and Wang, B. (2022). Decentralized federated averaging. *IEEE Transactions on Pattern Analysis and Machine Intelligence*, 45(4): 4289–4301.
[23] Efe, Y. (2021). A vertical federated learning method for multi-institutional credit scoring: Mics. arXiv preprint arXiv:2111.09038.
[24] Lu, Z., Pan, H., Dai, Y., Si, X. and Zhang, Y. (2024), Federated learning with non-IID data: A survey. *IEEE Internet of Things Journal*, 11(11): 19188–19209.
[25] Berkani, M. R. A., Chouchane, A., Himeur, Y., Ouamane, A., Miniaoui, S. et al. (2025). Advances in federated learning: Applications and challenges in smart building environments and beyond. *Computers*, 14(4): 124.
[26] Shenoy, D., Bhat, R. and Krishna Prakasha, K. (2025). Exploring privacy mechanisms and metrics in federated learning. *Artificial Intelligence Review*, 58(8): 223.
[27] Zhao, C., Zhao, S., Zhao, M., Chen, Z., Gao, C. -Z., Li, H. et al. (2019). Secure multi-party computation: Theory, practice and applications. *Information Sciences*, 476: 357–372.

[28] Jin, W., Yao, Y., Han, S., Gu, J., Joe-Wong, C., Ravi, S., Avestimehr, S., He, C. et al. (2023). FedML-HE: An efficient homomorphic-encryption-based privacy-preserving federated learning system. arXiv preprint arXiv:2303.10837.

[29] Yin, X., Zhu, Y. and Hu, J. (2021). A comprehensive survey of privacy-preserving federated learning: A taxonomy, review, and future directions. *ACM Computing Surveys (CSUR)*, 54(6): 1–36.

[30] Moshawrab, M., Adda, M., Bouzouane, A., Ibrahim, H. and Raad, A. (2023). Reviewing federated learning aggregation algorithms: strategies, contributions, limitations and future perspectives. *Electronics*, 12(10): 2287.

[31] Zhang, S., Tay, J. and Baiz, P. (2024). The effects of data imbalance under a federated learning approach for credit risk forecasting. arXiv preprint arXiv:2401.07234.

[32] Mu, S., Liu, B., Lien, C. and Nadia, N. (2023). Optimization of personal credit evaluation based on a federated deep learning model. *Mathematics*, 11(21): 4499.

[33] Abbassi, H., El Mendili, S. and Gahi, Y. (2025). Adaptive, privacy-enhanced real-time fraud detection in banking networks through federated learning and VAE–QLSTM fusion. *Big Data and Cognitive Computing*, 9(7): 185.

[34] Arora, S., Beams, A., Chatzigiannis, P., Meiser, S., Patel, K., Raghuraman, S. et al. (2024). Privacy-preserving financial anomaly detection via federated learning & multi-party computation. In *2024 Annual Computer Security Applications Conference Workshops (ACSAC Workshops)*, IEEE, pp. 270–279.

[35] Building privacy-preserving federated learning to help fight financial crime, https://research.ibm.com/blog/privacy-preserving-federated-learning-finance, accessed: 2025-11-26 (5 May 2023).

[36] The sum of parts-federated learning enables anti-financial crime cross-entity collaboration, https://medium.com/soteria-initiative/the-sum-of-parts-federated-learning-enables-anti-financial-crime-cross-entity accessed: 2025-11-26 (27 March 2025).

[37] Federated learning in fincrime: How financial institutions can fight crime without sensitive data sharing, https://lucinity.com/blog/federated-learning-in-fincrime-how-financial-institutions-can-fight-crime-wit accessed: 2025-11-26 (19 Nov 2024).

[38] Teo, Z. L., Jin, L., Liu, N., Li, S., Miao, D., Zhang, X. et al. (2024). Federated machine learning in healthcare: A systematic review on clinical applications and technical architecture. *Cell Reports Medicine*, 5(2).

[39] Kim, K., Raghavan, K., Kotevska, O., Dorier, M., Madduri, R., Ryu, M. et al. (2024). Privacy-preserving federated learning for science: Challenges and research directions. In *2024 IEEE International Conference on Big Data (BigData)*, IEEE, pp. 7849–7853.

[40] Guembe, B., Misra, S. and Azeta, A. (2024). Privacy issues, attacks, countermeasures and open problems in federated learning: A survey. *Applied Artificial Intelligence*, 38(1): 2410504.

[41] Ye, M., Fang, X., Du, B., Yuen, P. C. and Tao, D. (2023). Heterogeneous federated learning: State-of-the-art and research challenges. *ACM Computing Surveys*, 56(3): 1–44.

[42] Tariq, A., Serhani, M. A., Sallabi, F., Qayyum, T., Barka, E. S. and Shuaib, K. A. (2023). Trustworthy federated learning: A survey. arXiv preprint arXiv:2305.11537.

[43] Zhang, F., Zhang, Y., Ji, S. and Han, Z. (2024). Secure and decentralized federated learning framework with non-IID data based on blockchain. *Heliyon*, 10(5).

[44] Tu, X., Zhu, K., Luong, N. C., Niyato, D., Zhang, Y. and Li, J. (2022). Incentive mechanisms for federated learning: From economic and game theoretic perspective. *IEEE Transactions on Cognitive Communications and Networking*, 8(3): 1566–1593.

[45] Brecko, A., Kajati, E., Koziorek, J. and Zolotova, I. (2022). Federated learning for edge computing: A survey. *Applied Sciences*, 12(18): 9124.

[46] Raza, S. A., Syed, D., Rizwan, S. and Ahmed, M. (2025). Regulatory, governance and future trends in the financial system. In *The Global Evolution, Changing Landscape and Future of Financial Markets*, Emerald Publishing Limited, pp. 97–118.

10 Cross-Border Collaboration and Data Exchange

Donkor Nawaah,[1,*] Joseph Tufuor Kwarteng[2] and Solomon Jeresa[3]

As financial institutions worldwide seek to harness the transformative potential of artificial intelligence (AI), cross-border data collaboration has become both a strategic imperative and a complex challenge. Conventional data-sharing models often struggle under the pressures of divergent regulatory regimes, geopolitical sensitivities, and ethical concerns surrounding privacy and control. In this context, federated learning emerges as a compelling alternative, enabling institutions to collaboratively develop AI models while preserving data sovereignty and minimizing regulatory exposure. This chapter critically examines federated learning as a mechanism for enabling secure and effective cross-border collaboration among financial institutions operating in heterogeneous legal and technological environments. Drawing on illustrative global case studies, it explores partnerships among European banks operating under the General Data Protection Regulation (GDPR), Asian financial institutions constrained by stringent data residency requirements, and African fintech ecosystems striving for innovation, inclusion, and protection against data exploitation. Through these cases, the chapter highlights both the technical feasibility and the institutional complexities of operationalizing federated AI across jurisdictions. Beyond technological architecture, the discussion interrogates the broader sociopolitical and ethical dimensions that shape cross-border data exchange. Key tensions are examined, including trust versus transparency, innovation versus regulatory compliance, and global scalability versus local accountability. The chapter emphasizes that successful implementation requires not only robust infrastructure but also shared

1 Assistant Professor and Area Chair, Department of Finance and Accounting, Woxsen University, Hyderabad, Telangana, India.
2 Professor, Department of Business and Social Sciences Education, University of Cape Coast, Cape Coast, Central Region, Ghana.
3 Research Assistant, Huddersfield Business School, University of Huddersfield, West Yorkshire, United Kingdom.
Emails: jtkwarteng@ucc.edu.gh; solomon.jeresa@hud.ac.uk
* Corresponding author: donkor.nawaah@woxsen.edu.in

DOI: 10.1201/9781003710059-10

governance frameworks, mutual trust, and ethical alignment among participating entities. By integrating insights from AI governance, financial regulation, and international collaboration, this chapter challenges prevailing assumptions about data ownership, power asymmetries, and cooperation in a fragmented digital economy. It ultimately positions federated learning as a pragmatic yet transformative pathway for advancing responsible financial AI while respecting national boundaries, institutional autonomy, and societal values.

1. Introduction

Financial institutions increasingly rely on artificial intelligence to enhance operational efficiency, reduce fraud, automate risk assessment, and deliver personalized services. Yet, the transformative promise of AI is fundamentally inhibited by the limitations of the data on which it learns [1–5]. Financial data is inherently fragmented across jurisdictions, shaped by regulatory environments, and influenced by national agendas that prioritize privacy, autonomy, and economic competitiveness. Traditional approaches to cooperation rely on centralized databases, interbank exchanges, or secure clearinghouses; these models were originally designed for transaction sharing or compliance documentation, not for training complex machine learning algorithms at scale. As the world's financial landscape becomes increasingly digitized, centralized datasets no longer suffice to address evolving security threats, cross-border money laundering, and discriminatory lending outcomes. The resulting asymmetry in access to data creates a new form of digital inequality that disproportionately affects emerging markets and institutions lacking computational capacity or technical maturity [6], [7]. The rise of global digital finance coincides with the proliferation of regulatory regimes that restrict the movement of raw data [8–10]. Laws such as the General Data Protection Regulation (GDPR) in the European Union, the Personal Data Protection Act of Singapore, China's Personal Information Protection Law (PIPL), and various African data protection legislations have shifted the paradigm of data ownership and accountability [11], [12]. These frameworks were designed to protect citizens from surveillance capitalism, misuse of personal information, and predatory analytics. Yet, they inadvertently limit collaborative innovation by restricting cross-border data flows. The digital economy is thus trapped between two competing imperatives: the need for secure, responsible data governance, and the strategic demand to develop AI systems capable of learning from diverse global patterns of financial behavior. This paradox has motivated interest in alternative forms of collaboration that do not require the relocation or disclosure of sensitive information.

Federated learning offers an elegant, systemic solution to this challenge [13]. It reshapes the technical architecture of machine learning by allowing models to be trained on distributed datasets without centralizing them. Instead of moving data across borders, institutions exchange encrypted model parameters that reflect aggregated learning. This preserves the sovereignty of local data while enabling institutions to benefit from collective intelligence. Techniques such as differential privacy, secure aggregation, and homomorphic encryption prevent reverse engineering of model updates and reduce the risk of unauthorized access. Federated learning therefore provides a framework to achieve cross-border interoperability without undermining national regulatory frameworks or ethical principles. Its potential is particularly significant for financial institutions that must reconcile innovation with compliance.

The purpose of this chapter is to examine how federated learning can transform transnational financial collaboration by enabling secure, privacy-preserving artificial intelligence. Using a comparative geographic lens, the chapter explores how federated systems function within regions governed by disparate regulatory traditions. By situating European, Asian, and African financial institutions within their respective governance ecosystems, the chapter highlights both the risks and opportunities of cross-border AI cooperation. The inquiry moves beyond technical feasibility and asks deeper questions of equity, inclusion, and power distribution. It evaluates whether federated learning democratizes digital participation or whether it merely introduces a new form of algorithmic colonialism in which model hosts dominate the value chain. Ultimately, the chapter proposes a conceptual framework for cross-border federated learning that emphasizes trust, shared governance, and algorithmic accountability.

1.1 The Fractured Landscape of Financial Data

The digital financial ecosystem is characterized by systemic fragmentation [14], [15]. Financial transactions, customer identities, credit histories, biometric markers, and behavioral patterns are housed in insulated institutional silos. Even within nations, banks and fintech platforms rarely share proprietary customer data due to competitive pressures, intellectual property concerns, or cybersecurity vulnerabilities. Cross-border fragmentation is even more acute, as institutions must comply simultaneously with domestic regulatory regimes and international reporting obligations [16], [17]. Fragmentation is not merely a technical inconvenience; it is a structural barrier to collaboration. Large multinational banks typically possess access to diversified datasets, while regional or community-based financial institutions often lack scale. This asymmetry results in biased machine learning models that reinforce existing inequalities. Models trained solely on localized populations frequently fail when deployed across demographic or cultural contexts, generating misclassifications, denial of access to credit, or false-positive fraud alerts. Academic evidence shows that the accuracy and fairness of AI systems in finance are highly dependent on data diversity. Kairouz et al. demonstrate that distributed datasets combined through secure aggregation significantly improve model generalization compared with isolated learning approaches [18]. Such diversity is critical in domains such as anti-money laundering (AML), where the financial behavior of cross-border criminal networks often cannot be captured within regional datasets. Canhoto argue that global patterns of fraud require institutions to learn from transaction behaviors across cultures and currencies, and that fragmentation creates blind spots that sophisticated criminal actor's exploit [19]. The disjointed configuration of data ecosystems therefore limits the capacity of financial institutions to respond to emerging threats.

Fragmentation is reinforced by divergent interpretations of privacy and data ethics. Europe's regulatory culture privileges individual rights and consent-based governance [20], [21]. Asia tends to view data as a socioeconomic resource to be optimized at state or industrial scale [22]. African jurisdictions, while varied, often prioritize development, inclusion, and digital sovereignty. These values influence how data is collected, stored, and shared [23]. They also shape the willingness of governments and institutions to participate in collaborative models of intelligence. In Singapore, state-led regulatory sandboxes have encouraged experimentation in data exchange between banks and fintech companies. In the European Union, the same experiments would face strong legal scrutiny due to GDPR's provisions against data repurposing and cross-border transfers [24]. The overfitting of financial technology to local governance norms creates what can be described as regulatory silos, each mechanical in maintaining privacy but inefficient for global AI deployment.

The complexity of data governance extends beyond privacy law. Data localization mandates increasingly require firms to store and process data within national borders. China's PIPL explicitly prohibits unapproved export of critical financial or biometric data. India's Digital Personal Data Protection Act similarly classifies financial identifiers as sensitive assets. These laws are rooted in nationalism, cybersecurity, and economic sovereignty. They reflect a fear that external entities may extract digital value or exert asymmetric control over domestic markets. From a data ethics standpoint, localization protects citizens. From an innovation standpoint, it prohibits the development of models that benefit from global learning. A conceptual tension emerges: governance regimes protect personal identity but endanger collective intelligence. Traditional institutions have responded to fragmentation with ad hoc cooperation. Bank consortia sometimes engage in pseudonymized data exchange. Regulatory reporting frameworks such as Basel III encourage unified risk models but do not provide mechanisms for shared learning. Industry clearinghouses are inadequate for modern AI because they only facilitate transaction validation, not pattern recognition. The result is a financial AI landscape that is hyperlocal, poorly generalized, and often incompatible with transnational objectives.

1.2 Why Traditional Data Sharing Fails?

Attempts to overcome fragmentation typically involve centralizing datasets [25], [26]. Common approaches include pooling customer records into neutral repositories or establishing shared analytics platforms. While seductive in theory, centralization raises substantial political and ethical risks. When institutions relinquish their datasets to collective platforms, they fundamentally lose control. Data breaches become catastrophic, as a single compromised server may expose millions of personal records. Central repositories also become attractive targets for state surveillance, cybercrime, and industrial espionage. Deep-seated distrust among banks prevents organizations from participating in data pooling even when regulators endorse cooperation. Data replication practices introduce further inefficiencies. When multiple institutions store similar datasets, discrepancies and synchronization failures frequently arise. The same customer may be represented differently across banks or jurisdictions. Replication inherently increases privacy attack surfaces. Even when personal identifiers are removed, adversarial reidentification techniques can reconstruct sensitive attributes using demographic or behavioral correlations. Studies in privacy engineering show that de-identified datasets are vulnerable to inference attacks once combined with external data sources. De Montjoye et al. demonstrate that even generous anonymization does not guarantee privacy when datasets contain behavioral traces typical of financial transactions [27]. The myth of safe anonymization has therefore collapsed.

Legacy data-sharing architectures also produce heavy operational friction. They require complex legal agreements, standardized taxonomies, and harmonized reporting formats. The costs of negotiation and compliance far exceed the potential benefits of collaboration. Institutions face reputational and legal consequences if shared data is misused or misinterpreted. These liabilities discourage innovation, particularly among risk-averse financial entities such as commercial banks and insurance providers. The failure of traditional sharing is rooted not merely in law or technology, but in structural misalignment of incentives. Centralized collaboration redistributes power. Firms with high-value datasets are disincentivized to share because they risk losing competitive advantages. Firms with lower-value data seek access upward. Relationships become extractive rather than cooperative. Institutions in the Global North gain disproportionate analytical leverage from global pooling because they possess superior computational capability [28], [29]. Emerging market institutions, in contrast, become passive sources of raw information. The result is algorithmic asymmetry, where the exporting institution loses agency and the importing institution exploits global insights.

1.3 Federated Learning as Transformational Architecture

Federated learning overturns the assumptions of centralization by separating model training from data ownership [30], [31]. Rather than consolidating data into a central warehouse, each institution retains its dataset locally. The AI model is sent to these endpoints, trained on their internal data, and returns aggregated learning updates to a coordinating server. At no point do raw transaction logs or customer histories leave the local environment. Institutions control their data, regulate its usage, and avoid violating localization mandates. The innovation of federated learning lies in its capacity to preserve statistical richness without compromising privacy. Secure aggregation prevents institutions from viewing individual contributions of others. Differential privacy introduces controlled noise to model gradients, making it statistically impossible to reverse-engineer raw inputs while preserving learning quality. Homomorphic encryption enables mathematical operations on encrypted vectors, removing the need to decrypt sensitive content. The result is a mathematically rigorous ecosystem in which institutions collaborate without mutually exposing risk. Yang et al. provide a seminal overview of federated learning as a systematic paradigm for distributed machine learning [32]. Their work demonstrates that models can achieve comparable or superior accuracy to centralized models when trained across diverse participants.

Federated architectures come in variants. Horizontal federated learning is suitable when institutions share similar feature spaces, such as banks across jurisdictions with common transaction formats. Vertical federated learning applies when institutions hold complementary features of the same individuals, such as telecom companies and insurance firms sharing distinct behavioral attributes. Federated transfer learning supports scenarios where participants possess neither common samples nor overlapping features. Each approach accommodates specific structures of financial datasets. Horizontal models typically address transaction classification, credit scoring, and fraud detection. Vertical models support identity verification, AML evaluation, and underwriting. Transfer models facilitate cross-sector cooperation when datasets are highly heterogeneous. The ability to train across borders without relocating data has transformative implications. Federated learning harmonizes the interests of regulators, institutions, and consumers. Regulators ensure data sovereignty compliance while enabling collective intelligence. Institutions gain broader analytical insight without surrendering proprietary value. Consumers benefit from improved fraud detection, enhanced credit access, and reduced bias. This triadic alignment is unprecedented in the history of financial technology.

1.4 Foundations of Financial Application

In global finance, trust is a scarce resource. Federated learning redefines trust not as a matter of interpersonal cooperation but as an infrastructural guarantee. The learning process embeds trust into its pipeline. Institutions do not need to trust each other; they need to trust the protocol. When properly designed, the protocol enforces privacy by default. Cryptographic guarantees replace contractual promises [33]. Secure enclave computation further strengthens confidence by confining model execution to verifiable hardware environments. Financial institutions also benefit from stronger resilience against cyberattacks. Distributed training reduces the incentives for central breach attempts. Even if an endpoint is compromised, attackers do not gain access to aggregated data. They may only expose a fragment of the ecosystem. Such compartmentalization is essential under contemporary cybersecurity threats. A federated system is therefore not merely a machine learning architecture; it is a cyber-physical security strategy. Federated learning also enables proportional contribution. Institutions with limited datasets can still participate, provided their information possesses unique predictive value. For example, a fintech that serves microcredit borrowers in West Africa may offer transaction behaviors unseen in European banking datasets. Even if its samples are limited, their contribution increases model performance. This democratizes the AI ecosystem, reducing data monopolization. Kaminski argues that data governance should prioritize distributed mechanisms that equalize power among participants [34]. Federated learning operationalizes this principle by aligning value creation with autonomy.

2. Federated Learning and the Politics of Cross-Border Finance

Federated learning exists at the intersection of computational innovation and global regulation [35], [36]. Its importance cannot be understood purely in terms of technical efficiency; rather, it must be contextualized within the legal infrastructures that have emerged to control digital capital, citizen privacy, and the power asymmetries generated by data ownership. Financial institutions operate within an environment where the sovereign rights of nations, the expectations of regulators, and the obligations to individual clients coexist in uneasy tension. The very concept of cross-border data sharing is not simply an engineering problem, but a political one [37]. It implicates questions of jurisdictional authority, national security, and economic self-determination. States treat financial data as strategic capital capable of revealing consumer behavior, market networks, illicit fund flows, and the health of domestic economies. This transforms data from a mere digital resource into an instrument of geopolitical leverage. Digital sovereignty has therefore emerged as a central principle of financial regulation. Sovereignty is expressed through the authority to determine how data is collected, how it is stored, and under whose jurisdiction it may be processed. Across continents, financial regulators increasingly interpret data sovereignty as an integral part of national competitiveness. The European Union frames sovereignty around personal autonomy and the primacy of individual rights. China grounds sovereignty in the primacy of state interests and collective stability. Several African states, in contrast, view sovereignty as protection from digital extractivism and unequal bargaining positions with multinational technology corporations. These competing interpretations profoundly shape the feasibility of cross-border AI collaboration. A federated architecture capable of traversing such an environment must therefore be more than secure; it must be politically legible.

Federated learning is best understood as a form of algorithmic diplomacy. Unlike traditional diplomacy, which negotiates territorial boundaries, algorithmic diplomacy negotiates informational boundaries. It creates a channel through which institutions can collaborate without surrendering jurisdictional integrity. This channel is encoded into the architecture of the learning process itself. By allowing model parameters to cross borders rather than raw data, federated learning supports national interests while facilitating international benefit. In this sense, it functions as a governance framework that translates the principle of noninterference into computational protocols. A federated system is effective not because participants trust one another, but because it converts distrust into mathematically enforced constraints. The security of collaboration is not reliant on goodwill or ethical promises, but on cryptographic irreversibility. Federated learning therefore challenges older conceptions of financial data exchange. In historical practice, cross-border cooperation relied on memoranda of understanding, bilateral exchanges, or treaty-based sharing mechanisms. These approaches assume that compliance is guaranteed through contractual enforcement. Yet, such agreements seldom account for informational asymmetry or institutional power. A large multinational bank may have the capacity to benefit disproportionately from pooled datasets, while a smaller institution from an emerging economy may have little influence over how learned insights are deployed. Federated collaboration reverses the directionality of this extraction. Because each institution retains control of its own dataset, cooperation becomes non-extractive by design, provided the system does not centralize model authority. The political neutrality of the framework depends not on central administrators, but on the absence of incentives for exploitation.

2.1 Sovereignty in the Age of Financial AI

Financial sovereignty cannot be reduced to mere control of domestic bank records. It encompasses the authority to decide how predictive systems classify citizens, how lending algorithms interpret risk, and how fraud detection mechanisms determine guilt. When money laundering is detected by centralized algorithms developed outside the jurisdiction of the transactions, it raises legal and moral questions about accountability [38], [39]. Who determined the model thresholds? Which population informed the baseline distribution? Should a fraud classifier developed from European consumer behavior apply to clients in Kenya or Vietnam? These questions are not academic abstractions but pragmatic issues of regulatory compliance. The sovereign rights embedded in privacy statutes are therefore inseparable from the sovereign rights embedded in algorithmic interpretation [40], [41]. Nations resist data transfer not only because they fear disclosure of sensitive information, but because they fear transfer of interpretive power. Federated learning responds to this concern by preserving local agency over training. A bank in Ghana or South Africa retains the authority to determine how its data is used, what segments are included in the learning pipeline, and whether model updates align with domestic compliance norms. Sovereignty becomes an active function of participation rather than a passive assertion of refusal.

The implications of sovereignty extend further when considering digital colonialism. Scholars in data justice have warned that global AI ecosystems often reproduce historic patterns of resource extraction. Multinational actors harvest behavioral signals from emerging markets, train models in advanced economies, and commercialize predictive services without returning value to the original data contributors. This is particularly acute in financial services where unbanked or underbanked populations serve as providers of high-risk credit profiles that are monetized elsewhere. Federated learning provides a partial antidote to this pattern because it enables knowledge transfer without information expropriation. Model parameters flow in a bidirectional circuit rather than unidirectional extraction [42], [43]. Each participant contributes locally, influences shared global weights, and retains its underlying dataset. The effectiveness of this non-extractive cycle, however, depends on how federated governance is designed. If aggregation authority is centralized in a powerful institution, federated systems can become hierarchical. The entity that receives and updates the model gains disproportionate control over its optimization. Smaller financial institutions may find themselves shaping global models without receiving proportional benefit. Governance must therefore prevent federated learning from becoming a subtle continuation of data colonialism through algorithmic hegemony. Distributed aggregation or regulator-led aggregation may provide alternatives to entrenched structural power.

2.2 Regulatory Cultures and Their Impact on Federated Systems

Federated learning does not exist in a vacuum. It operates within a thick regulatory environment where law, policy, and compliance requirements intersect. These ecosystems vary significantly across continents. The European Union exemplifies a rights-based regulatory culture. GDPR treats personal data as an extension of human identity and therefore a possessive right [44]. Its restrictions on data export, profiling, and automated decision-making reflect a normative suspicion of corporate surveillance. GDPR Article 44 and related provisions establish strict limits on cross-border transfers to third countries without adequate protections [45]. Federated learning interacts with this environment not as an exception but as a compliance mechanism. Because personal data never leaves local servers, model training does not constitute cross-border transfer as defined by law. Institutions thus gain access to global statistical redundancy without violating privacy provisions. Academic analyses confirm this compatibility. De Montjoye et al. note that decentralized architectures can mitigate GDPR constraints while retaining strong accountability requirements [27].

Asia presents a contrasting orientation. In China, the Personal Information Protection Law and associated national security legislation enact sovereignty not as a function of individual autonomy but as an extension of state power [46]. Data that may influence public order or economic stability is treated as a national resource. This principle extends to foreign investment, antitrust regulation, and cybersecurity enforcement. In China's model, federated learning becomes an instrument of state-coordinated innovation [47]. Financial institutions can collaborate internally within domestic boundaries while complying with national cybersecurity protocols. Cross-border federated systems, however, are subject to strict screening. The political logic prioritizes protection of strategic national datasets from external inference. Singapore, by contrast, embraces a developmentalist orientation. Regulatory sandboxes and accreditation frameworks are used to manage risk while accelerating industrial pilots. Federated experiments are promoted as a way to capture regional competitive advantage without violating residency mandates.

Africa represents a third regulatory culture characterized by pluralism, developmental needs, and postcolonial caution [48–50]. Countries such as Kenya, Ghana, and Nigeria have adopted data protection regimes inspired by European legislation, yet these are often implemented in environments where data infrastructure is immature and fintech adoption is rapid. Legal frameworks serve dual purposes: protecting citizens from algorithmic exploitation and asserting national control over domestic innovation. Federation is particularly attractive to African regulators because it eliminates the need to convey sensitive consumer data to multinational banks or overseas analytics firms. Local fintech institutions can contribute to predictive modelling without surrendering ownership. Such model participation empowers emerging markets to generate financial intelligence on their own terms rather than being recipients of imported inference.

2.3 Interoperability as Political Negotiation

Interoperability is often treated as a technical challenge. Financial institutions use distinct schemas, transaction payloads, and regulatory taxonomies [51]. The difficulty of harmonizing these attributes is emphasized in many industries' white papers. Yet, interoperability is fundamentally political. The process of aligning distributed financial institutions requires reconciliation of incentives. Large institutions have little motivation to invest in infrastructure that benefits smaller competitors. Regulators may be reluctant to support harmonization initiatives if they believe such efforts serve foreign interests. Even when shared technical standards exist, financial institutions resist coordination due to reputational risk, perceived legal liability, or uncertainties around intellectual property of derived models.

Federated learning reframes interoperability by decoupling model alignment from institutional alignment. Participants do not need to adopt identical schemas to participate. Instead, they rely on metadata normalization and federated routing protocols. For instance, vertical federated systems allow institutions to maintain domestic feature structures while contributing to unified training. The process of negotiation is therefore less contentious than in traditional data pooling. However, interoperability still requires shared governance. Institutions must agree on the terms of participation, the distribution of model weights, and the mechanisms for dispute resolution. They must also negotiate how updates are validated and aborted. These agreements often resemble international treaties. They codify what is permissible and what constitutes a violation. In federated learning, the treaty is operationalized as a protocol rather than a legal document.

The political nature of interoperability is especially visible when financial institutions span high-trust and low-trust jurisdictions. Western institutions may demand assurances that contributions from developing countries are accurate or free from deliberate manipulation. Institutions from emerging economies may fear that their contribution will be undervalued or appropriated. These are not hypothetical anxieties. They reflect historical patterns in financial governance where large economies dictate standards, and smaller economies must comply. The federated approach offers a mechanism to soften this asymmetry, because knowledge is not transferred through static data exports but through dynamic model gradients. Local actors retain control of their inputs and therefore retain leverage. The negotiation focuses on how global models evolve rather than how data is surrendered.

2.4 Privacy as Legal Obligation and Ethical Imperative

Privacy is often treated narrowly as the right to shield personal information from unauthorized access. However, in financial ecosystems, privacy extends to questions of agency, dignity, trust, and political autonomy [52]. When personal transaction histories are pooled into centralized repositories, individuals lose control over the context in which their data is interpreted. Federated learning preserves contextual integrity because an individual's data never leaves its native institutional environment. Contextual integrity refers to the principle that information is generated under a specific set of relational assumptions and should not be interpreted under foreign assumptions without consent. By preserving locality, federated systems enable institutions to respect not only privacy laws but deeper ethical commitments to community norms. Privacy is therefore not a constraint on innovation; it is a precondition for sustainable trust. Federated systems help maintain this trust by eliminating the need for blind acceptance. Institutions can verify their own privacy guarantees. A bank does not need to trust another bank. It needs to trust its own cryptographic implementation. Because trust is anchored locally rather than externally, federated collaboration strengthens institutional resilience. The result is a more ethically robust ecosystem that encourages cooperation through enforced mutual restraint.

3. The Geopolitics of Algorithmic Power

Algorithmic systems do not merely automate decision-making; they structure economic power. In global finance, the entities capable of training superior predictive models acquire advantages in risk pricing, fraud detection, credit allocation, and market forecasting [53]. These advantages compound. Institutions with strong models attract more customers and capital, which produce more data, which further improves their models. The feedback loop produces structural concentration of analytical power that mirrors the economic concentration of capital. This dynamic converts AI into a geopolitical technology. Countries possessing advanced model capabilities gain leverage over less technologically mature economies. They can dictate compliance norms, credit ratings, transaction thresholds, and cross-border surveillance expectations. Federated learning alters the geography of algorithmic power. It reduces the ability of single actors to monopolize global datasets, because collaboration becomes embedded in the architecture of model training. However, federation does not eliminate power imbalances; it transforms them. The locus of control shifts from institutions that own the most data to institutions that control the aggregation process. The aggregation node becomes the geopolitical fulcrum. Whoever coordinates the model updates indirectly shapes the model's learning direction. If the aggregator is a large Western bank, a central bank, or an international consortium, it can prioritize objectives consistent with its own policy preferences. Global AI infrastructures therefore reproduce the politics of coordination.

This dynamic is reminiscent of international economic institutions such as the International Monetary Fund (IMF) or the World Bank, where governance structures allow powerful nations disproportionate influence over global economic policy. Federated learning can replicate this asymmetry if model aggregation is not democratized. A multinational platform may provide local institutions the technical infrastructure to participate in distributed training, but retain exclusive rights to evaluate model performance, classify anomalies, or deploy updates. The partnering institutions become data endpoints rather than autonomous decision-makers. Their contribution enriches global model capacity while their own domestic models remain derivative. In this way, federated learning risks transforming into a new modality of algorithmic colonialism, where knowledge flows upward and value flows outward. Literature on global AI systems warns of these risks. Birhane argues that dominant AI systems often reflect colonial logics, framing human experience according to Western epistemic assumptions and ignoring context-specific interpretations of behavior [54]. In financial contexts, these assumptions translate into risk profiles that categorize populations based on credit consumption habits common in industrialized economies. When applied in regions where informal lending, cash-based transactions, or mobile money ecosystems dominate, such models misclassify risk or criminalize everyday economic practices. The geopolitical consequences of these misclassifications are profound. They influence microfinance schemes, migration-based remittances, and digital trade networks.

Federated systems can counteract these harms when they incorporate heterogeneous perspectives [55]. If African fintech institutions contribute training signals from mobile money environments, the model learns alternative patterns of legitimate behavior. If Asian digital banking platforms contribute transaction patterns from super-app ecosystems, fraud detection becomes less Eurocentric. The model becomes global in representation rather than imperial in orientation. The geopolitics of federated AI is therefore a balancing act. The architecture must prevent centralization of interpretive authority while enabling equitable exchange of model intelligence. The ethics of the system are not determined by its cryptography alone, but by its governance.

3.1 Regulator-Led Federations and Public–Private Coordination

A significant question in cross-border AI governance is who should coordinate federated systems. Private-sector consortia may be motivated by commercial interests that align poorly with public welfare [56]. Banks often prioritize profit over social inclusion. Fintech start-ups prioritize growth over compliance. Technology vendors prioritize lock-in over transparency. Entrusting these actors with control of federated infrastructures may generate perverse incentives. In contrast, public-sector regulators such as central banks, financial supervision authorities, and data protection commissions embody broader mandates. Their objective is to balance systemic stability, innovation, and citizen welfare. Regulator-led federations may provide the most legitimate foundation for cross-border collaboration. Under such models, national regulators do not share raw datasets. Instead, they establish oversight frameworks that allow banks within their jurisdiction to participate in distributed learning while maintaining compliance. These regulators may negotiate international treaties that define the permissible boundaries of model exchange. The coordinating role is democratized because the aggregation node is not an individual institution but a multi-stakeholder body accountable to law. Such arrangements mitigate fears of digital colonialism because no single bank or technology vendor controls the training pipeline.

The European Banking Authority offers a partial example. Although it does not currently operate federated AI systems, its supervisory frameworks envision transnational risk analytics under data privacy constraints. The Monetary Authority of Singapore similarly pioneers regulatory sandboxes that allow cross-sector AI experimentation under the watchful eye of government auditors [57]. African central banks, particularly in Nigeria and Kenya, have begun developing digital payment intelligence networks designed to share behavioral indicators of fraud without disclosing transactional identities. These initiatives illustrate that regulators can act as reliable custodians of model governance, as they possess statutory authority and direct access to compliance infrastructures. A regulator-led federation also addresses economic asymmetry. Smaller institutions that lack computational power can still contribute to global models without being exploited. Their participation is not governed by market bargaining but by public policy principles. This structure aligns with the philosophy of developmental economics, which argues that growth must be supported through institutional scaffolding rather than laissez-faire competition. It helps safeguard inclusion, preventing the concentration of digital value in large multinational platforms.

There are, however, operational challenges. Regulators rarely possess the technical expertise required to supervise federated architectures. They may rely on third-party vendors or private institutions to host the aggregation nodes. This creates new dependencies. Governance structures must therefore stipulate strict auditing, transparency, and dispute resolution mechanisms to prevent vendor-based capture. Trust is achieved not through centralized ownership but through procedural safeguards, multi-institutional oversight boards, and cryptographic proof systems.

3.2 Risk Regulation, Liability, and the Ethics of Shared Outcomes

Federated learning complicates traditional ideas of liability in financial decision-making [58], [59]. When a bank makes an erroneous classification, regulators examine the internal decision systems of that institution. Under federated collaboration, the bank's classifier is partially derived from contributions made by foreign institutions. If a credit scoring model overestimates the risk of a borrower in Rwanda because of gradients contributed by institutions in Hong Kong or Madrid, who bears responsibility? The institution deploying the model, the nodes that contributed data, or the aggregator that optimized global weights? Legal scholars increasingly advocate for distributed accountability frameworks. Decisions derived from federated architectures must preserve traceability [60]. Institutions should be able to determine which training signals influenced which model weights. The goal is not to expose individual contributors but to allow regulators to understand how systemic bias emerged. This requirement challenges existing implementations of differential privacy, as they intentionally obscure the origin of training signals. A balance must be achieved between privacy protection and forensic transparency. The introduction of cryptographic auditing mechanisms may provide this balance, allowing regulators to trace model evolution without accessing raw data.

Ethics in federated finance is also temporal. A model may be valid at the time of training but invalidated by changing social or economic conditions [61]. Consider fraud detection models trained during a pandemic when digital transactions spike and cash withdrawals decrease. Such models may incorrectly treat resurgence of cash-based transactions as suspicious. Under centralized AI systems, regulatory bodies can intervene, recalibrate, or deprecate outdated models. Under federated systems, retraining requires coordinated participation. Institutions must agree to contribute fresh gradients. If powerful institutions refuse to participate in recalibration because it benefits them to maintain an older model that favors their market position, systemic bias persists. This illustrates why governance must include mandatory update protocols. Participants must commit to ongoing recalibration as a condition of federation. Model refresh cycles must be codified as legal obligations, not optional arrangements. Ethical integrity is not preserved through initial training alone but through continuous adjustment. Federated learning is therefore less a technical method than a temporal governance regime.

3.3 A Framework for Cross-Border Federated Collaboration

A conceptual model can help clarify how federated learning aligns with governance and regulatory principles [62], [63]. The conceptual model for this chapter is shown in Figure 1.

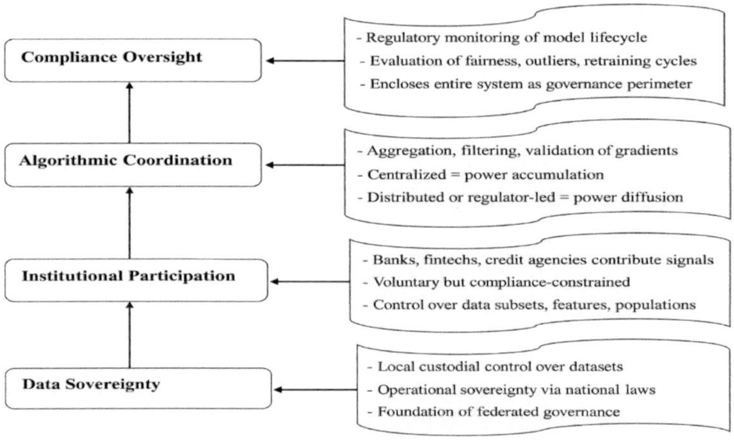

Figure 1: Conceptual model of federated learning governance.
Source: Authors' construct (2025).

The model consists of four interacting domains: data sovereignty, institutional participation, algorithmic coordination, and compliance oversight. The relationships among these domains determine whether a federated system becomes extractive or equitable. Data sovereignty is placed at the foundation. Each institution retains ownership and custodial control over its datasets. Sovereignty is not symbolic but operational; local laws determine the permissible scope of training. Institutional participation occurs above this layer. Banks, fintech companies, and credit agencies contribute localized training signals. Their participation is voluntary but constrained by compliance. They can choose which subsets of their data to expose to the model, which features to include, and which populations to exclude. Algorithmic coordination resides at the center of the model. It represents the mechanism through which gradients are aggregated, filtered, validated, and redistributed. The political significance of coordination cannot be overstated. If coordination is centralized, model power accumulates. If coordination is distributed or regulator-led, power diffuses. Compliance oversight encloses the system. Regulators monitor not the data but the model life cycle. They evaluate fairness metrics, detect outlier contributions, and ensure retraining cycles occur. The dynamics of the system are bidirectional. Sovereignty influences participation; participation influences coordination; coordination determines performance; performance shapes regulatory interpretation. In federated ecosystems, credit classification is not a purely technical output. It reflects the ideological landscape in which the model operates. This framework depicts federated learning not as a software architecture but as a governance engine. The model does not merely compute. It distributes agency. It ensures that cross-border collaboration respects national laws, institutional autonomy, and global ethics. It harmonizes local authority with global benefit.

4. Implementation Pathways in Cross-Border Financial Ecosystems

Turning federated learning from theoretical promise into operational infrastructure requires institutions to navigate three intersecting realities: regulatory commitment, institutional trust, and technological maturity [64–66]. These realities are not independent variables. Regulatory commitment shapes institutional trust. Institutional trust influences technological adoption. Technological maturity feeds back into regulatory confidence by providing evidence of responsible deployment. Federated collaboration therefore emerges not through technical pilots alone but through multilayered institutional agreements that embed cooperation into legal and organizational culture.

The most successful implementations begin from legal alignment rather than technical innovation. Regulators must define the boundaries of acceptable participation, the classification of model outputs, and the conditions for ongoing audits. Without this foundation, federated pilots risk devolving into informal partnerships that may violate privacy norms or expose participants to unintended liabilities. The Monetary Authority of Singapore provides an instructive example. Its regulatory sandbox approach permits institutions to experiment with cross-sector analytics, but every experiment is bounded by terms of use, anti-abuse clauses, and mandatory reporting. Technologists iterate within a controlled environment where regulators remain informed, reducing the shock of policy surprises. By contrast, European attempts at federated collaboration often begin with compliance rather than experimentation. Institutions must navigate GDPR clauses on legitimate interest, profiling constraints, and automated decision-making. The technology is framed as a compliance mechanism rather than a source of innovation. These cultural differences shape adoption trajectories.

Institutions also need to acknowledge that federated learning is as much an organizational transformation as a technical one. Banks accustomed to hierarchical decision-making are unprepared for models that require distributed contributions. Chief data officers must negotiate the internal politics of dataset prioritization. Legal departments must interpret model participation as a contractual responsibility. These adjustments transform corporate governance. Federated systems require cross-functional dialogue between risk departments, IT branches, business units, and ethics committees. Collaboration becomes internal long before it becomes external. The willingness of a bank to contribute gradients depends on its confidence that its own institution understands the purpose of the contribution. This internal coherence cannot be taken for granted. Technological maturity influences adoption differently. Institutions with modern cloud infrastructures and sophisticated machine learning pipelines are more ready to participate. Smaller banks, community lenders, or early-stage fintechs face hardware limitations, sparse security protocols, and limited talent pools. A federated ecosystem must therefore provide capacity-building. If participation is restricted to the most technologically advanced institutions, the federated model will reproduce existing inequalities. The governance framework must include support mechanisms: standardized toolkits, subsidized infrastructure, and open-source training modules. These interventions democratize participation and prevent the emergence of digital oligarchies.

4.1 Ethical Risk Management in Federated Finance

Ethical risk management in federated systems must address five categories of harm: distributive harm, representational harm, procedural harm, temporal harm, and geopolitical harm [67], [68]. Distributive harm occurs when the benefits of model training accrue disproportionately to powerful participants. If a multinational bank receives improved fraud detection capabilities while smaller institutions gain only marginal uplift, the model amplifies existing inequality. Representational harm emerges when local behavioral patterns are misinterpreted because they deviate from dominant transactions. For example, cash-based micro-entrepreneurial activity common in West Africa may be classified as anomalous or fraudulent because it diverges from digital spending norms in Europe. Procedural harm arises when the architecture obscures the mechanisms of decision-making. Federated learning can provide strong privacy guarantees but weak interpretability. If individuals cannot challenge algorithmic determinations because the training process is opaque, procedural fairness is undermined. Temporal harm arises when models age badly. Economic cycles, migration patterns, social shocks, and pandemics reshape financial behavior. A federated system that does not mandate frequent retraining risks codifying outdated assumptions as stable truths. Finally, geopolitical harm emerges when global models encode the economic preferences of dominant economies. If fraud detection systems are optimized to protect Western payment infrastructures, they may prioritize risk categories aligned with Western concerns rather than those of the Global South. Ethical risk management must therefore be multidirectional, providing safeguards not just against individual harms but against systemic harms that operate at scale.

Three strategies help mitigate these risks. First is data representativeness. Institutions must commit to inclusive sampling. They cannot train models exclusively on profitable demographics or digitally active populations. Including marginalized users is not simply a social justice preference; it is a technical requirement for accuracy. Second is algorithmic transparency. Regulators should require institutions to provide model-provenance information. This does not mean exposing raw datasets, but providing explanations of how model updates influenced architecture. Third is participatory governance. Communities affected by financial decisions should influence how models interpret fairness. This may involve consumer rights groups, civil society organizations, or public sector agencies. The principle is not adversarial oversight but participatory co-creation. Ethics must be embedded at the design stage. Post-hoc remediation is insufficient because federated systems resist intervention. Bias cannot be corrected merely by adjusting the final model output; it must be addressed during the federated training cycle. This requires long-term cooperation and institutional humility. No organization should assume it knows the correct distribution of fairness. Participatory ethics recognizes that fairness is negotiated, not inherited.

4.2 Institutional Incentives and Power Asymmetries

Even with strong governance, federated learning must confront economic realities. Institutions care about return on investment, not only compliance or ethics. If the benefits of model participation are diffused while the costs of infrastructure are concentrated, federated ecosystems will collapse. Incentive design must therefore create proportional value. Institutions that contribute rare data must receive meaningful enhancements. Institutions that hold informational monopolies must not treat federation as charity. Financial incentives must align with strategic goals. The most fragile federated ecosystems are those dominated by large banks that treat smaller institutions as feeders [69]. When this occurs, collaboration resembles a vendor–client relationship rather than a network of peers. Smaller institutions learn little, while larger institutions absorb their behavioral patterns to train global models. These dynamics mimic digital colonialism. The learning process becomes extractive rather than cooperative. Governance must prevent this. Model update mechanisms can restrict weight absorption if contributions do not enhance mutual performance. Differential weighting strategies can prioritize shared benefit rather than raw accuracy.

The private technology sector introduces a parallel asymmetry. Cloud providers, AI vendors, and analytics platforms frequently seek to insert themselves as indispensable intermediaries. Their interest is rarely purely collaborative. If third-party companies gain exclusive rights to host aggregation nodes or interpret model performance, they accumulate informational monopolies. Vendors gradually become the arbiters of fairness, optimization, and security. This is not a hypothetical risk. The history of digital infrastructure demonstrates that corporations frequently absorb public-sector functions once they dominate technical ecosystems. Federated finance must remain wary of this trajectory. Regulatory frameworks must explicitly prevent vendor-led capture. The solution is not to exclude private actors but to decentralize their authority. Vendors can maintain the computational layer while regulators and institutions retain governance. Model design, update frequency, exclusion protocols, and audit mandates must remain the domain of law and finance. Technology serves the participants, not the reverse. Federated learning becomes sustainable only when institutions maintain epistemic authority over the models, they collectively train.

4.3 Cross-Continental Case Reflections

Cross-border collaboration manifests are differently based on regional histories and institutional culture. Europe tends to view federated learning as a compliance tool. It provides a way to achieve innovation without violating rights-based legal frameworks. Financial institutions in the EU prioritize the reduction of liability through privacy-preserving methods [70], [71]. Their calculus is defensive rather than expansionist. Conversely, China views digitization as a strategic asset [72], [73]. Financial and technological infrastructures are instruments of state power and civil stability. The objective is not merely to comply with law but to orchestrate public order, economic security, and technological supremacy. In such contexts, federated systems serve national rather than transnational interests. Their deployment is inward-facing and tightly supervised. Africa presents a distinct configuration. Its financial innovation emerges from necessity. A large portion of its population remains outside the formal banking sector, relying on mobile transactions, informal credit schemes, and remittance channels [74], [75]. Fintech companies in Kenya, Ghana, and Nigeria have pioneered digital inclusion, but their datasets remain fragmented and vulnerable to exploitation [76]. They stand at risk of becoming laboratories of foreign extraction, where behavioral signals are harvested for models developed in Western firms.

Federated learning offers a countermeasure, but only if governed locally. African regulators must treat federated infrastructures as components of digital sovereignty. The goal is not to participate in global analytics merely to contribute data, but to shape global models in ways that protect local economic realities. These regional differences underscore that federated learning is not a universal solution. Its implementation must reflect local power structures, socio-economic priorities, and regulatory philosophies. What works in Singapore may not work in Nairobi. What succeeds in Frankfurt may fail in Ho Chi Minh City. Federated architectures must therefore be adaptive, not prescriptive. Governance is not a question of importing frameworks; it is a question of coproducing them.

4.4 Toward Accountable Global Models

The future of federated finance lies not in perfection of cryptography but in perfection of governance capacity. Cryptographic systems are necessary but insufficient [77]. Mathematical guarantees do not solve questions of fairness, legitimacy, or welfare. These questions require political negotiation. They demand recognition that financial AI is a regulatory technology, not merely a predictive tool. The primary role of federated learning is to create institutional environments where innovation does not undermine autonomy [78]. Global cooperation will depend on three structural commitments. The first is reciprocity. Federated ecosystems must ensure that participants benefit proportionally from what they contribute. This principle guards against exploitation and promotes long-term engagement. The second is transparency. Governance structures must reveal how models evolve, which metrics determine performance, and how errors are corrected. Transparency does not require exposure of sensitive data. It requires legibility of decision dynamics. The third is sovereignty. Local institutions must retain the authority to limit participation. Opt-out rights, red lines, and privacy boundaries must be enforceable. Sovereignty is not obstruction; it is the condition of ethical cooperation.

Federated systems can build a world where algorithmic infrastructures do not merely inherit geopolitical divisions but transform them into equitable relationships. They can foster infrastructures of mutual intelligence. Yet this promise remains contingent. Without active governance, federated learning can become a new instrument of power concentration. The responsibility lies not only with technologists or financial institutions but with regulators, civil society, and global policy communities.

5. Conclusion

The transitional era of digital finance confronts humanity with a fundamental challenge: how to reconcile the fluidity of global information flows with the grounded demands of legal sovereignty, ethical equity, and economic stability. Traditional approaches to financial collaboration have treated data as a commodity that can be traded, anonymized, or pooled. These approaches are no longer adequate. They expose individuals to invasive surveillance, amplify institutional inequality, and erode national autonomy. Federated learning offers a paradigm shift. It reframes collaboration not as the movement of data, but as the movement of knowledge. Through its decentralized architecture, federated learning operationalizes trust. It allows financial institutions to collaborate without compromising the rights of citizens or the integrity of national policy. Yet its promise is not inherent. Federated learning can also reproduce global asymmetries if poorly governed. The risk of algorithmic colonialism persists, particularly when aggregation is controlled by powerful actors or when interpretive authority is centralized.

Governance, therefore, is the main determinant of whether federated systems become emancipatory or extractive. Regulator-led federations hold the greatest potential for equitable coordination. They align technological innovation with statutory legitimacy. They provide neutral governance layers insulated from private profit motives. They can embed social goals such as inclusion, consumer protection, and developmental equity. But regulators must evolve. They require technical education, institutional innovation, and international cooperation. Cross-border financial AI cannot be governed by isolated bodies. Sovereignty must be multidirectional: nations defend their autonomy while recognizing their interdependence. Federated finance is not merely a computational technique. It is a governance strategy for an era of digital interdependence. Its success will depend on humanity's ability to design infrastructures that respect diversity while enabling collective intelligence. The chapter thus concludes not with technological determinism, but with institutional optimism. The future of global financial collaboration lies in architectures that convert sovereignty into strength, not isolation; that transform compliance into cooperation, not resistance. The path forward is neither naïve nor simple, but it is possible, if policymakers, scholars, technologists, and financial institutions commit to reshaping global AI through shared responsibility rather than unilateral dominance.

References

[1] Cao, L. (2025). Trans-AI/DS: Transformative, transdisciplinary and translational artificial intelligence and data science. *International Journal of Data Science and Analytics*, 20(2): 1617–1629. doi: 10.1007/s41060-023-00384-x.

[2] Gruetzemacher, R. and Whittlestone, J. (2022). The transformative potential of artificial intelligence. *Futures*, 135: Art. no. 102884. doi: 10.1016/j.futures.2021.102884.

[3] Helbing, D. (2018). Societal, economic, ethical and legal challenges of the digital revolution. In *Towards Digital Enlightenment: Essays on the Dark and Light Sides of the Digital Revolution*, Cham, Switzerland: Springer, pp. 47–72. doi: 10.1007/978-3-319-90869-4_6.

[4] Nawaah, D., Kwarteng, J. T. and Quarshie, M. A. (2025). Blockchain for sustainable finance and green investments in the era of sustainability. In *Blockchain Technologies for Smart Circular Economy and Organisational Sustainability*, Cham, Switzerland: Springer Nature, pp. 253–270. doi: 10.1007/978-3-031-89183-0_16.

[5] Quarshie, M. A., Djimatey, R., Akhtar, S. and Nawaah, D. (2025). Maximizing financial efficiency through technological synergy: Unleashing ICT for enhanced cash management in SMEs. *Journal of the International Council for Small Business*, pp. 1–31. doi: 10.1080/26437015.2025.2461025.

[6] Cinnamon, J. (2020). Data inequalities and why they matter for development. *Information Technology for Development*, 26(2): 214–233. doi:10.1080/02681102.2019.1650244.

[7] Jafar, S. H., Oyedele, O. M., Nawaah, D. and Bolanle, A. S. (2025). Exploring leadership challenges for adoption of digital innovation and sustainability. In *Innovation Ecosystems and Sustainable Technologies*, Emerald Publishing, pp. 253–269. doi: 10.1108/978-1-83662-368-720251012.

[8] Bongomin, G. O. C. and Ntayi, J. M. (2020). Mobile money adoption and usage and financial inclusion: Mediating effect of digital consumer protection. *Digital Policy, Regulation and Governance*, 22(3): 157–176. doi: 10.1108/DPRG-01-2019-0005.

[9] Foucault, T. and Menkveld, A. J. (2008). Competition for order flow and smart order routing systems. *The Journal of Finance*, 63(1): 119–158. doi: 10.1111/j.1540-6261.2008.01312.x.

[10] Quarshie, M. A., Akhtar, S. and Nawaah, D. (2025). Barriers to breakthroughs: The crucial role of support services in advancing accounting practices, financial literacy and performance in disability-led SMEs. *Quality & Quantity*, 59(Suppl. 2): 955–977. doi: 10.1007/s11135-024-02050-1.

[11] Andanda, P. (2019). Towards a paradigm shift in governing data access and related intellectual property rights in big data and health-related research. *IIC—International Review of Intellectual Property and Competition Law*, 50(9): 1052–1081. doi: 10.1007/s40319-019-00873-2.

[12] Fadler, M. and Legner, C. (2022). Data ownership revisited: Clarifying data accountabilities in times of big data and analytics. *Journal of Business Analytics*, 5(1): 123–139. doi: 10.1080/2573234X.2021.1945961.

[13] Wen, J., Zhang, Z., Lan, Y., Cui, Z., Cai, J. and Zhang, W. (2023). A survey on federated learning: challenges and applications. *International Journal of Machine Learning and Cybernetics*, 14(2): 513–535. doi: 10.1007/s13042-022-01647-y.

[14] Bheemaiah, K. (2017). Fragmentation of finance. In *The Blockchain Alternative: Rethinking Macroeconomic Policy and Economic Theory*, Berkeley, CA, USA: Apress, pp. 25–82. doi: 10.1007/978-1-4842-2674-2_2.

[15] Iheanachor, N., Umukoro, I. and Aranega, A. Y. (2023). Ecosystem emergence in emerging markets. *Technological Forecasting and Social Change*, 190: Art. no. 122426. doi: 10.1016/j.techfore.2023.122426.

[16] Lehmann, M. (2017). Legal fragmentation, extraterritoriality and uncertainty in global financial regulation. *Oxford Journal of Legal Studies*, 37(2): 406–434. doi: 10.1093/ojls/gqw028.

[17] Sun, P., Doh, J. P., Rajwani, T. and Siegel, D. (2021). Navigating cross-border institutional complexity: A review and assessment of multinational nonmarket strategy research. *Journal of International Business Studies*, 52(9): 1818–1836. doi: 10.1057/s41267-021-00438-x.

[18] Kairouz, P. and McMahan, H. B. (2021). Advances and open problems in federated learning. *Foundations and Trends in Machine Learning*, 14(1-2): 1–210. doi: 10.1561/2200000083.

[19] Canhoto, A. I. (2021). Leveraging machine learning in the global fight against money laundering and terrorism financing. *Journal of Business Research*, 131: 441–452. doi: 10.1016/j.jbusres.2020.10.012.

[20] Gefenas, E., Lekstutiene, J., Lukaseviciene, V., Hartlev, M., Mourby, M. and Cathaoir, K. Ó. (2022). Controversies between regulations of research ethics and protection of personal data. *Medicine, Health Care and Philosophy*, 25(1): 23–30. doi: 10.1007/s11019-021-10060-1.

[21] Hallinan, D. and Friedewald, M. (2015). Open consent, biobanking and data protection law. *Life Sciences, Society and Policy*, 11(1): Art. no. 1. doi: 10.1186/s40504-014-0020-9.

[22] Thavasi, V. and Ramakrishna, S. (2009). Asia energy mixes from socio-economic and environmental perspectives. *Energy Policy*, 37(11): 4240–4250. doi: 10.1016/j.enpol.2009.05.061.

[23] Bühler, M. M., Calzada, I., Cane, I., Jelinek, T., Kapoor, A., Mannan, M. et al. (2023). Unlocking the power of digital commons. *Digital*, 3(3): 146–171. doi: 10.3390/digital3030011.

[24] Bolatbekkyzy, G. (2024). Legal issues of cross-border data transfer in the era of digital government. *Journal of Digital Technologies and Law*, 2(2): 286–307. doi: 10.21202/jdtl.2024.15.

[25] Abdalla, H. and Artoli, A. M. (2019). Towards an efficient data fragmentation, allocation, and clustering approach. *Information*, 10(3): Art. no. 112. doi: 10.3390/ info10030112.

[26] Nashat, D. and Amer, A. A. (2018). A comprehensive taxonomy of fragmentation and allocation techniques. *ACM Computing Surveys*, 51(1): 1–25. doi: 10.1145/3150223.

[27] De Montjoye, Y. A., Radaelli, L., Singh, V. K. and Pentland, A. S. (2015). Unique in the shopping mall. *Science*, 347(6221): 536–539. doi: 10.1126/science.1256297.

[28] George, A. S. (2024). Bridging the gender gap in STEM. *Partners Universal Innovative Research Publication*, 2(2): 89–105. doi: 10.5281/zenodo.10956569.

[29] Lehdonvirta, V., Wú, B. and Hawkins, Z. (2024). Compute North vs. Compute South. In *Proc. AAAI/ACM Conf. on AI, Ethics, and Society*, 7(1): 828–838, doi: 10.1609/aies.v7i1.31683.

[30] AbdulRahman, S., Tout, H., Ould-Slimane, H., Mourad, A., Talhi, C. and Guizani, M. (2020). A survey on federated learning. *IEEE Internet of Things Journal*, 8(7): 5476–5497. doi: 10.1109/JIOT.2020.3030072.

[31] Zhang, C., Xie, Y., Bai, H., Yu, B., Li, W. and Gao, Y. (2021). A survey on federated learning. *Knowledge-Based Systems*, 216: Art. no. 106775. doi: 10.1016/j.knosys.2021.106775.

[32] Yang, Q., Liu, Y., Chen, T. and Tong, Y. (2019). Federated machine learning: Concept and applications. *ACM Transactions on Intelligent Systems and Technology*, 10(2): 1–19. doi: 10.1145/3298981.

[33] Fernandes, A., Garg, K., Agrawal, A. and Bhatia, A. (2021). Decentralized online voting using blockchain and secret contracts. In *Proc. Int. Conf. on Information Networking (ICOIN)*, pp. 582–587. doi: 10.1109/ ICOIN50884.2021.9333966.

[34] Kaminski, M. E. (2019). Binary governance: Lessons from the GDPR's approach to algorithmic accountability. *SSRN Working Paper*. doi: 10.2139/ssrn.3351404.

[35] Lazaros, K., Koumadorakis, D. E., Vrahatis, A. G. and Kotsiantis, S. (2024). Federated learning: Navigating the landscape. *Electronics*, 13(23): Art. no. 4744. doi: 10.3390/electronics13234744.
[36] Prieto, J. (2024). Case studies in federated learning for healthcare. In *Federated Learning and Privacy-Preserving in Healthcare AI*, p. 91. doi: 10.4018/979-8-3693-1874-4. ch007.
[37] Aaronson, S. A. (2019). Data is different. *Digital Policy, Regulation and Governance*, 21(5): 441–460. doi: 10.1108/DPRG-03-2019-0021.
[38] Khan, A., Jillani, M. A. H. S., Ullah, M. and Khan, M. (2025). Regulatory strategies for combatting money laundering. *Journal of Money Laundering Control*, 28(2): 408–423. doi: 10.1108/JMLC-07- 2024-0113.
[39] White, M. and Lyn, A. (2024). Ethical implications in money laundering detection. In *Ethical Quandaries in Business Practices*, IGI Global, pp. 123–158. doi: 10.4018/979-8-3693-3948-0.ch006.
[40] Elliott, M. and Young, A. L. (2019). Privacy international in the supreme court. *The Cambridge Law Journal*, 78(3): 490–496. doi: 10.1017/S0008197319000813.
[41] Pollicino, O. and De Gregorio, G. (2021). *Constitutional Challenges in the Algorithmic Society.* Cambridge, U.K.: Cambridge University Press. doi: 10.1017/9781108914857.
[42] Bryant, A. T., Kang, X., Santi, E., Palmer, P. R. and Hudgins, J. L. (2006). Two-step parameter extraction procedure. *IEEE Transactions on Power Electronics*, 21(2): 295–309. doi: 10.1109/TPEL.2005.869742.
[43] Ide, T., Shimizu, M., Shen, X. Q., Morita, T., Ueda, T. and Tanaka, T. (2012). Equivalent circuit model for a GaN gate injection transistor. *IEEE Transactions on Electron Devices*, 59(10): 2643–2649. doi: 10.1109/ TED.2012.2211020.
[44] van Ooijen, I. and Vrabec, H. U. (2019). Does the GDPR enhance consumers' control over personal data? *Journal of Consumer Policy*, 42(1): 91–107. doi: 10.1007/s10603-018-9399-7.
[45] Juliussen, B. A., Kozyri, E., Johansen, D. and Rui, J. P. (2023). The third country problem under the GDPR. *International Data Privacy Law*, 13(3): 225–243. doi: 10.1093/idpl/ipad013.
[46] Zhao, B. and Feng, Y. (2021). Mapping the development of China's data protection law. *Computer Law & Security Review*, 40: Art. no. 105498. doi: 10.1016/j. clsr.2020.105498.
[47] Guo, R. (2025). Governing through participation. *SSRN*. doi: 10.2139/ssrn.5376419.
[48] Nawaah, D., Bosu, L. and Akhtar, S. (2025). Transitioning from a perceived threat of climate change to an established reality. doi: 10.1108/978-1-83708-088-520261012.
[49] Abrahamsen, R. (2003). African studies and the postcolonial challenge. *African Affairs*, 102(407): 189–210. doi: 10.1093/afraf/adg001.
[50] Wa Muiu, M. (2010). Colonial and postcolonial state and development in Africa. *Social Research*, 77(4): 1311–1338. doi: 10.1353/sor.2010.0034.
[51] Ionescu, S. A., Diaconita, V. and Radu, A. O. (2025). Engineering sustainable data architectures. *Electronics*, 14(8): Art. no. 1650. doi: 10.3390/electronics14081650.
[52] Faria, I. (2019). Trust, reputation and ambiguous freedoms. *Journal of Cultural Economy*, 12(2): 119–132. doi: 10.1080/17530350.2018.1547986.
[53] Bello, O. A. (2023). Machine learning algorithms for credit risk assessment. *International Journal of Management*, 10(1): 109–133. doi: 10.37745/ijmt.2013/ vol10n1109133.
[54] Birhane, A. (2021). Algorithmic injustice. *Patterns*, 2(2): Art. no. 100205. doi: 10.1016/j.patter.2021.100205.
[55] Ye, M., Fang, X., Du, B., Yuen, P. C. and Tao, D. (2023). Heterogeneous federated learning. *ACM Computing Surveys*, 56(3): 1–44. doi: 10.1145/3625558.
[56] Jost, G., Dawson, M. and Shaw, D. (2005). Private sector consortia working for a public sector client. *European Management Journal*, 23(3): 336–350. doi: 10.1016/j.emj.2005.04.012.

[57] Singhal, N., Goyal, S. and Singhal, T. (2024). Emerging trends in regulatory and legal frameworks for decentralized insurance. In *Potential, Risks, and Ethical Implications of Decentralized Insurance*, pp. 211–260. doi: 10.1007/978-981-97-5894-4_5.
[58] Pingulkar, S. and Pawade, D. (2024). Federated learning architectures for credit risk assessment. In *Proc. IEEE Int. Conf. on Blockchain and Distributed Systems Security (ICBDS)*, pp. 1–7. doi: 10.1109/ICBDS61829.2024.10837430.
[59] Shi, Y., Song, H. and Xu, J. (2023). Responsible and effective federated learning in financial services. In *Proc. IEEE Conf. on Decision and Control (CDC)*, pp. 4229–4236. doi: 10.1109/CDC49753.2023.10384119.
[60] Kavasidis, I., Lallas, E., Mountzouris, G., Gerogiannis, V. C. and Karageorgos, A. (2023). A federated learning framework for enforcing traceability. *IEEE Access*, 11: 57585–57597. doi: 10.1109/ACCESS.2023.3282316.
[61] Cho, I. K. and Kasa, K. (2015). Learning and model validation. *The Review of Economic Studies*, 82(1): 45–82. doi: 10.1093/restud/rdu026.
[62] De Almeida, P. G. R., Dos Santos, C. D. and Farias, J. S. (2021). Artificial intelligence regulation. *Ethics and Information Technology*, 23(3): 505–525. doi: 10.1007/s10676-021-09593-z.
[63] Beltrán, E. T. M., Pérez, M. Q., Sánchez, P. M. S., Bernal, S. L., Bovet, G. and Pérez, M. G. et al. (2023). Decentralized federated learning. *IEEE Communications Surveys & Tutorials*, 25(4): 2983–3013. doi: 10.1109/COMST.2023.3315746.
[64] Akande, O. A. (2022). Integrating blockchain with federated learning. *International Journal of Computer Applications Technology and Research*, 11(12): 622–637. doi: 10.7753/IJCATR1112.1025.
[65] Chen, C., Liu, J., Tan, H., Li, X., Wang, K. I. K., Li, P. et al. (2025). Trustworthy federated learning. *Knowledge and Information Systems*, 67(3): 2321–2356. doi: 10.1007/s10115-024-02285-2.
[66] Hasan, M. T. and Kudapa, S. P. (2021). Data privacy-aware machine learning. *American Journal of Interdisciplinary Studies*, 2(3): 1–34. doi: 10.63125/vj1hem03.
[67] Fan, Y. (2025). The role of artificial intelligence in the digital transformation of government. *Frontiers in Public Health*, 13: Art. no. 1694996. doi: 10.3389/fpubh.2025.1694996.
[68] Van Den Meerssche, D. (2022). Virtual borders. *European Journal of International Law*, 33(1): 171–204. doi: 10.1093/ejil/chac007.
[69] Anagnostopoulos, I. Y., Sails, T. and Alexandrou, G. (2025). FinTechs, BigTechs and diminishing bank franchise values. *Technological Forecasting and Social Change*, 212: Art. no. 123924. doi: 10.1016/j.techfore.2024.123924.
[70] He, P., Lin, C. and Montoya, I. (2024). DPFedBank. arXiv preprint, arXiv:2410.13753.
[71] Kalodanis, K., Feretzakis, G., Anastasiou, A., Rizomiliotis, P., Anagnostopoulos, D. and Koumpouros, Y. (2025). A privacy-preserving and attack-aware AI approach. *Electronics*, 14(7): Art. no. 1385. doi: 10.3390/electronics14071385.
[72] Lee, C. C., Jiang, L. and Wen, H. (2024). Two aspects of digitalization affecting financial asset allocation. *Emerging Markets Finance and Trade*, 60(4): 631–649. doi: 10.1080/1540496X.2023.2244142.
[73] Yang, F., Luo, C. and Pan, L. (2024). Do digitalization and intellectual capital drive sustainable open innovation. *Resources Policy*, 88: Art. no. 104345. doi: 10.1016/j.resourpol.2023.104345.
[74] Mago, S. and Modiba, F. S. (2022). Does informal finance matter for micro and small businesses in Africa? *Small Business International Review*, 6(1): Art. no. e415, doi: 10.26784/sbir.v6i1.415.
[75] Mpofu, O. and Sibindi, A. B. (2022). Informal finance: A boon or bane for African SMEs? *Journal of Risk and Financial Management*, 15(6): Art. no. 270. doi: 10.3390/jrfm15060270.

[76] Tsanis, K., Aina, S. and Olubiyi, T. O. (2025). Creating enabling FinTech ecosystems across the continent. In *The Palgrave Handbook of FinTech in Africa and Middle East*, Singapore: Springer Nature, pp. 805–853, doi: 10.1007/978-981-96-6143-5_34.
[77] Schneier, B. (2002). Cryptographic design vulnerabilities. *Computer*, 31(9): 29–33. doi: 10.1109/2.708447.
[78] Long, G., Shen, T., Tan, Y., Gerrard, L., Clarke, A. and Jiang, J. (2021). Federated learning for privacy-preserving open innovation future on digital health. In *Humanity Driven AI*, Cham, Switzerland: Springer, pp. 113–133. doi: 10.1007/978-3-030-72188-6_6.

11 Federated Learning for ESG Disclosure Analytics: A Study on NSE Sectoral Indices

Silpa M.* and R. Naveena

The proposed study will utilize federated learning (FL), a decentralized and privacy-preserving machine learning approach, to analyze the environmental, social, and governance (ESG) disclosure performance of National Stock Exchange (NSE)-listed firms, and to compare them against some sector-specific indices such as Nifty 50, Nifty IT, and Nifty Bank. The research is valuable considering the need to increase transparency regarding ESG on financial markets and the necessity to accomplish secure and collaborative frameworks that enable successful ESG assessment without breaching the privacy of a dataset. In emerging economies, ESG factors are increasingly playing an important role in affecting the valuation of corporations, investment decisions, and regulation. A federated analytical model is established to empower the consolidation and analysis of ESG performance indicators across the various entities, making sure that data are safe and in compliance with the regulatory aspects. There are statistical models to analyze the correlation between ESG scores and the financial performance metrics, including return on equity (ROE), return on assets (ROA), and stock returns, and the way ESG performance has been affecting the required investor return and investment patterns. The outcomes reveal that ESG disclosure quality has a positive correlation with financial performance, meaning that companies with better ESG will have better financial performance and are more likely to be of interest to socially responsible investors. The research demonstrates that the federated learning can be used to improve transparency, analytical precision, and ethical financial analysis when adopted in ESG evaluation. The study has significant implications to institutional investors, regulators, and corporate managers because they advocate advanced and privacy-sensitive technologies in assessing ESG and developing scalable, secure, and intelligent ESG systems that will assist in responsible investing and better corporate responsibility within the Indian capital market.

Assistant Professor, Karpagam Academy of Higher Education, Coimbatore-641021.
Email: naveenasriram@gmail.com
* Corresponding author: silparathnakaran@gmail.com

DOI: 10.1201/9781003710059-11

1. Introduction

In the modern business environment, the environmental, social, and governance (ESG) factors are important when assessing the performance and sustainability of corporations, as well as their long term value creation. To investors, regulators, and stakeholders, ESG practices are not only an ethics responsibility, but a strategic resource that has an operational influence on profitability, risk management, as well as market reputation. When firms perform well in ESG, they attract socially responsible investors, minimize operational and regulatory risks, create trust in the stakeholders, and eventually enhance financial results. Sustainable investing has led to the rise in significance of ESG issues in the financial markets. The trend demands a high level of analytic technique to assess the effect of ESG on firm's performance [1]. AI is currently being incorporated into ESG systems, which has provided better evaluations of financial operations and sustainable objectives [2]. AI assists financial institutions in balancing the intricate nature of the financial operations and sustainability goals, in particular during the increased regulation and increased demands of the stakeholders [2]. The increase in the number of ESG reports and globally binding companies, such as China, committing to be carbon neutral by 2060, compels to integrate environmental protection into the governance process, which requires more complex tools to analyze it [3]. However, there are still difficulties—the lack of disclosure functions, high expenses, and low incentives in the emerging markets contribute to the fact that companies are not able to comply with ESG requirements and regulators and investors cannot get credible data [4]. The issues are multiplied in those countries where the mandatory ESG reporting is still in its infancy, such as in India, which requires superior analytical methods to deliver superior-quality ESG data [5].

ESG disclosure has become a major concern in India following the increased regulatory requirements, increasing investor awareness, and global interests in sustainable finance. Yet challenges remain. Lots of researches involve data collection centralization and traditional statistical tools that might jeopardize the privacy of data, restrict cross-company collaboration, and fail to consider industry-specific dynamics. These sectoral variations particularly between high impact industries such as banking, information technology, and telecommunication are easily overlooked and the generalized conclusions made do not necessarily represent real performance [6]. In order to address these drawbacks, the present paper relies on federated learning (FL), a privacy-sensitive, decentralized machine learning structure, to examine ESG disclosure of companies listed on the National Stock Exchange (NSE). FL enables joint analysis without exchanging raw data and maintaining confidentiality, as well as increasing the accuracy of analysis. The paper examines the relationship among ESG scores and some of the financial key metrics such as return on assets (ROA), return on equity (ROE), and stock returns. It also discusses the issue of ESG practices on investor behavior and expected rate of return. The predictive and risk assessment process is enhanced with the adoption of AI, in particular, federated learning, which offers the holistic perspective of corporate sustainability [2]. Nevertheless, the increase in the number of ESG scores of different standards has become an added cost, confusion, and risk to investors in the primary aspect of poor data quality and the various approaches taken by rating agencies, which has raised greenwashing concerns [7–15]. The solution to this can be provided by FL: it is a method of developing common analytical models that do not consolidate sensitive ESG data, maintaining privacy and enhancing insights [16]. Such a decentralized method is useful in achieving credible, holistic ESG analysis, which is necessary when investing in messy environments [17–26].

The need to develop such approach is in the absence of standardization between ESG rating agencies, and inconsistency in ESG data. Existing approaches are varied and are likely to be opaque, which generates uncertainty in methodology [18–19]. Financial institutions will be able to counter these shortcomings by using federated learning and enhance collaboration through the respect of data sovereignty and greater accuracy and depth of ESG analytics. The approach is essential to the analysis of the wide and frequently delicate ES data points and consequently creating a more subtle perspective on corporate sustainability performance. It has become critical to include nonfinancial ESG data in the investment process and impact profitability projection and require sophisticated analytical processes to evaluate multifaceted factors [5]. In this paper, the author analyzes the potential of federated learning, a paradigm of distributed AI, to address these issues. It allows the joint training of models among different financial institutions and corporations without sharing sensitive information, protecting sensitive information, and improving the overall ESG disclosure analytics [16].

In this paper, we will discuss ways to overcome these challenges of data through FL. It enhances the analysis of ESG of NSE sectoral indices since it provides models trained on a variety of datasets without sensitive data exchange [24]. FL solves the problem of data silos, which allows several companies to create powerful machine learning models deprived of sharing proprietary data [15]. Recent studies also highlight the efficiency and security advantages of federated learning in financial applications, further supporting its adoption in ESG analytics [27]. This method is mostly useful in ESG analytics, where the data heterogeneity issue and privacy concerns frequently restrict the perceptions of the corporate sustainability practices [15]. With the help of federated learning, we demonstrate that financial institutions can develop more precise and detailed ESG performance evaluations based on dispersed data, which improve decision-making and knowledge of corporate fundamentals [6–15]. The approach decreases information asymmetry and provides more insight into the ESG performance of a firm by combining different sources of data [6–15]. This work provides a secure and transparent ESG performance analysis of the Indian capital market, which is sector-sensitive and composed of sectoral indices such as Nifty 50, Nifty IT, and Nifty Bank. The findings are likely to support the institutional investors, the corporate managers, and the policymakers in designing effective ESG policies, enhancing responsible investing, and encouraging sustainable corporate behavior. In the end, this research is relevant to a better comprehension of how ESG performance may lead to the financial prosperity and long-term sustainability in the emerging markets.

2. Review of Literature

In the emerging markets, such as India, ESG factors have emerged as important factors of corporate performance, investor decision-making, and market value. Research has shown that increased ESG disclosure is likely to be linked to better financial performance, increased investor confidence, and better stock returns. Nevertheless, the efficiency of ESG assessment is restricted by issues such as the privacy of the data, differences in sectors, and irregular reporting regulations. FL with its recent developments is a privacy-preserving, decentralized method of analyzing ESG performance across companies without access to sensitive information. This review summarizes the existing empirical and theoretical literature on the aspect of the ESG disclosure, sectoral variations, and the use of advanced analytics, which forms the basis of the analysis of the outcome of ESG scores on the financial performance of NSE-listed firms.

Giudici and Wu (2025) [21] suggest ensemble machine learning models to determine the variation of ESG scores on credit ratings and overcome the issues of poor explainability of the model and its strength. They propose the use of the SAFE (Sustainable, Accurate, Fair, and Explainable) framework that is specific to financial use. According to their findings, the short-term forecasts of credit ratings using ESG factors are more precise than long-term ones. Predictive performance is also increased through the combination of the data across time. The research provides good information on the application of machine learning in ESG evaluation, without losing transparency and ethical principles.

The article by Deshpande (2025) [18] critically examines the trends of ESG disclosure for Nifty 50 firms. Based on content analysis and index comparison, the article demonstrates that Nifty 50 companies excel in India in terms of the embrace of global sustainability frameworks and production of full ESG reports. Nevertheless, the quality and richness of disclosures are very diverse: IT companies are generally ahead of banking and manufacturing. The paper highlights the importance of ESG standards being increased by regulatory efforts and investor pressure. Challenges related to such aspects as inconsistency, the lack of a third-party guarantee, and the lack of integration of material issues (sector-specific) are critical. Even though ESG reporting is on the rise, comparability and sector benchmarking are still in progress.

Singh (2025) [14] analyzes Nifty 50 companies' ESG disclosure practices in terms of regulatory compliance, reporting forms, and industry differences. The author discovers that there was a significant rise in the volume and frequency of ESG reporting following the sustainability requirements by Securities and Exchange Board of India (SEBI). Many IT companies that are in Nifty tend to be the first in setting industry standards by giving comprehensive climate and social impact data. Conversely, Nifty Bank firms, despite their improvements, remain low in terms of transparency and engagement of stakeholders. Singh notes that voluntary disclosures have the tendency of emphasizing the positives and not disclosing controversial or other not-so-enthusiastic information. The study recommends that there should be tightening of standards and alignment of sectoral ESG reporting in India.

Rahman (2025) [8] surveys federated learning structure, communication system, and issues of technical challenges in distributed machine learning. The barriers that are investigated in the study include non-IID data, communication overhead, system heterogeneity, and privacy preservation through differential privacy and secure aggregation. It also examines the new trends in personalized federated learning, cross-silo and cross-device, and their combination with other computational paradigms. The survey identifies the research directions in developing scalable, efficient, and trustworthy federated learning systems that are applicable to financial applications with the need to conduct collaborative analysis while maintaining data sovereignty.

Zeng et al. (2025) [30] evaluate the impact of disagreements in ESG ratings on equity markets in terms of the risk of return volatility and stock returns. It is indicated by the results that an increased ESG rating divergence is related with an increase in the risk of return volatility, which may raise the stock returns to compensate uncertainty. The study highlights that to reduce information asymmetry in financial markets, there is a need to have consistent ESG ratings and standardized assessment procedures. The results underscore the role of the powerful, transparent, and privacy-sensitive analytics, including federated learning, that will be able to intelligently synthesize ESG data across multiple sources and still ensure data security and narrow the spread in ratings.

Fildisi et al. (2025) [20] in order to map ESG disclosures on both structured and unstructured data, combine the natural language processing methods of AI. Their study links international financial measurement scales to local financial reporting and demonstrates the increase in decision-making accuracy by computational models. The findings indicate that federated models have the potential to combine datasets on ESG across jurisdictions and ensure the proprietary information of companies.

Hamdouni (2025) [23] investigates the impact of ESG disclosure on the financial performance of Saudi Arabia's heavy-pollutant firms by a two-step system Generalized Method of Moments (GMM) to adjust the endogeneity. The researcher concludes that there is a positive association among ESG performance and the major financial indicators, ROA, ROE, and Q of Tobin, which suggests the fact that good ESG performance increases firm's value, stakeholder confidence, and operational efficiency. It also highlights the significance of ESG to managers, investors, and policymakers, and calls on more disclosures to increase transparency and promote sustainable development in accordance with the Vision 2030 of Saudi Arabia.

Gladstone (2025) [22] upgrades ESG disclosure standards through the commentary of SEBI's 2025 ESG circular, which belongs to the Business Responsibility and Sustainability Report (BRSR) core framework. The implication on boards and stakeholders is discussed in the commentary that focuses on accountability, transparency, and repetitive reporting in the Indian capital markets. It highlights how the demand is rising to have standardized ESG analytics and mentions that federated solutions are able to provide privacy-compliant and accurate performance metrics.

The empirical research of Tripathi (2024) [28] is focused on the impact of ESG ratings on accounting and market performance of the Nifty 50 companies. The author uses regression analysis to determine that there is a positive but moderate connection between ESG scores and profitability, especially in large-cap Indian companies. The higher the ESG score, the more robust the company seems to be with regard to financial shocks and market turbulence. Nevertheless, Tripathi cautions that causality is not a universal truth and the impact may differ according to sector. Another area that has been identified by the article as a shortfall in Indian ESG disclosures is the lack of data availability and standardization. On the whole, it comes to the conclusion that there are long-term financial gains of investing in ESG practices, although short-term consequences vary.

Li et al. (2024) [16] study the relationship between overall ESG ratings and corporate performance measures ROE and ROA in trades with an environmental impact. A regression analysis shows that there is a significant positive correlation between the ESG implementation and financial performance. The environmental dimension in the specific case has a very good influence ($p < 0.01$). The paper gives empirical statistics that more investment in environmental protection benefits the firms in the high-impact industries, which makes the business case to integrate ESG.

Robai (2024) [11] studies the use of federated education to provide privacy-preserving and secure data analytics in the context of heterogeneous networks that have variety of devices, data distributions, and network conditions. The study summarizes the important privacy techniques such as differential privacy, secure multi-party calculation, and homomorphic encryption, and compares their performance in dynamical, resource-constrained settings. Scalability, communication efficiency, and adversarial robustness are some of the most problematic issues addressed in the study and provide researchers and practitioners with an in-depth process of deploying federated learning to more complex network ecosystems applicable to financial data analysis.

Shobhwani and Lodha (2024) [13] explore the effect of ESG disclosure scores on different types of firms listed at the NSE in India. Based on the analysis of 38 firms, they use fixed-effects panel regressions to demonstrate that improved operational (ROA), financial (ROE), and market-based (Tobin Q) performance is caused by higher ESG scores. The scores on ESG explain 71.15 and 75.25 of variance in ROA and ROE, respectively, which provides good evidence of financial benefits of ESG transparency in Indian capital markets. These findings justify the establishment of privacy-sensitive systems of ESG analysis.

The research by Veeravel et al. (2024) [29] determines the impact of the ESG disclosure scores on the performance of the companies on the NSE of India. They discover that more powerful ESG disclosures are always better in enhancing firms' performance in various statistical models. The research question is whether transparency of ESG brings any financial gain or not in the wake of new regulatory developments, including the BRSR requirement. These findings support the need to make ESG reporting more transparent.

In August 2024, KPMG International [25] discussed the ways to enhance accuracy and validation of the ESG data analysis by its AI-driven automation. The report shows that machine learning produces no human error or standardization of scoring, which increases the comparability of data. It provides a distinct connection between the analytical capability of AI and efficiency requirements of privacy-conscious data-sharing algorithms, such as federated learning, in ESG evaluation.

On November 18, 2024, to identify financial crimes without sensitive customer data being compromised, Lucinity [31] describes the practical implementation of FL. The article describes a model-aggregation and local-training strategy which enables institutions to take advantage of collective intelligence, but at the same time, maintain data sovereignty. It highlights the similarity in the application of federated learning principles to protect corporate disclosures in multilateral ESG analyses.

The business report of Ricago Consultancy [10] discusses the new relaxation and gradual introduction of the ESG value-chain disclosure requirements by SEBI. It narrates how the focus on proportional reporting, voluntary reporting, and guaranteed reporting has been shifting in the Indian sustainable business environment. The article confirms the necessity of digital governance solutions that can facilitate real-time ESG reporting using developing compliance systems.

Ramakrishna and Abhishek (2024) [9] use multifactor models and the longitudinal analysis of NSE's ESG-listed companies to determine the connection between ESG integration and profitability, ROE, and risk. Findings indicate that, among Indian corporates, a positive relationship of greater ESG scores and stronger ROE and enterprise value exists. They discover that open ESG reporting eliminates information asymmetry and is a factor that appeals to institutional investors. However, the authors observe that infrastructure and energy are other sectors that experience high costs of adaptation and this may dilute financial benefits. The paper concludes that the adoption of ESG is a dynamic practice in India and is gaining more criticality with regard to international competitiveness. The results confirm the opinion that ESG can be considered a risk-mitigating and growth-promoting driver in the Indian setting.

Makkar (2023) [32] uses in comparison Nifty 50 and Nifty IT, as sectoral ESG indices, and conventional indices to evaluate the performance under various market conditions. The article concludes that ESG indices work better than traditional indices in volatile markets, particularly in the post-COVID-19 period. Sector analysis indicates that IT and FMCG sectors have a high level of ESG activity, and banking and industries are less rapid. Makkar emphasizes the institutional diversification of ESG data as a reason to build a portfolio. However, the research indicates that there are difficulties in data accuracy and relevancy to the Indian investors. The article finds that sectoral ESG benchmarking will be more and more severe in the context of the progress of India to global standards of disclosure.

The article by Aydoğmuş et al. (2022) [33] expresses the connection between the ESG performance and the financial figures in publicly traded firms. They demonstrate the fact that the ESG scores are highly correlated. The association between ESG scores and conventional financial metrics such as ROA and Q of Tobin is complicated, however. These results defy common beliefs regarding the links between ESG and finance and underscore the importance of sophisticated methodologies of analysis, especially in developing markets where institutional structures are in the process of development.

Saxena (2016) [12] employs panel data provided by the NSE companies to examine the direct and indirect impacts of ESG screening on returns of the firms, quality of assets, and investor sentiment. The discussion indicates that ESG-positive companies tend to do better than their counterparts in terms of market-capitalization expansion and investor retention. Nonetheless, not every dimension of ESG is equally important; in India, governance aspects are more likely to have a close connection to financial measures. There is a significant difference based on the sector—the strongest ties of ESG performance are disclosed by the IT and consumer-goods companies as compared to heavy industries and banks. To further refine their analysis in future, Saxena suggests narrower ESG measures and increased participation of more stakeholders.

3. Research Gap

Although the linking between ESG performance and financial results keeps on evolving and being studied, there is still a strong gap that exists in the emerging markets, India in particular. A majority of the researches indicate a positive relationship between ESG disclosure and corporate financial performance, yet use centralized data and conventional statistical techniques, which casts doubts on privacy and collaboration issues. The differences related to sectors, particularly within banking and IT, tend to be disregarded, which leads to general conclusions. Although machine learning and AI have been implemented in ESG analytics around the world, this technology is not widely used in India, and the centralized model presents confidentiality and compliance issues. FL is a privacy-preserving, decentralized alternative that has not been implemented on ESG evaluation of NSE-listed companies. Additionally, there is no empirical research in India that combines FL evaluation of ESG based on financial performance such as ROE, ROA, and stock returns. This research will fill these gaps by utilizing FL in the new study to examine ESG disclosure and its effects on financial performance in the NSE-listed companies and sectoral index and offer theoretical and practical policy implications toward sustainable finance.

4. Statement of the Problem

ESG has emerged as one of the most important aspects in the past few years as it defines the long-term sustainability of a company, the confidence of the investor, and the financial outcome of a company. Although more and more regulators and investors demand ESG disclosure, there is one significant challenge—assessing the performance in the field of ESG complying with the regulations while not disclosing sensitive information. Centralization of data analysis usually involves the firms exchanging confidential data, and it brings up issues of privacy, security, and inter-organizational cooperation.

The majority of existing studies on ESG cover global markets or apply common statistics and machine-learning frameworks that do not take into account sector-specifics and do not deal with decentralized data. In India, there are limited studies that reconcile the ESG analysis and privacy-preserving techniques such as FL. The absence of safe collaborative technologies restrains investors, policymakers, and executives who require quality ESG evaluations to make effective choices and encourage responsible business practices.

Several research works have associated ESG performance with financial performance such as ROE, ROA, and stock returns. Nevertheless, it is still unclear what is the exact relationship between the quality of ESG reporting and sector-specific financial outcomes in India. This gap demonstrates the necessity of a powerful, decentralized, and sector-sensitive framework which would be able to assess ESG, maintain confidential data, and provide clear informed insights regarding sustainable investing and governance.

Our research is primarily going to address the gap in privacy-sensitive, cooperative, and reliable approaches to assessing ESG disclosure and its impact on financial results in the Indian markets. We accomplish this by utilizing the federated learning to the companies in the NSE listed in key sectors.

5. Scope of the Study

We use federated learning to test ESG disclosures of NSE-listed companies, particularly in Nifty 50, Nifty IT, and Nifty Bank indices. To indicate the relationship between sustainability practices and ROE, ROA, and stock returns as the key financial measures, we consider the relationship between ESG quality and these financial metrics in India.

The sample only consists of publicly listed companies in India that report on ESG. This constrains its results to institutional investors, policymakers, and managers that are interested in responsible investing and governance in areas that consider data privacy. Federated learning helps us to examine ESG in a group of the firms without exchanging confidential information.

We also analyze the variations in ESG performance by industry, particularly in the banking and IT industries, and provide some useful insights on the industry strategy and policymaking as applied to investments. The framework despite focusing on India can be expanded to other emerging markets requiring secure and scalable ESG assessment.

Concisely, our study contributes to the development of ESG analytics using a combination of federated learning technology and financial performance analysis. This model can be used to appreciate the impact of ESG revelation on corporate value and justify responsible investment in India.

6. Objectives

- To assess the relationship between the ESG score and financial performance of NSE-listed companies.
- To examine the ESG disclosure performance of NSE-listed companies across sectoral indices such as Nifty 50, Nifty IT, and Nifty Bank.

7. Research Methodology

The current research has a quantitative, empirical research design, which covered the relationship between ESG disclosure and financial performance in companies listed on the NSE. It combines FL, a decentralized data-privacy, privacy-respecting machine-learning approach, with conventional statistical algorithms to establish a confidential and scalable data analysis system. The study is descriptive-cum-analytical where both cross-sectional and longitudinal data on a number of financial periods have been used to make the study robust. The sample is composed of NSE-traded companies that publicly report on ESG. To ensure industry-specific variations, a stratified sample is used based on sectoral indices (Nifty 50, Nifty IT, and Nifty Bank). Corporate ESG reports, NSE filings, annual reports, and established ESG rating databases obtain secondary data, whereas financial performance indicators (ROE, ROA, and stock returns) are publicly available. FL enables companies to cooperate in training the models without the necessity of sharing raw data, and hence, it preserves privacy and satisfies the regulations. The correlation and regression measures involve quantifying the relations between ESG disclosure and financial performance, and sectoral comparison shows industry-specific trends. Python, TensorFlow Federated, scikit-learn, and statistical packages, including SPSS and R, are among the tools utilized in the study, and visualization tools are also used to illustrate all patterns of ESG clearly. The ethical protection is stringent to guarantee that the sensitive corporate information is kept confidential during the analysis. Although the approach is constrained by the number and quality of ESG revelations and the sample of the NSE-traded firms, the methodology provides a solid, safe, and informative framework to evaluate the ESG performance and its financial consequences in the Indian capital market.

8. Significance of the Study

The study is scholarly and practice- and policy-focused in the dynamic specialty of sustainable finance. On the academic side, it contributes to the literature by fusing federated learning with ESG assessment, which offers a decentralized and privacy-sensitive framework that compensates the flaws of existing centralized frameworks. In practice, the results provide institutional investors, portfolio managers, and corporate decision-makers with tangible evidence that high-quality ESG disclosure is related to improved financial performance of better ROE, ROA, and stock returns. The information supports the responsible investment policy, risk-management strategies, and industry-related portfolio allocation particularly in banking and IT sectors where ESG is currently being embraced. Concerning policymaking, the report notes that there should be safe, transparent, and standardized ESG reporting systems. This provides the regulators and policymakers with a ground on which to come up with effective disclosure norms and sustainability incentives. Ethical, privacy-conscious, and technology-oriented corporate sustainability evaluation is possible with the work. It demonstrates that federal learning can be used in ESG assessment, which allows preserving sensitive information but also allows cross-firm analysis to be successful. All in all, the study underwrites to the knowledge on interconnection of ESG and financial performance, justifies responsible investment, and provides a scalable framework that will enhance the practice of governance and sustainability in new economies such as India.

9. Analysis and Interpretation

Return on Equity: Table 1 compares the 5-year ROE patterns of NSE-listed companies with the focus on the trend in the sector and profitability.

Table 1: Comparison of 5-year ROE trends across NSE-listed companies by sector.

	Return on Equity					
	SBI	*BHARTI AIRTEL*	*HDFC BANK*	*ICICI BANK*	*INFOSYS*	*TCS*
2021	10.13	−38.44	16.5	13.1	27.4	38.55
2022	13.61	6.8	16.6	14.8	29.1	44.13
2023	18.44	11.6	17.1	17.2	31.2	47.26
2024	18.97	9.4	17.2	18.8	32.1	51.04
2025	18.66	34.3	14.5	17.9	29	52.94
Average	15.962	4.732	16.38	16.36	29.76	46.784
SD	3.937381	26.51096226	1.094075	2.3501064	1.879628	5.724485
Covariance	4.484	29.616	−0.68	2.72	1.24	7.138

The ROE analysis (2021–2025) discloses of variations in the sector. TCS and Infosys have good, steady IT profitability of 46.78 and 29.76, respectively. Bharti Airtel was very volatile, ranging between −38.44% and 34.3%. The returns provided by SBI, HDFC Bank, and ICICI Bank were consistent, and they were about 16 years of age, which showed consistent equity efficiency. The overall results are that IT firms performed better, whereas telecom and banking industries had moderate and fluctuating profitability.

Return on Assets: Table 2 of ROA measures asset efficiency and utilization of the selected NSE-listed companies within the period of 5 years, and it reveals the sector performance, performance consistency, and variability.

Table 2: 5-year ROA trends of NSE-listed companies: a comparative assessment of asset efficiency and sectoral performance.

	Return on Assets (Including Revaluations)					
	SBI	*BHARTI AIRTEL*	*HDFC BANK*	*ICICI BANK*	*INFOSYS*	*TCS*
2021	284.47	140.86	381.74	241.72	167.01	235.49
2022	313.84	134.14	447.29	270.22	163.31	245.54
2023	367.08	140.76	520.27	315.67	161.18	249.26
2024	422.7	166.79	614.89	382.53	195.56	252.4
2025	494.32	245.13	698.29	458.69	210.27	264.7
Average	376.482	165.536	532.496	333.766	179.466	249.478
SD	84.41049058	46.22023723	126.89891	87.780919	22.12719	10.62387
Covariance	105.712	48.238	160.14	109.25	23.754	13.056

ROA (2021–2025) shows high and stable rates of increase of the majority of firms. Bank of HDFC has 532.50 on average, which is above that of SBI and ICICI Bank, emphasizing on the efficiency of the banking sector. TCS and Infosys have stable returns and moderate returns. The performance of Bharti Airtel is lowest and most volatile. On the whole, the banking companies are better in assets efficiency; the IT companies increase consistently; telecommunications industry changes more.

Return on Equity: Table 3 ROE summary shows the differences, variability, and trends of performance of NSE-listed companies within a period of 5 years.

Table 3: Comparative ROE statistics of NSE-listed companies: 5-year sectoral performance overview.

	N	*Mean*	*Std. Deviation*	*Minimum*	*Maximum*
SBI	5	15.9620	3.93738	10.13	18.97
BHARTI AIRTEL	5	4.7320	26.51096	−38.44	34.30
HDFC BANK	5	16.3800	1.09407	14.50	17.20
ICICI BANK	5	16.3600	2.35011	13.10	18.80
INFOSYS	5	29.7600	1.87963	27.40	32.10
TCS	5	46.7840	5.72449	38.55	52.94
Total	30	21.6630	17.02384	−38.44	52.94

The returns are very robust and steady with TCS (46.78) and Infosys (29.76) both performing well in the business of IT. The HDFC Bank, ICICI Bank, and SBI remain at about 16% ROE. The mean ROE of Bharti Airtel is 4.73% and very volatile. The wide variation of −38.44 to 52.94 is indicative of strong IT performance and telecom instability.

Analysis of Variance (ANOVA)—Return On Equity: Table 4 of ANOVA compares the ROE values of the chosen NSE-listed companies in the 5 years to identify statistically significant differences in ROE.

Table 4: Analysis of variance (ANOVA) on ROE: assessing differences among selected NSE-listed companies over 5 years.

	Sum of Squares	*df*	*Mean Square*	*F*	*Sig.*
Between Groups	5359.091	5	1071.818	8.447	0.000
Within Groups	3045.427	24	126.893		
Total	8404.518	29			

The ANOVA indicates that there is a noteworthy difference in ROE of the six companies ($F = 8.447$, $p = 0.000$). This means that the level of profitability differs significantly in terms of the sectors and that IT firms perform better than others.

Return on Assets: Table 5 sums the statistics of ROA of NSE-listed companies. It indicates differences and variability and performance trends in the sector over a period of 5 years.

Table 5: Comparative ROA statistics of NSE-listed companies: sectoral performance and stability overview.

	N	*Mean*	*Std. Deviation*	*Minimum*	*Maximum*
SBI	5	376.4820	84.41049	284.47	494.32
BHARTI AIRTEL	5	165.5360	46.22024	134.14	245.13
HDFC BANK	5	532.4960	126.89891	381.74	698.29
ICICI BANK	5	333.7660	87.78092	241.72	458.69
INFOSYS	5	179.4660	22.12719	161.18	210.27
TCS	5	249.4780	10.62387	235.49	264.70
Total	30	306.2040	145.57423	134.14	698.29

The descriptive statistics of ROA indicate obvious differences between sectors. HDFC bank has the highest ROA of 532.50, while SBI has the same of 376.48 and ICICI Bank has the same of 333.77. These values demonstrate good use of assets in the banking sector. The ROAs of TCS (249.48) and Infosys (179.47) are moderate and regular, indicating a stable efficiency of the IT. The lowest and most erratic ROA is of Bharti Airtel (165.54). On the whole, the aggregate mean ROA is 306.20 and the spread is 134.14–698.29, which highlights the differences in sectors. Due to the higher level of asset returns, banking firms are the most successful; however, telecom is more variable.

ANOVA—Return on Assets: Table 6 of ANOVA establishes whether ROA is significantly different across the sampled NSE companies that are listed in the NSE in the past 5 years.

Table 6: Analysis of variance (ANOVA) on ROA: testing differences among selected NSE-listed companies over 5 years.

	Sum of Squares	*df*	*Mean Square*	*F*	*Sig.*
Between Groups	479872.882	5	95974.576	17.101	0.000
Within Groups	134690.971	24	5612.124		
Total	614563.853	29			

The findings indicate that the six companies have a big difference in ROA (F 17.101, p 0.000). The levels of assets and efficiency vary significantly among sectors. Banking organizations are the most stable, and telecommunication firms are more unstable.

Correlation Analysis:

SBI: Table 7 shows the correlation analysis conducted to examine the association between ESG score, ROE, and ROA of SBI and evaluate the impact of ESG performance on equity and asset returns.

Table 7: Influence of ESG performance on SBI's ROE and ROA: a correlation analysis.

		ESG Score	*ROE*	*ROA*
ESG Score	Pearson Correlation (PC)	1	−0.957	−0.060
	Sig.		0.187	0.962
	N	3	3	3
ROE	PC	−0.957	1	0.346
	Sig.	0.187		0.775
	N	3	3	3
ROA	PC	−0.060	0.346	1
	Sig.	0.962	0.775	
	N	3	3	3

The connection between ESG score and ROE is significant and negative (r = −0957), although this result is not statistically significant (p = 0.187) because the sample size (N = 3) is small. ESG score and ROA have a very small correlation (r 0.060, p 0.962). The correlation between ROE and ROA is moderate (r = 0.346, p = 0.775), which is also not significant. In general, the few data fragments do not allow drawing the definite conclusion regarding the ESG performance and financial indicators of SBI.

Bharti Airtel: Table 8 presents the correlation analysis conducted to identify the direct connection between ESG ratings and financial indicators (ROE and ROA) in Bharti Airtel and to extract information as to whether the ESG disclosure has any effect on financial performance.

Table 8: Influence of ESG disclosure on financial metrics (ROE and ROA) of Bharti Airtel.

		ESG Score	*ROE*	*ROA*
ESG Score	PC	1	−0.315	−0.599
	Sig.		0.796	0.591
	N	3	3	3
ROE	PC	−0.315	1	0.949
	Sig.	0.796		0.205
	N	3	3	3
ROA	PC	−0.599	0.949	1
	Sig.	0.591	0.205	
	N	3	3	3

The correlation outcomes of Bharti Airtel indicate that there is a weak negative correlation between ESG score and ROE ($r = -0.315$, $p = 0.796$) and moderate negative correlation among ESG score and ROA ($r = -0.599$, $p = 0.591$). These results recommend that the connection between ESG scores and financial performance might be positive but not statistically significant due to a small size of the sample ($N = 3$). ROE and ROA show a strong positive correlation ($r = 0.949$, $p = 0.205$), representing that asset efficiency is closely linked to equity returns, but this is also statistically insignificant. Overall, no conclusive relationship between ESG performance and financial metrics can be drawn for Bharti Airtel.

HDFC Bank: Table 9 presents the correlation analysis between ESG score, ROE and ROA of HDFC Bank. The table highlights how ESG performance is associated with key financial indicators, offering insights into the sector-specific effects of ESG on banking financial performance.

Table 9: Impact of ESG performance on HDFC Bank's ROE and ROA: a sectoral analysis.

		ESG Score	*ROE*	*ROA*
ESG Score	PC	1	0.471	−0.884
	Sig.		0.687	0.310
	N	3	3	3
ROE	PC	0.471	1	−0.829
	Sig.	0.687		0.377
	N	3	3	3
ROA	PC	−0.884	−0.829	1
	Sig.	0.310	0.377	
	N	3	3	3

For HDFC Bank, the correlation analysis shows a reasonable positive relationship between ESG score and ROE ($r = 0.471$, $p = 0.687$) and a solid negative relationship with ROA ($r = -0.884$, $p = 0.310$). ROE and ROA are also strongly negatively correlated ($r = -0.829$, $p = 0.377$). However, all correlations are not statistically significant due to the small sample size ($N = 3$). These results suggest no definitive connection between ESG performance and financial metrics for HDFC Bank in this period.

ICICI Bank: Table 10 shows the examination of the correlation between disclosure of ESG and financial results (ROE and ROA) of ICICI Bank, bringing out any positive or negative relationship.

Table 10: Impact of ESG disclosure on ICICI Bank's financial performance: ROE and ROA analysis.

		ESG Score	*ROE*	*ROA*
ESG Score	PC	1	−0.758	−0.902
	Sig.		0.452	0.284
	N	3	3	3
ROE	PC	−0.758	1	0.402
	Sig.	0.452		0.736
	N	3	3	3
ROA	PC	−0.902	0.402	1
	Sig.	0.284	0.736	
	N	3	3	3

In the case of ICICI Bank, correlation analysis reveals that the ESG score and ROA ($r = -0.902$, $p = 0.284$) and ROE ($r = -0.758$, $p = 0.452$) have a strong negative correlation. There is a low positive correlation between ROE and ROA ($r = 0.402$, $p = 0.736$). All these correlations are however nonsignificant because the sample size ($N = 3$) is small. In general, the connection between the ESG performance and the financial values in the case of ICICI Bank cannot be concluded.

Infosys: Table 11 presents the analysis of the relationship between ESG performance and financial performance indicators- Return of Equity(ROE) and Return of Assets(ROA).

Table 11: Impact of ESG performance on financial outcomes of Infosys: an analysis of ROE and ROA in the IT sector.

		ESG Score	*ROE*	*ROA*
ESG Score	PC	1	−0.282	−0.682
	Sig.		0.818	0.522
	N	3	3	3
ROE	PC	−0.282	1	−0.509
	Sig.	0.818		0.660
	N	3	3	3
ROA	PC	−0.682	−0.509	1
	Sig.	0.522	0.660	
	N	3	3	3

In the case of Infosys, the correlation analysis shows that there is a weak negative correlation between ESG score and ROE (r = −0.282, p = 0.818) and a moderate negative correlation between ESG score and ROA (r = −0.682, p = 0.522). There is also a moderate negative relationship between ROE and ROA (r = −0.509, p = 0.660). All those correlations are not statistically significant due to the small sample size (N = 3). All in all, no conclusive evidence can be found on the relation between ESG performance and financial measures of Infosys.

TCS: Table 12 presents the correlation among ESG scores and financial performance (ROE and ROA) in TCS and whether the high ESG practices lead to increased returns.

Table 12: Relationship among ESG scores and financial performance of TCS: assessing the impact of ESG practices on ROE and ROA.

		ESG Score	*ROE*	*ROA*
ESG Score	PC	1	0.982	0.946
	Sig.		0.120	0.210
	N	3	3	3
ROE	PC	0.982	1	0.868
	Sig.	0.120		0.330
	N	3	3	3
ROA	PC	0.946	0.868	1
	Sig.	0.210	0.330	
	N	3	3	3

In the case of TCS, the correlation analysis indicates that there is a strong positive correlation among the ESG score and ROE (r = 0.982, p = 0.120) and between ESG score and ROA (r = 0.946, p = 0.210). There is also a strong positive correlation among ROE and ROA (r = 0.868, p = 0.330). These correlations are not significant (the small sample size, N = 3) but indicate that an increased ESG performance could be correlated with the increased financial performance of the TCS.

All these tables are aimed at investigating the sector-specific correlation between ESG performance and monetary indicators of six NSE-listed companies and finding a pattern, a strong side or a weak side of the connection between the ESG disclosures, and equity and asset performance.

Correlation: Table 13 shows that there are strong positive correlations between the Nifty 100 ESG index and the leading NSE indices, which have been used to show that ESG stocks follow the market and sector trends.

Table 13: Correlation between Nifty 100 ESG index and Major NSE indices: evidence of alignment between ESG stocks and market trends.

NSE		*NIFTY 100 ESG Index*	*NIFTY 50*	*NIFTY IT*	*NIFTY BANK*
NIFTY 100 ESG Index	PC	1	0.981	0.651	0.849
	Sig.		0	0	0
	N	2476	2476	2476	2476
NIFTY 50	PC	0.981	1	0.615	0.888
	Sig.	0		0	0
	N	2476	2476	2476	2476
NIFTY IT	PC	0.651	0.615	1	0.381
	Sig.	0	0		0
	N	2476	2476	2476	2476
NIFTY BANK	PC	0.849	0.888	0.381	1
	Sig.	0	0	0	
	N	2476	2476	2476	2476

The correlation analysis provides an empirical perspective of the relation between the key indices in the Indian market, namely, the NIFTY 100 ESG index, NIFTY 50, NIFTY IT, and NIFTY BANK. It demonstrates the market forces influencing the sustainable-investment choices. The research results revealed a very high rate of positive correlation ($r = 0.981$, $p = 0.01$) between NIFTY 100 ESG index and NIFTY 50. This shows that the portfolios based on ESG follow the overall equity market closely. The idea of ESG investments in India is not vacuum-packed; it is closely tied to the general market dynamics and indicates that corporate sustainability practice is getting integrated into financial performance. The NIFTY 100 ESG index and NIFTY BANK are also strongly correlated ($r = 0.849$, $p = 0.01$) with each other. This explains the significant contribution of banking industry to the cause of ESG via green financing, sustainable credit policy, and responsible investment structures. Conversely, the relationship with NIFTY IT is medium ($r = 0.651$, $p = 0.01$). IT sector has the momentum of ESG in terms of digital transformation and transparency of governance but the contribution is less than other sectors. The existence of the weak correlation between NIFTY IT and NIFTY BANK ($r = 0.381$, $p = 0.01$) highlights the heterogeneity of the industrial sector and the diversification of the Indian capital market. The pattern of correlation reveals in general that the ESG indices in India are largely driven by the macro-market trends and performance of the financial sector. This once again reinforces the opinion that sustainable investments are slowly becoming part of the traditional market, and not an alternative asset.

10. Suggestions

- Promote the assimilation of ESG in IT companies: TCS and Infosys determine a positive connection among ESG performance and monetary performance, which is that sustainable and accountable practices can enhance profitability and the efficiency of assets. IT firms ought to continue enhancing ESG efforts in order to draw socially responsible investors.
- Enhance ESG activities in the banking industry: Banks such as SBI, HDFC Bank, and ICICI Bank have neutral or adverse relationships between ESG scores and financial performances. They ought to implement more powerful ESG strategies and more effective disclosure efforts in order to align sustainability and financial outcomes with investor expectations and anticipations.
- Stabilize ESG implementation in telecom industry: Bharti Airtel recorded low ROE and ROA volatility and poor ESG correlations. Telecom industry needs to concentrate on regular ESG policies, disclosure, and reporting to eliminate the performance variations and enhance investor trust.
- Sector-specific ESG plans: The analysis demonstrates a high level of variation in different sectors. Businesses are advised to use specific ESG strategies that alter the risks and opportunities in the sector as opposed to generic models.
- Federated learning in ESG analytics: Due to privacy implication and sensitive information, companies can adopt federated-learning-based ESG measurement framework to enhance transparency, cooperation, and accuracy in reporting without jeopardizing the confidentiality.
- Connect ESG to investor communications: Businesses ought to communicate the ESG performance better to investors, and should highlight its effects on financial performance, particularly in industries where ESG has a positive correlation with ROE and ROA.
- ESG impact tracking: Firms would need to track ESG indicators during a long period to see the way the relationship with financial performance develops to make better decisions and follow the sustainability objectives.
- Regulatory compliance and standardization: Firms ought to implement standardized norms of ESG reporting to enable comparability, attract investment, and help in benchmarking the sector.
- Incorporate ESG training and awareness: Businesses ought to provide continuous employee education on ESG principles which should be implemented as part of their culture and decision-making.
- Be technologically monitored: Implement blockchains and AI solutions to monitor real-time ESG data, increase transparency, responsibility, and prevent fraud.

- Promote joint ventures: Interact with companies, investors, and regulators by communicating best practices and setting up shared ESG standards, as well as sponsoring combined sustainability efforts.
- Connect executive compensation to ESG: Initiate managerial compensation and bonuses to ESG accomplishments, which would promote long-term sustainable profits.
- Publish and participate: Report on the ESG progress frequently and engage the stakeholders of the company, including investors, customers, and communities, to establish trust and credibility.
- Develop industry scorecards: Exchanges or regulators should come up with industry-specific ESG scorecards to compare their performance and make targeted improvements.
- Use green finance: Encourage companies to finance green projects with green bonds, sustainability-linked loans, and funds with an ESG focus.
- Policy integration: Governments and regulators are to increase the rules of ESG disclosure and give tax breaks to sustainable investments and clean operations.
- Employ data-driven risk management: To reduce the environmental and social risks that endanger financial stability, incorporate ESG factors in risk assessment models.
- Educate investors: Investment education programs on ESG must be organized that emphasize the long-term financial benefits.

11. Conclusion

The current research gives a detailed evaluation of the correlation between the ESG performance and the financial measures of the NSE-listed companies with detailed references to the sectoral variations in IT, banking, and telecom sectors.

The outcomes indicate the presence of a positive and significant correlation amid ESG scores and financial performance indices such as ROE and ROA in IT companies and companies in particular, TCS and Infosys. It would reflect that sound ESG practices within the IT industry do not only help to generate profitability, but also to effectively use assets, reduce risks, and increase stakeholder confidence, which would support the business argument in favor of sustainable corporate practices.

On the other hand, the banking industry, which is represented by SBI, HDFC Bank, and ICICI bank, portrays moderate or even negative relations between the financial measurements and ESG performance. This is an issue of the industry, where the application of ESG strategies to both operational and financial models is not taken seriously. Telecom companies as demonstrated by Bharti Airtel are highly volatile in terms of ROE and ROA implying that the inconsistent disclosure and implementation of ESG may restrain its effects on financial performance. These findings indicate the relevance of sector-specific ESG policies, as opposed to a universal strategy.

Critically, the paper indicates how useful FL is as a decentralized, privacy-sensitive system of analyzing ESG. FL helps organizations to collaborate safely and without jeopardizing sensitive financial or ESG data, and increases the accuracy of the analysis, as well as staying in compliance with regulations. This approach to methods may be used as an example of future ESG assessments of emerging markets, where the issue of information privacy is a severe problem.

In general, the research reveals two significant roles of ESG performance: this area leads to the financial performance of companies whose ESG is strong, as well as it fosters investor trust, openness, and responsible investment. The implications on corporate managers and institutional investors and policymakers are practical, with recommendations being that the standard, transparent, industry-specific ESG disclosure systems be adopted. Companies would find it possible to create lasting value, ensure sustainable growth, and meet global sustainability objectives by incorporating ESG principles in corporate strategies and investment choices.

12. Scope for Further Research

Although this research offers useful information around the association among ESG performance and financial performance of NSE-listed firms through federated learning, there are a number of possibilities to conduct further research to enhance the knowledge and make it applicable to a wider audience.

To start with, a bigger sample should be used in future research with increased diversity. This would involve the inclusion of small- and middle-cap firms and firms belonging to other industries such as manufacturing, energy, and pharmaceuticals. In such a way, the researchers will be able to estimate the validity of the observed trends to a more limited set of industries and make more general conclusions about the ESG practices in the Indian capital market.

Second, a longitudinal study over a long duration would be able to analyze the long-standing impact of ESG adoption on financial performance and investor behavior. These studies would represent the changing effect of sustainability practices and changes in regulation, the lagged effects of ESG investment, and provide the long-run benefits or costs of varying degrees of ESG involvement.

Third, the comparative research across countries may be conducted covering ESG disclosure and performance between emerging and developed markets. This would emphasize local variations, regulatory factors, as well as market-specific investor interests. The results of such research would be useful in learning how applicable ESG strategies are globally and offer guidelines that Indian companies wishing to have foreign investors can use.

Fourth, predictive accuracy could be enhanced by the implementation of the latest machine-learning approaches, such as hybrid AI–federated learning architectures or deep-learning models. These methods would be able to identify nonlinear associations among ESG performance and financial measures that statistical frameworks may not identify. The research may also focus in the future by considering the sectoral and component-level impacts by predicting the environmental, social, as well as governance factors individually, and determine which of these factors leads to the biggest impact on financial performance, stock returns, and investor decisions.

Lastly, the behavioral features of ESG-based investment could be investigated in future studies. This would involve the interaction between investor sentiment, perception of risk, and reputation of corporation with ESG disclosure in capital allocation. Researching these dimensions would give a more detailed insight into the complex roles of ESG in corporate finance, sustainable investing, and policymaking. Together, these sources imply that there is a fertile future of ESG research in India and other countries to facilitate the creation of evidence-based models of corporate governance and investment policies.

References

[1] Oza, P. and Patekar, A. (2024). Does environmental, social, and governance strategy lead to better firm performance: Analysis of NIFTY 500 companies. *Corporate Governance and Sustainability Review*, 8(2): 24. https://doi.org/10.22495/cgsrv8i2p2.

[2] Jun, X. (2024). *AI in ESG for Financial Institutions: An Industrial Survey*. https://doi.org/10.2139/ssrn.4949354.

[3] Zhang, C. and Wu, X. (2023). Analyst coverage and corporate ESG performance. *Sustainability*, 15(17): 12763. https://doi.org/10.3390/su151712763.

[4] Fu, T. and Li, J. (2023). An empirical analysis of the impact of ESG on financial performance: The moderating role of digital transformation. *Frontiers in Environmental Science*, 11. https://doi.org/10.3389/fenvs.2023.1256052.

[5] Desai, R. (2023). Nexus between mandatory ESG disclosure regulation and abnormal stock returns: A study of an emerging economy. *International Journal of Law and Management*, 66(2): 236. https://doi.org/10.1108/ijlma-07-2023-0154.

[6] Rohendi, H., Ghozali, I. and Ratmono, D. (2024). Environmental, social, and governance (ESG) disclosure and firm value: The role of competitive advantage as a mediator. *Cogent Business & Management*, 11(1). https://doi.org/10.1080/23311975.2023.2297446.

[7] Pavlova, M., Casey, B. and Wang, M. -Z. (2024). ESG-FTSE: A corpus of news articles with ESG relevance labels and use cases. *arXiv (Cornell University)*. https://doi.org/10.48550/arxiv.2405.20218.

[8] Rahman, R. (2025). Federated learning: A survey on privacy-preserving collaborative intelligence. arXiv preprint arXiv:2504.17703. https://doi.org/10.48550/arXiv.2504.17703.

[9] Ramakrishna, V. and Abhishek, P. (2024). Impact of ESG scores on financial performance in Indian NSE (ESG) listed companies. *Journal of Research Administration*, 6(2): 102–121. https://journlra.org/index.php/jra/article/view/1982.

[10] Ricago Consultancy. (2024, December 31). SEBI's latest ESG disclosure reforms: Impact on Indian businesses and compliance strategies. Retrieved from https://www.ricago.com/blog/sebi-latest-esg-disclosure-reforms-impact-on-indian-businesses-and-compliance-strategies.

[11] Robai, M. P. (2024). Federated learning for secure and privacy preserving data analytics in heterogeneous networks. *GSC Advanced Research and Reviews*, 21(2): 527–555. https://doi.org/10.30574/gscarr.2024.21.2.0451.

[12] Saxena, S. (2016). An analysis of the impact of ESG screening on financial performance of Indian firms. *SSRN Electronic Journal*. https://papers.ssrn.com/sol3/Delivery.cfm/SSRN_ID3376752_code1845090.pdf?abstractid=3376752&mirid=1.

[13] Shobhwani, K. and Lodha, S. (2024). Impact of ESG disclosure scores on financial, operating and market-based performance of NSE-listed companies. *Journal of Indian Business Research*, 16(4): 421–445. https://doi.org/10.1177/09711023241306219.

[14] Singh, R. (2025). ESG reporting in Nifty 50 companies: Navigating sustainability challenge. *Indian Journal of Accounting*, 57(1): 51–71. https://doi.org/10.63637/ija.v57i1.51-71.

[15] Taleb, M. and Kadhum, H. J. (2024). The role of artificial intelligence in promoting the Environmental, Social and Governance (ESG) Practices. In *Lecture Notes in Networks and Systems* (pp. 256). Springer International Publishing. https://doi.org/10.1007/978-3-031-63717-9_17.

[16] Li, Q., Zhou, Y., Chen, H. and Wang, X. (2024). ESG systems and financial performance in industries with significant environmental impact. *Frontiers in Sustainability*, 5: Article 1454822. https://doi.org/10.3389/frsus.2024.1454822.

[17] Beltrán, E. T. M., Gómez, Á. L. P., Feng, C., Sánchez, P. M. S., Bernal, S. L., Bovet, G. et al. (2023). Fedstellar: A platform for decentralized federated learning. *Expert Systems with Applications*, 242: 122861. https://doi.org/10.1016/j.eswa.2023.122861.

[18] Deshpande, B. (2025). Performance through the ESG lens: A review of sustainable reporting in Nifty companies. *Kristu Jayanti Journal of Management Sciences (KJMS)*, 3(2): 39–51. https://doi.org/10.59176/kjms.v3i2.2470.

[19] Elhady, A. M. and Shohieb, S. M. (2025). AI-driven sustainable finance: Computational tools, ESG metrics, and global implementation. *Future Business Journal*, 11(1). https://doi.org/10.1186/s43093-025-00610-x.

[20] Fildisi, B., Vakaj, E., Dridi, A., Imran, A. S. and Azad, R. M. A. (2025). Integrating AI-driven analytics for enhanced ESG mapping: Aligning local and global perspectives. *Sustainable Futures*, 10: 101231.

[21] Giudici, P. and Wu, L. (2025). Sustainable artificial intelligence in finance: Impact of ESG factors. *Frontiers in Artificial Intelligence*, 8: 1566197. https://doi.org/10.1186/s40854-024-00689-2.

[22] Gladstone, L. S. (2025, September 21). Navigating SEBI's 2025 ESG Circular: An Independent Director's Lens on Sustainability, Transparency, and Regulatory Coherence. SCC Online Blog. https://www.scconline.com/blog/post/2025/09/22/navigating-sebis-2025-esg-circular-an-independent-directors-lens-on-sustainability-transparency-and-regulatory-coherence/.

[23] Hamdouni, A. (2025). The role of artificial intelligence in enhancing ESG outcomes: Insights from Saudi Arabia. *Journal of Risk and Financial Management*, 18(10): 572.

[24] Heidari, A., Javaheri, D., Toumaj, S., Navimipour, N. J., Rezaei, M. and Ünal, M. (2023). A new lung cancer detection method based on the chest CT images using federated learning and blockchain systems. *Artificial Intelligence in Medicine*, 141: 102572. https://doi.org/10.1016/j.artmed.2023.102572.

[25] KPMG International. (2024, August). ESG in the age of AI. Retrieved from https://assets.kpmg.com/content/dam/kpmgsites/in/pdf/2024/08/esg-in-the-age-of-ai.pdf.

[26] Li, M., Xu, P., Hu, J., Tang, Z. and Yang, G. (2025). From challenges and pitfalls to recommendations and opportunities: Implementing federated learning in healthcare [review of *from challenges and pitfalls to recommendations and opportunities:*

Implementing federated learning in healthcare]. *Medical Image Analysis*, 101: 103497. Elsevier BV. https://doi.org/10.1016/j.media.2025.103497.

[27] Liu, T., Wang, Z., He, H., Shi, W., Lin, L., An, R. et al. (2023). Efficient and secure federated learning for financial applications. *Applied Sciences*, 13(10): 5877.

[28] Tripathi, M. (2024). Impact of ESG rating on financial performance of NIFTY 50 firms. *International Journal of Social Science*, 12(4): 223–234. https://journal.sijss.com/index.php/home/article/view/144.

[29] Veeravel, V., Vijaya, P. M. and Vijayakumar, N. (2024). Does ESG disclosure really influence the firm performance in India? *Quarterly Review of Economics and Finance*, 95: 193–202. https://doi.org/10.1016/j.qref.2024.03.008.

[30] Zeng, Q., Xu, Y., Hao, M. and Gao, M. (2025). ESG rating disagreement, volatility, and stock returns. *Finance Research Letters*, 72: 106602.

[31] Lucinity. (2024, November 18). Federated learning for secure data sharing in FinCrime. Retrieved from https://lucinity.com/blog/federated-learning-in-fincrime-how-financial-institutions-can-fight-crime-without-sensitive-data-sharing.

[32] Makkar, M. K. (2023). Performance of conventional and sustainable index in pre and post COVID-19 periods: Evidence from India. *Indian Journal of Finance*, 17(2): 77–92. https://www.indianjournaloffinance.co.in/index.php/IJF/article/view/172736.

[33] Aydoğmuş, M., Gülay, G. and Ergun, K. (2022). Impact of ESG performance on firm value and profitability. *Borsa Istanbul Review*, 22: S119–S127.

12 | Application of Machine Learning for Detecting Financial Irregularities in Local Government Revenue Collection Information System

Said M. Mohamed,[1] Gilbert M. Gilbert,[2]
Tabu S. Kondo[2] and George S. Ulomi[2,*]

Financial irregularities (FI) remain a significant challenge for collection of revenue generated internally by local government authorities (LGAs). Such irregularities result from a combination of fraudulent and legitimate transactions in the local government revenue collection information system (LGRCIS). Consequently, LGA continues to receive recommendations and adverse audit opinions driven by unresolved audit queries identified in the auditor's report. In this paper, we investigate the application of machine learning (ML) techniques in detecting and classifying fraudulent and nonfraudulent transactions for fraud risk and fraud attempts in LGRCIS. We experiment on six ML algorithms and compare their performance based on accuracy and F1 score. Datasets were gathered from LGRCIS and classified in terms of point-of-sale (POS) management and back-office adjustments for FI detection. Out of six investigated models, XGBoost offers acceptable accuracy performance of 99.87% and 99.76%, and F1-scores of 99.98% and 99.87% for both POS management and back-office adjustments, respectively.

1. Introduction

Technological advancements in information and communication technology (ICT) infrastructure provide a foundation for countries worldwide to transition from manual-based to electronic-based revenue collection [1–2]. A system-based approach not only saves time but also makes it easy to store and retrieve completed and pending transactions. Nevertheless, the presence of fraudulent behaviors conducted by dishonest employees hinders the government's efforts to

[1] Department of Information, Communication and Technology, IFAKARA, Tanzania.
[2] College of Informatics and Virtual Education, The University of Dodoma, Dodoma, Tanzania.
Emails: said.mohamed3@ifakaratc.go.tz; gilbert.gilbert@udom.ac.tz; tabu.kondo@udom.ac.tz
* Corresponding author: ulomi.george@udom.ac.tz

DOI: 10.1201/9781003710059-12

collect an adequate amount of revenue to finance its economic development and growth [1], [3]. As part of cherishing the advancement of ICT, Tanzania decided to shift from a manual-based system to electronic revenue collection and payment systems [4–5]. With a target of improving revenue collection, the government decided to establish, install, and operate the local government revenue collection information system (LGRCIS) in 185 local government authorities (LGAs) for the collection of own source revenue (OSR) in 2016 [6–7].

LGRCIS is expected to reduce both operational costs and expenditures while increasing the percentage of tax collection during OSR collection processes [8], [6], [9]. Moreover, the system is anticipated to enhance accountability and transparency in revenue collection, while serving as a reliable tool for examining revenue sources and lowering bribery instances [7].

However, the LGRCIS initiatives encounter several challenges, including financial irregularities in OSR collection. Financial irregularities can be defined as acts that engage the use of cheating to gain an illegal benefit, as argued in reference [10]. Financial irregularities manifest through a spectrum of malpractices, including embezzlement, fraudulent activities, inappropriate utilization and misappropriation of assets, falsification of accounting records, and nonadherence to legal and regulatory frameworks in financial management.

Currently, the LGRCIS usage in Tanzania faces massive financial discrepancies and irregularities, including fraud risks and attempts [11–13]. Dishonest employees developed a means of revenue theft by initiating fraudulent transactions in LGRCIS [14]. Over time, fraudsters employ new tactics and plans, posing a challenge for humans to analyze every financial transaction [15]. Such circumstances result in an under-collection of OSR, ineffective internal controls, and significant monetary loss [16–17].

Several studies attempt to address fraudulent detection using a machine-learning approach. Researchers [18] combined natural language processing (NLP), queen genetic algorithm (QGA), and support vector machine (SVM) to develop a fraud detection method for narratives in financial annual reports. This study aimed to improve fraud detection mechanisms while mitigating risks to investors' assets. However, the study is conducted with a limited training dataset, thereby providing limited insight for a large sample size.

Moreover, reference [4] focused on leveraging financial social media data for corporate fraud detection through machine learning classifiers. The researchers focused on three observations. The research process involves three key stages. First, data are periodically collected from social media platforms to automatically extract latent features. Second, these latent social media features, combined with financial ratios and language-based indicators, are integrated into a machine learning framework to classify firms as fraudulent or nonfraudulent. Third, the trained model is subsequently employed to monitor and predict the probability of potential firms engaging in fraudulent activities. Nevertheless, researchers pointed out the dataset availability as a major limitation since financial social media platforms are relatively new.

Furthermore, the demographic profiles of staff members implicated in financial irregularities and other similar activities within public institutions at Chibombo District (Zambia) are presented in reference [10]. Guided by the fraud-triangle and fraud-diamond frameworks, the study investigated the determinants that predispose public servants to financial irregularities. The findings highlight major forms of misconduct, notably the creation of unauthorized payrolls, misuse of accountable imprest, and irregular disbursement of subsistence and meal allowances. While the study provides means for minimizing financial irregularities, it lacks adequate suggestions and variables for technical mechanisms to detect such financial irregularities effectively.

A machine-learning-based method introduces for analyzing annual financial statements to estimate the probability of significant financial irregularities within companies [19]. The model assesses the risk of such irregularities based on financial disclosures, recognizing that some forms of financial fraud may not directly affect the statements themselves. Moreover, the study suggests that algorithms can be trained to detect fraudulent patterns using data that may not explicitly reflect fraudulent behavior. The proposed models achieved approximately 95% accuracy, though their applicability is limited to annual financial statements of both publicly listed and privately held firms.

Text mining and guard techniques for identifying financial fraud are reported in reference [20]. To achieve better accuracy, an optimized deep belief network (DBN) with three layers of restricted Boltzmann machines (RBMs) is used for the classification process. The work proposed a model with lower computational costs. Yet, the study lacks model measurement results such as recall, sensitivity, F-measure, specificity, and classification accuracy.

A multi-classifier framework is developed to address the complexities of credit card fraud classification [21]. Their ensemble model integrates several machine learning algorithms and utilizes the behavior-knowledge space (BKS) approach to aggregate predictions across classifiers. The results demonstrate that BKS significantly outperforms the majority voting technique, with statistical significance confirmed at the 95% confidence level. The model effectively distinguishes between fraudulent and legitimate credit card transactions, although its performance is constrained when applied to large, noisy datasets.

In this work, a machine learning approach for financial irregularities in LGRCIS is presented. To address the dataset limitation, we employ 186,079 instances from the live database to investigate and predict fraudulent activities. A rigorous investigation based on six ML algorithms is reported, and the best-performing algorithm is pointed out based on accuracy and F1-score. As far as the authors are aware, existing literature has not utilized such an extensive dataset sourced from a live database for the purpose of detecting financial irregularities.

2. Methodology

In this paper, a transaction-based approach is used to collect financial transactions from LGRCIS reports. The financial irregularities detection variables were derived from document review of related works, LGAs' administration reports, LGAs' financial statements and budgets, LGRCIS's financial reports, and fraud risks assessment performance reports. We combine variables into a dataset, followed by feature selection, data cleaning, feature extraction, data integration, data transformation, and data reduction.

2.1 Financial Irregularities Detection Process

The financial irregularities detection process aims to inspect all transactions involving revenue collection in LGAs and highlight whether transactions are fraudulent or not. This serves as a basis for detecting financial irregularities in LGRCIS using the ML approach. Figure 1 illustrates the procedures we use in detecting and classifying transactions in LGRCIS.

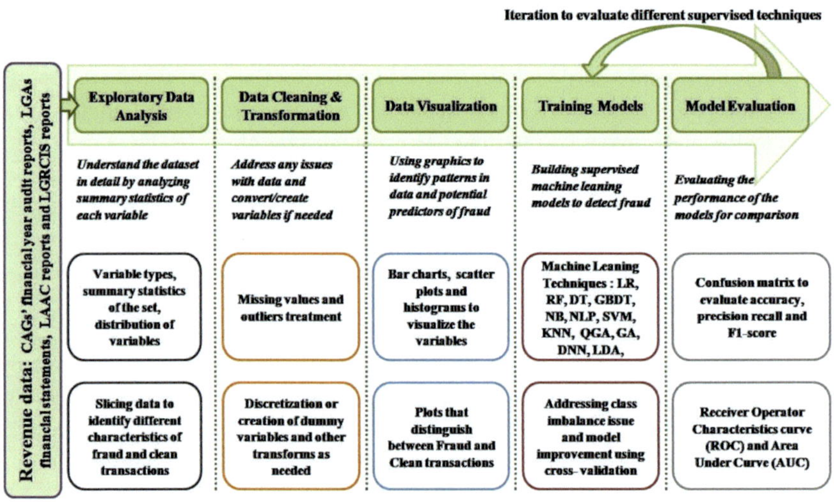

Figure 1: Procedures for irregularity detection and classification.

2.2 Data Preprocessing

We analyzed the collected data from the LGRICS system using Microsoft Excel (2016) before data filtering and feature selection. Rows possessing invalid numbers, negative numbers, blank or missing data, and characters are omitted. Additionally, we use the filter method technique for feature selection to capture the most important characteristics or attributes of the dataset from LGRCIS financial data (as inputs) to the anticipated output. The mechanism plays a role in modeling unrelated variables before the machine learning modeling by understanding the relation between dependent variables during the data preprocessing stage, based on statistical approaches. It should be noted that not all features that appeared in the collected dataset are used for training ML algorithms; rather, only those features deemed relevant to enhancing the efficiency of machine learning algorithms are utilized.

Moreover, the proposed model is intended for a real-world system; therefore, features are derived from both the back-office adjustment and POS management datasets.

Finally, the obtained features comprise nine attributes (*LGA_Code, Case Type, Original_Amount, Adjusted_Amount, Requested By, Requested Date, Approved By, Approved Date, and Class*) for the back-office adjustments dataset and eight attributes (*LGA_Code, Device IMEI, Payer_Id, Collected, Banked, Out_Standing, Date_was_last_online, and Class*) for the POS management dataset.

2.3 Financial Irregularities Detection Model

The dataset used for model development was partitioned into two subsets, with 80% allocated for training and 20% for testing. The model is trained until a pleasing accuracy is achieved while avoiding model generalization of the dataset. We employ random state hyperparameters for dataset reshuffling and regulate the unpredictability present in machine learning models. We investigated different ML algorithms such as XGBoost, K-nearest neighbors (KNN), multi-layer perceptron (MLP), random forest (RF), logistic regression (LR), and decision tree (DT), and recommend a suitable ML algorithm to detect financial irregularities in LGRCIS.

2.4 ML Performance Measurement

To assess the effectiveness of the created approach in identifying financial abnormalities in LGRCIS, the most recent financial dataset is used. The confusion matrix for detecting financial irregularities in LGRCIS is composed of false positive (FP), true negative (TN), true positive (TP), and false negative (FN). The model performance is characterized by accuracy and F-score. As shown in Table 1 TP means the result that detects an irregularity whenever it is present. TN means the result that does not detect financial irregularity, even if it is present. FN means the result that does not detect financial irregularity, even if the irregularity is not present. While a false positive rate means the result that detects financial irregularity when the financial irregularity is not present.

Table 1: Evaluation indicators for financial irregularities detection in LGRCIS.

Metric	*Definition of Terms*	*Formula*
Accuracy	The proportion of the total number of correct predictions	$\frac{TP + TN}{TP + FP + TN + FN}$
F1 score	Harmonic mean for precision and recall values	$\frac{2 \times Precision \times Recall}{Precision + Recall}$

3. Experiment Setup

3.1 Datasets

A comprehensive dataset serves as the backbone for a robust machine learning model for producing plausible results [22]. Having obtained detector variables from document review, related works, and LGRCIS reports, we extract financial data from various sources at LGRCIS to form a dataset. Investigated financial data are from the 2015 to 2024 financial years.

In LGRCIS, POS refers to a mobile application for Android-based smartphones and smart POS devices created by PORALG and the World Bank for processing financial transactions [22].

Also, the back-office adjustment refers to a module in LGRCIS used to correct transactions having improper amounts as required to be paid by taxpayers [23]. Table 2 presents a summary of the ML training and testing processes for the financial irregularities detection model, based on data extracted from back-office adjustments and POS management.

Table 2: Datasets summary on ML training and testing processes.

Dataset Component	*Variables*	*Instances*	*Training set*	*Test and validation set*	*# of fraud*	*# of non-fraud*	*% of fraud*	*% of non-fraud*	*Outlier fraction*
Back-office adjustment	9	73,703	58,962	14,721	60,641	13,062	82.28	17.72	4.64
POS management	8	112,376	89,901	22,475	12,258	100,118	10.91	89.09	0.12

3.2 Data Visualization

Data visualization is employed to provide readers with easy access to key insights on data patterns and trends. For simplicity, we use a bar chart to visualize event counts versus LGA codes.

In the POS management dataset, we explored 112,376 rows of financial transactions using frequency distribution. Among 100,118 financial transactions, 89.09% are nonfraudulent, and 10.91% of the transactions were fraudulent, with an outlier fraction of 0.12. Moreover, in the back-office adjustments dataset, we explored 73,703 rows of financial transactions using frequency distribution. Among them, 13,062 financial transactions (17.72%) were non-fraud, and 60,641 financial transactions (82.28%) were fraud, with an outlier fraction of 4.64. Figure 2 illustrates the LGA code versus financial transaction counts for both POS management and back-office adjustment. Nonfraudulent and fraudulent cases are presented by Class-Id zero (Class 0) and Class-Id one (Class 1), respectively.

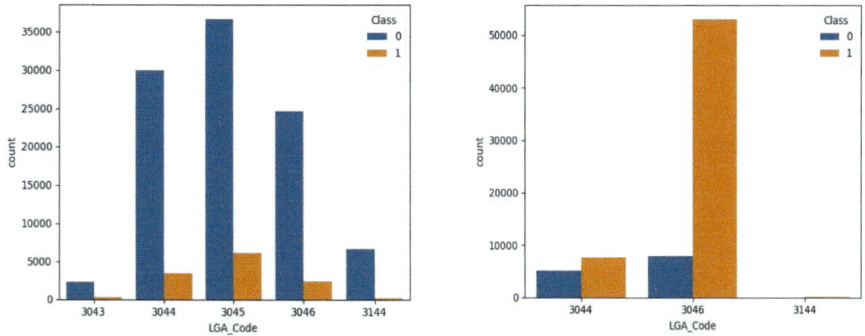

(a) (b)

Figure 2: LGA code versus financial transactions count for (a) POS management and (b) back-office adjustment.

Furthermore, the *Date_was_last_online* feature is removed during model training as it does not influence performance. Figure 3 depicts the relationship between the derived variables in POS management and back-office adjustment using a heat map.

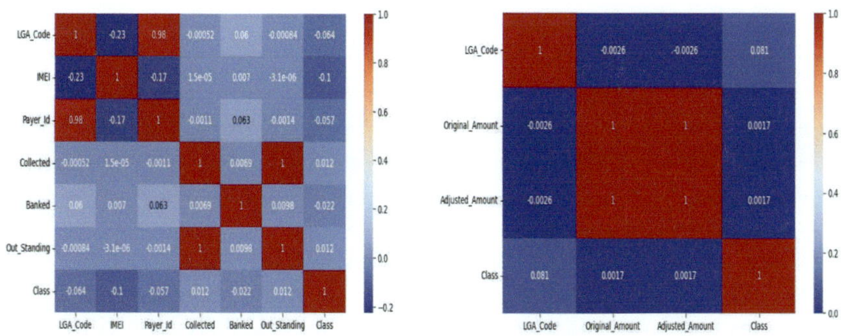

(a) (b)

Figure 3: Relationship between variables in (a) POS management and (b) back-office adjustment.

3.3 Model Training Platform

We conduct an experiment using an NVIDIA RTX 3090 GPU-powered computer with 23.50 GB of GPU memory and a 10.1 CUDA version. The Ubuntu Linux version 20.04 operating system is installed. For model building and training, we utilize the Scikit-learn's deep learning framework. Additionally, we use several Python libraries, including Seaborn (v0.11.2), SciPy (v1.7.1), and Matplotlib (v3.4.3) for data plotting and visualization.

4. Results and Discussion

4.1 Model Performance

F1-score and accuracy evaluation metrics were employed to determine the models performance in the detection of LGRCIS financial irregularities using the testing set. Because this research aimed to solve the classification problem, a confusion matrix is used to describe and compare detections and test findings with actual values. Tables 3 and Table 4 show a confusion matrix (CM) summary for the training model with back-office adjustments and POS management datasets, respectively.

Table 3: Confusion matrix for a model trained with the back-office adjustment dataset.

ML Model	*Training*				*Validation*				*Testing*			
	TP	*TN*	*FP*	*FN*	*TP*	*TN*	*FP*	*FN*	*TP*	*TN*	*FP*	*FN*
XGBoost	1211	`2592	20	18	6060	1297	9	5	6051	1295	11	13
KNN	12100	2597	15	29	6054	1297	9	11	6046	1300	6	18
DT	11974	2462	150	155	5987	1238	68	78	5987	1224	82	77
RF	12068	2227	385	61	6037	1122	184	28	6031	1105	201	33
MLP	12129	0	2612	0	6065	0	1306	0	6064	0	1306	0
LR	0	2612	0	12129	0	1306	0	6065	0	1306	0	6064

Table 4: Confusion matrix for a model trained with the POS management dataset.

ML Model	*Training*				*Validation*				*Testing*			
	TP	*TN*	*FP*	*FN*	*TP*	*TN*	*FP*	*FN*	*TP*	*TN*	*FP*	*FN*
XGBoost	2427	2016	8	25	1961	16019	0	0	7844	64075	0	1
KNN	2365	20023	1	87	1916	16019	0	45	7629	64074	1	216
DT	2204	20010	14	248	1795	16009	10	166	7168	64050	25	677
RF	2132	20023	1	320	1721	16019	0	240	6953	64074	1	892
MLP	0	20024	0	2452	0	16019	0	1961	0	64075	0	7845
LR	0	20024	0	2452	0	16019	0	1961	0	64075	0	7845

The experimental results revealed elevated false-negative rates across training, testing, and validation phases for the logistic regression (LR) model, as illustrated in Figure 4. This outcome suggests that LR is not well-suited for classifying financial irregularities using the LGRCIS back-office adjustment dataset. In contrast, a high true-positive rate is indicative of a well-performing machine learning model. A true-negative outcome reflects the model's correct identification of non-irregular cases, demonstrating its ability to accurately classify negative instances within the test data.

We utilize a test set to evaluate the trained machine learning algorithm, allowing us to determine the value of key evaluation metrics, including correctly classified classes, incorrectly classified classes, F1 score, and accuracy. XGBoost, KNN, MLP, RF, LR, and DT are ML algorithms in both the back-office adjustments and POS management datasets. The accuracy was utilized to identify the best-trained ML algorithms for improved generalization to the testing dataset for financial irregularities detection in LGRCIS.

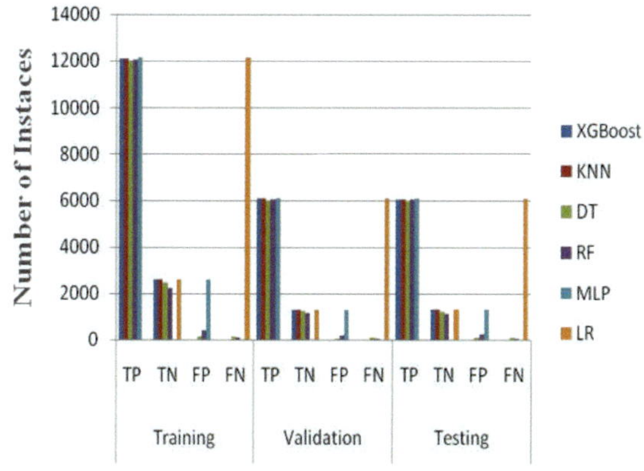

Figure 4: ML models' performance with the back-office adjustment dataset.

Model evaluation was conducted using accuracy as the primary validation metric. Among the tested approaches, the XGBoost algorithm demonstrated superior performance, achieving accuracy rates of 99.81% and 99.89% on the back-office adjustment and POS management datasets, respectively. Figure 5 presents the comparative performance of the machine learning models across these datasets. Additionally, F1-score metrics were assessed, with the outcomes summarized in Table 5 and Table 6. Based on these results, XGBoost is recommended as the most effective model for predicting financial irregularities within LGRCIS.

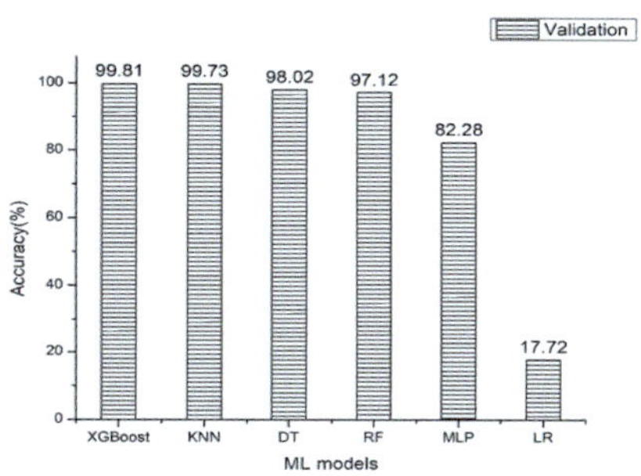

(a)

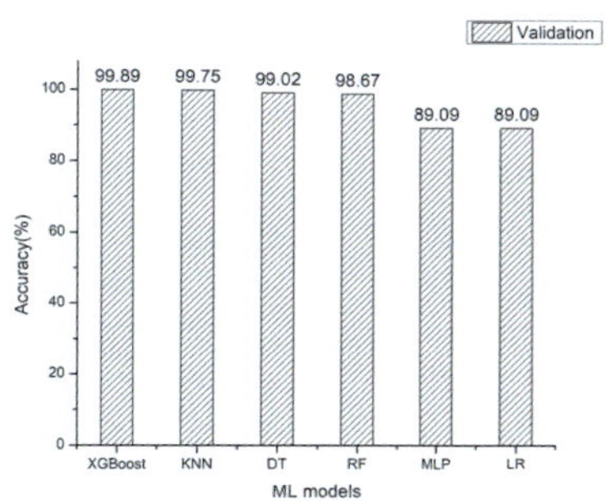

(b)

Figure 5: Model's performance for (a) back-office adjustment and (b) POS management.

Table 5: F1-scores for trained ML models on the back-office adjustments dataset.

ML Model	*F1 Score*		
	Training	*Validation*	*Testing*
XGBoost	99.84	99.89	99.80
KNN	98.82	99.83	99.80
DT	98.74	98.80	98.69
RF	97.79	98.28	98.10
MLP	90.28	90.28	90.27
LR	0.00	0.00	0.00

Table 6: F1 scores for trained ML models on the POS management dataset.

ML Model	*F1 Score*		
	Training	*Validation*	*Testing*
XGBoost	99.33	99.52	99.48
KNN	98.17	98.84	98.60
DT	94.39	95.33	95.33
RF	93.00	93.48	93.97
MLP	0.00	0.00	0.00
LR	0.00	0.00	0.00

The machine learning algorithms were evaluated using a tenfold cross-validation approach alongside a separate validation set comprising 10% of the data. Following the application of K-fold cross-validation, the resulting performance metrics were aggregated and analyzed to identify the most effective technique. Tables 7 and 8 present the outcomes of the tenfold validation for the models applied to the POS management dataset.

Table 7: Evaluation of ML techniques using tenfold validation on back-office adjustment data.

ML Technique	*K-Fold Cross-Validation (K=10)*										*Avg*
	1	*2*	*3*	*4*	*5*	*6*	*7*	*8*	*9*	*10*	
XGBoost	**99.83**	**99.66**	**99.78**	**99.75**	**99.66**	**99.86**	**99.89**	**99.63**	**99.80**	**99.83**	**99.76**
KNN	99.80	99.61	99.73	99.73	99.71	99.73	99.73	99.76	99.71	99.76	99.73
DT	98.02	98.17	98.15	98.05	98.02	98.00	97.81	97.98	97.59	97.98	97.98
RF	96.76	96.61	96.29	96.34	96.30	96.96	96.01	96.86	96.30	96.52	96.50
MLP	81.82	82.19	100	94.74	82.65	81.80	99.98	82.90	81.65	99.25	88.70
LR	18.18	17.81	17.79	17.27	99.85	18.20	18.11	17.10	18.35	17.08	25.97

Table 8: Tenfold validation results of ML techniques in POS management.

ML Technique	*K-Fold Cross-Validation (K=10)*										*Avg*
	1	*2*	*3*	*4*	*5*	*6*	*7*	*8*	*9*	*10*	
XGBoost	**99.81**	**99.89**	**99.78**	**99.84**	**99.89**	**99.88**	**99.90**	**99.91**	**99.90**	**99.92**	**99.87**
KNN	99.54	99.72	99.54	99.63	99.64	99.54	99.64	99.63	99.67	99.70	99.63
DT	98.84	98.93	98.81	99.03	99.07	99.04	99.09	98.89	98.97	99.17	98.98
RF	98.81	98.83	98.65	98.84	98.67	98.63	98.68	98.54	98.63	99.00	98.73
MLP	89.14	89.54	89.24	89.56	88.85	89.12	89.12	88.80	88.65	88.89	89.09
LR	89.14	89.54	89.24	89.56	88.85	89.12	89.12	88.80	88.65	88.89	89.09

5. Conclusion

This study examined the effectiveness of six machine learning algorithms—XGBoost, DT, KNN, MLP, RF, and LR—in identifying financial irregularities within the LGRCIS. Model validation was conducted using tenfold cross-validation, with performance assessed through accuracy and F1-score metrics. The results indicate that XGBoost delivers strong predictive performance, achieving an average accuracy of 99.89% and an F1-score of 99.87% on the POS management dataset. On the back-office adjustment dataset, the model attained an average accuracy of 99.81% and an F1-score of 99.76%, confirming its suitability for financial irregularity detection in LGRCIS. Based on performance, the deployment of the algorithm in conjunction with LGRCIS is proposed to enhance system capability in handling fraudulent transactions. The findings provide a roadmap for authorities to improve methods for detecting financial irregularities, thereby enhancing revenue collection at the local government level.

References

[1] United Nations. (2019). Digital Economy Report 2019: *Value Creation and Capture—Implications for Developing Countries*. (1st ed.). United Nations Publications.

[2] Clos, J. (2015). The challenge of local government financing in developing countries. In *United Nations Human Settlements Programme* (1st ed., Vol. 1, Issue 1). UN-HABITAT.

[3] Mawejje, J. and Sebudde, R. K. (2019). Tax revenue potential and effort: Worldwide estimates using a new dataset. *Economic Analysis and Policy*, 63(1): 1–24. https://doi.org/10.1016/j.eap.2019.05.005.

[4] Mvungi, S. H. (2019). *Factors Affecting the Adoption of E-Payment Systems on Ride Sharing Business in Tanzania a Case of Uber: Dar Es Salaam, Tanzania (Masters Dissertation)*. The University of Mzumbe.

[5] Dong, W., Liao, S. and Zhang, Z. (2018). Leveraging financial social media data for corporate fraud detection. *Journal of Management Information Systems*, 35(2): 461–487. https://doi.org/10.1080/07421222.2018.1451954.

[6] Rajabu, Y. (2020). *Prediction of Annual Revenue Collection by using Data Mining Techniques: A Case of Local Government Authorities in Tanzania (Masters Dissertation)*. University of Dodoma.

[7] Nguyen, N. et al. (2022). A proposed model for card fraud detection based on catboost and deep neural network. *Res. Sq.*, 1(1): 1–19.

[8] Edwin, U. (2019). *The Impact of Revenue Collection in Local Government Authorities in Tanzania on Improvement of Social Services: The Case of Dodoma City (Masters Dissertation)*. The University of Dodoma.

[9] Msenga, E. (2021). *Factors Affecting Implementation of Pÿcontroller and Auditor General's Recommendations in Selected Local Government Authorities in Tanzania*. The University of Dodoma.

[10] Kafula, L. (2020). *Applying an Integrative Model in Predicting Financial Irregularities in Chibombo District (Masters Dissertation)* (Issue 1). The University of Zambia.

[11] Kessy, S. S. A. (2019). Electronic payment and revenue collection in local government authorities in Tanzania: Evidence from kinondoni municipality. *Tanzanian Economic Review*, 9(2): 89–106.

[12] NAOT. (2021). *Annual General Report of the Controller and Auditor General for the Financial Year 2019/20: Information Systems Audit.*

[13] Nyomeye, E. (2020). *Factors for Declining Revenues Collection in Local Government Authorities in Tanzania: A Case of Mbinga District Council (Master Dissertation)*. Mzumbe University.

[14] Kassam, N. B. (2020). *Organisational and Individual Behaviours and their Influence on Revenue Collections in Local Government Authorities in Tanzania: Implication of Electronic Fiscal Device Usage (Masters Dissertation)*.

[15] Kasasbeh, B., Aldabaybah, B. and Ahmad, H. (2022). Multilayer perceptron artificial neural networks-based model for credit card fraud detection. *Indonesian Journal of Electrical Engineering and Computer Science*, 26(1): 362–373. https://doi.org/10.11591/ijeecs.v26.i1.pp362-373.

[16] Mahyoro, A. K. (2020). *The Effectiveness of Internal Audit on Performance of Internal Audit Services in Selected Local Government Authorities in Tanzania (Master Dissertations)*. The University of Dodoma.

[17] Msigwa, B. B. (2018). *Data Integrity Risk Assessment of Local Government Revenue Collection Information System in Tanzania (Masters Dissertation)*. The University of Dodoma.

[18] Chen, Y. J., Wu, C. H., Chen, Y. M., Li, H. Y. and Chen, H. K. (2017). Enhancement of fraud detection for narratives in annual reports. *International Journal of Accounting Information Systems*, 26(June): 32–45. https://doi.org/10.1016/j.accinf.2017.06.004.

[19] Wyrobek, J. (2020). Application of machine learning models and artificial intelligence to analyze annual financial statements to identify companies with unfair corporate culture. *Procedia Computer Science*, 176: 3037–3046. https://doi.org/10.1016/j.procs.2020.09.335.

[20] Singh Yadav, A. K. and Sora, M. (2021). Fraud detection in financial statements using text mining methods: A review. *IOP Conference Series: Materials Science and Engineering*, 1020(1). https://doi.org/10.1088/1757-899X/1020/1/012012.

[21] Nandi, A. K., Randhawa, K. K., Chua, H. S., Seera, M. and Lim, C. P. (2022). Credit card fraud detection using a hierarchical behavior-knowledge space model. *PLoS One*, 17(1 January): 1–16. https://doi.org/10.1371/journal.pone.0260579.

[22] Nguyen, N., Chi, H., City, M., Duong, T., Chi, H., City, M. et al. (2022). A proposed model for card fraud detection based on catboost and deep neural network. *Research Square*, 1(1): 1–19.

[23] PO-RALG. (2016). *LGRCIS User Manual on LGRCIS and GePG Integration* (2nd ed.). PO-RALG.

13 Regulatory and Ethical Considerations in Federated Finance

Silvio Andrae

The growing adoption of federated learning and decision-making architectures in the financial sector represents a significant transformation in the organization of data-driven modeling and control. Although federated finance is frequently characterized as a technical response to challenges in data protection and inter-institutional cooperation, its regulatory and ethical dimensions remain insufficiently systematized. Established governance and supervisory frameworks that prioritize institution-centered oversight and transparent responsibility allocation face structural challenges under federated conditions. This chapter examines the regulatory and ethical challenges posed by federated financial architectures from a governance and regulatory standpoint. The analysis employs conceptual governance theory, regulatory frameworks, and ethical perspectives on fairness, responsibility, and legitimacy. Rather than addressing technical implementation, the focus is on institutional conditions necessary for controllability and accountability. The findings indicate that explainability, fairness, and responsibility in federated systems should be understood as relational properties of institutional arrangements, rather than as technical attributes of individual models. Federated financial architectures inherently entail trade-offs among model performance, transparency, and controllability, which evolve over time and often defer risks to the future. Consequently, effective governance should prioritize explicit, risk-based, and internationally coordinated management of these trade-offs, rather than their elimination. Federated finance thus emerges as a critical testing ground for contemporary artificial intelligence (AI) governance in the financial sector.

1. Introduction

The growing adoption of federated learning and decision-making architectures represents a significant transformation in the organization of data-driven financial

Independent Researcher, Germany.
Email: andrae@zedat.fu-berlin.de

DOI: 10.1201/9781003710059-13

decision-making. Federated finance encompasses not only a privacy-preserving technical approach to machine learning, but also an institutional reconfiguration of modeling, responsibility, and control. Decision-making processes now emerge from distributed contributions by multiple institutions, platforms, and infrastructure providers, rather than from clearly defined organizational units. This development fundamentally challenges established regulatory and ethical assumptions within the financial sector.

Existing supervisory and governance frameworks are predominantly designed for institution-centric models. Traditional concepts such as model risk management (MRM), explainability, and responsibility attribution presuppose adequate organizational control over data, models, and their application. Federated financial architectures disrupt this logic by systematically distributing control, knowledge, and intervention capabilities across multiple actors and organizational levels. As a result, new forms of regulatory uncertainty arise that cannot be addressed solely through technical optimization or by extending current compliance mechanisms.

This chapter does not seek to evaluate federated financial systems from a technical standpoint or to provide specific implementation guidelines. Instead, the analysis adopts a governance and regulatory perspective, examining the regulatory, institutional, and ethical conditions that enable the legitimate, controllable, and accountable use of federated models in the financial sector. Federated finance is conceptualized as a potentially enduring organizational form for data-driven decision-making, whose implications warrant consideration regardless of the maturity of individual applications.

The chapter follows a systematic line of argument. Section 2 analyzes the implicit assumptions underlying classical risk management in the classical model and demonstrates why federated architectures challenge them. Section 3 explores the role of explainability, arguing that, in federated contexts, explainability functions more as a relational governance resource than as a purely technical attribute. Section 4 expands the analysis to ethical considerations, interpreting autonomy, fairness, and legitimacy as system-level properties of distributed decision-making architectures. Building on this foundation, Section 5 investigates the requirements for governance structures and institutional responsibilities, including multi-level control models and collective arrangements. Section 6 articulates the inherent trade-offs between model performance, explainability, and controllability, framing these trade-offs as a central design challenge for federated governance. Section 7 extends the analysis to the international context, positioning federated finance as a testing ground for cross-border artificial intelligence (AI) governance amid regulatory fragmentation. Section 8 concludes with a synthesis of the key findings.

2. Regulatory Framework and Model Risk Management in Federated Systems

Model regulation in the financial sector has traditionally relied on an institution-centered approach to risk and responsibility. Models, whether econometric, statistical, rule-based, or algorithmic, are viewed as internal tools of individual institutions designed to support or automate business-critical decisions. MRM, as outlined in international guidelines, national supervisory expectations, and established governance structures [1–2], is predicated on this perspective. However, federated finance fundamentally challenges this foundational assumption at a structural level.

2.1 Model Risk Management as a Model-Agnostic Regulatory Framework

MRM is intentionally structured to be model-agnostic. Rather than differentiating between specific model types, it addresses models as decision-making technologies that can significantly affect risk profiles, capital requirements, customer relationships, and market behavior. Consequently, MRM frameworks emphasize overarching principles: ensuring a model's suitability for its intended purpose, maintaining traceability of its operations, enabling monitoring and adjustment, and clearly allocating institutional responsibility throughout the model's life cycle.

These principles do not mandate complete transparency or simple explainability of models. Instead, they require that key assumptions, input variables, and causal relationships remain fundamentally verifiable, and that institutions can assume organizational responsibility for decisions based on models. Thus, MRM serves less as a technical control mechanism and more as an organizational framework to ensure regulatory accountability.

The risk-based logic underlying the regulatory treatment of federated financial models is explicitly reflected in the European AI regulation. This establishes a graduated regulatory regime in which the scope and intensity of regulatory requirements are systematically linked to the potential damage and risk profile of an AI system. For high-risk AI systems, including specific applications in the financial sector, the regulation establishes binding requirements for risk management, data quality, technical documentation, transparency, and human oversight. This makes it clear that regulatory expectations do not apply to the mere use of AI, but rather to its integration into risk-relevant decision-making processes. For federated financial architectures, this means that performance gains from distributed learning are only regulatory acceptable to the extent that they are accompanied by risk-adequate control, monitoring, and documentation capabilities [3].

2.2 Implicit Assumptions of Classic MRM Logic

Although MRM is formally model-agnostic, its practical implementation relies on several implicit assumptions. First, institutions are presumed to have sufficient control over model inputs, including data, parameters, and rule-based decision logic. Second, it is assumed that key model assumptions can be documented, tested, and modified as needed. Third, MRM ties responsibility to organizational accountability, designating the institution using the model as the primary subject of regulatory expectations, regardless of whether the model is developed internally or externally. Fourth, MRM presumes a manageable model life cycle that permits review, monitoring, and intervention.

Conceptually, MRM represents a form of organized uncertainty, in which formalized processes, testing, and documentation requirements primarily serve to manage and legitimize risks institutionally rather than eliminate them. As Power demonstrates, risk management establishes a particular order of uncertainty that conveys a sense of controllability without fully resolving underlying complexity [4]. This perspective highlights that MRM chiefly functions as a governance practice, stabilizing expectations of control and accountability rather than serving as a purely technical risk-control mechanism.

These implicit assumptions are rarely questioned in the literature on model and explainability governance, and are generally accepted as functional norms. In the financial sector, explainability concepts are primarily designed to facilitate controllability, trust, and responsibility attribution within well-defined institutional contexts, rather than to achieve full disclosure or causal reconstruction of complex decision-making processes [5]. This logic serves as a central reference point for traditional model governance, against which the distinctive characteristics of federated architectures can be more precisely analyzed.

These prerequisites can largely be met in classic, institution-specific model landscapes. They form the basis for supervision, internal control functions, and management to not only identify model risks, but also actively limit them. In federated model architectures, however, they are subject to structural pressure because control, knowledge, and intervention options are distributed across multiple actors and levels.

2.3 Structural Disruption Caused by Federated Model Architectures

Federated models are constructed by aggregating distributed model contributions from multiple actors. The decision-making logic in these models emerges from collective processes that extend beyond the control of any single institution. As a result, neither the full set of underlying inputs nor the complete aggregation logic resides within a single institution.

This situation is not limited to specific model classes, but is intrinsic to the core of federated architectures. The regulatory challenge thus stems not from the technical design of individual models, but from the distributed generation, use, and evolution of decision-making foundations. In federated settings, model risks primarily emerge from the interplay of institutionally distinct model contributions, governance frameworks, and incentive structures, rather than from isolated erroneous assumptions.

2.4 Responsibility and the Limits of Institution-Centered Attribution

This structural disruption is especially apparent in the context of responsibility. Traditional supervisory frameworks closely associate responsibility with model use, assigning regulatory accountability to the institution that employs the model. Federated models complicate this principle, as institutions make decisions based on models whose behavior is substantially shaped by external contributions.

This dynamic generates a tension between formal responsibility and actual influence. Although supervisory authorities continue to address the designated responsible institution, that institution's control capacity remains constrained. This situation increases the risk of responsibility diffusion, making it challenging to attribute systemic effects. Federated finance thus demonstrates that traditional liability and responsibility frameworks are approaching their functional limits, even as their normative objectives of accountability and controllability remain intact.

2.5 Model Testing and Monitoring under Federated Conditions

In federated contexts, the emphasis of model testing changes. Rather than seeking comprehensive insight into every model component, the central question becomes whether institutions possess adequate organizational, contractual, and procedural mechanisms to identify and mitigate risks associated with federated models. Consequently, model testing shifts from technical completeness to a focus on institutional robustness.

From a regulatory standpoint, the critical issue is not the traceability of every detail within a federated model, but the existence of clear protocols for managing uncertainty, deviations, and unforeseen effects. This requires transparent governance structures, well-defined responsibilities, mechanisms for monitoring model impact, and the capacity for targeted intervention in model usage.

2.6 Cross-Border Dimension and Regulatory Inconsistencies

The federated structure of these models underscores the necessity of cross-border coordination. Models are frequently deployed across multiple jurisdictions, where governance and supervisory requirements differ by country. This variability introduces the risk of inconsistent regulatory assessments for the same model, contingent on institutional context and supervisory practices.

This fragmentation increases institutional complexity and complicates the implementation of coherent risk management. As a result, model risk management becomes a coordination challenge, requiring the alignment of regulatory expectations both technically and institutionally.

2.7 Functional Redefinition of MRM in Federated Systems

In light of these developments, model risk management requires functional redefinition. The objective is no longer to achieve complete transparency across all model components. Instead, the emphasis shifts to determining whether federated models can be employed responsibly despite their distributed nature. Consequently, MRM is transitioning from controlling individual models to managing complex model ecosystems.

Although current explainability and model governance frameworks correctly regard explainability as essential for institutional control, federated architectures demonstrate that this assumption is no longer universally valid. Therefore, model risk management should be decoupled from explainability-based control assumptions and instead prioritize governance, process, and accountability structures [5].

This redefinition establishes the conceptual foundation for the subsequent sections. Section 3 examines the role of explainability as a regulatory control tool under conditions of limited transparency. Sections 4 and 5 demonstrate that ethical requirements and governance structures are essential elements of contemporary federated model risk management. The focus thus shifts from whether models are explainable to the role explainability can fulfill under distributed control conditions.

3. Explainability and Accountability in Federated Model Architectures

Explainability has emerged as a central concept in the regulation of model-based decision-making processes. Within financial supervision, it primarily serves as a functional tool to ensure responsibility, accountability, and control, rather than as an epistemic ideal. Federated model architectures intensify these challenges by diminishing the transparency of individual model components and prompting fundamental questions regarding the reasonable expectations and inherent limitations of explainability in distributed decision-making systems.

3.1 Explainability as a Regulatory Function

From a regulatory standpoint, explainability is neither an end in itself nor solely a technical attribute of models. It serves distinct functions by enabling management, internal control units, and supervisory authorities to review model-based decisions, identify risks, and assign responsibility. Consequently, explainability should be conceptualized as relational, emerging from the interplay between the model, the organization, and the institutional context, and must be evaluated within the framework of governance structures.

Existing explainability frameworks in the financial sector make it clear that explainability should not be understood as an epistemic completeness, but rather as a governance-related communication service that supports institutional control, trust, and the assignment of responsibility without claiming complete understanding or causal reconstruction [5].

This functional perspective is especially significant in federated systems. When models are developed across multiple institutions, the notion of complete interpretability becomes less tenable. From a regulatory viewpoint, the critical issue is not the full disclosure of internal model mechanisms, but whether an institution can justify its decisions comprehensibly and manage risks effectively despite limited transparency.

3.2 Epistemic Boundaries and Irreducible Uncertainty

Federated model architectures are characterized by distributed knowledge bases, heterogeneous inputs, and emergent system behavior. These characteristics create forms of irreducible uncertainty that cannot be fully resolved, even with greater transparency or technical explanatory methods. The loss of explainability is not primarily an expression of technical complexity, but rather a consequence of institutional fragmentation of knowledge and control.

A security-oriented perspective underscores that responsible action does not necessitate complete knowledge, but rather institutional capacity to manage uncertainty. In the context of federated financial models, explainability should not be interpreted as a pursuit of exhaustive epistemic insight. Instead, its regulatory function is to render uncertainty visible, communicable, and manageable within organizations. In this way, explainability delineates the boundaries of knowledge and fulfills a central governance function [5].

3.3 Explainability and Attribution of Responsibility

A primary function of explainability is to facilitate the attribution of responsibility. In traditional model environments, erroneous decisions can, in principle, be traced to specific assumptions or decision-making rules. In federated systems, however, this traceability is constrained, as decisions are derived from aggregated outputs that cannot be entirely attributed to any single organization.

This situation creates tension between formal responsibility and practical explainability. Institutions retain regulatory responsibility for model usage, even when their ability to explain decision-making logic is limited. In this context, explainability serves as a normative mediator—it does not substitute for responsibility, but operationalizes it under conditions of limited transparency. From a regulatory perspective, the key consideration is whether explanations are adequate to support control, intervention, and escalation, rather than whether they offer complete causal reconstruction.

3.4 Addressee-Specific and Graded Explainability

Explainability is inherently addressee-dependent, as various stakeholders—such as supervisors, management, and affected individuals—require distinct forms of explanation to evaluate, control, or challenge decisions. This insight was systematically articulated in early governance-oriented explainability frameworks [5]. Supervisory authorities require information to assess controllability and appropriateness; management and control functions need explanations that inform operational decisions and interventions; affected individuals require comprehensible reasons to understand and, if necessary, contest decisions.

Regulatory and ethical discussions often treat explainability as a uniform attribute of AI systems. However, this perspective overlooks the fact that explanations serve diverse purposes and audiences. Early research on interpretable AI emphasized that explainability is not an inherent property of models, but must be defined relative to specific objectives, user groups, and decision-making contexts [6]. Building on this, Mittelstadt et al. distinguish between explanations aimed at technical understanding and those supporting normative justification, accountability, or control. This distinction is particularly relevant in federated financial architectures, where developers, institutions, supervisors, and stakeholders all require different forms of explanation, and a single comprehensive explanation is unattainable [7].

In federated systems, this challenge is intensified because no single actor possesses complete knowledge of the data, the model logic, or the aggregation mechanisms. Comprehensive transparency is structurally unattainable; instead, explainability can serve only to support control, monitoring, and responsibility attribution. As such, explainability becomes a relational governance resource, with its scope and limitations requiring institutional determination.

A uniform, all-encompassing explanation is neither feasible nor required in federated systems. Instead, tiered explainability concepts that integrate varying degrees of transparency are necessary. Consequently, explainability becomes a governance design issue—it must be generated, communicated, and embedded within organizational decision-making processes, rather than being regarded solely as a characteristic of individual models.

3.5 Explainability, Learning, and Institutional Control

Another critical dimension is the role of explainability in institutional learning. Federated models disrupt traditional feedback loops between model assumptions and outcomes. In this context, explainability primarily facilitates observation and understanding, rather than merely reducing uncertainty. It enables organizations to detect and address deviations, drift, and unforeseen consequences, even when their underlying causes remain partially unexplained.

Explainability thereby functions as a component of institutional control in the face of uncertainty. It enables organizations to respond to anomalies without necessitating complete explanations. This perspective directly connects explainability to governance and security frameworks, highlighting its significance as an ongoing practice rather than a singular disclosure.

In this context, explainability does not signify a claim to complete knowledge, but rather delineates the institutionally relevant boundary between adequate controllability and regulatory problematic uncontrollability. This distinction explicitly frames explainability as a governance artifact rather than a model attribute [5].

3.6 Systemic Risks of Limited Explainability

The limited explainability of federated models presents not only challenges for individual traceability but also introduces systemic risks. Aggregated decision models may produce distortions, risk concentrations, or exclusion effects that emerge only gradually or indirectly. In the absence of institutionally embedded explainability, there is a danger that such problematic effects become normalized due to their diminished identifiability or attribution.

Empirical studies of explainable artificial intelligence (XAI) in the financial sector support this functional and context-dependent view. A recent systematic literature review demonstrates that XAI approaches in financial applications are highly fragmented and primarily serve as post-hoc explanations, with considerable variation in their significance, stability, and regulatory suitability [8]. These findings indicate that, in practice, explainability functions more as a situational support mechanism than as a uniform standard, further illustrating the limitations of explainability-based control in federated model architectures.

From a regulatory standpoint, explainability should not be considered in isolation. It must be integrated into monitoring, governance, and escalation mechanisms. When direct explanation encounters epistemic boundaries, organizational safeguards are necessary to uphold responsibility and controllability.

In summary, explainability assumes a distinct role in federated model architectures compared to traditional model environments. It functions less as an attribute of individual models and more as an element of institutional governance. The quality of explainability is assessed not by the depth of technical insight, but by the system's capacity to ensure responsibility, control, and learning under conditions of irreducible uncertainty.

This perspective establishes the conceptual foundation for the subsequent sections. Section 4 examines the ethical implications of these uncertainty constellations, while Section 5 discusses how governance structures can institutionally anchor and operationalize explainability.

4. Ethical Dimensions of Federated Financial Architectures

The ethical evaluation of federated financial architectures presents significant challenges to classical models of individual responsibility and normative attribution. Traditional ethical frameworks typically emphasize clearly identifiable actors, intentional actions, and discrete decision-making errors. In contrast, federated systems involve distributed decision-making, collective model development, and emergent effects. Ethical concerns in these systems stem less from individual rule violations or errors and more from the structural processes by which decisions are formulated, aggregated, and institutionalized.

Given these complexities, a harm-based approach is particularly appropriate. Rather than isolating abstract principles such as fairness or transparency, this approach examines the specific forms of harm that federated systems may cause, the mechanisms by which harm accumulates, and the institutional arrangements required to mitigate such harm under conditions of persistent uncertainty.

4.1 From Individual Blame to Systemic Responsibility

A central ethical feature of federated financial systems is the transition from individual blame to systemic responsibility. Decisions in areas such as lending, risk assessment, or portfolio management increasingly rely on aggregated model outputs that cannot be entirely attributed to any single organization. Consequently, the traditional ethical framework that links responsibility to the intentional actions of individual actors is insufficient in this context.

Responsibility thus becomes a systemic property of institutional arrangements. The critical consideration shifts from identifying individual decision-makers to evaluating how decision-making processes are structured, the feedback mechanisms they produce, and their effectiveness in limiting foreseeable and cumulative harm. This perspective aligns with security-oriented approaches that conceptualize responsibility as a prospective design task rather than a retrospective attribution of blame.

4.2 Dimensions of Harm in Federated Financial Systems

A harm-based approach enables the ethical risks of federated financial architectures to be organized according to distinct dimensions of harm. While direct physical harm is uncommon in economic contexts, financial misjudgments can produce significant indirect consequences, such as the systematic exclusion of borrowers or the destabilization of local markets. Damage occurs where federated decision-making systems undermine autonomy, for example, through non-transparent risk classifications, a lack of appeal options, or the perception of algorithmic arbitrariness. Social damage resulting from the aggregation of individual decisions is particularly relevant: structural discrimination, reinforcement of existing inequalities, or the erosion of institutional trust.

A defining feature of federated systems is that harm can seldom be attributed to individual model components. Instead, it emerges from the interplay of distributed contributions, feedback effects, and the scaling of ostensibly neutral decision rules. The primary ethical issue, therefore, is not the individual decision but the absence of effective mechanisms to identify and limit cumulative effects.

4.3 Emergence, Aggregation, and Moral Blind Spots

The primary ethical challenge of federated financial architectures stems from their emergent nature. Aggregated models may generate effects that are neither intended nor observable at the local level. This emergence leads to moral blind spots, as harm often becomes apparent only after it has produced systemic consequences, while individual actors can credibly claim limited involvement.

A security-oriented ethical approach emphasizes that these blind spots should be understood as structural risks rather than individual failures. Ethical assessment must therefore commence at the system design level. The key consideration is whether institutional arrangements are capable of identifying emergent risks early, facilitating learning processes, and enabling corrective action.

4.4 Precautionary Ethics under Irreducible Uncertainty

Federated financial systems function under conditions of irreducible uncertainty. Achieving complete transparency or precise predictability of their effects is not feasible. Consequently, ethical assessments that demand full explainability or the elimination of all risk are impractical in these contexts.

Instead, a precautionary ethical approach is increasingly important. This perspective views security and responsibility as ongoing processes of institutional vigilance rather than static conditions. Precaution in this context does not inhibit innovation but requires the design of decision-making architectures that anticipate, monitor, and mitigate potential harm, even when its precise causes cannot be fully explained.

Accordingly, ethical legitimacy is not contingent upon perfect control, but rather on the capacity to manage uncertainty responsibly. Federated systems are ethically defensible if they incorporate mechanisms that render uncertainty visible, ensure responsiveness, and provide affected parties with opportunities for protection and redress.

4.5 Autonomy, Fairness, and Legitimacy as System Properties

Traditional ethical frameworks often conceptualize autonomy and fairness as attributes of individual decisions. In federated financial architectures, however, these concepts must be understood at the systemic level. Autonomy is constrained not only by information asymmetries but also by the structure of the decision-making architecture. Fairness emerges as an aggregate effect across multiple decisions rather than as a property of individual model outputs.

The ethical challenges of algorithmic systems extend beyond issues such as bias or misclassification to include a wide range of risks, including lack of transparency, diffusion of responsibility, power imbalances, and limitations on individual autonomy. Mittelstadt et al. demonstrate that these challenges are structurally embedded in socio-technical decision-making systems and cannot be addressed through isolated technical interventions [9]. Normatively, this perspective aligns with the guiding principles of a "good AI society" as articulated by AI4People, which regard autonomy, justice, harm avoidance, and social welfare as institutional responsibilities and view ethical quality as the outcome of responsible governance of socio-technical systems rather than a technical by-product [10].

The discourse on fairness in machine learning has demonstrated that algorithmic justice cannot be reduced to a technical optimization problem. Competing fairness criteria are frequently in irresolvable tension and necessitate normative decisions that are shifted, rather than eliminated, through model and data selection [11]. Legal perspectives further reinforce this point—Wachter et al. argue that European anti-discrimination law requires context-dependent considerations and justifications that cannot be fully automated or delegated to algorithms, but instead demand institutional evaluation and human judgment [12]. In federated financial architectures, this challenge is intensified by local data heterogeneity and distributed model contributions, which can produce divergent fairness profiles that are only partially reconcilable at the aggregate level.

Ethical evaluation should therefore concentrate on the institutional conditions that enable the attribution and exercise of responsibility. From a hermeneutic standpoint, responsibility is not linked to discrete individual authorship but emerges relationally within social practices, where action and identity are constituted through interaction with others. In distributed decision-making architectures, responsibility is necessarily mediated by institutions and cannot be definitively assigned to specific actors [13]. Legitimacy, in this context, derives not from the accuracy of individual decisions but from procedural transparency, effective control and correction mechanisms, and the capacity for institutional learning.

4.6 Ethics as an Integral Component of Federated Governance

Overall, ethics in federated financial systems should not be regarded as an external benchmark or a subsequent evaluation. Instead, it constitutes an integral element of system architecture. Harm-based, precautionary ethics redirects attention from assessing the correctness of individual decisions to evaluating whether institutional arrangements are effective in preventing harm, ensuring accountability, and maintaining trust over the long term.

This perspective sets the stage for Section 5, which examines how governance structures can operationalize these ethical requirements. Ethics functions not as a supplementary moral consideration, but as a normative framework guiding the design and management of federated financial architectures.

5. Governance Structures for Federated Financial Architectures

Federated financial architectures transfer central control challenges from individual models to the domain of institutional coordination. Traditional governance in the financial sector emphasizes clearly defined organizational boundaries, explicit responsibilities, and hierarchical control mechanisms. In contrast, federated systems rely on distributed responsibilities, shared decision-making, and collective learning. Consequently, governance emerges as the primary mediating authority among regulatory expectations, ethical requirements, and operational controllability.

5.1 Governance as a Response to Distributed Responsibility

A defining characteristic of federated systems is the separation of decision-making authority from direct control. Decisions are based on aggregated model outputs, yet individual institutions exert only limited influence over the entire system. Governance structures must address this asymmetry while maintaining the normative foundation of regulatory responsibility.

Instead of linking responsibility exclusively to ownership or complete control, functional attribution comes to the fore. Governance defines which actors are responsible for which aspects of the system, how decision-making powers are distributed, and under what conditions interventions are permissible or necessary. Responsibility is thus not dissolved, but reorganized.

The growing adoption of federated model architectures alters the technical organization of data processing and model training, yet it does not change the core regulatory logic of institutional responsibility. From a regulatory standpoint, the institution utilizing the system remains the principal subject of governance, control, and liability expectations, even when central model components, aggregation mechanisms, or infrastructure services are delivered collaboratively or externally. Federated architectures, therefore, modify operational processes without shifting regulatory responsibility.

This continuity of responsibility is evident in the European Banking Authority's (EBA) guidelines on outsourcing arrangements. The EBA emphasizes that even technologically complex cooperation models do not relieve institutions of their duty to manage, monitor, and control outsourced functions effectively. Specifically, for critical or essential functions, governance, risk, and exit responsibilities remain entirely with the outsourcing institution [14]. In federated financial architectures, collective model development or reliance on external aggregation or orchestration services does not justify a diffusion of responsibility.

Regulatory expectations for cloud-based infrastructure further specify this logic. The European Central Bank's guide to outsourcing cloud services underscores that institutions must maintain adequate transparency, access rights, and control options always, irrespective of technical complexity or geographic distribution. Even in highly distributed architectures, auditability, resilience, and exit capability must be ensured [15]. Thus, from a regulatory perspective, technical federation does not justify reduced governance requirements; instead, it heightens the need for formalized control and coordination mechanisms. The AI regulation also establishes a clear normative framework for governance and institutional responsibilities. It makes it clear that the use of complex AI systems—regardless of their technical architecture—requires a transparent allocation of roles, duties, and control responsibilities. For high-risk AI systems, the regulation requires robust governance structures that ensure continuous risk management, transparent decision-making processes, effective monitoring mechanisms, and opportunities for human intervention. This is particularly important for federated financial systems, as technical decentralization and model architectures based on the division of labor carry the risk of diffusion of responsibility. The AI regulation counteracts this risk by defining governance not as an optional best practice, but as a legally binding prerequisite for the permissible use of robust AI systems. Federated architectures thus exacerbate not only the technical but also the institutional requirements for governance capability [3].

5.2 Multi-Level Governance Architectures

Federated financial systems necessitate multi-level governance architectures that integrate various levels of control. At the institutional level, individual entities remain accountable for model-based decisions. Simultaneously, systemic-level collective governance mechanisms are required to address overarching risks. These arrangements represent collaborative governance, in which autonomous actors exercise collective control through institutionalized processes without entirely displacing hierarchical oversight [16]. This approach is particularly apt for analyzing federated financial architectures, as it frames governance as a dynamic process of coordination and accountability rather than a static allocation of responsibilities.

This multi-level structure typically comprises:

- local governance within the participating institutions (e.g., model approval, usage control, escalation);
- consortium governance at the level of the federated network (e.g., common standards, coordination bodies);
- external governance by supervisory authorities, audit bodies, or independent third parties.

The critical factor is not merely the formal existence of governance levels, but their effective functional integration. Governance failures frequently occur when responsibilities are formally assigned but lack practical interconnection.

Empirical work on explainable federated learning confirms this perspective and shows that governance in federated financial architectures must be decentralized and organized across multiple levels. Applications to institutionally fragmented datasets make it clear that identical federated models can deliver consistent results at the aggregate level, while their explanatory drivers vary systematically at the local level. This shows that effective governance cannot be based solely on global model approvals or central control authorities, but requires procedures that functionally combine local interpretation, institutional accountability, and collective aggregation [17].

5.3 The Role of Orchestrators

Beyond local and consortium governance levels, federated financial architectures require explicit recognition of orchestrators. Orchestrators are entities that perform central coordination, integration, or control functions within federated model environments, even though they may not be end users of model-based decisions. In practice, orchestrators include platform operators who supply technical infrastructure and aggregation mechanisms, consortium leaders who coordinate standards and decision-making, and specialized service providers who manage training, model updates, or monitoring. Despite their significant influence on federated models, orchestrators are often insufficiently defined in traditional regulatory frameworks.

From a governance standpoint, this situation raises critical questions about the location of actual control and intervention capabilities within federated architectures. Orchestrators frequently set key parameters such as aggregation rules, update cycles, and escalation thresholds, thereby shaping the system's risk profile. However, their formal responsibilities often remain ambiguous: while individual institutions are liable for model outputs, orchestrators manage technical system dynamics, including model drift, adversarial effects, and participant integration. Effective governance design in federated financial systems requires explicit allocation of responsibilities at these interfaces. It is essential to clarify who determines and reviews aggregation logic, who authorizes or resets updates, and under what circumstances orchestrators share responsibility for systemic failures. In absence of such clarification, structural diffusion of responsibility may occur, which cannot be adequately addressed by local controls or downstream supervision.

5.4 Governance and the Institutionalization of Precaution

As discussed in Section 4, precaution in the face of irreducible uncertainty is a central ethical principle in federated systems. Governance structures serve as the primary means of institutionalizing this precaution by translating abstract normative requirements into concrete decision-making and escalation processes.

This approach encompasses mechanisms for early identification of systemic risks, continuous monitoring of aggregate effects, and coordinated responses to unforeseen developments. Governance thereby becomes a learning-oriented practice focused on ongoing risk limitation rather than complete risk elimination.

5.5 Role of Committees, Standards, and Procedures

A recurring element of effective governance in federated systems is the creation of dedicated committees and procedures. Examples include joint governance boards, risk or ethics committees, and clearly defined decision-making and escalation pathways. These committees serve as forums for collective responsibility rather than operational bodies. They create a minimum common language for risk assessment, documentation, and decision-making logic without forcing complete harmonization. Standards enable comparability and coordination without suppressing the necessary heterogeneity of federated systems.

5.6 Governance Beyond Technical Control

A fundamental aspect of federated governance is the move away from the expectation of complete technical control. Governance addresses epistemic limitations through organizational and procedural safeguards. When models cannot be fully explained or controlled, established rules, roles, and procedures substitute for technical understanding.

This shift should be viewed not as a deficiency, but as a reflection of realistic control logic in complex systems. Governance serves to manage uncertainty by clearly assigning decision-making authority, defining response strategies, and ensuring accountability through institutional mechanisms. Individual actors can exert disproportionate influence on the overall system due to their database, technological capabilities, or coordination role. Governance structures must therefore not only enable coordination, but also limit concentrations of power.

This necessitates transparency regarding roles and influence, along with mechanisms for rebalancing, such as rotating responsibilities, veto rights, or external oversight. In absence of these mechanisms, federated governance may become superficial, allowing centralized control to persist.

5.7 Cross-Border Governance and Regulatory Embedding

The federated structure of many financial systems extends beyond national jurisdictions. As a result, governance structures must align with diverse regulatory requirements, underscoring the importance of procedural rather than solely substantive control approaches.

Rather than imposing detailed content requirements, regulators emphasize framework requirements for governance, documentation, and responsiveness. Supervisory acceptance of federated systems relies more on the credibility of their governance structures than on technical design. Governance thus becomes the primary reference point for regulatory evaluation.

Overall, governance structures serve as a bridge between ethical imperatives and regulatory implementation. They operationalize precaution, responsibility, and fairness in a manner compatible with the epistemic constraints of federated systems. Governance is not solely normative or technical, but constitutes an institutional practice of mediation.

This mediating role enables the trade-offs outlined in Section 6. While governance cannot eliminate tensions among efficiency, transparency, and control, it can structure and manage them. As such, governance is the central mechanism for the responsible design of federated financial architectures.

6. Trade-Offs and Conflicting Objectives in Federated Financial Systems

Federated financial architectures are defined not only by emerging regulatory, ethical, and governance requirements but also by heightened structural conflicts of interest. These trade-offs are often inherent and persistent, reflecting fundamental tensions among efficiency, control, transparency, and collective responsibility. While governance in federated systems cannot eliminate these conflicts, it can render them visible, structure their management, and maintain their manageability at the institutional level.

6.1 Efficiency, Model Performance, and Controllability

A central tension in deploying advanced AI systems in the financial sector arises from the conflict between model performance and controllability, particularly regarding explainability. High-performance models, such as deep neural networks or complex ensemble methods, frequently deliver substantial forecasting improvements over traditional, interpretable models. However, these models often lack intuitive comprehensibility. Reviews of XAI literature in finance indicate that explainable models' performance gains are frequently limited or achieved at the expense of increased complexity, intensifying the conflict between performance and controllability [8]. Federated financial architectures amplify this tension, as the diversity of distributed datasets, institutional contexts, and business models encourages the adoption of highly complex model architectures.

From a methodological perspective, explainability is not a scalable commodity, but rather depends on the application and context, so that performance gains from complex models are regularly accompanied by epistemic losses that cannot be compensated for technically, but only through institutional arrangements and governance mechanisms [6].

Recent research demonstrates that the trade-off between model performance and explainability is not strictly binary. Federated approaches utilizing inherently interpretable models, such as logistic regression, can achieve competitive performance under heterogeneous data distributions and adversarial conditions when paired with robust aggregation techniques. These findings indicate that explainability need not always compromise performance and can be enhanced through deliberate model and architectural choices. Furthermore, the selection of explainable models constitutes a normative and regulatory design decision, rather than a purely technical outcome [18].

From a regulatory perspective, explainability is not a purely technical property, but a scarce control resource. It enables supervision, management, and internal control functions to identify risks, question decisions, and assign responsibility. Where explainability is limited, the requirements for alternative safeguards increase. In federated systems, complete explainability is structurally unachievable because no single actor has full knowledge of the data, model logic, or aggregation mechanisms.

As a result, supervisory authorities must evaluate explainability relative to a model's risk profile rather than in absolute terms. The required level of explainability should correspond to the model's potential impact [19]. This risk-based approach is especially pertinent in federated architectures, where performance improvements often entail increased opacity. Recent reviews of federated learning in finance support this perspective by categorizing financial use cases according to their regulatory and compliance exposure. These reviews demonstrate that requirements for explainability, governance, and control intensify with the model's impact, and that performance gains are justifiable only when accompanied by enhanced security and supervisory mechanisms. The evidence underscores that trade-offs among performance, transparency, and data protection must be institutionally balanced rather than optimized in isolation [20].

The aforementioned governance requirements directly influence the design and deployment of federated models. In decision-critical applications, conflicts intensify among model performance, automation levels, and the controllability mandated by regulators. These tensions are most pronounced when federated models are integrated into operational decision-making processes that directly affect customers or market stability.

In credit-related contexts, the European Banking Authority's guidelines on lending and monitoring explicitly articulate these requirements. The guidelines stipulate that automated models may assist decision-making but cannot autonomously replace human judgment. Institutions must retain the capacity to justify, challenge, and override credit decisions at any time, particularly in high-risk or atypical cases [21]. Consequently, requirements for explainability, documentation, and human-in-the-loop mechanisms are heightened and are further complicated, rather than alleviated, by federated model architectures.

A key regulatory approach to addressing this conflict of objectives is therefore to introduce graduated explainability requirements. Models with a high impact depth—such as those that influence credit decisions, regulatory capital requirements, or systemically relevant risk classifications—are subject to stringent requirements for traceability, governance, and institutional control. In such cases, it may be necessary from a regulatory perspective to either use inherently interpretable models or to prescribe particularly robust forms of explanatory support.

Conversely, less transparent models may be allowed in applications with lower individual or systemic significance, provided that adequate monitoring, escalation, and intervention mechanisms are in place. Federated systems are especially pertinent in this context, as their performance frequently derives from aggregating complex local patterns that are not fully explainable.

Against this backdrop, the possibility of so-called explainability waivers is increasingly being discussed in the regulatory debate. These waivers represent conditional exemptions from stringent explainability requirements, granted under specific, well-defined circumstances. Institutions must demonstrate that employing a less explainable yet more powerful model yields substantial added value unattainable with simpler alternatives. However, such exemptions are only justifiable under strict conditions. These include, in particular, increased external auditing, continuous performance and bias monitoring, clearly defined intervention thresholds, and the ability to take the model out of service at any time. Explainability waivers are therefore not a regulatory carte blanche, but rather an expression of pragmatic risk management in the face of technical imperfection.

A further critical element of risk-based regulation involves documentation and justification requirements for institutions. In federated architectures, it is insufficient to describe a model's technical operation merely. Institutions must articulate the necessity of adopting a federated structure, outline considered alternatives, and identify additional risks associated with the selected architecture. This justification becomes especially crucial when employing complex, difficult-to-explain models.

6.2 Transparency Versus Protection of Legitimate Interests

The conflict of objectives between efficiency and controllability is closely linked to another fundamental tension—that between transparency and the protection of legitimate interests. In federated systems, regulatory expectations for traceability and disclosure often clash with requirements for data protection, trade secret protection, or the preservation of institutional autonomy. Federated architectures are emerging precisely as a response to the limitations of complete data and model disclosure.

This conflict cannot be resolved in a binary manner. Greater transparency can promote trust, but, at the same time, undermine incentives to participate or disclose sensitive information. Conversely, excessive isolation can jeopardize regulatory assessment and social acceptance. The trade-off is therefore not between transparency and opacity, but between different forms of openness, each with its own risks and benefits.

6.3 Local Autonomy Versus Collective Coherence

A further structural conflict emerges from the tension between local autonomy and collective coherence. Federated systems benefit from the capacity of individual institutions to contribute unique data, contexts, and risk profiles. However, aggregating these contributions necessitates a baseline level of harmonization, achieved through common standards, aggregation rules, or governance requirements.

Increased local autonomy leads to greater system heterogeneity, complicating control. Conversely, heightened harmonization risks erasing context-specific features and diminishing institutional acceptance. Governance in federated systems thus centers on balancing this conflict by delineating permissible deviations while preserving overall system integrity.

6.4 Innovation Versus Precaution

Federated financial architectures facilitate innovation, primarily through privacy-preserving collaboration and collective learning. However, they also heighten the complexity and uncertainty of decision-making. This dynamic creates a classic conflict between innovation and precautionary risk management. Prioritizing innovation may marginalize precautionary measures, while excessive caution can stifle innovation. In federated systems, this conflict is intensified because risks often emerge only in aggregate. Here, precaution should be viewed not as a barrier to innovation, but as an adaptive capacity to address unforeseen consequences.

Trade-offs in federated financial architectures are not only structured by content but also by time. Performance gains from complex, distributed models often manifest in the short term as improved forecasting quality or efficiency, while the associated risks—such as model consolidation, creeping drift, diffusion of responsibility, or dependencies on central orchestrators—only become apparent after a time lag. Federated systems thus tend to defer uncertainty rather than resolve it. Based on concepts of organized uncertainty, governance can be understood here as an intertemporal control task that not only evaluates current performance but also focuses on the long-term stability, adaptability, and reversibility of model architectures [4], [22]. Precautionary governance of federated financial systems must therefore explicitly evaluate trade-offs over time and provide mechanisms that do not sacrifice long-term control and learning capabilities in pursuit of early performance gains.

6.5 Individual Responsibility Versus Collective Liability

Another significant conflict involves the tension between individual responsibility and collective liability. Regulatory frameworks have traditionally assigned responsibility to particular institutions. Yet, federated models generate risks that are explicable only at the collective level.

An exclusively collective liability model would erode individual duties of care, whereas strictly individual liability does not reflect participants' actual influence. Federated governance must therefore establish hybrid responsibility frameworks that integrate individual obligations with collective oversight. This conflict cannot be fully resolved, but must be managed institutionally.

6.6 Standardization Versus Context Sensitivity

Federated systems also encounter a conflict between standardization and context sensitivity. Common standards are essential for comparability, interoperability, and regulatory evaluation. However, standardized models may fail to adequately address local market conditions, social distinctions, or legal specifics.

This conflict is especially pronounced in international contexts. Excessive standardization can erode local legitimacy, whereas excessive context sensitivity can threaten the coherence of federated systems.

6.7 Trade-Offs as a Core Task of Federated Governance

In summary, the primary challenges of federated financial architectures stem not from isolated technical or legal issues, but from the coexistence of multiple, often conflicting objectives. Trade-offs reflect the inherent complexity of socio-technical systems rather than regulatory shortcomings. In federated architectures, performance improvements frequently arise from aggregating diverse, locally embedded patterns, whereas regulatory expectations emphasize consistent, traceable, and overridable decision-making processes.

This tension highlights a core feature of contemporary risk governance—uncertainty is not eradicable, but must be managed institutionally. Scientific and technical literature cautions against simplistic approaches that attempt to control complexity through unilateral optimization. As Stirling notes, such reductionist strategies often introduce new vulnerabilities, whereas resilient governance is grounded in acknowledging and constructively addressing complexity [22].

Regulators regard explainability in this context as a scarce control resource rather than a purely technical feature. It underpins supervision, management, and internal control by enabling risk identification, decision scrutiny, and the assignment of responsibility. Consequently, supervisory authorities do not endorse all forms of technical optimization; instead, they require a risk-appropriate balance between predictive accuracy and controllability.

Federated systems intensify this tension because no individual actor possesses comprehensive knowledge of the data, the model logic, or the aggregation mechanisms. Complete transparency is structurally unattainable. Consequently, limited explainability necessitates more robust governance, monitoring, and intervention mechanisms.

However, this trade-off has boundaries. In highly intervention-intensive scenarios, some researchers intentionally emphasize the conflict for normative purposes. Rudin contends that, for critical decisions, inherently interpretable models may be required for regulatory and ethical reasons, since post hoc explanations of complex black-box models do not ensure robust control or reliable attribution of responsibility [23].

This underscores that trade-offs should not be assessed solely on technical or efficiency grounds, but are constrained by legal and normative considerations. In this context, explainability serves as a threshold for legitimate automation rather than an optimization objective.

Accordingly, governance should not aim to resolve these conflicting objectives permanently, but rather to make them explicit, structure them institutionally, and manage them responsibly. Effective governance is defined not by the absence of tensions, but by transparent processes, clear accountability, and the capacity for controlled intervention amid uncertainty.

This perspective redirects regulatory attention from the internal mechanics of models to the conditions under which they can be deployed safely, fairly, and controllably in real-world settings. Simultaneously, it establishes a substantive link to the subsequent Section 7, which explores the international aspects of federated financial architectures and the associated coordination challenges.

7. Cross-Border Coordination and Standardization

Federated finance operates inherently across borders. The collaborative development, calibration, and deployment of models across institutional and jurisdictional boundaries constitute the standard practice within federated financial architectures. This transnational character generates significant regulatory tensions. Historically, national supervisory regimes have been designed to oversee individual institutions within clearly defined legal domains. Federated models challenge this framework by systematically distributing risks, responsibilities, and decision-making effects across multiple jurisdictions. In the absence of coordinated international supervision, federated finance may catalyze regulatory fragmentation.

This complex situation can be analytically characterized as a hybrid governance arrangement in which state, private, and mixed-organizational actors assume distinct control functions. The governance triangle framework developed by Abbott and Snidal offers a relevant reference, as it elucidates how global regulation emerges beyond traditional state hierarchies through the interaction of diverse actors [24]. From a political-economic perspective, this dynamic is further informed by the observation that global order is shaped less by formal hierarchy and more by the diffusion of dominant regulatory standards and strategic interactions [25]. In the context of emerging cross-border technologies, Shackelford et al. argue that effective regulation under technological uncertainty must increasingly adopt resilience-oriented and polycentric approaches to integrate risk anticipation, institutional learning, and international coordination [26].

This fragmentation creates legal uncertainty for institutions and may constitute a systemic risk in its own right. Divergent requirements for explainability, governance, or accountability can result in inconsistent risk management or the transfer of risks to less-regulated domains. Consequently, federated architectures risk enabling regulatory arbitrage rather than advancing regulatory objectives such as data protection, fairness, and risk limitation, which are frequently intended.

7.1 Regulatory Fragmentation as a Systemic Risk

Significant differences already exist between national and regional regulatory approaches to AI, model risk management, and algorithmic transparency. Some jurisdictions are developing AI-specific governance requirements, while others maintain technology-neutral, abstract principles. As a result, federated financial models may be subject to divergent valuation standards across jurisdictions.

From a political-economic perspective, this development can be understood against the backdrop of the realization that global power and coordination structures increasingly shape national regulatory decisions in highly interdependent policy areas. As Drezner shows, global order arises less from formal hierarchy than from the diffusion of dominant regulatory standards and the strategic interaction of state and non-state actors. This mechanism can reinforce regulatory asymmetries [25].

This fragmentation creates legal uncertainty for institutions and may constitute a systemic risk in itself. Divergent requirements for explainability, governance, or accountability can result in inconsistent risk management or the transfer of risks to less-regulated domains. Consequently, federated architectures risk enabling regulatory arbitrage rather than advancing regulatory objectives such as data protection, fairness, and risk limitation, which are frequently intended.

The regulatory assessment of federated models varies not only formally, but also in terms of the underlying supervisory logic. While some regimes emphasize transparency and formal explainability, others place greater emphasis on robustness of results, governance structures, or systemic stability. Federated systems must address these heterogeneous expectations simultaneously, which can lead to conflicting goals in design and operation.

For institutions, this results in increased compliance complexity. Federated models must function technically and organizationally, while also being interpretable in regulatory terms. This dynamic creates tension between the risk of regulatory arbitrage and the potential for excessive caution when systems are aligned to the strictest regulatory standards.

7.2 The Role of International Standard-Setting Bodies

In this context, international standard-setting institutions play a critical role. Organizations such as the Basel Committee on Banking Supervision (BCBS), the

Financial Stability Board (FSB), and the International Association of Insurance Supervisors (IAIS) have established mandates to harmonize supervisory expectations. The Bank for International Settlements has also contributed significantly through its work on explainable AI, model risks, and governance [19].

To date, these initiatives have primarily addressed institution-specific models or general AI risks. Federated financial architectures, however, constitute a qualitatively distinct use case that necessitates the explicit advancement of existing principles. Specifically, there is a need for standard guidelines regarding responsibility allocation, collective model testing and validation, risk-based minimum requirements for explainability, and the management of third parties and orchestrators within federated systems.

Given the limited scope of current soft law approaches, the European AI regulation assumes significance that extends beyond its formal territorial boundaries. While the regulation primarily targets providers and operators of AI systems within the European Union, it exerts extraterritorial influence whenever AI-supported decision-making affects the European market or is utilized by European institutions [3]. Similar to data protection law, this framework compels global actors to adapt their systems to maintain access to European financial markets.

Federated financial architectures significantly amplify this extraterritorial effect. In federated consortia, models, training processes, and aggregation mechanisms are regularly distributed across multiple jurisdictions. In contrast, the resulting model outputs are used by European institutions or integrated into European decision-making processes. This means that even non-European participants in federated systems are indirectly subject to European governance requirements, for example, regarding risk management, documentation obligations, or human oversight. For international consortia, this means that regulatory compliance can no longer be assessed in isolation at the national level, but becomes a characteristic of the entire federated system. It thus effectively functions as a unilaterally set but globally adequate governance standard that even non-European players must adhere to.

7.3 Risk-Based Minimum Standards as an Alternative to Complete Harmonization

Comprehensive international harmonization of detailed regulatory requirements appears neither feasible nor necessary. Establishing risk-based minimum standards that can be adapted at the national level without compromising their essential function is a more effective approach. For federated finance, such minimum standards could encompass the following elements:

- Clear governance requirements for federated consortia.
- Minimum requirements for collective model testing, validation, and monitoring.

- Risk-based expectations for explainability and transparency.
- Binding rules to prevent diffusion of responsibility.

These minimum standards would not supplant national supervision, but would provide a common reference framework that promotes regulatory consistency while preserving institutional diversity.

7.4 The Concept of a Federated Model Passport

An additional approach to operationalizing international minimum standards is the federated model passport. Similar to existing passport systems in financial market law, this passport could certify that a federated model satisfies fundamental internationally agreed requirements for governance, fairness, explainability, and risk control.

A federated model passport would not preclude national supervisory authorities from conducting their own audits. Instead, it could function as a confidence-building pre-certification, reducing redundant audits and facilitating cross-border cooperation. Simultaneously, it would enhance transparency regarding the institutional safeguards associated with a federated model and the risks that are deliberately accepted.

7.5 Developing International Supervisory Capacities

However, effective international coordination necessitates not only standard rules but also robust institutional capabilities. Federated financial models are highly complex from technical, organizational, and ethical standpoints. Without adequate expertise, supervisory authorities risk evaluating formal governance structures without the capacity to assess their actual effectiveness.

The coordination agenda should therefore encompass the development of joint supervisory capacities, such as international audit networks, shared model sandboxes, coordinated audit methodologies, and systematic exchanges of expertise. Federated financial architectures could thereby become not only subjects but also catalysts for enhanced international supervisory cooperation.

Federated finance can be viewed as an institutional experiment that highlights the limitations of national regulation. The tensions among efficiency, transparency, responsibility, and precaution are especially pronounced in the financial sector, though not exclusive to it.

If effective forms of internationally coordinated supervision can be established for federated finance models, they may serve as a blueprint for other data-intensive, cross-border AI applications. Federated finance will thus become a benchmark for global AI governance, not primarily in terms of technical feasibility, but in the capacity of regulatory institutions to organize collective responsibility and control within highly distributed systems.

8. Conclusion

This chapter demonstrates that federated finance should be regarded not as a marginal technical variant of data-driven financial models, but as a structural challenge to established regulatory, governance, and ethical frameworks. Federated financial architectures are transforming both the development and deployment of models, while also altering foundational assumptions regarding the organization of responsibility, control, and legitimacy within complex socio-technical systems.

From a regulatory standpoint, traditional institution-centric control logics are reaching their functional limits. Model risk management, explainability, and liability rely on assumptions of closed organizational life cycles, transparent responsibility allocation, and traceable decision-making processes. Federated systems challenge these assumptions at a structural level by distributing decision-making, risks, and knowledge across institutional and legal boundaries, while regulatory expectations of individual responsibility persist. The primary regulatory challenge is thus to functionally redefine controllability in the context of distributed control, rather than merely adapting individual regulatory instruments.

Within this context, explainability emerges not as an epistemic ideal, but as a limited governance resource. Its primary value lies in facilitating accountability, intervention, and institutional learning, rather than in fully disclosing internal model mechanisms. Federated architectures highlight that explainability is inherently dependent on the addressee, context, and organizational mediation. When complete transparency is structurally unattainable, regulatory priorities shift from explanation to governance, monitoring, and escalation. Consequently, explainability becomes a relational concept that achieves its regulatory function only through effective institutional arrangements.

Ethical analysis indicates that federated financial systems are defined less by isolated errors and more by cumulative, emergent potential for harm. In such systems, responsibility must be viewed not only as retrospective attribution of blame, but as a prospective task focused on shaping future outcomes. A harm-based, precautionary ethical approach enables this perspective without imposing unrealistic expectations of complete control or predictability. Ethical legitimacy, in this context, derives not from flawless individual decisions but from institutional arrangements that render uncertainty visible, limit risks, and maintain opportunities for corrective action.

Governance structures play a central mediating role in federated financial architectures. They form the interface where regulatory expectations, ethical requirements, and operational control converge. Hierarchical control is replaced by a multi-level governance logic that combines local responsibility, collective coordination, and external oversight. Governance not only addresses epistemic boundaries but also structures unavoidable conflicts among efficiency, transparency, autonomy, and precaution. In this sense, federated systems are governance-intensive not despite, but because, of their inherent trade-offs.

Analysis of these trade-offs demonstrates that federated financial architectures do not permit clear-cut optimal solutions. Performance improvements frequently entail increased opacity, local autonomy may conflict with systemic coherence, and innovation can compete with precautionary risk management. These trade-offs are not indicative of regulatory failure, but are inherent features of complex socio-technical systems. Consequently, regulatory quality is assessed less by the elimination of such tensions and more by the capacity to make them explicit and maintain institutional manageability.

Finally, it became clear that federation exacerbates the international dimension of regulatory governance. The cross-border nature of federated models collides with nationally fragmented supervisory regimes and carries the risks of regulatory arbitrage and excessive caution. International coordination cannot resolve these tensions through complete harmonization, but it can do so through risk-adequate minimum standards, confidence-building instruments, and the development of joint supervisory capacities. In this context, federated finance appears less as a specific problem of the financial sector than as a testing ground for the performance of global AI governance as a whole.

In summary, this chapter contends that federated finance should be viewed primarily as an institutional challenge rather than a technological innovation. The central issue is not the power or explainability of federated models, but the adequacy of regulatory, ethical, and governance structures in ensuring collective responsibility, precaution, and long-term controllability under distributed control. From this vantage point, federated finance serves as a prism that reveals the fundamental tensions inherent in contemporary data-driven regulation.

References

[1] Basel Committee on Banking Supervision (BCBS). (2012). Principles for financial market infrastructures. *Bank for International Settlements.*

[2] Basel Committee on Banking Supervision (BCBS). (2023). Principles for financial market infrastructures. *Bank for International Settlements.*

[3] European Commission, Regulation (EU) 2024/1689 of the European Parliament and of the Council of 12 July 2024 laying down harmonised rules on artificial intelligence (Artificial Intelligence Act). Official Journal of the European Union, L 1689/1.

[4] Power, M. (2027). *Organized Uncertainty: Designing a World of Risk Management.* Oxford University Press.

[5] Andrae, S. (2024). Explainable Artificial Intelligence in Risk Management: A Framework. In *Artificial Intelligence and Beyond for Finance* (pp. 149–206).

[6] Doshi-Velez, F. and Kim, B. (2017). Towards a rigorous science of interpretable machine learning. *arXiv preprint arXiv:1702.08608.*

[7] Mittelstadt, B., Russell, C. and Wachter, S. (2019, January). Explaining explanations in AI. In *Proceedings of the Conference on Fairness, Accountability, and Transparency* (pp. 279–288).

[8] Yildiz, K. and Cil, A. E. (2025). A systematic literature review on applications of explainable artificial intelligence in the financial sector. *Internet of Things*, 101696.

[9] Mittelstadt, B. D., Allo, P., Taddeo, M., Wachter, S. and Floridi, L. (2016). The ethics of algorithms: Mapping the debate. *Big Data & Society*, 3(2). https://doi.org/10.1177/2053951716679679.

[10] Floridi, L., Cowls, J., Beltrametti, M., Chatila, R., Chazerand, P., Dignum, V. et al. (2018). AI4People—An ethical framework for a good AI society: Opportunities, risks, principles, and recommendations. *Minds and Machines*, 28(4): 689–707. https://doi.org/10.1007/s11023-018-9482-5.

[11] Barocas, S., Hardt, M. and Narayanan, A. (2023). *Fairness and Machine Learning: Limitations and Opportunities*. MIT Press.

[12] Wachter, S., Mittelstadt, B. and Russell, C. (2021). Why fairness cannot be automated: Bridging the gap between EU non-discrimination law and AI. *Computer Law & Security Review*, 41: 105567. https://doi.org/10.1016/j.clsr.2021.105567.

[13] Ricœur, P. and Blamey, K. (1994). Oneself as Another University of Chicago Press, 10992. DOI: 10.7208/chicago/9780226844541.001.0001.

[14] European Banking Authority (EBA). (2019). Guidelines on outsourcing arrangements (EBA/GL/2019/02). EBA.

[15] European Central Bank (ECB). (2020). Guide on outsourcing cloud services. *ECB Banking Supervision*.

[16] Ansell, C. and Gash, A. (2008). Collaborative governance in theory and practice. *Journal of Public Administration Research and Theory*, 18(4): 543–571. doi: 10.1093/jopart/mum032.

[17] Carta, L., Spadea, F. and Seneviratne, O. (2025). Explainable federated learning for US state-level financial distress modeling. arXiv preprint arXiv:2511.08588.

[18] Yang, K., Krishnan, N. and Kulkarni, S. R. (2025). Financial data analysis with robust federated logistic regression. arXiv preprint arXiv:2504.20250.

[19] Pérez-Cruz, F., Prenio, J., Restoy, F. and Yong, J. (2025, September). Managing Explanations: How Regulators Can Address AI Explainability.

[20] Kennedy, C. H., Hilal, A. and Momeni, M. (2025, November). The role of federated learning in improving financial security: A survey. In *2025 IEEE Global Conference on Artificial Intelligence and Internet of Things (GCAIoT)* (pp. 1–8). IEEE.

[21] European Banking Authority (EBA). (2022). Guidelines on loan origination and monitoring. EBA.

[22] Stirling, A. (2010). Keep it complex. *Nature*, 468(7327): 1029–1031.

[23] Rudin, C. (2019). Stop explaining black box machine learning models for high stakes decisions and use interpretable models instead. *Nature Machine Intelligence*, 1(5): 206–215.

[24] Snidal, K. and Abbott, D. (2009). The governance triangle. *The Politics of Global Regulation*, 44–88.

[25] Drezner, D. W. (2008). All politics is global: Explaining international regulatory regimes.

[26] Shackelford, S. J. (2012). Toward cyberpeace: Managing cyberattacks through polycentric governance. *Am. UL Rev.*, 62: 1273.

14 Emerging Trends and Future Innovations

Somdatta Patra* and Ankit Sharma

With the increasing dependence of the financial industry on artificial intelligence (AI), it is in a dire collision with increasing data privacy regulations, such as the General Data Protection Regulation (GDPR) in Europe and the Digital Personal Data Protection (DPDP) Act in India. This chapter examines federated learning (FL) as the breakthrough architecture that is destined to address this paradox, and set the stage of the coming decade for safe financial innovations. A few of which include the immutable auditability of blockchain, strong security through the application of differential privacy, and hardware-level integrity through trusted execution environments, possible due to the synergy of FL with enhancements of technologies. The discussion seeks into pivotal algorithmic innovations, such as personalized and clustered FL, to address non-IID (non-independent and identically distributed) data problem endemic to finance, and also the need of algorithmic fairness. On top of that, the chapter identifies transformative uses within anti-money laundering, credit risk modelling, and decentralized finance that reveal how collaborative intelligence may be applied to drive precision and fairness. It subsequently critically assesses the moral-governance labyrinth, the content of which requires model explainability, cross-border compliance, and counter-adversarial threat. Lastly, the chapter includes a strategic prediction for the upcoming decade, as per which the monetary environment would be outstanding, transparent, and intelligent, based on the premises of decentralized and privacy-assuring AI.

1. Introduction: The Dawn of a New Financial Intelligence Paradigm

Digital transformation and the increasing global need of data privacy are the two forces that define the global financial services market as they converge at an intersection. Initially introduced as a conceptual novelty in the last two decades, artificial intelligence (AI) evolved into a must-have innovation and efficiency

Apex Institute of Technology (CSE), Chandigarh University, Mohali-140413, Punjab, India.
* Corresponding author: somdattapatra151@gmail.com

DOI: 10.1201/9781003710059-14

factor. With high-frequency trading algorithms running millions of transactions per second, and powerful machine learning models estimating creditworthiness, detecting fraud, and giving personalized financial recommendations as robo-advisors, AI is pervasive in the operational culture of contemporary finance. This algorithmic breakthrough has created more opportunities than ever before, as institutions are now more risk-efficient, capital-productive, and capable of offering highly personalized products and services to a worldwide client base. The insatiable consumption of these sophisticated algorithms by large and varied datasets has, until recently, been regarded as a precondition to their success. Simple wisdom has done the trick—the more the data, the better, more robust, and illuminative models. Figure 1 shows the difference between basic architecture about centralized learning and federated learning (FL) regarding communication overhead. Unlike centralized schemes, yellow-headed systems need the constant exchange of raw data to a central server, federated learning anonymously, and almost incurring no exposure due to the transfer of model parameters alone. This analogy underscores how federated models are more compatible with privacy-sensitive financial models [1].

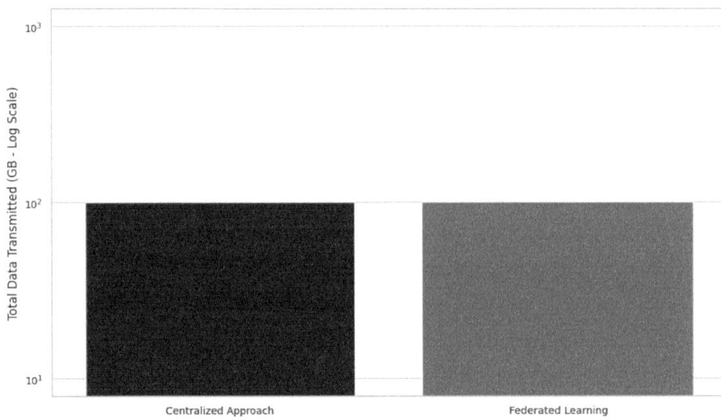

Figure 1: Communication overhead: centralized vs. federated.

A significant and even insensible conflict has emerged as a result of this data-centric paradigm, however. Since financial institutions have developed enormous databanks of sensitive client data—such as personal identities, transaction history, asset holdings, and behavioral traces—they have been targets of advanced cyberattacks too. Data centralization is analytically convenient, but it leaves a single point of failure, where an effective breach will impact millions of people negatively and threaten the survival of the institution itself. At the same time, the awareness of the world about the sacredness of individual information has solidified into strict legal provisions. It is not only the nature of the legal aspect of data processing that has been drastically changed today by some laws such as the European Union General Data Protection Regulation (GDPR) and the relatively newer Indian Digital Personal Data Protection (DPDP) Act among others in various countries around the world, but also the ethical consideration aspect of data processing [22]. These laws require data fiduciaries with high demands that advance the precepts of data minimization, purpose limitation, and user consent. In the case of the financial sector, the message is simple—harvesting and centralizing client information without restraint is no longer a sustainable policy option in the medium term. That poses a dilemma of critical implementation—how will the industry be able to press ahead with its innovation and development of AI when the source of the same data, that is, the fuel, becomes a subject of even stricter limitations and the risk of serious security breaches? It is against this difficult backdrop that FL steps into the scene as not just another technical instrument, but as a paradigm shift into a new era of financial intelligence. Federated learning provides a solution to this implicit vice, introducing a direction toward a new era of secure, private, and collaborative AI by flipping that age-old paradigm and taking the algorithm to the data, and not the data to an algorithm [8].

The chapter assumes federated learning to be a fundamental technological change that will trigger the advancement of innovation in finance in the next decade. It is much more than a privacy-enhancing technology measured in small monthly steps; it is a strategic enablement of a new decentralized financial intelligence. Through the prism of FL, by enabling many competing or siloed institutions to jointly create potent machine learning models on their distributed data, without ever sharing or revealing any of the underlying highly sensitive raw data itself, the inter-organizational collaboration is broken down at the very structural points which have long been impeding such collaboration historically [11]. This feature is what gets the industry out of a zero-sum game of proprietary data hoarding and into the production of a positive-sum ecosystem. The collective good in this ecosystem can be that collective intelligence emerges on systemic risks such as fraud, money laundering, and credit defaults, and none of this is hindered by the strict protection of client confidentiality or compliance with the most rigorous privacy legislation in the world. The thesis behind this chapter, then, is that federated learning will form the base on which a more resilient, transparent, and intelligent financial ecology is founded; the aspects of security, privacy, and corporate responsibility successfully aligning the goals of technological innovation [2].

To fully develop this transformative potential, this chapter is designed in such a way that it takes the reader through the surface-level aspects of the influence of FL on the financial sector. We will start with a discussion of the paradigm shift in moving beyond centralized data silos toward a new kind of collaborative financial modelling, and further discuss the technical restrictions and regulatory pressures which make the shift both necessary and inevitable. The chapter will then consider the impactful synergistic technologies including blockchain, differential privacy (DP), and the secure hardware environment that are enhancing the security, auditability, and scale of federated learning systems. The following will delve into the algorithmic edges of FL, with attention to the state-of-the-art studies that seek to address the practical issues of scaling these methodologies to the complex, heterogeneous, non-identically distributed data of the financial world. After this technical exposition, we will also overview an assortment of transformative use cases, including next-generation fraud detection and high-frequency trading, to the increasingly popular fields of decentralized finance and insurance. Having acknowledged that technological growth is not achieved in isolation, we will then journey through the most significant ethical, regulatory, and governance issues that need to be resolved, such as model explainability, cross-border data governance, and novel security vulnerabilities. The chapter will end with a final sentence in which the author projects the vision of the 10-year future of federated financial intelligence, and proposes strategic insights to guide researchers, industry leaders, and policymakers to make responsible and effective advances in this promising field.

2. The Paradigm Shift: From Centralized Data Silos to Collaborative Financial Modelling

Financial services industry architecture has long been ruled by a centralizing logic when it comes to the data management architecture. Over the decades, the dominant approach to leveraging the power of data has been aggregation, that is, the formation of large, centralized storage facilities, or data lakes, into which all accessible data is injected. A method that proved instrumental in the creation of first-generation AI and machine learning models is now proving that it is exceptionally limited. The rising security risks, excessive and untenable regulatory burdens, and the very nature of competition in the market are questioning its underlying assumptions. It is the same structure that was constructed to generate value that is setting fire to the whole system and preventing innovation in the future. This discussion addresses the inevitable change process that is occurring away from this old paradigm to a new paradigm of decentralized and collaborative financial intelligence, a transformation in which federated learning is serving as the key engine [3].

2.1 Flaws of the Centralized Traditional AI Models

A traditional model of centralized AI operates on the principle of data silos, both external and internal to various institutions and across the industry. Internally, one large bank can occasionally be a feudal system of semi-autonomous fiefs. Each of the retail banking departments—the wealth management segment, the investment banking division, and the mortgage section—collects its own specific datasets, and treats them separately. This fragmentation does not allow the institution to establish a truly holistic, 360-degree perspective of its clients, which results in the inability to cross-sell, ineffective risk assessment, and a fragmented customer experience. A portfolio of investments that their client, an affluent client, has spent the majority of their money on may not be fully taken into account when the algorithm decides whether they should be given a commercial loan, resulting in a false judgment regarding their creditworthiness. Figure 2 illustrates the trade-off between privacy of data and model utility of traditional and federated learning model. In federated learning, utility can be optimized more evenly unlike in centralized systems in which utility may tend to improve at the expense of privacy. This change is essential when financial institutions work under stringent rules of data protection.

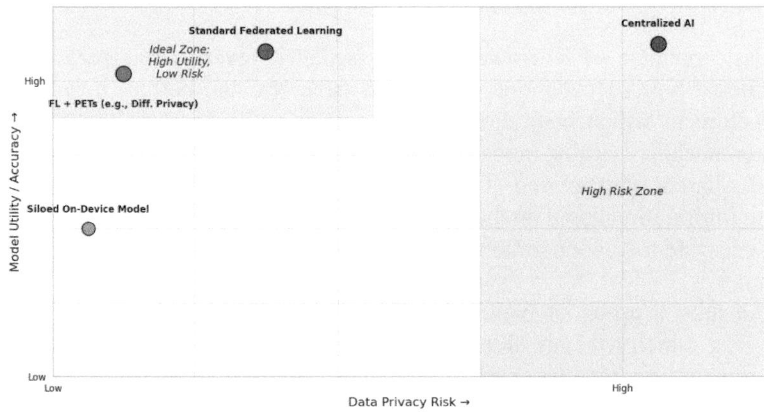

Figure 2: The privacy–utility paradigm shift.

These silos are then extended externally to the level of an industry. Every financial institution, whether a global bank or a local credit union or an agile fintech start-up or a credit rating agency, treats its information as its key proprietary asset and protects it accordingly. Such a competitive hoarding generates a partial and disjointed image of the entire market. A model that has only been trained on the data of a single bank can quickly develop a strong ability to identify the patterns of fraud or credit risk that are present in its own customer base, but will fail to detect new attack vectors or emerging economic behavior that is now first appearing among the customers of the competition [10]. This closed system disadvantages individual institutions and makes the financial system as a whole more vulnerable because systemic risks can spread through the informational cracks between these fortified data silos.

In addition to this strategic myopia, there are extreme and rapidly increasing risks caused by centralization of data. These huge reserves of vulnerable personal and financial data are a honeypot to bad actors. One effective cyberattack can result in a data breach of apocalyptic levels, putting millions of customers at risk of credit card theft and identity fraud, causing massive regulatory penalties, and systematically causing massive reputational harm to the institution. There are also the significant operational risks. A centralized data platform is a single point of vulnerability; a loss of communication, whether through technical failure or a targeted attack, can turn countless important AI-enabled processes, such as automated trading or the fraud detection system, into a standstill. Lastly, the logistical and financial hurdles toward real-world data exchange within a centralized model are virtually unbearable. Tremendous cost, legal barriers, and technical complexity involved in securely aggregating raw, sensitive customer information across several competing organizations have made the idea of a shared, industry wide data lake a theoretical dream, but not a reality [4].

2.2 Collaborative Ecosystems on the Rise

The basic premise of federated learning is that it reverses this paradigm and facilitates a type of collaboration that has never existed before. It presents an architecture in which institutions can join together to create a higher-quality, stronger machine learning model without the underlying sensitive data ever being moved, shared, or disclosed. This is a giant step out of sharing data and into sharing information based on that data. The mechanism enables the establishment of an ecosystem of cooperation, which is based on mutual benefit and ensured privacy.

Consider a group of banks, fintech, and insurance agencies that want to develop a state-of-the-art framework to identify more sophisticated money laundering networks. This cannot be the case under the traditional model. No institution would accept to submit its confidential transactions logs to a central server, much more one that is controlled by its rival. Federated learning is the way to change the process. The process is broken down to start with a coordinating server that disseminates a base model to all the other members of the process. This model is in turn trained in each individual institution within its own firewall, using its own proprietary and non-shared data. The important next step is when each institution there sends only the resulting model updates, a set of abstract numerical weights and parameters that captures what its local data have learned. These updates are mathematical derivatives, not raw data, and are intended to be added together without disclosing what particular data point actually gave rise to them. These updates are then safely averaged with a central server to produce a better global model, which is in turn sent back to the participants to be used in the subsequent round of training [15].

Such a cyclic process enables the global model to be taught by the experience and data of the whole consortium. The resulting model is able to recognize cross-institutional patterns of fraudulent activity which would not be visible to an individual participant. It is able to acquire a degree of accuracy and generalization that is well beyond what could be learned by any single member in isolation. Most importantly, this collaborative advantage is realized without compromising the two most valuable assets of each organization: client confidentiality and competitive advantage. Raw data never has to move outside a safe perimeter, and privacy is designed in. Moreover, as the specialized data of any single institution is never shared, they preserve the essence of their competitive advantage and at the same time contribute to and gain the benefit of the aggregate intelligence of the ecosystem. This paradigm also turns the competitors into the collaborators of precompetitive market in the management of systemic risks to make financial system safer and healthier; more secure and stable to everyone [5].

2.3 Regulatory Pressure to Decentralize

When the pull factors that lead the industry to a new model are the technical constraints of centralization, the key catalyst is the global wave of data privacy regulation. Nonfinancial and legal implications of noncompliance have become so great they are even compelling the re-architecture of data governance. Federated learning is specifically well placed not only as a technology to help institutions escape penalties, but as a technical construct that reflects the fundamental ideals of new privacy laws.

The principle of the federated approach fits like a glove with the principles of the European Union GDPR which is the global standard of data protection. It implies data protection both by design and by default, that is, the privacy issues are to be taken into account even during the development of a system, not dealt with afterward [20]. One of the best examples of this idea is federated learning. The concept of data minimization, stating that data must be processed in accordance with the requirement of a particular necessity only, is fulfilled per se, as the central model aggregator never even accesses the raw personal data at all. Likewise, "purpose limitation" is easier to implement in cases where data remains locally available, avoiding the risk of the type of functional creep that frequently arises in a large, centralized data lake.

This is not the European trend in regulation. These themes are reflected in the DPDP Act of India and the California Consumer Privacy Act (CCPA), which give an individual more control over his or her data, imposing strict requirements upon any data fiduciary. It is an operational and legal nightmare to a financial institution with a centralized data strategy navigating this complex and occasionally conflicting patchwork of regulations, when operating globally. Having all the data in a single place might break the data residency rules, and transferring the data across any boundaries entails complicated legal liaisons. Federated learning avoids many of these problems in a graceful manner. Retaining data in their domestic jurisdictions, and only sending anonymized model updates, also gives it a valid avenue to construct global models that adhere to laws on national data sovereignty. The regulatory environment in essence is providing a strong incentive toward decentralization, both economically and legally. The technological solution that empowers the financial institution to satisfy this demand and enables regulatory compliance to become a driver of safe collaborative innovation is federated learning. Figure 3 puts in perspective the development of significant worldwide laws on data protection that affect the use of AI in the financial sector. The history also reveals how laws such as GDPR and DPDP Act of India have increased the urgency of decentralized learning structure. Federated learning is inherently in line with such regulatory paths [6].

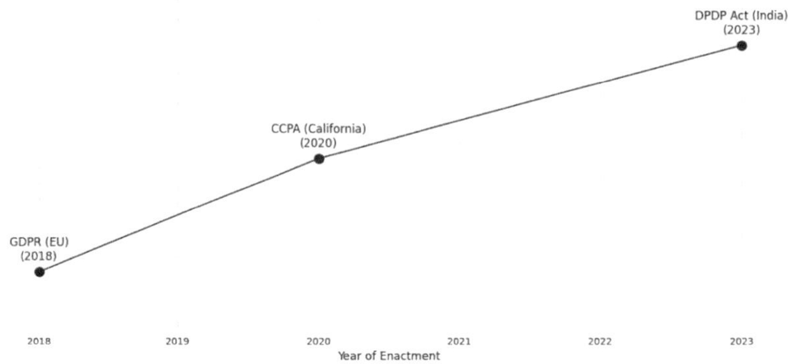

Figure 3: Timeline of key global data privacy legislation.

3. Synergistic Technologies: Federated Learning on Steroids

Federated learning offers the fundamental model of privacy-preserving AI, but its potential is fully opened when combined with a set of other advanced technologies. These integrative combinations result in a multilayer defense against a broad range of threats to security and privacy, making what appears to be a good idea a strong, enterprise-grade security system in the financial sector. The typical FL model, where a central server is used to coordinate the training process, still has potential vulnerabilities and areas of centralization that may be further hardened. By integrating technologies, such as blockchain, advanced cryptography, and secure hardware, we can create a federated ecosystem which can be not only private, but also transparent, auditable, and resilient. This part explores these key technological integrations, and how they reinforce each other in supporting the highly demanded federated paradigm.

3.1 Auditability and Trust with the Use of Blockchain

A traditional FL structure is based on the use of a central orchestrator to control the training process—to transmit the original model, to receive updates, and to sum them up. Although the raw data is not accessed by this entity, it nevertheless possesses the critical power and confidence. In principle, a rogue or hacked server can inject malicious elements or sabotage the process of aggregation, or lock out some participants, or even reverse-engineer participant data based on the updates in the model. A promising answer to decentralize this trust and bring radical transparency to the process is blockchain technology [1].

With FL combined with permissioned blockchain, we can trace the complete life cycle of the machine learning model to an immutable distributed ledger. All of the steps can be recorded as a transaction—the hash of the initial model was published, the names of people who gave updates to that model during a particular round were recorded, and the final cumulative model is a hash of the world model. This gives an audit trail that cannot be changed and is cryptographically encrypted. The people involved in a training process, alongside the regulators and auditors, can independently verify the integrity of the training process without having to trust a central administrator. It can be shown that the end model was, in fact, the outcome of the intended aggregation of updates made by all competent participants and nothing more [7].

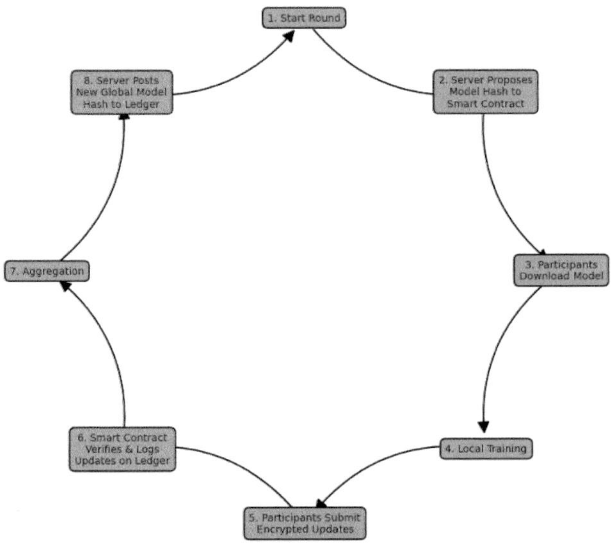

Figure 4: FLoB (Federated learning on blockchain).

In addition, the federated learning workflow can be automated and controlled by smart contracts. Following are the participation rules—participation criteria, training round schedule, the exact aggregation algorithm to apply (e.g., Federated Averaging), incentive mechanisms to reward quality contributions, etc. All this might be defined by a smart contract [4]. This eliminates confusion and the possibility of manual error or manipulation, substituting the trusted central server with confidence in the transparent auditable code. This combination is sometimes called federated learning on blockchain (FLoB), and it can be especially effective in cross-institutional partnerships when one party (these institutions) does not wish to concede power to the other. It creates a democratized and trustless space of co-creation of common intelligence. Figure 4 illustrates how federated learning can be integrated with blockchain so as to improve on transparency and trust. The blockchain allows capturing a history of training events and contributions of people, which will not be changed by a central aggregator that people can trust them. This architecture enhances audit within multi-institutional financial partnerships [8].

3.2 Secure Multi-Party Computation (SMPC) and Enhanced Differential Privacy

By itself, federated learning is not a privacy panacea. Although it eliminates data leakage on a case-by-case basis, advanced attacks have shown that one can potentially extract information regarding the underlying training data by looking at the sequence of model updates that a participant has given. Incidentally, a model inversion attack could seek to construct a representative data sample that would have created a specified update. FL systems need to be hardened in response to these remaining risks with powerful cryptographic and statistical privacy measures [9].

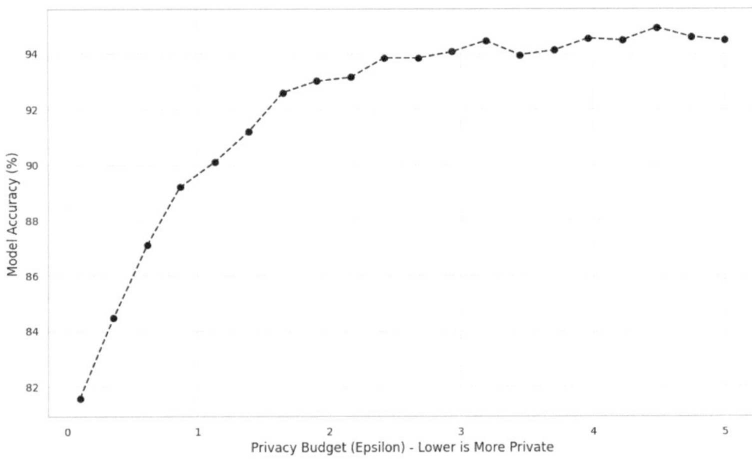

Figure 5: Trade-off between privacy and model accuracy.

DP is a potent, mathematically sound privateness promise. The key concept is to add just the right level of statistical noise to the data or, more typically in FL, to the model updates which the participant device then transmits [23]. This noise is chosen with care to be sufficiently large to obscure the input of any single person, so that it is computationally infeasible to decide (as the attacker) whether the information of a concrete person was included in the training set. It does have a trade-off inherent in it—more noising means better privacy, at the cost of a slightly weaker final model, but this means that institutions can optimize the balance as needed by their regulatory and performance needs. It introduces a layer of anonymization which is provable and resists the strongest inference attacks. The natural trade-off between preserving privacy and predictive accuracy is marked by Figure 5 when the processes of differential privacy are being implemented. Controlled noise helps to keep sensitive financial data out of reach of the bad but can have marginal impacts on performance. The number highlights the relevance of the choice of the best privacy budgets in controlled financial frameworks [10].

Another cryptograph-based approach is known as SMPC. SMPC is a scheme of protocols to enable two or more parties to jointly compute a function on shared inputs, without the parties learning about one another. Within the framework of FL, it is possible to completely substitute the central aggregation server with SMPC. Participants can participate in an SMPC protocol to get the average of the updates, instead of transmitting their model updates to a central point [3]. The update of each participant is cryptographically divided into parts and shared among the other participants. The protocol also guarantees that not one party (nor even a coalition of up to a corresponding degree of groups) can reconstruct the original update of another, but the proper aggregate (the average) can be computed by all. This eliminates the support of an ideally trusted aggregator and people can give strong security assurances, so that the model updates they achieve themselves are confidential during the procedure. Together with FL and DP/SMPC or both, it creates an imposing defense-in-depth security architecture.

3.3 Edge Computing/Trusted Execution Environments (TEE) Role

To implement federated learning at scale, especially in applications where latency is a critical issue, such as real-time fraud detection or high-frequency trading, the underlying hardware and network infrastructure should also be taken into consideration. Edge computing is one of the enabling factors in this situation. The edge here is the local computing facilities in each of the participating financial institutions—the servers behind their firewalls where the data lives. The FL paradigm is intrinsically consistent with the principles of edge computing that suggested processing data at proximity to its source. Using the high-powered edge servers, the computationally intensive local training rounds can be effectively performed by institutions without constricting the network with a large dataset.

Nevertheless, the integrity of the computation itself can be of concern even in cases where training is done locally. What can a consortium do to make certain that a member is executing the proper, pure training code? How does a participant know that the model it gets as part of the orchestrator has not been manipulated? TEEs are a hardware solution to these issues. TEEs are protection domains in the primary processor (e.g., those delivered by the Intel Software Guard Extensions (SGX) or AMD Secure Encrypted Virtualization (SEV) [16]. The code and information stored in a TEE are hardware-locked, that is, it cannot be accessed, read, or viewed by the operating system or even any privileged administrator on the host machine. As shown in Figure 6, trusted execution environments play a role in ensuring local model training. TEEs provide isolation of sensitive computations both among the operating systems and administrators. This hardware solution provides confidence in the federated members of high-value financial use cases [11].

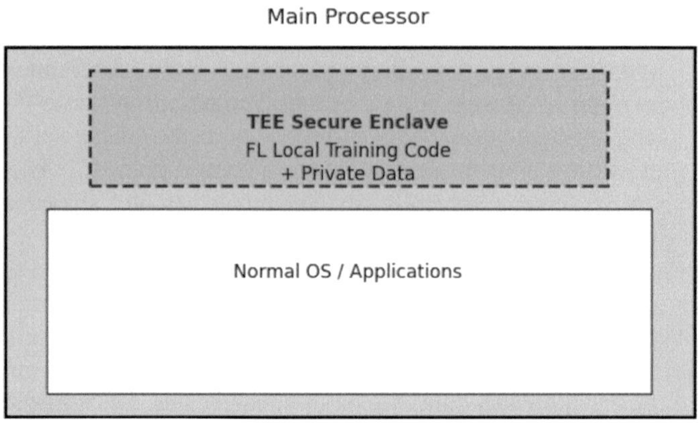

Figure 6: Conceptual diagram of a trusted execution environment (TEE).

In a federated system, the entire local training process can be made verifiable and tamper-proof with the help of TEEs. Remote attestation allows the participants to demonstrate to the consortium in a cryptographic manner that they are executing the official, untampered training algorithm within a secure TEE. On the other hand, the TEE could secure the proprietary model itself against being stolen or reverse-engineered by the local institution. This establishes a strong level of confidence on both ends, ensuring the integrity of the process and confidentiality of the model intellectual property, thus creating the trust necessary in large-scale, high-stakes financial partnerships.

4. Algorithmic Frontiers: Developing FL to Real-World Financial Data

Federated learning is a theoretically promising method of model training without sharing data. But to translate this promise into effective, production-grade financial applications is to overcome huge algorithmic challenges. The clean, well-mannered datasets of academic theory have little in common with the messy, multifaceted, and heterogeneous data of the actual world of finance. Initial FL algorithms, including the canonical Federated Averaging (FedAvg), were formulated assuming that participant data is independent and identically distributed (IID). In financial settings, this assumption inherently fails, generating issues of model convergence, model performance, and even equitableness. This section discusses the state of the art of FL research, including the novel algorithms that are being developed to address the statistical heterogeneity of financial data and to harness the full capabilities of federated intelligence. Figure 7 depicts a layer security architecture that consists of federated learning, blockchain, differential privacy, and secure hardware. Different vulnerabilities are handled by each of the layers making it a defense-in-depth strategy. Enterprise-grade financial AI systems need this kind of multilayered protection.

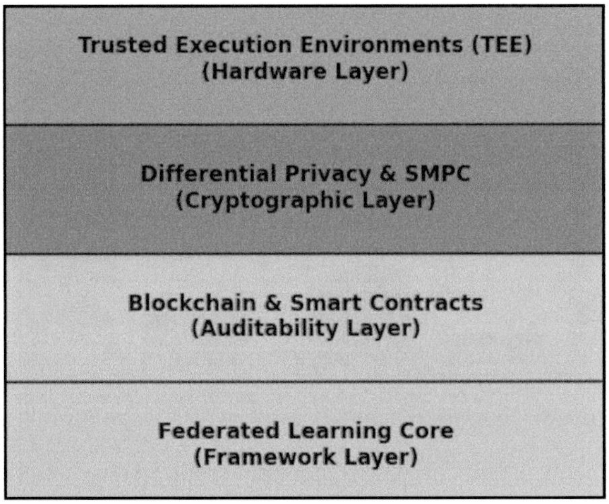

Figure 7: Multilayered defense with synergistic technologies.

4.1 What Is the Non-IID Data in Finance?

The most critical issue faced on implementing FL to finance is the concept of non-IID data. It implies that the data possessed by each institution involved in the study assume a different underlying statistic. Instead, this heterogeneity is the rule of the system rather than an exception, and is the result of the nature of the financial ecosystem. The client base and product portfolio of a global investment bank in New York are completely dissimilar to that of a regional bank in rural India that deals with agricultural loans. The risk profile of a micro-lender of workers in the gig economy is entirely foreign to the risk profile of a well-established mortgage lender. The data of a credit card provider will reveal the different spending habits of a metropolitan center and a suburban population even within the same country [12].

Figure 8 plots the heterogeneity of the distribution of financial data of institutions. There are non-IID customer demographics, products, and risk profiles leading to differences in the customer demographics, products, and the risk profiles, and this is obstruction of the standard federated algorithms. The only point that is important in the design of adaptive federated models is the realization of this variability. This statistical divergence appears in a variety of forms: feature distribution skew (e.g., income levels differ dramatically among the participants), label distribution skew (e.g., one bank has a much higher rate of fraud than the others), and concept drift (e.g., the definition of a risky investment varies over time or among institutions). The performance of a basic algorithm, such as FedAvg, when used in this type of non-IID environment can become much worse. The algorithm is based on searching for a single group of global model parameters, which reduces the overall loss of all individuals. But the local training of each participant causes the model to be drawn to the specific data

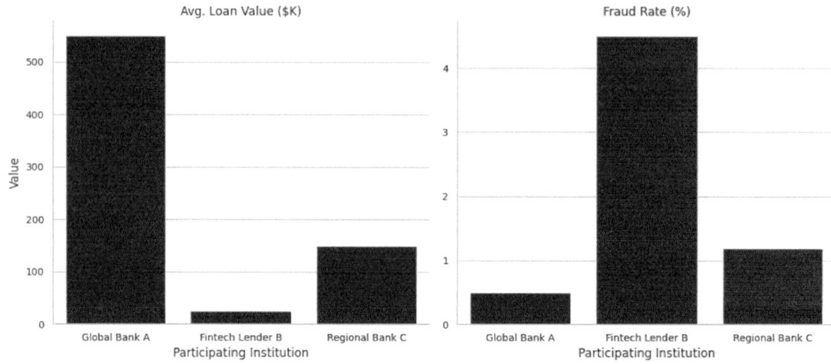

Figure 8: Example of non-IID financial data across institutions.

distribution. This is called client drift and may result in the global model moving back and forth between competing goals that will never arrive at an answer that optimally satisfies anyone. The final global model can be a dismal compromise, performing worse than a model that all participants could have trained themselves on, thus defeating the very idea of collaboration.

4.2 The History of the Development of Adaptive and Personalized Algorithms

It has become evident that a single global model may suffer from sub-optimality, leading the research of academic interest to move firmly in a direction that focuses on adaptive and personalized federated learning. The new generation of algorithms recognizes and embraces the heterogeneity of the data and aims to deliver more specific and effective models to each member without compromising the ability to utilize the cumulative shared wisdom of the network [6].

Personalized federated learning (PFL) is one of the best-known approaches. PFL is not aimed at generating a single global model, but at training an individual, participant-specific, model that is conditioned to a local data distribution. One typical method is a hybrid method—the system is trained on a global model that represents general trends, but the individual participant can shape or customize that model based on its own private data. A powerful algorithm in this area is FedProx that transforms the local training goal. It includes an extra proximal variable that punishes enormous variation of the parameters of the global model [12]. This serves as a kind of regularization whereby local models are encouraged to take advantage of the global consensus without deviating to such an extent that they push the overall training off track. This will enable every institution to settle on a final model as a complex amalgamation of worldwide acumen and regional particularity. The performance of advanced federated optimization methods on convergence in non-IID conditions is also presented in Figure 9. Individualized

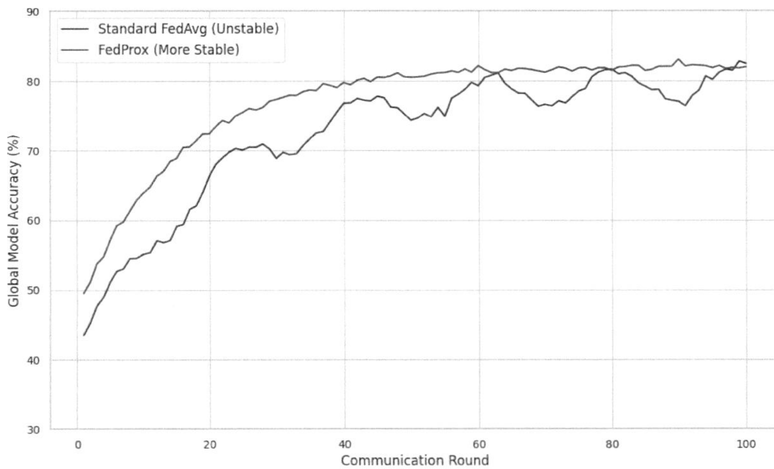

Figure 9: Algorithm convergence on heterogeneous (non-IID) data.

and normalized algorithms minimize client driftage as well as stabilizing global training. The behavior is important to implement federated learning in the real financial environment.

Another good strategy is clustered federated learning (CFL). CFL algorithms do not make assumptions about the membership of all participants to a single group, but instead seek to dynamically subdivide the participants into groups based on how similar their data distributions are. An individual model is then trained per cluster [19]. As an example, a consortium of financial institutions could have algorithmically recognized a set of retail banks, a set of investment companies, and a set of insurance companies. With training a model per cluster, the system can perform significantly better, since the model of the "retail bank" cluster is not watered down by meaningless data of the "insurance" cluster. The financial sector finds this very intuitively appealing, as natural clusters of institutions are already established on the basis of business models and demographic profiles of clients. Figure 10 demonstrates clustered federated learning where participants can be grouped together, depending on the similarity of the data. The advantages of collaboration are also maintained, and the use of different models, one trained on each cluster, also improves the accuracy. It is the best strategy that fits well into the fragmented nature of the financial industry [13], [14].

Outside of such changes in architecture, there are also innovations in the process of aggregation. Algorithms such as FedNova have been designed to address client drift by normalizing the updates each participant transmits—this is because some may have done more local calculation than others. This ensures the aggregation is fairer, which increases the convergence rate and stability on non-IID. These adaptive strategies may be regarded as a paradigm shift as far as imposing consensus to intelligently managing diversity is concerned [15].

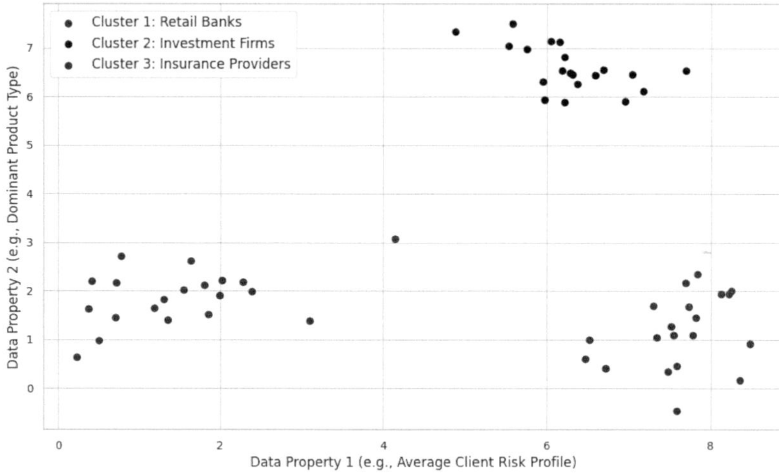

Figure 10: Conceptual visualization of clustered federated learning.

4.3 Algorithmic Fairness on a Federated Axis

Another critical question that arises as a result of the promise of FL to be able to train on more diverse data is that of algorithmic fairness. Unwittingly, a simple cumulative aggregation of model updates may create a biased model on a global scale, which is commonly called the tyranny of the majority. Larger institutions that have millions of clients will automatically contribute more heavily to the updates of the global model than smaller specialized institutions in a financial consortium. When these smaller institutions represent a demographic or geographic minority, the aggregation process will risk outvoting or averaging out their patterns of data [5].

Think of a federated credit scoring model. When low-income rural residents are the main clients of a small set of community banks in the consortium, their financial behaviors could be systematically dissimilar to the urban, high-income clientele who comprise most of the information at larger banks. A typical FedAvg model may fit well most of the population yet work poorly, and unfairly, on the rural minority, and so deprive creditworthy people of access only because their data profile is underrepresented. This poses serious ethical and regulatory risks, because the financial models are, by law, supposed to be competitive and not discriminatory. Figure 11 brings into focus how fairness-conscious aggregation influences the results of loan approval. Fairness-conscious federated learning enhances a just decision-making process by reducing the dominance of big institutions. It is especially significant in regard to regulatory compliance and ethical implementation of AI in finance.

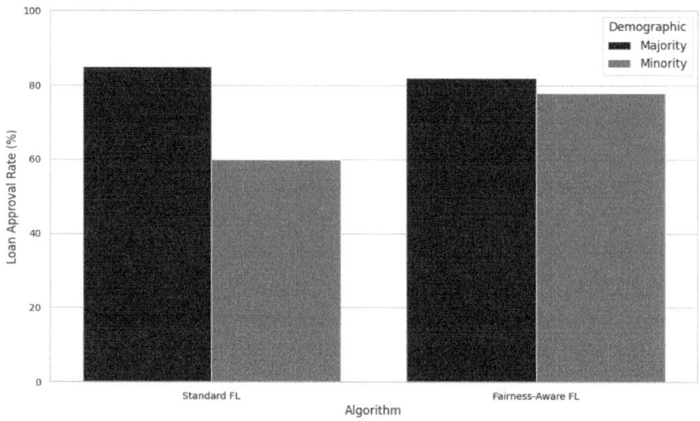

Figure 11: Impact of fairness-aware algorithms on loan approval rates.

To deal with this, fairness-conscious federated learning algorithms have to be developed. There is one field of study aimed at altering the aggregation process. As one of them, the central server can increase heaviness of updates by participants who represent underserved groups so their information can be used in the final model with a larger share. The other strategy is to establish fairness constraints as part of local training goals. Not only would each participant be asked to train an accurate model, but also to meet some measure of fairness (i.e., demographic parity or equal opportunity) on a variety of sensitive attributes, such as race, gender, or location. This is a daunting yet important frontier. As FL gains traction, establishing the technical infrastructure to demonstrate that the resulting models are not only correct but also fair will be the primary challenge to gain the confidence of the public and pass regulatory inspection scrutiny [16].

5. The Case of Transformative Use in Finance

The resulting combination of progressive federated algorithms, strong security technology, and the business case of cooperation is setting the stage for a new wave of financial applications. Federated learning is not just a theoretical model, but a practical framework that can address some of the most acute and the most timeless issues in the sector. The potential of FL to unlock the transformative potential of the entire value chain, including risks management and compliance alongside investment strategies and customer service, lies by providing institutions with the ability to harness collective intelligence, while maintaining the highest data privacy standards. Here, we examine a range of high-impact applications of federated learning that will soon prove to be an invaluable instrument, leading to innovation and establishing a more secure, efficient, and fair financial ecosystem [17].

5.1 Next-Generation Fraud and Anti-Money Laundering (AML) Detection

Financial crime is becoming an ever-growing arms race. Money launderers and fraudsters work in elaborate, international networks and continuously adapt to new methods of abusing vulnerabilities in the financial system. On a case-by-case basis, these threats are difficult to fight. Bank fraud detectors trained on just the bank transaction information are necessarily limited. It is only able to look at one side of a far bigger puzzle. It can learn to detect familiar patterns of fraud but will be susceptible to new vectors of attack that are yet to manifest themselves among its clients. A typical money laundering scheme such as this one tends to consist of a web of transactions across a variety of financial institutions, with each particular transaction per se seeming innocuous.

Federated learning is a radically new solution to the issue. Federated AML fintechs may be trained with a much broader and richer dataset than any individual institution might ever have access to by building a consortium of banks, payment processors, and fintechs [24]. This common model can be trained to recognize the obscure, cross-institutional successes that are the marks of advanced financial crime. As an example, it may be able to identify a set of small, organized deposits in five different banks that, when grouped with each other, explicitly point to an effort to avoid reporting limits. These systemic patterns are learned by the global model through the aggregate, anonymized updates of all system players. As each new transaction is made at any member institution, this globally trained model would be able to evaluate its risk with much more situational sensitivity. This results in a radical enhancement of detection fidelity, substantially decreasing false-positive rates which plague conventional systems, while substantially increasing the likelihood of deterring the emergence of new and elaborate fraudulent activities. Most importantly, all this is done without a single bank of the financial system having to share their confidential customer transaction information with their competitors, thereby maintaining confidentiality and competitive independence [18].

Figure 12 illustrates that federated learning is effective in enhancing fraud and AML detection by learning institutional cross-institutional patterns. The international model embraces various transactional habits without exiting crude information. This cooperative intelligence goes a long way to boost financial prevention of crimes.

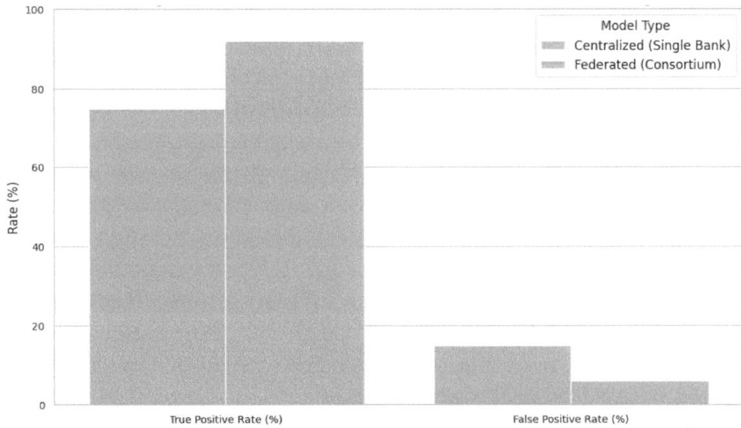

Figure 12: Enhanced fraud detection with federated learning.

5.2 Improving Credit Risk Modelling

The basis of a healthy lending market is accurate credit risk assessment. Conventional credit rating systems are based on past credit data that is collected by credit agencies and the personal relationship of the applicant with the lender. This approach is likely to be incomplete, and in practice, also to strengthen existing prejudices. It frequently has difficulty in determining those who have thin credit files (young people, new immigrants, any person on the margins of the cash economy), and excludes them financially. Also, a model that is trained with data provided by one lender just represents the risk profile of that lender's portfolio and may not scale up to wider economic changes.

With federated learning, more complex, more precise, and more fair credit risk models can be made. A federated consortium may include traditional banks and the alternative lenders (i.e., fintech micro-lenders) and even the telecommunication or utility companies. Both participants have valuable and unique data that offers a new dimension to the financial stability and creditworthiness of an individual. A telecom firm has information about payment patterns, and a micro-lender could possess information about the creditworthiness of the self-employed. This allows the consortium to create a deep profile of credit risk that is much more accurate and predictive than any single source of data would ever tell with training a federated model [14]. To take one example, for even a person with no previous credit card history, the model might come to learn that on-time utility payments are a powerful predictor of mortgage repayment. This enables the lenders to make better choices and offer credit to the deserving and previously ignored groups of the population. By applying advanced algorithms, including the personalized and fairness-aware algorithms mentioned in the earlier text, the resulting model is not only more accurate to the lender, but also more just to the borrower, avoiding the threat of discriminatory results [19].

5.3 Asset Management and High-Frequency Trading

Informational advantage is what drives the world of algorithmic trading and asset management. Companies invest enormous amounts of money acquiring exclusive datasets and creating proprietary models, which can react to market movements a few seconds quicker than their rivals do. Even though this has inspired innovation, it also has a very competitive, zero-sum environment. Federated learning presents the opportunity of a new cooperative approach to alpha generation.

Consider the case of a collection of hedge funds or asset management firms each holding their own proprietary data and signals to trade. They would never give up this fundamental intellectual property, but they may contribute to a federated learning net to learn a common market prediction model. The global model could be used by each firm as a starting point and, using its local data, it would specialize the model and generate a personalized model through PFL methods. The global model would incorporate the different views of all players. One firm may be experts at analyzing satellite shots of oil tankers, the other at processing social media sentiment, and the third at macroeconomic evidence. The federation model learns to combine all these types of signals without any single firm being exposed to its proprietary secret sauce. This can lead to more stable and robust trading strategies that are not at risk of being overfitted to one data source. Similarly, companies might jointly develop risk management models, where a federated model is trained to detect systemic market risk or liquidity crisis by learning the aggregate, anonymized portfolio positions of the entire consortium, and serve as an early warning system on the common good.

5.4 Future of Decentralized Lending/Insurance

Decentralization as a value embodied in federated learning closely aligns with the newly emerging industries of decentralized finance (DeFi) and future insurance. Within DeFi, there is a challenge of determining the creditworthiness of pseudo-anonymous borrowers through peer-to-peer lending without a central intermediary. Federated learning may enable a group of DeFi protocols to work together to create a reputation or credit-scoring model. The transaction history on one system could be contributed (in a privacy-conscious way) by users to a global model that could in turn be utilized by other systems to provide them with improved lending conditions, without the need to store this history as a centralized database of user behavior.

FL also presents the insurance industry with an avenue to more precise and personalized underwriting. Insurance companies, car manufacturers, and even healthcare providers could form a consortium to train federated models that would perform risk assessment better. Considering the above as an example, telematics devices anonymously monitor the driving behavior of millions of cars and would therefore create a highly accurate model of accident risk, enabling the insurers to offer more accurate and precise usage-based insurance policies. Federated models using anonymized data collected through wearable health devices and hospital records could also transform the process of health and life insurance underwriting, where a limited number of broad demographic categories are replaced by risk analysis on an extremely personalized level [9]. The collective solution enables the industry to develop models with unprecedented precision while addressing the high privacy sensibilities of individual health and behavioral information [20].

6. To Tread the Ethical, Regulatory, and Governance Labyrinth

A federated financial intelligence paradigm shift, as appealing as it would be from the technology's standpoint, is not a technological problem only. The key to its responsible and successful adoption lies in finding the way through a convoluted maze of ethical concerns, shifting regulatory conditions, and new forms of governance. The same qualities that are attractive in federated earning—decentralization, minimization of data, and cooperation between competitors—are also a source of new types of risk and unpredictability that has to be addressed. As financial institutions transition pilot projects to production infrastructures, they need to design not only the technical structures, but also the effective governance mechanisms essential to make these powerful structures transparent, fair, safe, and accountable. This part of the paper analyzes the key nontechnical aspects that will ultimately shape long-term sustainability and social functionality of federated learning in finance.

6.1 Admonition of Model Explicability and Auditability

Regulators in the financial industry are already facing a large-scale issue with the black-box problem of complex AI models making decisions without giving any apparent, human-understandable explanation. Regulators can request the data and the model reasoning that went into a decision when a centralized institution refuses a customer a loan. Federated learning makes this picture much more complicated. What does an institution say about a decision that has been benchmarked against a global model that was trained on data that it never saw or can look at? Who is the responsible party when a decision turns out to be an emergent property of the whole federated network?

The issue puts an increased premium on the discipline of explainable AI (XAI). More classical XAI methods such as LIME (local interpretable model-agnostic explanations) or SHAP (SHapley Additive explanations), which explore the behavior of a model through probing, need to be customized to the federated setting. It is also an ongoing field of study, and some new concepts, such as "federated XAI" [21], are already appearing. One of these can be to ask every participant to generate localized explanations of the predictions made by the global model on its own data. These local descriptions can be added up (in a privacy-sensitive manner) to construct a larger world view of the logic of the model. The other approach involves making federated models more interpretable by design, even at the cost of a small predictive accuracy loss. To be auditable, blockchain integration, as was said in the earlier text, becomes essential. A ledger powered by blockchain can offer the irrevocable history of the training process—of who contributed, what aggregation technique was employed, and the change history of the global model. This is not a description of the internal logic of the model, but it does give a verifiable and clear chain of custody with respect to the development of the model, which is an essential initial step to any regulatory audit. In the absence of obvious solutions to explainability and auditability, federated models may just be pushed into low-stakes applications, in which they cannot achieve the regulatory acceptance necessary to support high-stakes tasks such as credit scoring or lending underwriting [21].

6.2 The Swamp of Data Governance across Borders

Federated learning is commonly described as a remedy to the problem of international data transfer regulation policies such as GDPR, where the movement of personal data beyond a specific jurisdiction is limited. FL seems to gracefully avoid these limitations by storing raw data locally, and only sending abstract model updates. But the legal fact is much more complex and, in most jurisdictions, is unclear. Regulators are also asking questions about whether model parameters may be personal data in some circumstances, in particular when they may be used to draw inferences about the data individuals they represent [7].

This puts any financial consortium across multiple countries in a complex compliance quagmire. Are the model updates that are sent by a bank in Europe to a central server in the United States subject to the data transfer provisions of GDPR? What are the interactions between the regulations in one country (e.g., the ones that mandate data localization) with the regulations in another country? Legal and compliance costs to responding to these questions related to a multi-jurisdictional FL network can be high. It takes a sound legal structure to be adopted by all involved parties to forge such a network, and this would have to be negotiated through a maze of national legislation. This framework must specify clearly how model changes are defined as lawful or illegal, define clearly the roles and responsibilities of each participant as data controller or processor, and establish clear procedures to respond to data subject access request or national regulator orders. The jurisdictional tension can reduce international FL activity until the jurisdictional questions become more clearly institutionalized in statute and regulation—by the creation of international standards or by conciliating safe harbor agreements regarding federated learning.

6.3 Novel Security Vulnerability Threats and Adversarial Threats

The distributed nature of federated learning provides a new and different attack surface while resolving the problem of centralized data risk. Security in a centralized system is centered at hardening the edge of the data center. With a federated system, each individual participant becomes a possible target for an attacker and a possible danger to the integrity of the global model. This leads to the development of a series of adversarial attacks that are specifically crafted to attack the FL process [2].

The most well-known threat is data poisoning. There is a possibility of a malicious member of the consortium adding a deliberately corrupted or mislabelled data to its local training set. These "poisoned" learnings are incorporated into the global model when it is submitting its model update, and they slightly diminish its overall performance or, more perniciously, perpetrate a deliberate backdoor. To demonstrate this point, a malicious actor might threaten to poison an AML model in such a way that transactions with a certain signature will always be treated as nonfraudulent. One related threat is model poisoning, in which the malicious participant directly modulates the outgoing model update itself toward a similar end. These attacks are difficult to defend against since the main server cannot monitor the information of the participants. This may be addressed by designing high-effort anomaly detectors on the server that reject model updates that appear suspicious, encouraging reputation systems where a person can be graded based on the quality of their contributions over time, and use powerful statistics algorithms to design aggregation processes that are not as often affected by outlier updates [17]. Such defenses play a key role in instilling trust in the federated ecosystem because the final model can only be as secure as the weakest component. Figure 13 shows how model performance is adversely affected by attacks of adversarial poisoning. It identifies the flaws of decentralized training systems. The figure highlights why federated systems need powerful strategies of aggregation and anomaly detection [22].

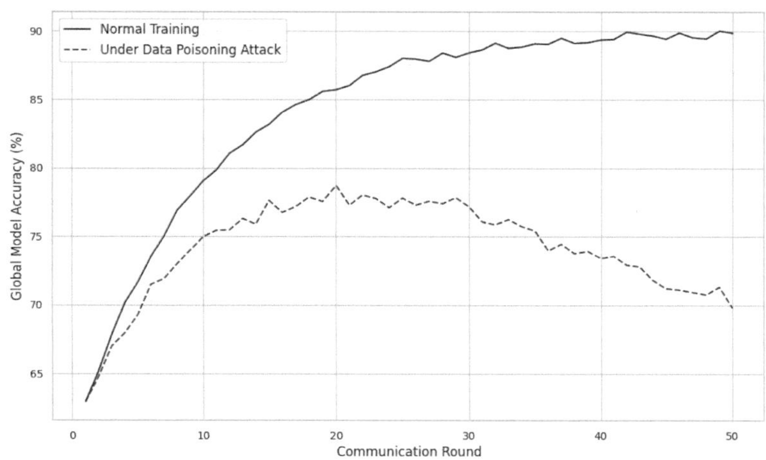

Figure 13: Effect of an adversarial poisoning attack on model accuracy.

6.4 Defining Governance Models toward Federated Consortia

The ultimate organizational issue underlying the technical and legal problems is the problem of governance. What would a collection of rival institutions do with a common, useful object, such as a federated model? This involves answering some hard questions. Who is the owner of the original IP of the model at the end of the world? Is it owned all together among the participants or by some different legal entity created by the consortium? When the model results in a measurable business gain, what is the sharing of the gains? Is a larger portion of the benefits due to those who provide more quality data to the participants?

Moreover, what is the liability? Who is into the fray? If it is discovered that the federated credit scoring model is discriminatory and results in regulatory fines? Is it the institution that engaged the model to make a decision or is it a collective responsibility of the whole consortium? All the questions require an elaborative governance framework to be established prior to any training. This paradigm, potentially encoded in the terms of a legal agreement or even a smart contract based on a blockchain, has to be clearly defined regarding the guidelines of IP ownership, data quality, incentives to contribution (e.g., via micropayment or revenue sharing), and the allocation of liability [18]. It must also set out a well-defined decision-making mechanism in the consortium, how new members are accepted, how the model architecture is revised, and how conflicts are resolved. These socio-economic governance structures will contribute as much to the success of financial FL as the complexity of the underlying algorithms [23], [24].

7. Conclusion

Looking at the future, we can say that within the next 10 years, federated learning will not be a fad but one of the cornerstones of the next generation of financial system. Decentralized, collaborative intelligence ecosystems of tomorrow are not that far off in the future, with the irresistible power of regulatory pressure, security demands, and the undying drive to develop competitive advantage through AI pushing the current centralized, siloed data models to their limits. The above-mentioned sections have described the radical shift FL facilitates, the technologies that can enhance its effect, the algorithmic innovation(s) that the success of this massive change demands, the radical uses of FL, and the governance issues that this drastic shift raises. This final section is a synthesis of these threads in an attempt to project a vision of the 10-year horizon and how federated financial intelligence might evolve within it and provides strategic advice to the stakeholders who will determine its future.

7.1 Maturing the Federated Ecosystem

In the coming 10 years, federated learning will be a mainstream, enterprise-grade system built on roots as a niche, specialist technology. The ad-hoc, experimental consortia of today will become institutionalized, industry-wide utilities, especially in pre-competitive areas such as fighting financial crime. We will see the introduction of so-called federated learning as a service (FLaaS), provided by large cloud vendors and dedicated fintechs, which will layer away a lot of complexity. These will offer standard legal agreements, turnkey governance frameworks, and a comprehensive library of privacy-enhancing technologies that have been built, which reduce the entry threshold to smaller institutions by an order of magnitude. It will be a way to democratize access to the state-of-the-art AI, so that community banks and credit unions can enjoy the scale of collective data of the larger banks without sacrificing their autonomy. Integration of FL and synergistic technologies will become smooth technologically. TEEs will become a standard practice with high-stakes applications, offering not only hardware-level assurances of process integrity, but also model confidentiality. In the future, even further cryptographic approaches such as SMPC will probably be powerful enough to be alternative to the trusted aggregator model in most cases, resulting in actually decentralized training protocols. The algorithmic frontiers will also keep on going further. Federated learning will be personalized by default, systems will automatically form clusters of participants and provide models that are highly adapted to their local data distributions, overcoming the non-IID challenge. We will also witness the emergence of so-called federated reinforcement learning, where several companies jointly train more complex trading or risk management agents that acquire the best strategies via interaction with a common (simulated) market environment [13]. Figure 14 shows a future projection of the spread of federated learning in the financial services in the decade. The trend indicates an increasing degree of regulatory pressure, maturity in technology, and need of privacy-preserving AI. It is projected that federated learning will be a central financial infrastructure.

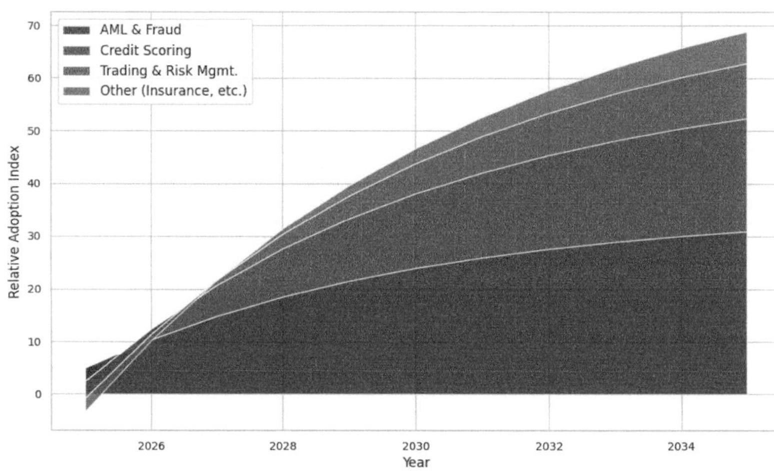

Figure 14: Projected adoption of FL in financial services (next 10 years).

7.2 Strong Interaction with Web3 and the Data Economy

Far beyond that, the concepts of federated learning will be entwined with the development of Web3 and the data economy as a whole. The philosophy of ownership of data as pertaining to the user, which is the foundation of the Web3 vision, is fully consistent with the FL paradigm. One way to imagine the future is that people, as well as institutions, can actively participate in federated networks. Customers may decide to release their personal financial information that they keep safely in a personal data vault or in a self-sovereign identity wallet to be used in the training of federated models in return for direct compensation or opportunities to highly-personalized, niche-level financial services. This might open up data dividend markets, where people receive compensation due to the intelligence performance their data adds to a federated model, without ever needing to give up the data itself. With FL and the combination of blockchain-powered micropayment systems and smart contracts, this procedure can be automated and lead to a more fair and transparent data economy. The smart car of an individual could be feeding some driving data to an insurance model, their smart meter could be feeding some energy-trading model, and their own spending history could be feeding a retail analytics model, with value flowing back to the individual in a safe and automated manner. In this vision, FL is the technology that will enable people to extract the monetary value out of the latent intelligence within their data without losing their privacy, essentially rebalancing power between consumers and corporations. Figure 15 shows the growing ecosystem of federated learning participants, such as institutions, individuals, and decentralized platforms. The model indicates the intersection between federated learning and Web3 and data ownership paradigms. The development is toward a more decentralized data economy which is more inclusive.

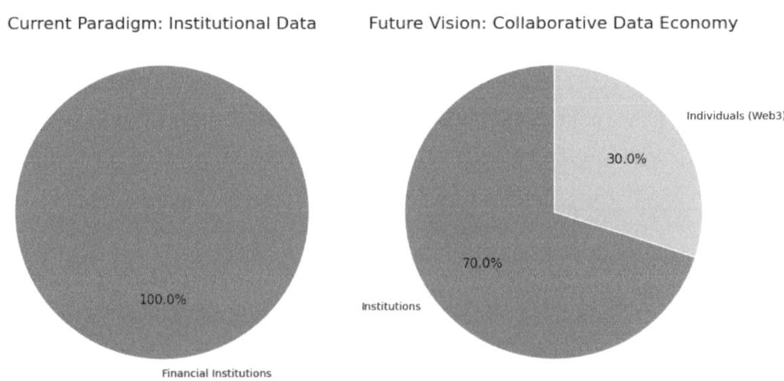

Figure 15: Evolution of participants in federated networks.

7.3 Strategic Recommendation Ideas of a Federated Future

The accomplishment of this ambitious vision would only be possible through a concerted and aggressive action of all stakeholders. The way forward is a process of co-evolution, in which technology, policy, and business strategy should progress together. With that in mind, we provide the following strategic recommendations:

To Researchers and Technologists: It needs to be based on solving the underlying practical problems. This involves designing more communication-efficient FL algorithms to decrease network overhead, devising stronger countermeasures to sophisticated adversarial attacks such as model poisoning, and inventing new federated XAI algorithms that offer useful and understandable by regulators explanations of how the model works. Moreover, there are economic and game-theoretic works on FL relevant to determine stable and fair incentive plans in consortia.

To Financial Industry Leaders: Time to do it. Leaders need to transition beyond a wait-and-see strategy and start spending money on pilot projects to develop internal experience and learn about the practical challenges of FL implementation. This means focusing on high-impact/low-risk, first use cases, for example, improving internal fraud detection models by federating learning across business units within a single organization. Most importantly, the leaders in the industry should also be the promoters of shared governance standards. They can anticipate the legal and operational frameworks under which future federated consortia will operate, and, by coordinating their actions through industry associations and standards bodies, can make them practical, equitable, and supportive of innovation.

To Policymakers and Regulators: A reactionary regulatory position will suppress innovation. Associations should look to involve technologists and industry leaders in proactive discussion of the federated learning concepts. This involves the creation of effective guideline on the legal status of model updates that are available under the prevailing data protection laws and the consideration of establishing regulatory sandboxes. Such sandboxes would enable financial institutions to test cross-border federated systems within a controlled environment, so regulators can have the empirical data they need to develop informed, innovation-friendly policies. International collaboration in developing similar standards of federated data ownership will be a necessary step toward realizing the full potential of the technology on a global scale.

Overall, federated learning is not a normal technological invention, but a corporate requirement. It represents a practical, exciting way out of the data quagmire that now puts pressure on financial sector. It provides a means of allowing further development of potent AI and at the same time accommodating the mandatory worldwide data privacy and protection requirement. The path forward is complicated and involves solving algorithmic, cryptographic, legal, and organizational problems simultaneously. But it is a worthwhile end, the more intelligent, more resilient, more transparent, and more equitable global financial ecosystem we are just starting to work on. The seeds of this future are being planted today, and those institutions that embrace the challenge of constructing this new paradigm not only will have gained competitive advantage, but will also be shaping the very fabric of the 21st-century finance.

References

[1] Ali, A., Almaiah, M. A., Hajjej, F., Pasha, M. F. and Almomani, O. (2022). A sustainable blockchain framework for the halal food supply chain: A case study of the OIC countries. *Sustainability*, 14(18): 11627. https://doi.org/10.3390/su141811627.

[2] Bagdasaryan, E., Veit, A., Hua, Y., Estrin, D. and Shmatikov, V. (2020). How to backdoor federated learning. In *Proceedings of the 23rd International Conference on Artificial Intelligence and Statistics* (pp. 2938–2948). PMLR.

[3] Bonawitz, K., Ivanov, V., Kreuter, B., Marcedone, A., McMahan, H. B., Patel, S. et al. (2020). Practical secure aggregation for privacy-preserving machine learning. In *Proceedings of the 2019 ACM SIGSAC Conference on Computer and Communications Security* (pp. 1175–1191). ACM. [https://doi.org/10.1145/3133956.3133982].

[4] Cui, Z., Zhang, S., Wu, Z. and Chen, Z. (2021). FedCredit: A secure and verifiable federated learning framework for credit scoring. *IEEE Transactions on Dependable and Secure Computing*, 19(5): 3241–3254. https://www.google.com/search?q=https://doi.org/10.1109/TDSC.2021.3090623.

[5] Du, L., Cui, P. and Wang, X. (2021). Fairness in federated learning: A survey. *ACM Computing Surveys*, 54(9): 1–36. https://www.google.com/search?q=https://doi.org/10.1145/3472322.

[6] Fallah, A., Mokhtari, A. and Ozdaglar, A. (2020). Personalized federated learning with theoretical guarantees: A model-agnostic meta-learning approach. In *Advances in Neural Information Processing Systems*, 33: 3557–3568. Curran Associates, Inc.

[7] Hardjono, T. and Lipton, A. (2020). *Federated Learning and Privacy*. MIT Press.

[8] Kairouz, P. and McMahan, H. B. (2021). Advances and open problems in federated learning. *Foundations and Trends in Machine Learning*, 14(1-2): 1–210.

[9] Khan, L. U., Saad, W., Han, Z., Hossain, E. and Hong, C. S. (2021). Federated learning for internet of things: A comprehensive survey. *IEEE Communications Surveys & Tutorials*, 23(3): 1835–1877. https://www.google.com/search?q=https://doi.org/10.1109/COMST.2021.3075439.

[10] Lao, H., Cheng, Q. and Shao, Z. (2022). A survey on federated learning in the finance industry. *Journal of Financial Data Science*, 4(2): 108–124. https://www.google.com/search?q=https://doi.org/10.3905/jfds.2022.1.066.

[11] Li, T., Sahu, A. K., Talwalkar, A. and Smith, V. (2020). Federated learning: Challenges, methods, and future directions. *IEEE Signal Processing Magazine*, 37(3): 50–60. https://doi.org/10.1109/MSP.2020.2975749.

[12] Li, T., Sahu, A. K., Zaheer, M., Sanjabi, M., Talwalkar, A. and Smith, V. (2020b). Federated optimization in heterogeneous networks. In *Proceedings of Machine Learning and Systems*, 2: 429–450.

[13] Lim, W. Y. B., Luong, N. C., Hoang, D. T., Jiao, Y., Liang, Y. C., Yang, Q. et al. (2020). Federated learning in mobile edge networks: A comprehensive survey. *IEEE Communications Surveys & Tutorials*, 22(3): 2031–2063. https://doi.org/10.1109/COMST.2020.2986024.

[14] Long, G., Tan, Y., Jiang, J. and Zhang, C. (2020). Federated learning for privacy-preserving credit scoring. In *2020 IEEE International Conference on Big Data (Big Data)* (pp. 2577–2586). IEEE. https://doi.org/10.1109/BigData50022.2020.9378038.

[15] McMahan, H. B., Moore, E., Ramage, D. and y Arcas, B. A. (2021). Federated learning of deep networks using model averaging. *Journal of Machine Learning Research*, 22(196): 1–27.

[16] Mo, F., Li, Y., Liang, X. and Liu, J. (2021). PPFL: Privacy-preserving federated learning with trusted execution environments. *IEEE Transactions on Information Forensics and Security*, 16: 4022–4035. https://www.google.com/search?q=https://doi.org/10.1109/TIFS.2021.3090635.

[17] Pillutla, K., Kakade, S. M. and Harchaoui, Z. (2022). Robust aggregation for federated learning. *IEEE Transactions on Signal Processing*, 70: 1142–1154. https://www.google.com/search?q=https://doi.org/10.1109/TSP.2022.3153136.

[18] Rieke, N., Hancox, J. and Li, W. (2020). The future of digital health with federated learning. *NPJ Digital Medicine*, 3(1): 119. https://doi.org/10.1038/s41746-020-00323-1.

[19] Sattler, F., Müller, K. R. and Samek, W. (2020). Clustered federated learning: Model-agnostic distributed multi-task learning under data heterogeneity. *IEEE Transactions on Neural Networks and Learning Systems*, 32(11): 4976–4987. https://www.google.com/search?q=https://doi.org/10.1109/TNNLS.2020.3032559.

[20] Shastri, S. and Choubey, A. (2024). A study of data protection and privacy laws: The GDPR and DPDP Act, 2023. *Journal of Legal Studies and Research*, 10(1): 1–15.

[21] Truex, S., Liu, L., Gursoy, M. E. and Yu, L. (2020). A survey on federated learning and explainable AI. In *Proceedings of the 1st ACM Workshop on Explainable AI for the Web* (pp. 1–7). ACM. https://www.google.com/search?q=https://doi.org/10.1145/3375899.3375900.

[22] Voigt, P. and Von dem Bussche, A. (2021). *The EU General Data Protection Regulation (GDPR): A Practical Guide*. Springer.

[23] Wei, K., Li, J., Ding, M., Ma, C., Yang, H. H., Farokhi, F. et al. (2020). Federated learning with differential privacy: Algorithms and performance analysis. *IEEE Transactions on Information Forensics and Security*, 15: 454–3469. https://doi.org/10.1109/TIFS.2020.2988575.

[24] Yang, S., Zhang, J. and Wang, L. (2022). Federated learning for financial fraud detection: A survey. *Journal of Network and Computer Applications*, 201: 103348. https://www.google.com/search?q=https://doi.org/10.1016/j.jnca.2022.103348.

15 | Evaluation of Logistic Regression and Decision Tree Classifiers to Detect Smurf Attacks on a Network Interface

Aisha Aneesa Abubakar,[1] Amit Mishra[2,*] and Usman Bello Abubakar[1]

Reliable cyber-attack detection is important to safeguard systems and networks. A Smurf attack is a resource consumption attack using Internet Control Message Protocol (ICMP) to overwhelm a network with ping traffic which consumes available bandwidth. The research provides a solution using machine learning classifiers (logistic regression and decision tree) to classify malicious packets from a generated dataset. The researchers used the dataset KDD99 Cup, which is a rich pcap (packet capture) dataset that contains malicious Smurf packets. The experiment was carried out using python programming language and results show that logistic regression outperformed the decision tree with accuracy of 92% in classification, with the decision tree having 86%. The results archived using the classifiers show the need for more cyber security firms to adopt the implementation of ML algorithms for better detection rates.

1. Introduction

A Smurf attack is a resource consumption attack using Internet Control Message Protocol (ICMP) to overwhelm a network with ping traffic which consumes available bandwidth. As a result, there is no available bandwidth for consumers. An ICMP echo attack is just one example. Smurf uses ICMP to send a fraudulent ping packet to the network broadcast address, identifying the victim as the source address. Many systems may respond over a multi-access network. The victim is bombarded with ping answers as a result of the assault.

A Smurf attack is based on improperly configured network gear that allows packets are routed to all computer hosts on a specific network through the network's transmission address rather than just one device.

[1] Baze University, Abuja, Nigeria.
[2] Dr. Vishwanath Karad MIT World Peace University, Pune, India.
Emails: anisaabubarkar@gmail,com; usman.abu@bazeuniversity.edu.ng
* Corresponding author: i.amitmishra@gmail.com

DOI: 10.1201/9781003710059-15

The perpetrator will send out a sizable number of Internet Protocol (IP) packets with a faked source address that impersonates the victim's address. Legitimate packets are unable to reach their destinations because the network's bandwidth rapidly runs out.

Ping flooding involves delivering an excessive volume of ping packets to the victim. Ping of death is based on sending the victim a malformed ping packet, which will lead to a system crash on a vulnerable system [1]. Smurf attacks have been used by malicious actors for distributed denial of service attacks (DDOS), and they have caused a lot of problems for network administrators to deal with, as traditional firewall systems have been ineffective to stop these attacks.

Smurf attacks have been very problematic for network administrators [1], and have led to a lot of system crashes. Many network intrusion detection systems are not able to detect these attacks [2]. In order to classify malevolent packets in a network, this study aims to assess two machine learning (ML) algorithms: logistic regression and decision tree classifiers.

The study's value lies in its evaluation of two machine learning algorithms—logistic regression and decision trees—to see how well they categorize Smurf attacks.

2. Literature Review

Protection against cyber-attacks is challenging. This is due to anti-detection techniques used by malware authors such as obfuscation. Unfortunately, existing solutions, such as data encryption methods, hardware and software firewalls, and user authentication, are inadequate to protect the computer network and meet the challenge of incoming demand.

Due to the faster, more severe evolution of intrusion systems, these traditional security structures are insufficient to protect the network.

2.1 Detection of Network Intrusions

Software program that watches a single computer system or a network of computers for malevolent activity is known as a detection of network intrusions (NID) system, including denial-of-service and cross-site scripting assaults that aim to steal or censor data or alter network protocols. The bulk of NID methods in use today are unable to handle how dynamic and intricate computer network cyberattacks are. Effective adaptive methods can therefore lead to reduced instances of false alarms, higher detection rates, and realistic computing with transmission price. Examples include machine learning techniques. In reference [3], the authors investigated and compared the performance of several intrusion detection techniques. They classified the approaches as either classical artificial intelligence (AI) or computational intelligence (CI). They also demonstrated how various properties of CI approaches can be used to construct effective Intrusion Detection System (IDS).

2.2 Related Works

In reference [4], the authors used a combination of two ML algorithms to classify any anomalous behavior in network traffic. The complete effectiveness of the suggested procedure was evaluated by calculating the exposure accuracy, false-positive (FP) rate, false-negative (FN) rate, and detection duration.

Compared to the traditional Support Vector Machine (SVM) based structure, which obtained a detection correctness of 88.03% and FP rates of 4.2% and 7.77%, respectively, the proposed methodology demonstrates the algorithm's efficacy in sensing the intrusion with a higher finding precision of 98.76% and a lower FP rate of 0.09% and a FN rate of 1.15%.

In reference [5], the authors present an intrusion detection model based on genetic algorithms and neural networks. The fundamental idea behind intrusion detection systems is to harness the categorization abilities of neural networks and evolutionary algorithms. The model is able to classify attacks into several categories, identify assaults, and—most importantly—sense new assaults by a high recognition proportion and a small incorrect negative rate. This method uses information progress and evolutionary theory to strain flow of data and decrease complication. To put this system in place and track its performance, they employed the KDD99 benchmark dataset and got a good detection rate.

The authors in reference [6] proposed a new strategy for unsupervised feature learning based on nonsymmetric deep auto encoder (NDAE). Furthermore, they proposed a novel deep learning classifier based with stacked autoencoders. The author's proposed classifier was run on Graphics Processing Unit (GPU) and evaluated using the KDD, Goblet 99, and NSL-KDD datasets. The result was assessed using network intrusion discovery investigation datasets, specifically the KDD99 Cup and NSL-KDD records.

In reference [7], several experiments had been performed and evaluated to assess various machine learning classifiers based on the KDD intrusion dataset. It was successful in calculating numerous performance measures to assess the chosen categorization. The emphasis remained on false-negative and false-positive routine measures to improve the intrusion recognition system's detection rate. The trials showed that the result slab classifier produced the fewest FN, while the random forest (RF) classifier had the maximum average precision rate.

In reference [8], the KDD99 Cup test sets of data were analyzed using certain machine learning algorithms: Bayes net, J48, random forest, and random tree. By categorizing these attacks into their different types, the accuracy of these algorithms was ascertained.

The trial findings showed that the algorithms such as random tree and random forest achieved the classification approach on the test dataset the most efficiently. WEKA is the experimental tool employed, and it performed an association-grounded feature categorization on the dataset using a best-first hunt approach, with the constraints precision, recall, and F-measure. The study reported in reference [8] demonstrates that soft computing techniques are receiving a lot of attention, since many people have used them there. Furthermore, several academics are concentrating on IDS classification, which is useful in determining known intrusion threats. It may, however, cause difficulties in identifying abnormal intrusions, and it may embrace innovative or improved intrusion occurrences.

Outliers are used in an extensive diversity of tenders such as soldierly observation for adversary actions, invasion uncovering in cyber security, deception discovery in credit cards, health insurance or personal care, and error finding in safety-critical structures. Their reputation in data is because they can interpret into wrong evidence in an eclectic variation of submissions. An anomalous traffic pattern in a computer network could mean that a hacked computer is sending out sensitive data to an unauthorized destination [9]. Outlier finding is an information investigation technique that has been applied to discover and delete aberrant data findings. With the awareness that deviation can be the crucial finding to be completed from huge databases, the discovery of outliers has attracted substantial curiosity in data mining. Machine-driven defects, variations in system performance, deceitful activity, humanoid mistake, and apparatus error are all causes of outliers. As a result, for many applications, discovering outliers yields more intriguing and relevant findings than discovering inliers. Outlier detection can result in the classification of system mistakes, allowing superintendents to take precautionary measures earlier than they intensify. Outliers are data patterns that do not fit a predefined definition of standard actions. Figure 1 demonstrates outliers in a modest two-dimensional dataset.

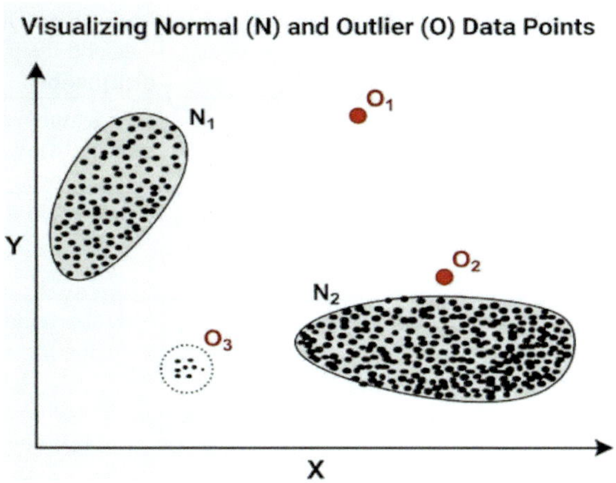

Figure 1: A simple example of outliers in a two-dimensional dataset.

The research in reference [10] offers a new graph-based descriptor for billing-related anomalies in cellular mobile networks. To detect invoicing abnormalities in Global System for Mobile (GSM) networks, it employs a graph-based algorithm. The approach employs graph-based descriptors, wherein the graph's bumps stand in for clients and its boundaries for communication events. In order to train the RF classifier, a supervised classification algorithm, to identify anomalous data, this paper described the procedure used to produce numerous graphs in each apex zone of a predefined size. It also presents the features that are extracted from the neighborhood graphs as shown in Figure 2 for different neighborhood sizes [10].

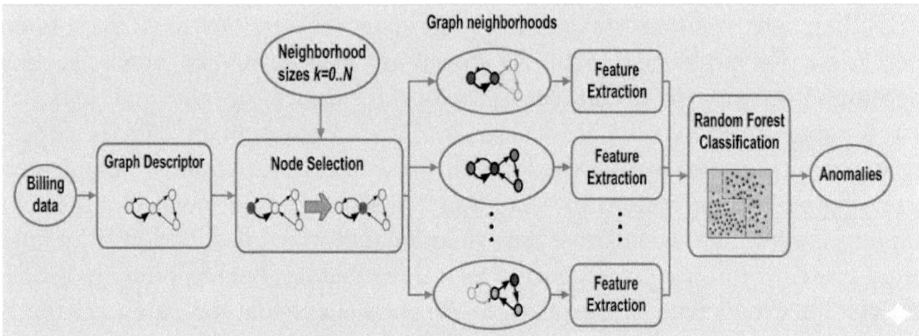

Figure 2: Graph-based descriptor.

Table 1: Anomaly detection rules.

Feature	*Description*	*Definition Range*	*Anomaly Detection*
Volume	Number of boundaries	$K \geq 1$	To find irregularities associated with a huge, abnormally large network
Edge Entropy	The randomness of the masses	$K \geq 1$	Variations in the amount of data and their underlying distribution
Graph Entropy	Graph organizational appearances	$K \geq 1$	This feature records how malware starts a conversation
Edge Weight Ratio	The ratio of the sum of the weight of outward to inward edges	$K \geq 0$	Check spam SMSs on edge
Average Outward/ Inward Edge Weight	The average weights of the outward/inward edges	$K \geq 0$	Neighborhoods that include participating servers

Table 1 details the specific graph-based features used for anomaly detection. It describes how structural graph properties are mathematically defined and what specific security threats they are designed to detect. The approach proposed by reference [11] originates from a perspective that appears to be nonparametric, despite the fact that the authors validate their findings using the Gaussian. It is an online technique stating that it will function without knowledge of the signal beforehand [11]. The problem is modeled so that the suggested method conserves system resources by only distributing data when a critical event arises in a medical wireless sensor network made up of sensors attached to various places of a patient's body to take physiological readings. By avoiding a covariance-aware distance metric that requires matrix inversion, the proposed technique minimizes the overall computational burden. The sensors in this method forecast the following data point to be measured by the sensor using an exponentially weighted moving average [11]. The actual measured value is then contrasted with this projected value. The values of the error and the actual measurement are then used to calculate an enclosing ellipse. For routine measurements, the error should be fairly modest. The bare minimum number of sensors that must provide aberrant data before further processing can begin as determined in the work. This was done due to the correlation between physiological data and the expectation that the recognition system drive will only transmit an alarm when a factual change in the patient is monitored. An inconsistent measurement is eventually identified as ace, which takes a different pdf from the rest, using a kernel concentration estimator on the windowed chi-squared remoteness of the faults. This approach has the drawback of only picking up on the edges of change because it only detects anomalies when there is a large departure from the norm. For instance, if a patient is in major difficulties in a hospital, this anomaly detection system will only signal an anomaly when the patient's condition significantly improves or worsens. It will not return detection until that moment. This may not be ideal, especially if the patient needs to be attended to constantly while ill; in this situation, it may be highly beneficial to have the system highlight anomalies when the condition of the patient is uncomfortable till the condition improves. This would provide ongoing input to healthcare professionals caring for the patient. The system was tested using medical records for heart rate, pulse, and so on, and it performed quite well as reported by the authors [11].

The authors in reference [12] present an application of anomaly detection to sensors in an agricultural environment using discrete wavelet transforms (DWT) and self-organizing maps (SOM). Multiple parameters are monitored by the system's feelers at once, and these remain arranged into a State Space Path. A DWT is used to first partition the measured standards into aspect quantities and estimate quantities. The detail factors define more of the fundamental properties of the data distribution, whereas the approximate coefficients are utilized to evaluate the system. By monitoring the remoteness among any state vector and the captivating neuron vector, the SOM establishes a threshold and, as is common, indicates an anomaly if it is exceeded. Else, the dataset is accepted as normal. The simulation findings for up to 99% confidence intervals have been published by the authors, and they show much lower false alarm rates when compared to alternative techniques. Although the system is substantially less expensive to utilize after training, it is still quite computationally expensive. Due to the fact that the distance between two possibly high-dimensional vectors is taken into consideration, results are identical for a slighter difference in all the vector essentials between two observed state directions and a huge alteration in only a rare of these vectors' constituents. This is very deceptive since, depending on the threshold, an abnormality can be correctly identified or overlooked. The authors mention a local choice to get around this issue, but this is only carried out after an anomaly is reported. Also, it is not certain whether all the parameters being monitored are all correlated, as this is probably when this method is most useful [12].

3. Methodology

3.1 Data Collection

The dataset that was utilized for the purpose of this study was sourced from Kaggle.com. The name of the dataset used is the KDD99.

This dataset was used as the starting point of the Fifth International Conference on Knowledge Discovery and Data Mining. The dataset was created with the intention of developing a system disturbance detector and an analytical prototypical that can differentiate between invasions. A typical collection of data to be audited is contained in this dataset, which also comprises an extensive range of simulated invasions into a military network situation. The details of this dataset are provided in Figure 3.

Out[1]:

	duration	protocol_type	service	flag	src_bytes	dst_bytes	land	wrong_fragment	urgent	hot	...	dst_host_srv_count	dst_host_same_srv_rate
0	0	tcp	http	SF	181	5450	0	0	0	0	...	9	1.0
1	0	tcp	http	SF	239	486	0	0	0	0	...	19	1.0
2	0	tcp	http	SF	235	1337	0	0	0	0	...	29	1.0
3	0	tcp	http	SF	219	1337	0	0	0	0	...	39	1.0
4	0	tcp	http	SF	219	2032	0	0	0	0	...	49	1.0
...	...	...	...	...	...	...	...	...	...	...	...	...	...
494015	0	tcp	http	SF	310	1881	0	0	0	0	...	255	1.0
494016	0	tcp	http	SF	282	2286	0	0	0	0	...	255	1.0
494017	0	tcp	http	SF	203	1200	0	0	0	0	...	255	1.0
494018	0	tcp	http	SF	291	1200	0	0	0	0	...	255	1.0
494019	0	tcp	http	SF	219	1234	0	0	0	0	...	255	1.0

494020 rows × 42 columns

Figure 3: Shape of dataset.

3.2 Data Pre-Processing

We made sure to eradicate unrelated features from the dataset. The resolution of this is to ensure the ML models are learning from only relevant features, which, in turn, improves model performance. Figure 4 in the following text shows the respective instances for the normal and Smurf occurrences in the dataset. The dataset contains 97,222 occurrences of normal and 280,790 occurrences of Smurf, clearly indicating a significant class imbalance between the two categories.

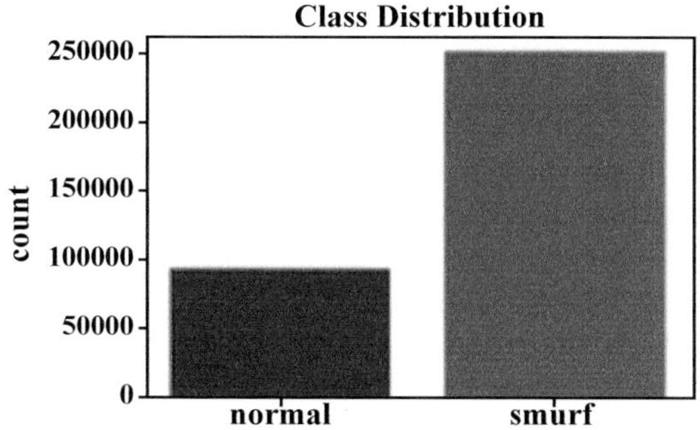

Figure 4: Dataset class distribution.

3.3 Data Distribution

Dataset was separated using 80% for training and 20% for testing.

3.4 Environmental Setup

Table 2 shows the hardware and software tools needed to apply the machine learning models.

Table 2: Development environment.

Hardware	*Details*
Computer operating system	Windows (Pavilion 15)
Memory (RAM)	12GB
Processor	Intel® Core i5, 1.60 GHz
Software	Jupyter Notebook
Python	Programming language software

3.5 Machine Learning Models

Decision Tree: The decision tree classifier is an administered machine learning algorithm that can be employed for use in deterioration as well as categorization problems. It is a classifier that is organized in a tree fashion in which the structures of the dataset given are represented by internal nodes in the decision tree. The branches of the decision tree are used to depict the decision rules, and lastly, the leaf represents the final result of the classifier. In every decision tree classifier, there exist two nodes: leaf node and decision node. A decision from the classifier is made based on the available decision nodes in the classifier and these decision nodes may have multiple branches. The leaf nodes do not have further branches from them, and as earlier stated, they are the final result or expected decision obtained from the decision tree classifier. The concept of the decision tree classifier is that it simply poses a question and based on the outcome of the question (example Yes or No), the algorithm further splits the tree into sub-trees.

The decision tree classifier has a topmost node which is referred to as the root node. Based on the root node, the decision tree learns to partition into sub-trees on the basis of the attribute value. This partitioning of the tree into sub-trees is done in a recursive way which is called recursive segmentation. This method in some cases is frequently referred to as "divide 'n' conquer" because it ruptures the data into subgroups, which are then split continually into even condensed subsets, and so on. The recursive subgrouping stops when the algorithm elects the data inside the subdivisions that are satisfactorily homogenous.

Logistic Regression: This is a predictive analysis to be used when the dependent variable of a given dataset is binary, although it can be appropriately used when the dependent variable is more than just two. It can be used to make data descriptive, and to simplify the understanding of the connection between one dependent binary inconstant and one or additional sovereign variable quantity, which are minimal, ordinal, intermittent, or ratio equal variables. Logistic regression employs the sigmoid function. The sigmoid function is an S-shaped curvature that takes in any real-valued quantity in its domain and provides a mapping to a value between 0 and 1.

3.6 Pseudo Code for the Machine Learning Algorithms Applied

1. Introduction Pandas
2. Import NumPy
3. Introduction Seaborn
4. Import (matplotlib).pyplot
5. Read CSV file
6. Get the count of dataset with class normal
7. Get the count of dataset with class Smurf
8. Shape the instances of the classes to make them equal
9. Initialize X variable
10. Initialize y variable
11. Assign the independent features as a data frame to X
12. Assign the dependent features as a data frame to y
13. Import train_test_split from sklearn.model_selection
14. Initialize four variables: X_train, X_test, y_train, y_test
15. Invoke train_test_split function with X,y and size as arguments

16. Set the variables in step 15 to be the result of step 16
17. Import decision tree classifier
18. Import logistic regression
19. Create an object of decision tree classifier
20. Create an object of logistic regression
21. Invoke the fit method on the object formed in step 20 for decision tree classifier with X_train, y_train as arguments
22. Invoke the fit method on the object formed in step 20 for logistic regression with X_train, y_train as arguments
23. Invoke the predict method on the object created in step 20 for decision tree classifier with X_test as argument
24. Invoke the predict method on the object created in step 20 for logistic regression with X_test as argument
25. Import confusion_matrix
26. Invoke confusion_matrix method with y_test and the result of step 24 as arguments for decision tree
27. Invoke confusion_matrix method with y_test and the result of step 25 as argument for logistic regression
28. Use Seaborn and matplotlib to show result of step 27 for decision tree
29. Use Seaborn and matplotlib to show result of step 28 for logistic regression

4. Results and Discussion

The models have been fit and trained as established in the previous step of this paper. The predict function has been applied to the trained models. What can be seen from the applied prediction from trained models? The accurateness score of the pronouncement tree classifier came to be 86%, while the accuracy score of the logistic regression came to be 92%. Therefore, the dataset and ensuing findings of our code suggest that in this instance, logistic regression is a better model than the decision tree classifier. A confusion_matrix (CM) is another way to visualize how well (or poorly) a classification model performs. When multiple classes exist (more than two) or when the number of observations across classes is imbalanced, accuracy alone can be misleading for a classification score. A confusion matrix allows for a more detailed viewpoint on model error. A confusion_matrix is an assembly of calculation results of a classification issue. The number of observations predicted correctly or incorrectly for each class is denoted by count values within a confusion matrix. A confusion matrix does not just tell you about the errors your classifier is making, but, more importantly, the classes within which the errors are happening. The confusion_matrix from the pronouncement tree classifier and the logistic regression prototypical are shown in Figures 5 and 6.

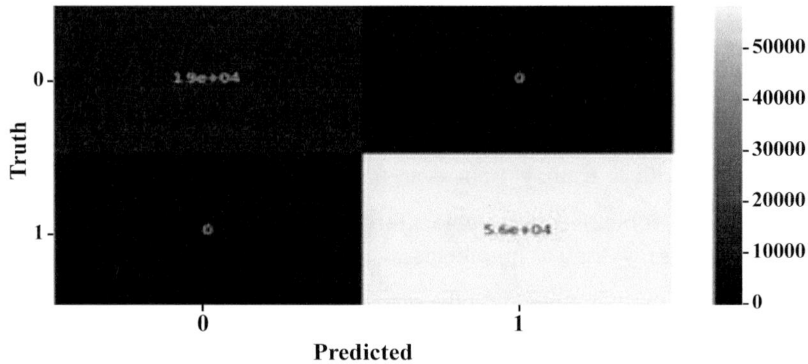

Figure 5: Decision tree CM.

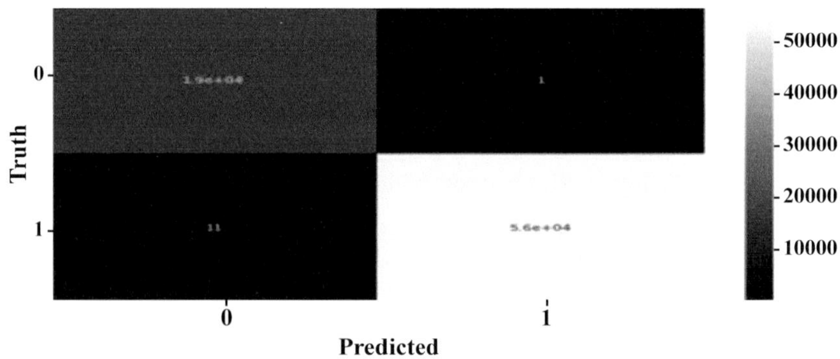

Figure 6: Logistic regression (CM).

5. Conclusion

With project completion, the initial goals are fulfilled. A machine learning network intrusion detection system was designed, focusing on the model's ability to detect anomaly in packets that transmit over the network. The implementations were done with the python programming language through Jupyter Notebook as the Integrated Development Environment (IDE). The specific library that helped to develop the model was scikit to implement the classifier algorithm. The entire project made use of the decision tree classifier and the logistic regression classifier. The confusion matrix metric and scikit-learn accuracy score validated each model's accuracy when comparing the two classifiers.

Both models do not have perfect accuracy, but we can see from the model assessment and the confusion matrix that they have both predicted the majority of the rows accurately in both circumstances. No machine model is 100% accurate.

References

[1] Rosenberg, J. (2017). Embedded security. In *Rugged Embedded Systems: Computing in Harsh Environments* (pp. e1–e74). Elsevier. https://doi.org/10.1016/B978-0-12-802459-1.00011-7.

[2] Chari, K. (2003). Firewalls. In *Encyclopedia of Information Systems* (pp. 313–329). Elsevier. https://doi.org/10.1016/B0-12-227240-4/00070-8.

[3] Ardad, V., Dhar, A. and Nema, S. (2013). Machine learning techniques for intrusion detection. *International Research Journal of Engineering and Technology*, 6(5): 4707–4712. https://arxiv.org/abs/1312.2177v2.

[4] Chowdhury, M. N., Ferens, K. and Ferens, M. (2016). Network Intrusion Detection Using Machine Learning. https://ijarsct.co.in/A15464.pdf.

[5] Akshaya, P. (2016). Intrusion detection system using machine learning approach. *International Journal of Engineering and Computer Science*, 5(10): 18249–18254. https://doi.org/10.18535/ijecs/v5i10.05.

[6] Gulghane, S., Shingate, V., Bondgulwar, S., Awari, G. and Sagar, P. (2020). A survey on intrusion detection system using machine learning algorithms. In *Lecture Notes on Data Engineering and Communications Technologies* (Vol. 46, pp. 670–675). Springer. https://doi.org/10.1007/978-3-030-38040-3_76.

[7] Almseidin, M., Alzubi, M., Kovacs, S. and Alkasassbeh, M. (2017). Evaluation of machine learning algorithms for intrusion detection system. *SISY 2017—IEEE 15th International Symposium on Intelligent Systems and Informatics, Proceedings* (pp. 277–282). IEEE. https://doi.org/10.1109/SISY.2017.8080566.

[8] Ugochukwu, C. J., Bennett, E. O. and Harcourt, P. (2019). An intrusion detection system using machine learning algorithm. *LAP LAMBERT Academic Publishing.*

[9] Kumar, V. (2005). Parallel and distributed computing for cybersecurity. *IEEE Distributed Systems Online*, 6(10). https://doi.org/10.1109/MDSO.2005.53.

[10] Papadopoulos, S., Drosou, A. and Tzovaras, D. (2016). A novel graph-based descriptor for the detection of billing-related anomalies in cellular mobile networks. *IEEE Transactions on Mobile Computing*, 15(11): 2655–2668. https://doi.org/10.1109/TMC.2016.2518668.

[11] Hawkins, D. M. (1980). *Identification of Outliers*. Chapman and Hall. https://doi.org/10.1007/978-94-015-3994-4.

[12] Rassam, M. A., Zainal, A. and Maarof, M. A. (2013). Advancements of data anomaly detection research in wireless sensor networks: A survey and open issues. *Sensors*, 13(8): 10087–10122. https://doi.org/10.3390/s130810087.

16 | Protecting the Sensitive Data: Federated Learning System Privacy Improvements

R. Prithviraj,[1,*] R. Saminathan[2] and R. Manishankar[3]

At a time when various regulations regarding data privacy including the General Data Protection Regulation (GDPR), the California Consumer Privacy Act (CCPA), and the data localization policy in India put forward by Reserve Bank of India (RBI) are redefining the area of financial data processing, federated learning (FL) has offered itself as a game-changer method that allows the joint training of a model without centralizing sensitive information. Nevertheless, although FL in theory decreases the likelihood of data exposure attacks, it cannot evade the risk of privacy attacks, such as model inversion attacks, gradient leakage, and adversarial client behavior. In this chapter, the researchers discuss innovative approaches to improving data privacy and security in federated learning systems that are specific to the financial services sector.

It starts with examining major weaknesses of existing FL framework and explore such highly developed privacy-preserving solutions as differential privacy (DP), secure multi-party computation (SMPC), homomorphic encryption (HE), and trusted execution environments (TEE). There is also the emergence of zero-trust security model and blockchain-based auditability integration when deciding the variables of trust in a federated network. In addition, breaking news in federated adversarial training, sturdy aggregation protocols, and client anomaly detection are also analyzed to mitigate threats posed by rogue or poisoned clients, which are very crucial issues in decentralized financial artificial intelligence (AI) environments.

The practical applications of federated learning frameworks in banking, insurance, and capital markets in the chapter show how federated learning is being applied in the leading institutions to detect frauds, arrive at credit scoring,

[1] Assistant Professor, Department of Artificial Intelligence (AI) and Data Science, Vel Tech Rangarajan Dr.Sagunthala R&D Institute of Science and Technology, Avadi, Chennai-600062.
[2] Professor, Department of Computer Science and Engineering, Annamalai University, Annamalainagar-608002.
[3] Research Scholar, Department of Computer Science and Engineering, Annamalai University, Annamalainagar-608002.
Emails: samiaucse@yahoo.com; manishankar2398@gmail.com
* Corresponding author: prithviraj0805@gmail.com

DOI: 10.1201/9781003710059-16

and counter money laundering activities without violating any of the regulatory requirements. Best tools such as TensorFlow Federated, PySyft, and OpenFL are examined with regard to the support of secure protocols and financial scalability.

This chapter is a complete guide to fellow researchers, data scientists, and financial organizations seeking to implement federated learning in a sustainable and safe manner by integrating the innovations present in technology with the policy-inspired needs. The intersection of secure FL and privacy engineering does not only help prevent sensitive financial data but also opens up new synergies of AI-based financial services.

1. Introduction

In the era of hyperconnectivity, data is the modern treasure of the financing industry, governments, and technology firms. The speed at which artificial intelligence (AI) and machine learning (ML) proliferate in banking, insurance, and capital markets has now transformed data into the backbone of decision-making, fraud detection, risk management, and customer interaction. Nevertheless, more privacy-aware methods of handling data processing became necessary due to the growing number of cyberattacks, the tighter global policies touching on data privacy, and the growing concern regarding the misuse of personal data among the population. Specifically, regulations of financial services abound in the forms of the General Data Protection Regulation (GDPR) in the Europe, the California Consumer Privacy Act (CCPA) in the United States, and the Indian policy to localize data, especially in the financial sector known as the Reserve Bank of India (RBI) [1]. It is against this context that federated learning (FL) has surfaced as a trendsetter in training machine learning models without relaying raw data to a centralized server.

In federated learning, different clients, such as banks, insurance companies, and edge devices, can cooperate to train a global model, no longer by sending raw data, but by exchanging model updates (weights or gradients) sent to an aggregator. This design seems to offer a spontaneous privacy bumper, as delicate financial information does not exit the company premises. Nevertheless, in reality, federated learning is also not resistant to privacy risks. Model updates are shown to be vulnerable to reconstruction by adversaries with methods such as gradient leakage, model inversion, and membership inference attacks [2]. Further, poisoning attacks, in which a malicious participant can intentionally modify its updates, may compromise the integrity of the global model. Those were the threats that have caused an increased level of concern among the financial institutions that needed to meet sets of regulations and still bear high predictability of accuracy in predictive models.

This chapter discusses the main concern of increasing privacy to the financial sector using federated learning systems. It starts with the consideration of the structural failures that the traditional FL framework possesses and the threats that, in their turn, compromise the security. It then explains advanced privacy-preserving techniques, including differential privacy (DP), secure multi-party computation (SMPC), homomorphic encryption (HE), and trusted execution environments (TEE), each of which introduces a different way of enhancing privacy promises [3]. Included in the chapter is the rise of blockchain-based auditability, zero-trust security models, and federated adversarial training as new ways of managing risks in the decentralized monetary AI system.

1.1 Motivation

Financial industry is the one with its own set of challenges in adopting AI technologies. Contrary to the case of consumer-oriented industries, financial institutions deal with delicate information such as bank transactions, credit card records, loan repayments, and insurance claims. Any unauthorized access or disclosure of such information does not only compromise privacy of the user but can lead to market instabilities and loss of confidence of the masses. Regulatory frameworks have placed stiff dictums concerning the storage, transmission, and processing of financial information. These regulations are opposed to traditional centralized machine learning techniques based on the aggregation of data across multiple institutions, thus FL represents an appealing alternative.

However, without mitigating the privacy threats of federated learning, it is not adaptable at scale. This chapter is thus motivated by the interest to find out how federated learning can be enhanced to satisfy the twin objectives of data privacy protection and model usefulness. Such balance is important in the financial domain, where accuracy and security are critical components in applications of fraud detection, credit scoring, anti-money laundering (AML), and algorithmic trading [4].

1.2 Problem Statement

As much as federated learning reduces the amount of data separation required, it does not automatically address all the privacy issues. Information provided by the gradient can leak sensitive information, and poisoning and free-riding attacks can sabotage training. Also, the aggregation server itself is subject to being a single point of failure should it be compromised. Each technique in current privacy-preserving methods has its own shortcomings: differential privacy decreases accuracy due to the injection of noise, and SMPC can be associated with enormous communication costs, and homomorphic encryption may be computationally inefficient [5].

The core question that we have answered in this chapter is: What are the options available to federated learning systems that can improve with sophisticated privacy-preserving methods to the rigorous scope of the financial services industry, and be scalable and compliant, along with fulfilling model performance?

1.3 Objectives of the Chapter

Various objectives have been achieved in the chapter:

1. Determine the gaps in the conceivable current federated learning structure, at least in monetary terms.
2. Survey state-of-the-art privacy-preserving systems such as DP, SMPC, HE, and TEE and trade-offs.
3. Consider novel approaches (aka solutions) to consider blockchain-based auditability, zero-trust models, and adversarial training of FL.
4. Illustrate practical use of FL in banking, insurance, and capital markets.
5. Identify regulatory and compliance issues, which influence the adoption of FL in the financial sector.
6. Suggest avenues of sustainable and privacy-resilient federated learning in the future.

1.4 Organization of the Chapter

The rest of this chapter will be in the following manner:

1. Section 2 discusses the history of federated learning and conducts a literature survey of studying approaches to privacy-preserving techniques.
2. Section 3 discusses the key privacy risks and weak points in the systems of federated learning.
3. In Section 4, privacy-enhancing techniques that are advanced are discussed with their strengths and weaknesses to financial applications mentioned.
4. Section 5 provides the case study on the federated learning in banking, insurance, and capital markets.
5. Section 6 discusses issues and research directions of secure FL.
6. The paper ends with concluding statements and practitioner and policymaker recommendations.

2. Background and Literature Review

2.1 Development of Data Privacy in the Digital Age

The development of data privacy practices can be attributed to the emergence of digital economies and the use of user data as a foundation to make decisions. During the early days of computing, the organizations were more concerned with access control and encryption in order to make their data secure whether it is at rest or at communications. With the proliferation of the internet in the late 20th century, data gathering became the norm and entire industries started storing sensitive information in vast databases. The model caused considerable worries about the single points of failure, both in the aspect of cyber-security and in the terms of personal privacy [1].

To resolve these fears, researchers have sought to apply privacy-enhancing methods that aimed to anonymize data such that personal identifiable information (PII) was stripped prior to analysis. But later research showed anonymization was not unassailable, and opponents could identify users by correlating anonymized databases with external data [2]. It gave rise to more sophisticated frameworks such as k-anonymity, l-diversity, and t-closeness, yet these methods were also too restrictive when applied to the financial data having high dimensions.

Big accidents such as the Cambridge Analytica case, ginormous credit card hacks, and identity theft scandals served as the impetus of the new modern era of privacy regulation and brought to people the awareness of how dangerous the centralization of data can be. Strict guidelines of data handling were given official status in the GDPR of 2018, which provided elements such as data minimization, right to be forgotten, and explicit consent [3]. In other countries, such as those with the CCPA in the United States and the RBI data localization directive in India, similar frameworks were imposing further limitations on the cross-border data flow. Together, these rules presented a problem of compliance as well as business opportunity—organizations now needed a solution that would allow them to generate data-driven insights without being in breach of law.

This is the situation in which FL appeared as a revolutionary method. The ability to leave data local and to share only model updates meant FL has provided potentially acceptable trade-offs between collaboration intelligence and data sovereignty.

2.2 Federated Learnings: The Mechanism and the Process

Google was first to popularize federated learning in 2016, where it was applied to keyboard prediction systems (Gboard) to train on-device data to make predictive typing more accurate without uploading sensitive text to central servers [4]. Since then, the technology has been applied beyond cryptocurrency into healthcare, finance, and IoT due to the importance of privacy.

The general process of federated learning includes these steps:

1. Initialization of a Model: One instance of a global model is initialized by a central server or coordinator.
2. Local Training: All clients in the collaboration (e.g., bank, insurance company, or mobile device) use their own data to train the model on their local systems.
3. Transmission of Update: Clients upload their model updates (gradients or parameters) to the aggregator that is at the center.

4. Aggregation: Updates are combined (e.g., with Federated Averaging) by the central server into a better global model.
5. Iteration: The new model is then repackaged and distributed to clients and the iterations repeated until convergence [5].

This decentralized method lowers the requirements of direct sharing of data and, in hypothetical terms, enhances privacy. Nevertheless, it creates a number of new challenges:

1. The central aggregator is a vulnerable part that once compromised may leak information.
2. Inference attacks against model updates—adversaries seek to recover sensitive information by gradients.
3. Non-IID distributions of client data cause model convergence to be more difficult.
4. Communication overhead may turn out to be high when thousands of clients are involved [6].

Nonetheless, federated learning has been extensively used in financial applications because it inherits the compliance advantages of not storing data in a centralized location and can aggregate collective intelligence.

2.3 Use Cases of Federated Learning in Financial Services

The financial sector especially provides a persuasive argument in favor of using federated learning as its operations require the use of sensitive and regulated data. Some application examples show what a revolutionary impact FL can have:

1. Fraud Detection: FL can also be used to detect cross-institutional fraud patterns that would otherwise go undiscovered by coordinating banks in training the models without sharing raw records [7].
2. Credit Scoring: The creation of predictive models may be collaborated with credit bureaus and financial institutions with the client confidentiality being preserved. Such a strategy covers fairness issues and makes it possible to make better risk assessment and still be on the safe side of compliance requirements.
3. Anti-Money Laundering (AML): With federated systems, institutions can provide information regarding suspicious activity without providing transaction level data. This is essential in complying with global AML codes.
4. Insurance Risk Modeling: Insurers will have the ability to pool claim and customer behavior data with more accuracy to the risk models without the privacy of policy holders being breached.
5. Algorithmic Trading and Risk Management: In an additional model, investment firms may band together to train models that extract

macroeconomic information without disclosing their proprietary trading strategies.

These applications show that federated learning is not just an abstract academics theory, but is a workable solution to find harmony between innovation and control in banking [8].

2.4 Privacy Problems in the Federated Learning

Although FL has high privacy benefits, it is not secure per se. There exist various types of privacy threats that were recorded in literature:

1. Gradient Inversion Attacks: During the training process, adversaries are able to compute gradients on a shared model. An example is that even a small number of times of gradient sharing can yield sensitive transaction information as the research indicates [9].
2. Membership Inference Attacks: The attacker is able to know the status of a particular record (e.g., if the customer loan history was included during training).
3. Model Poisoning: This occurs when malicious clients can trick updates into biasing the global model toward making incorrect predictions.
4. Free-Rider Attacks: There is a risk that some of the participants may seek to gain while those who have established their global model do not share their significant updates.
5. Threats to Communication: Any intercepted transmission may leak out model information and this might be a problem when not coded.

These vulnerabilities highlight that federated learning lessens but not completely obliterates privacy risks, especially when doing so in sensitive scenarios such as high-stakes financial ones.

2.5 Privacy-Preserving Techniques Review

Inadequacy with regard to baseline FL has led to the development of sophisticated privacy-saving approaches. The most important techniques are:

- Differential Privacy (DP): Introduces some statistical noise to the updates of the models, constraining the capacity of adversaries to retrieve dangerous information. Although effective, DP may lower model accuracy in the case of excessive noise [10].
- Secure Multi-Party Computation (SMPC): Shares the computations with two or more parties such that no participant gets full access to the dataset. This guarantees that during collaborative training, data is encrypted. But SMPC is often associated with high computational as well as communication overheads [11].

- Homomorphic Encryption (HE): The computations can be done on the encrypted data and the raw data will always be concealed. Despite this, HE is computationally expensive and possibly does not scale to large pools of financial data [12].
- Technologies That Enable Isolated Sensitive Computations: A secure hardware enclave (e.g., Intel SGX) enables TEE, in which sensitive computations run in isolation on a trusted hardware. Although they are effective, TEEs also create hardware trust issues, and they can be susceptible to side-channel attacks [13].
- Federated Learning Based on Blockchain: More recent articles suggest using distributed ledger technologies in relation to auditability, integrity, and decentralized trust management. Integration of blockchain allows tamper-evidence updates in the model, although its scalability is an issue [14].

Every one of these methods has its advantages and disadvantages. In the case of financial services, where accuracy, scalability, and compliance are all very important, it is increasingly viewed that multi-method hybrid approaches are the most feasible next step.

2.6 Discovered Literature Gaps

The federated learning privacy literature is expanding fast; however, there are still a few gaps:

- Sector-Specific: There has been extensive coverage on general methods of privacy protection, yet little is available on the needs of the financial sector.
- Trade-Off Optimization: Related works tend to focus only on privacy or accuracy but not balanced.
- Scalability Issues: Techniques such as SMPC and HE are computationally expensive, thus they cannot be applied practically in very large financial networks.
- Regulatory Integration: Not much study has been conducted to understand how FL privacy methods can be harmonized with the changing regulatory regimes across jurisdictions.
- Adversarial Resilience: Poisoning and adversarial client behavior have been insufficiently considered by most approaches to privacy, yet they are vital in financial partnerships where parties are no longer even as confident as they are in one another.

These deficiencies illustrate the need to fill these privacy attack vectors which will help to implement comprehensive privacy-preserving strategies that incorporate the technical, regulatory, and organizational concerns.

3. Federated Learning System Privacy Threats

Despite the fact that the risk of data leakage in FL is minimized in comparison to the centralized data collection, it is not danger-free. Indeed, studies have shown that even after an update on models, sensitive information is still shared, and malignant players are capable of jeopardizing the security of the whole system [1]. Financial services are high-stakes environments where privacy threats are prevalent, and their landscape needs to be understood in designing effective defenses. This part overviews the pertinent types of privacy risks in FL, such as inference attacks, reconstructions tactics, membership disclosures, poisoning efforts, and systematic exploits of communication and trust.

3.1 The Direct Privacy Attacks

Direct privacy attacks take advantage of the statistical characteristics of gradients or model updates sent between clients and the main server. Such attacks target in accessing confidential data which originates in seemingly harmless data.

3.1.1 Gradient Inversion Attacks

Gradient inversion, during which adversaries reproduce the training samples used in training over shared gradients, is one of the most examined threats in FL. As an example, a malicious aggregator would be able to back-engineer sensitive information including account balances or categories of transactions by using a gradient update issued by a client bank made using transaction data [2]. Researchers have demonstrated that high-resolution reconstructions can be made even with partial gradients and this poses a significant threat to financial applications where sensitive data involve transactions.

3.1.2 Inversion of the Attack Models

Model inversion attacks happen when adversaries use the global model itself to guess sensitive properties of the training data. An attack in the financial sector may disclose the credit worthiness of a client, chances of loan default by a customer, or the information concerning high-value transactions [3]. As opposed to gradient inversion, model inversion is facilitated without direct access to updates and relies on the trained model to obtain hidden patterns.

3.1.3 Membership Inference Attacks

Another grave issue, known as membership inference, is where the adversary tries to identify whether a specific record of data was included in the training set [4]. As an example, an attacker might test to check whether a particular credit card transaction made it into the dataset used to build the fraud detection model. This can represent a breach of customer privacy and the ability of others to lawfully identify personal data in some instances; inadequate regulatory compliance such as GDPR that ensures measures to counteract unauthorized identification of personal data.

3.2 Indirect Privacy Risks

In contrast to directly "stealing data out of the gradients or models" as described in indirect threats, these attacks abuse the infrastructure and protocols of federated learning.

3.2.1 Traffic Analysis

They can use traffic analysis to deduce sensitive data even in cases where the updates to the models have been encrypted. Attackers can use patterns in communication frequency, volume of updates, or timing, to determine which institutions are involved, or when valuable training sessions will take place [5]. Competitive intelligence or vulnerabilities within a system would be exposed in financial networks with such side-channel information.

3.2.2 Intercepting Communications

Depending on whether the communication between the clients and the aggregator is not adequately secured, intercepted updates can leak model parameters, or be used in a replay attack. Although encryption prevents this risk, the sheer complexity of federated systems provides an opening to sophisticated adversaries trying to take advantage of weak connections in the network [6].

3.2.3 Server Compromise

In numerous FL architectures, the central server which is commonly the aggregator is a point of failure. A compromised server could cheat aggregation, selectively suppress additional updates, or even put in malicious gradients. Such risk is especially problematic when it comes to financial collaborations since those involved are to trust that the aggregator will be honest [7].

3.3 Hostile Client Behavior

One unique challenge of federated learning is that there are malicious clients who will actively attempt to derail the training process. Such attacks contrast the passive inference since the model updates are deliberately interfered with.

3.3.1 Attack of Data Poisoning

Data poisoning attacks involve adversarial clients contaminating their local training data with poisoned data, and the effect of the poisoned data spreading to the global model via gradient updates [8]. As an example, a malicious member of a financial consortium might intentionally misclassify an abusive transaction as legitimate, undermining the work of the shared model in detecting fraud.

3.3.2 Model Poisoning Attack

Compared to data poisoning, models poison results when clients directly change their own gradients prior to submitting them to the aggregator. An insurance company acting maliciously may have an interest in influencing the model to discriminate against particular risk profiles so as to have a competitive advantage. Model poisoning attacks are usually low profile and can be disguised in basic anomaly detection [9].

3.3.3 Free-Rider Attacks

The clients have the possibility of free-riding where they have little or no useful update but they enjoy the better global model [10]. Free-riding is a counterproductive concept to the fairness in financial networks and it provides the disincentive mechanism of retaining honesty. The issue is extreme where the information processing, computer, or other communication resources are expensive.

3.3.4 Backdoors Attack

One particular form of poisoning is the backdoor attack, whereby attackers will add triggers that make the model act in a way that is wrong in some conditions. To give an example, an attacker may enter such sequence of operations knowing that whenever such an operation appears, it will be considered as being nonfraudulent by the system. These types of attacks can be especially threatening when applied to financial systems where seemingly minor manipulations of finances can lead to massive losses of money [11].

3.4 Vulnerabilities in the System

In addition to the risks of clients and servers, federated learning has systemic risks in its architecture and surroundings.

3.4.1 Data Distributions That Are not Non-IID

In reality, the financial institutions have non-independent non-IID datasets. To give an example, one bank can cater to the urban population with high online activities and the other can target rural users who have to carry a lot of cash. Non-IID data makes it difficult to aggregate, and may produce biased global models [12]. This diversity brings about a situation where it allows enemies to leverage weaknesses in the learning process.

3.4.2 Scalability and Communication Bottlenecks

Transmission overhead to different clients and computation cost of secure aggregation grow unacceptable as more clients are added [13]. These bottlenecks may be used as attack points by attackers using denial-of-service (DoS) strategies to stall or stop convergence.

3.4.3 Assumption of Trust

Most federated learning frameworks assume a semi-honest model in which clients and servers follow protocols but may still try to learn more. In financial partnerships, though, there is the likelihood that the participants can be completely adversarial, with outlooks that are based on competition or crime. Such a discrepancy between presumptions and reality reveals the weaknesses inherent in the systems [14].

3.5 Specific Risks in the Financial Sector

New challenges to federated learning privacy emerge in the financial sector:

- Regulatory Noncompliance: Because of privacy leaks in federated systems, a localization policy (GDPR, CCPA, or RBI) may be infringed, costing significant fines and reputational losses.
- Cross-Border Cooperation Risk: Financial institutions have to operate in a cross-border setting, and this brings about exposure to varied regulatory regimes.
- High-Value Targets: Financial data is of special attention to adversaries because it has direct monetary value. Leakage of gradients disclosing transaction histories or loans applications can be monetized without delay.
- Insider Threats: When an employee of a bank or insurance company serves as an FL participant, such party may use his position to accomplish poisoned updates.

These risks reflect the importance of establishing sector-specific protections to federated learning as opposed to generic privacy solutions.

3.6 Overview of Privacy Threats

Overall, the privacy risk of federated learning can be split into three general groups:

- Direct Attacks: Gradient inversion, model inversion, and membership inference.
- Indirect Attacks: Traffic analysis, communication interception, and compromise of the servers.

- Adversarial Behavior: Data poisoning, model poisoning, backdoor insertion, and free-riding.

In case of the financial industry, these risks are increased by sensitivity and nature of regulation of the data concerned. To overcome these obstacles, it is necessary to use a multi-level defense mechanism combining the cryptographic protection, powerful aggregation protocols, anomaly detection, and compliance with regulations.

3.7 Conceptual Privacy-Preserving Federated Learning Architecture in the Financial Service Industry

An architecture capable of supporting federated learning in the financial industry requires integrating the fundamental FL workflow with privacy-preserving layers at different levels to address the security threats mentioned previously by using a combination of primitives (such as G-Learning) and frameworks (like OpenFL) to further facilitate the generalization of federated learning. A theoretical framework that could be best suited to a financial application is represented in Figure 1.

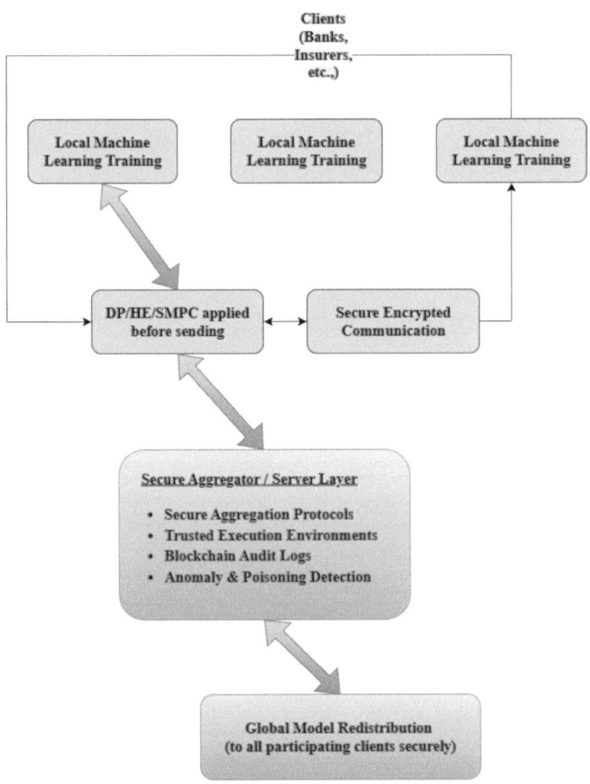

Figure 1: Privacy-preserving federated learning framework for financial services.

Framework Workflow:

1. Model Initialization: The aggregator initializes the global one.
2. Local Training: Local financial data is used to train each client.
3. Privacy Protection: Clients encrypt it or add DP noise prior to the sending of updates.
4. Secure Aggregation: Aggregation of updates is done securely with SMPC/TEE.
5. Model Validation: The ensemble of models is subject to adversary verifications (anomaly checks, robust averaging).
6. Rebalancing Model: Globally, model distribution will be optimized back to the clients.
7. Iterative Training: The steps 2–6 are carried out iteratively until convergence.

The Major Elements in the Framework:

1. **Interlocutor Clients (Financial Institutions/Edge Nodes)**
   - Every customer (e.g., banks, insurance companies, stock exchanges, payment gateways) has isolated financial information in the form of transaction histories, credit histories, or claims.
   - Clients train locally on their data, and produce model updates (gradients or parameters).
   - Updates can be encrypted using differential privacy (adding noise), and/or homomorphic encryption before transmission.
2. **Secure Communication Layer**
   - All updates are sent using encrypted channels (e.g., TLS, VPN tunnels).
   - Traffic analytics: Traffic analysis can be resisted using traffic obfuscation protocols.
   - Featherweight authentication is utilized to guarantee the participation of permitted clients.
3. **Publish Server/Central Server (Secure Protocols)**
   - The aggregator receives the updates made by clients and securely aggregates the updates, such that no single update is revealed in plaintext.
   - The aggregation process can be isolated using TEE (e.g., Intel SGX).
   - Ledgers used in blockchains can store transactions of updates to audit and be accountable to each other with no hidden backside deals.

4. **Worldwide Model Distribution**
    - The global model thus generated is redistributed to clients who participate in the global model.
    - In order to be resilient against poisoning, anomaly detection and Byzantine-resilient aggregation protocols (such as Krum, Trimmed Mean, Bulyan) are used to filter model updates prior to acceptance.
5. **Privacy-Preserving Layers**
    - DP guarantees that no reverse-engineering is possible of the individual client contributions.
    - SMPC is a way to distribute aggregation with the secret of raw updates.
    - HE allows computing on encrypted updates.
    - Zero-trust security model does not presuppose any implicit trust to exist among participants and will enforce exhaustive verification and monitoring.
6. **Layer Regulation and Compliance**
    - The architecture includes policies of GDPR, CCPA, and RBI localization regulations.
    - Geofencing systems do not allow data to be transited to prohibited jurisdictions.
    - During regulatory checks, the audit logs aid in compliance. Figure 2 shows the impact of adversarial attacks on model accuracy.

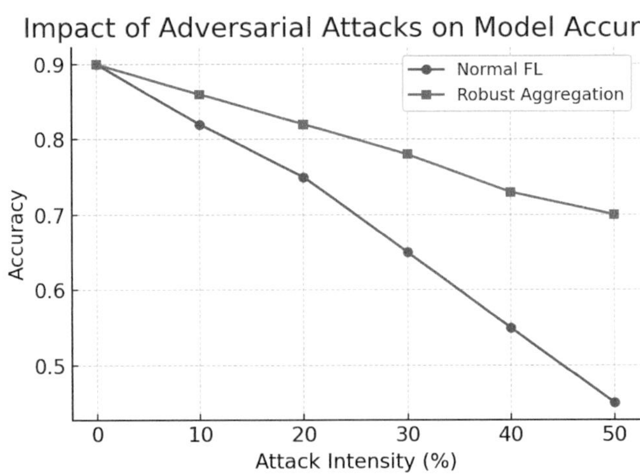

Figure 2: Impact of adversarial attacks on model accuracy.

Benefits of the Suggested Framework:

1. End-to-End Privacy: Sensitive information is never transmitted and updates have cryptographic/statistical privacy guarantees.
2. Trust System: Zero-trust architecture, anomaly, and blockchain-based audit implementations shift to blind trust.
3. Regulatory Compliance: Data localization and auditability allow staying compliant with financial regulations.
4. Bucking Attacks: Aggregation methods and poisoning are solved through the robust techniques, whereas encryption and DP provide resistance to inference.
5. Scalability: Modular orientation enables it to be implemented in multiple institutions and geographies.

4. Privacy-Sensitive Federated Learning

Though the architecture presented in the earlier text gives the conceptual understanding of how a secure FL system can be designed in a financial service, the real power of such a system is limited to the privacy-protective methods implemented into it. This section discusses the key strategies that are currently followed in research and industry, their principle of operation, their relevance to financial datasets, and their limitations.

4.1 Differential Privacy

DP is a mathematical model that guarantees that the result of a given computation does not disclose whether a particular individual was part of a dataset [1]. In FL, DP may be used locally (at the client side) or centrally (at the server side).

4.1.1 Local Differential Privacy

- Individual clients inject calibrated random noise into their model updates and send them to the aggregator.
- This is to make sure that when the updates are intercepted, an attacker cannot deduce precise sensitive data (e.g., a specific customer credit card transaction).

4.1.2 Central Differential Privacy

Use of DP is done by the server during the combination of model updates among clients.

- As an example, once averaging, the server adds Gaussian or Laplacian noise to the aggregated parameters.

4.1.3 Advantages

- Makes formal privacy guarantees, which can be quantified in terms of ε (epsilon) and δ (delta).
- Supports a broad range of current FL algorithms.

4.1.4 Limitations

- Noise can cause poorer model performance, particularly in finance where accuracy is an important factor (e.g., fraud detection).
- The privacy–utility trade-off is difficult to balance.
- Example: In finance, a group of banks that employs FL in anti-money laundering can apply local DP such that the transaction pattern of a single institution is not disclosed.

4.2 Secure Multi-Party computation

SMPC is a cryptographic research area that aims to guarantee confidentiality and integrity of the computation results of multiple parties. SMPC is a method that allows many parties to perform a computation on their respective inputs in a confidential manner [2]. SMPC gives the client certain assurances that the model will combine updates without exposing contributions in FL.

4.2.1 Techniques in SMPC

- Secret Sharing: A client divides its update into shares shared with other clients; the sum of share is only reassembled to create the original update.
- Additive Homomorphism: Summation of encrypted updates is enabled.

4.2.2 Advantages

- Good cryptographic assurances—no one gets to know the update of another.
- Precludes aggregation leakage on the server side.

4.2.3 Limitations

- There is high communication overhead because of several interaction rounds.
- The bottlenecks in performance can be experienced upon scaling to thousands of financial clients.
- Financial Example: Insurance companies that work together on risk models can operate SMPC such that no actuarial data is ever exchanged.

4.3 Homomorphic Encryption

HE enables computation to be performed on encrypted data without decryption [3]. In FL, the updates are encrypted by the clients and the aggregator runs computations on the ciphertext.

4.3.1 Types of HE

- Partially Homomorphic Encryption (PHE): Only a single operation (e.g., addition or multiplication) is supported.
- Somewhat homomorphic encryption (SHE): Limited operations.
- Fully Homomorphic Encryption (FHE): It is computationally costly, yet can support arbitrary computations.

4.3.2 Advantages

- High Protection: updates are never viewed by the server.
- Stokesy with untrusted aggregator.

4.3.3 Limitations

- Extremely large computational and communications overheads.
- Still not viable on big financial data in real-time systems.
- Financial Example: Agent models of credit score may be trained on a bank-by-bank basis with HE, so that even the aggregator does not know about the updates.

4.4 Trusted Execution Environments

A TEE is a hardware enclave that enables sensitive computations to be performed in isolation [4].

4.4.1 Working Mechanism

Aggregator receives encrypted updates.

- On the TEE (e.g., Intel SGX), updates are decrypted and summed up.
- Results are re-encrypted prior to leaving the enclave.

4.4.2 Advantages

- Isolates the hardware on a hardware basis with the rest of the system.
- More fast than pure cryptographic solutions such as HE.

4.4.3 Limitations

- Depends on hardware vendors (e.g., Intel), which can be one point of trust.
- Vulnerable to side-channel attacks unless configured to be resistant.
- Finance Example: The central bank might run a TEE-based aggregator to organize fraud detection models in commercial banks without exposing data to leakage.

4.5 Zero-Trust Security and Blockchain

4.5.1 Auditability with Blockchain

- Blockchain technology is capable of offering records of model updates and aggregation that cannot be tampered with [5].
- Every update is registered as a transaction.
- The ledger can then be audited by regulators or participants later to ensure compliance.

4.5.2 Zero-Trust Security Model

Conventional systems presuppose the reliability of some bodies. In a zero-trust design, all clients and servers have to keep demonstrating who they are and their intent.

- Constant authentication (with digital certificates).
- Behavioral monitoring (identify anomalies in updates by the client).
- Adaptive access control (weed out rogue clients).
- Financial Example: A blockchain-based FL network to detect fraud guarantees non-repudiation—when a malicious client produces a poisoned update, the audit trail will catch him.

4.6 Federated Adversarial Training

Federated learning is susceptible to poisoned gradients (adversarial attacks). In response, federated adversarial training adds adversarial robustness methods to the FL pipeline [6].

- Not only train on normal data, but also on adversarial perturbed data, produced locally.
- Aggregator applies strong averaging policies (Krum, Bulyan) so that poisoned updates are rejected.

- Finance Example: An attacker should not be allowed to add counterfeited credit histories to skew lending models.

Detection of anomalies in a client update is another security issue in accounting systems that can be resolved with an attack detection method.

4.7 Client Update Breakage Detection

Another security problem in accounting systems is the ability to detect anomalies in a client update, which can be addressed with an attack detection method..

- Monitoring the behavior of clients, to determine anomalies, is another essential mechanism.
- Gradient Similarity Analysis: Identify clients whose changes are abnormally different to the majority.
- Reputation Scores: Give weight to trust to the clients, de-emphasizing to unreliable participants.
- This improves resistance to Byzantine clients and collusion attacks.
- Finance Example: Detection of whether a compromised payment processor is injecting poisoned gradients into the fraud detection model.

4.8 Hybrid Approaches

Theoretically, one approach cannot work. Financial institutions commonly use hybrid architectures, which mix between several techniques:

- DP + SMPC (noise + secret sharing).
- HE + TEE (encryption + secure enclave).
- Blockchain + anomaly detection (audit + client monitoring).
- This tiered defense establishes defense-in-depth that is essential in risky financial settings.

Table 1: Comparative analysis of security approaches for financial systems.

Technique	*Strengths*	*Weaknesses*	*Suitability in Finance*
Differential Privacy	Formal privacy guarantees, lightweight	Reduces accuracy	High
SMPC	Strong cryptography, protects against server attacks	High communication overhead	Medium–high
Homomorphic Encryption	Strong protection, aggregator blind	Computationally expensive	Medium
TEE	Hardware-level security, fast	Vendor reliance, side-channel risk	High

Contd...

Technique	*Strengths*	*Weaknesses*	*Suitability in Finance*
Blockchain	Auditability, transparency	Scalability issues	Medium
Zero-Trust	Continuous verification	Complexity in deployment	High
Adversarial Training	Robust against poisoning	Extra training cost	High
Anomaly Detection	Detects rogue clients	False positives possible	High

Comparative analysis of security approaches for financial systems is shown in Table 1.

5. Financial Services Case Studies and Applications

The financial services industry has led in the uptake of federated learning technologies because its data is highly sensitive, privacy is a major concern, and the use of AI-based insights is growing prominent. This sub-book offers real-world examples and case studies illustrating how federated learning that benefits with privacy-preserving methodologies can be successfully implemented in the banking insurance credit scoring fraud detection and other financial sectors.

5.1 Fraud Detection

5.1.1 Background

Fraudulent activities are a worldwide problem and credit card fraud, identity theft, and synthetic fraud cost billions of dollars every year [7]. Conventional fraud detection models focus on data aggregation at the center, posing a privacy risk and regulatory challenges.

5.1.2 FL Application

Federated learning enables banks, payment processors, and fintech companies to cooperatively train fraud detection models, without having access to raw transaction data.

- Every institution is locally trained on transaction records.
- Aggregation of encrypted or noise-protected update is performed.
- The global model is trained on the trends of fraud in various datasets.

5.1.3 Privacy Enhancements

- Differential privacy is a guarantee where the pattern of transactions of one customer does not leak.
- Anomaly detection assists in detection of the malicious clients attempting to inject poisoned updates.

5.1.4 Example

A European group of banks is said to have conducted a pilot with an FL-based model of fraud detection, which enhanced the detection accuracy by approximately 20% yet was compliant with GDPR [8].

5.2 Credit Scoring and Risk Assessment

5.2.1 Background

One of the most important applications of credit scoring is to analyze the risk of borrowers. Nevertheless, consolidation of credit histories across institutions also presents data security and antitrust issues [9].

5.2.2 FL Application

- A credit scoring model can be trained by multiple banks.
- SMPC or HE is used to aggregate updates so that no raw credit history is exposed.
- Model: Captures more population behavior and is less biased.

5.2.3 Privacy Enhancements

- Homomorphic encryption is a concept that makes sure that the aggregator cannot see sensitive updates.
- Blockchain auditing will give regulators unalterable evidence of compliance.

5.2.4 Example

An Asian fintech consortium was using FL to score credit among banks to provide access to credit to small businesses more equally without consolidating sensitive loan histories in one pool [10].

5.3 Anti-Money Laundering Compliance

5.3.1 Background

One of the most controlled fields of finance is money laundering. Banks should record suspicious transactions without violating the privacy of customers or cross-border legislation on the security of data [11].

5.3.2 FL Application

- FL enables AML models to be trained across facilities without revealing sensitive customer information.

- Transactions across geographies can be used to share a common detection system.

5.3.3 Privacy Enhancements

- Zero-trust security models assure that every client node undergoes continual authentication.
- Adversarial training enhances resistance to attackers who seek to obscure any illegal transactions.

5.3.4 Example

One U.S. to EU financial partnership relied on FL to enhance AML compliance among institutions without actual data transfers, meeting both GDPR and FinCEN requirements [12].

5.4 Insurance Risk Modeling

5.4.1 Background

Actuarial predictions and fraud detection during claims are dependent on large datasets, which insurance companies use. Such centralization of this information creates the issue of breach of privacy and competitive sensitivity [13].

5.4.2 FL Application

- FL allows insurers to collectively train models on fraudulent claims.
- The use of collaborative actuarial models ensures improved determination of customer risk profiles.

5.4.3 Privacy Enhancements

- SMPC is a solution that makes sure that no insurer is exposed to proprietary information of another.
- An experience rating of the participants eliminates the possibility of rogue updates distorting risk models.

5.4.4 Example

FL was used on claims datasets by a federated consortium of health insurers to minimize false positives in fraud detection but in a way that met HIPAA regulations [14].

5.5 Personal Finance and Wealth Management

5.5.1 Background

The advisory services that are undertaken personally in finance require very sensitive information about the customer, including income, spending patterns, and investments [15].

5.5.2 FL Application

- Mobile banking apps incorporate small-scale FL systems to deliver risk evaluations and suggestions to users.
- Models are trained using local device data, and only updates are shared.

5.5.3 Privacy Enhancements

- Local differential privacy is specific privacy that secures the concealment of individual customer patterns.
- Federated adversarial training secures models against being manipulated by malicious clients.

5.5.4 Example

North American WealthTech startups experimented with FL-based personal finance advisors balancing personalization with privacy by ensuring that no raw client data is exited from user devices [16].

5.6 Stock Market Prediction and Algorithms Trading

5.6.1. Background

Huge volumes of high-frequency trading data are produced by financial markets. Nonetheless, the pooling of such data among companies poses competitive threats and insider trading [17].

5.6.2 FL Application

- Brokerage firms and hedge funds could utilize FL to educate market movement forecasting formulas.
- Training is done at home by each firm with aggregate updates.

5.6.3 Privacy Enhancements

- TEEs secure updates during aggregate.

- The combination of blockchain assures transparency and responsibility in model changes.

5.6.4 Example

An investigator with several investment companies considered FL to forecast volatility indexes (VIX), and showed enhanced model strength without disclosing their trading methods [18].

Figures 3 and 4 both show that there are trade-offs in the use of DP, SMPC, HE, etc.

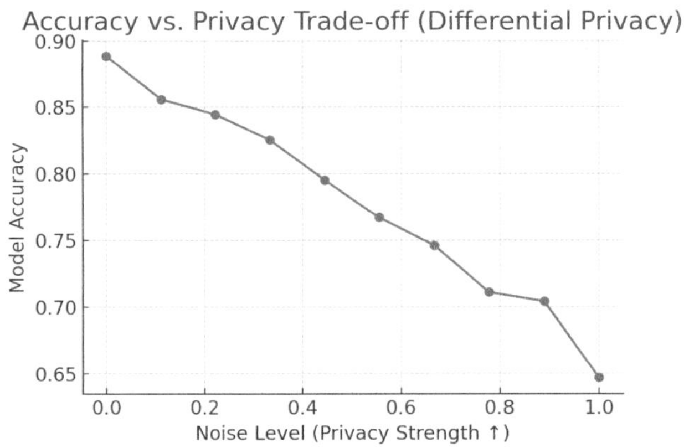

Figure 3: Accuracy versus privacy trade-off.

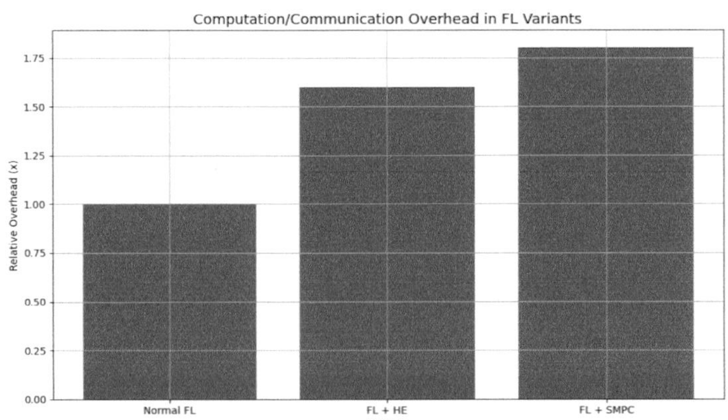

Figure 4: Computation/communication overhead in FL variants

5.7 Cross-Border Payment Security

5.7.1. Background

Transactions across borders are at high risk of fraud because of the presence of numerous intermediaries and variations in regulations [19].

5.7.2 FL Application

- FL allows shared fraud detection systems among banks in disparate countries without the need of raw data transfer.
- Regulatory authorities need not access sensitive data to regulate model training.

5.7.3 Privacy Enhancements

- Differential privacy provides adherence to GDPR and other laws concerning localization of data.
- Zero-trust security prevents insider threats.

5.7.4 Example

BIS has singled out FL as a possible solution to being able to monitor cross-border payments in accordance with FATF rules [20]. Table 2 shows the comparative analysis of case studies.

Table 2: Comparative analysis of case studies.

Application	*Privacy Technique*	*Benefits*	*Challenges*
Fraud Detection	DP + anomaly detection	Improved accuracy, GDPR compliance	Risk of degraded precision
Credit Scoring	HE + blockchain	Fairer credit access	High computational costs
AML Compliance	Zero-trust + adversarial training	Cross-border compliance	Complexity of deployment
Insurance	SMPC + reputation scores	Collaboration without data leaks	Communication overhead
Personal Finance	Local DP + adversarial training	Personalized insights	Limited device resources
Trading	TEE + blockchain	Protects proprietary models	Trust in hardware vendors
Cross-Border Payments	DP + zero-trust	Global fraud detection	Regulatory heterogeneity

5.8 Lessons Learned

Based on these case studies, one can make a few observations:

- Hybrid Techniques Work Best: No individual privacy mechanism is as effective as a combination (e.g., DP + SMPC) provides practical results.
- Regulatory Alignment Is Essential: Adoption is never truly technical at its core as it is typically driven by legal compliance (e.g., GDPR, HIPAA, FATF).
- Cost vs. Privacy Trade-Off: Institutions need to trade between computation/communication overhead and the desired privacy assurances.
- Trust via Transparency: Blockchain and auditing systems enhance institutional trust, which is vital in the multi-party relationships.
- Personalization vs. Privacy: Federated learning does not compromise privacy in the context of personalization (finance advisors, credit scoring).

Challenges and Open Research Directions: The possibilities that federated learning opens to financial services are transformative, yet its implementation on a large scale is anything but easy. Regardless of the positive improvements, a number of technical, organizational, and regulatory issues are yet to be resolved. These barriers are important to address to make sure that FL systems provide a high level of privacy protection, high performance, and practical usage. This part defines the key issues in the FL adoption to protect sensitive data, and presents open research directions in the following decade.

6. Technical Challenges

6.1.1 Communication Overhead

Among the most important problems of FL systems is the high cost of communication between client devices and the central aggregator [21]. Regular updates of parameters demand more bandwidth.

In finance across borders, the problem is aggravated by limited network bandwidth. Latency of communication reduces the convergence of the models.

Open Research Directions

- Update Compression: Methods such as quantization, pruning, and sketching minimize the size of updates with no loss of performance [22].
- Asynchronous Federated Learning: Clients synchronize models less often, which makes synchronization less expensive.
- Edge Caching and Model Distillation: Lightweight student models can substitute heavy global updates.

6.1.2 Non-IID and Imbalanced Data

Financial institutions are in the habit of dealing with non-independent and identically distributed (non-IID) data. Different geographies have diverse patterns of transactions. Small banks can possess small samples in relation to large institutions. Biased models are caused by data imbalance.

Open Research Directions:

- Personalized Federated Learning (PFL): Customizes global models to local needs of clients without having to exclude common knowledge [23].
- Domain Adaptation Techniques: Modify global models to local conditions.
- Data Rebalancing: Synthetic oversampling; weighted loss functions counteract imbalances in classes.

6.1.3 Model Robustness to Adversarial Attacks

FL systems can also be poisoned or attacked via inference as part of adversarial attacks on malicious clients that inject poisoned updates [24].

Open Research Directions:

- Byzantine-Resilient Aggregation: Strong algorithms (e.g., Krum, Bulyan) identify and block poisoned updates [25].
- Adversarial Training in FL: Training models trained on synthetic adversarial data increase resilience.
- Trusted Execution Environments: Secure computation enclaves but need hardware trust.

6.1.4 Scalability

Scalability is a sensitive issue with thousands of clients (banks, insurers, fintech firms) [26].

- The existing aggregation schemes have a problem with large client count.
- The involvement is hampered by resource limitations on edge devices.

Open Research Directions:

- Hierarchical FL: Multi-level aggregation (local to regional to global) enhances scalability.
- Federated Neural Architecture Search (NAS): Automates the design of models on resource-constrained devices.
- Hybrid Cloud-Edge FL: Strikes a compromise between rich data centers and thin clients.

6.1.5 Privacy–Utility Trade-Offs

More stringent privacy controls tend to impair the performance of the models [27].

- Differential privacy adds noise, which lowers accuracy.
- Homomorphic encryption and SMPC add high latency.

Open Research Directions:

- Adaptive Privacy Budgets: Privacy level dynamically adjusted to context.
- Hybrid Privacy Approaches: DP, HE, and SMPC complement each other.
- Utility-Aware Privacy Metrics: New models to measure accuracy and privacy.

6.2 Organizational and Governance Issues

6.2.1 Lack of Standardization

Varied financial institutions embrace diverse FL structures, and thus interoperability has proven to be challenging [28].

- Proprietary implementations curtail cross-institution cooperation.
- Absence of auditing standard makes compliance checks harder.

Open Research Directions:

- Federated Learning Standards: ISO like standards development in FL protocols.
- Open-Source Frameworks: More interoperable FL toolkits (e.g., TensorFlow Federated, PySyft).

6.2.2 Incentive Mechanisms

Institutions might not be willing to cooperate until there are advantages over disadvantages [29].

- Big banks could be able to provide more information, but also get equal reward as small participants.
- Threat of free riders who do not contribute.

Open Research Directions:

- Game-Theoretic Incentive Models: Incentives proportional to value of contribution.
- Tokenization Using Blockchain: Institutions get tokens in exchange of data/model contributions.

- Reputation-Based Systems: History trust is established based on past contributions.

6.2.3 Trust Between Participants

The lack of trust is the case when there is cooperation among competitors [30].

- Data inversion attack.
- Fear of unjust advantage in case one side alters the updates.

Open Research Directions:

- Zero-Knowledge Proofs (ZKP): Prove that you were correct without disclosing sensitive information.
- Decentralized FL: Eliminates the central aggregator, based on peer-to-peer or blockchain networks.
- Reputation and Accountability: Audits that are irrevocable build inter-institutional trust.

6.3 Regulatory and Legal Issues

6.3.1. Privacy Laws

FL should adhere to such regulations as GDPR (Europe), HIPAA (U.S.), and FATF (global AML standards) [31].

- The laws of data localization make cross-border cooperation complex.
- Regulators have no clear instructions on FL deployment.

Open Research Directions:

- Federated Regulatory Sandboxes: Joint tests between regulators and institutions.
- Auditable Privacy Certificates: Cryptographic attestations of compliance.
- Cross-Jurisdiction Frameworks: Internationalization of international privacy.

6.3.2 This Is Liability in Case of Breaches

In federated systems, liability does not clearly apply in case privacy breaches. Who bears responsibility—the aggregator, the clients, or the software vendor? Shared Models: The shared models confuse responsibility lines.

Open Research Directions:

- Liability Sharing Smart Contracts: Responsibility is defined by automated contracts.

- FL Insurance Mechanisms: Cyber-risk insurance designed to work with federated systems.

6.3.3 Ethical Considerations

FL may also serve to confirm biases accidentally, or construct opaque black-box models [33].

- Discriminatory results can be created by biased training data.
- Inability to explain lowers the confidence of regulators and customers.

Open Research Directions:

- Fairness-Conscious FL: Adding fairness restrictions to model training.
- Explainable Federated Learning (XFL): Increasing explainability of FL models.
- Ethical AI Governance: Policy-level fairness and responsibility.

6.4 Future Research Directions

Generalizing the challenges mentioned in the earlier text, the following research pathways that are of critical importance in the long term are:

- Privacy Performance Harmony: Making a compromise between high accuracy and strong privacy.
- Federated AI + Blockchain: FL with distributed ledgers to achieve trust and transparency.
- Cross-Sector Collaboration: Grow FL to healthcare, energy, and smart cities.
- Quantum-Resistant FL: Designing privacy protocols in the post-quantum world.
- Self-Adaptive FL Systems: Models that dynamically adapt to heterogeneity of clients and regulation.

6.5 Summary

Technical scalability, organizational trust, and regulatory compliance are the technical, organizational, and regulatory areas where challenges in adopting federated learning intersect in sensitive financial data. Although recent developments, such as DP, HE, and blockchain integration, solve aspects of the issue, new open research directions, such as fairness-aware FL, quantum-safe security, and ethical governance, will set the next stage. Finally, the effectiveness of FL in the financial industry will depend on joint innovation among technologists, policymakers, and stakeholders in the industry [34]. Model accuracy over training rounds is shown in Figure 5.

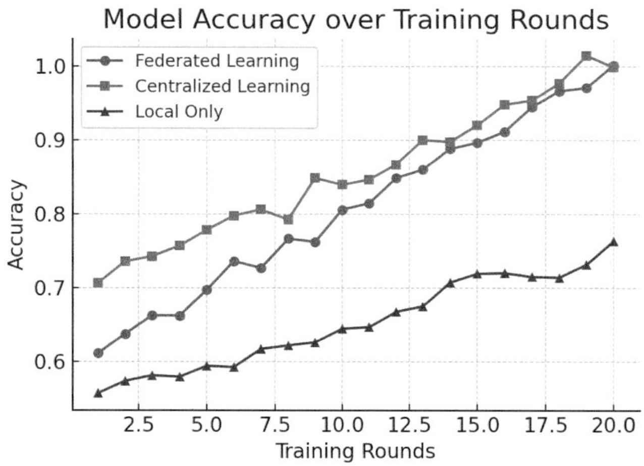

Figure 5: Model accuracy over training rounds (FL vs. centralized vs. local).

7. Conclusion

One of the most urgent issues in the context of digital transformation is the protection of sensitive financial data. Conventional centralized machine learning systems make organizations vulnerable to risk of information leakage, noncompliance with regulations, and adversarial exploitation. The power of federated learning paradigm has seen institutions cooperate with other institutions to develop a particular model, but they do not exchange raw data, thus improving privacy and security.

The chapter has examined the principles of FL, discussed privacy-aware methods including DP, HE, and SMPC, and suggested a framework/architecture specifically to financial services. Case studies have demonstrated that FL is successfully applicable in fields such as fraud detection, credit scoring, and risk assessment, which offers better accuracy, as well as high privacy assurance.

Although these advances have been made, a number of challenges are yet to be addressed. FL needs to solve problems of communication overhead, non-IID data distributions, scalability, and adversarial robustness. Organizational barriers such as inter-institutional trust, absence of standardization, and ambiguous liability structures are also of great importance. Moreover, adherence to the world privacy regulations and moral concerns on fairness and transparency are essential to sustainable adoption.

In the future, further developments on privacy–utility trade-offs, blockchain-based FL, quantum-resistant security schemes, and explainable federated models will determine FL in financial services. The meeting of technology, governance, and regulation will decide whether FL will live up to its invited functions as the de facto standard of secure collaborative learning in finance.

Finally, FL is not only a technological but also a strategic facilitator of privacy-sustaining digital transformation. Federated systems can be at the core of protecting sensitive financial information by promoting cross-industry cooperation and ongoing research, as well as open up a wider range of opportunities to innovate with data.

References

[1] Kairouz, P. and McMahan, H. B. (2021). Advances and open problems in federated learning. *Foundations and Trends in Machine Learning*, 14(1-2): 1–210.

[2] McMahan, B., Moore, E., Ramage, D., Hampson, S. and y Arcas, B. A. (2017, April). Communication-efficient learning of deep networks from decentralized data. In *Artificial Intelligence and Statistics* (pp. 1273–1282). PMLR.

[3] Bonawitz, K., Ivanov, V., Kreuter, B., Marcedone, A., McMahan, H. B., Patel, S. et al. (2016). Practical secure aggregation for federated learning on user-held data. *arXiv preprint arXiv:1611.04482*.

[4] Shokri, R. and Shmatikov, V. (2015, October). Privacy-preserving deep learning. In *Proceedings of the 22nd ACM SIGSAC Conference on Computer and Communications Security* (pp. 1310–1321).

[5] Gentry, C. (2009, May). Fully homomorphic encryption using ideal lattices. In *Proceedings of the Forty-First Annual ACM Symposium on Theory of Computing* (pp. 169–178).

[6] Dwork, C. (2006, July). Differential privacy. In *International Colloquium on Automata, Languages, and Programming* (pp. 1–12). Berlin, Heidelberg: Springer.

[7] Yang, Q., Liu, Y., Chen, T. and Tong, Y. (2019). Federated machine learning: Concept and applications. *ACM Transactions on Intelligent Systems and Technology (TIST)*, 10(2): 1–19.

[8] Hard, A., Rao, K., Mathews, R., Ramaswamy, S., Beaufays, F., Augenstein, S. et al. (2018). Federated learning for mobile keyboard prediction. *arXiv preprint arXiv:1811.03604*.

[9] Li, T., Sahu, A. K., Zaheer, M., Sanjabi, M., Talwalkar, A. and Smith, V. (2020). Federated optimization in heterogeneous networks. *Proceedings of Machine Learning and Systems*, 2: 429–450.

[10] Zhao, Y., Li, M., Lai, L., Suda, N., Civin, D. and Chandra, V. (2018). Federated learning with non-IID data. *arXiv preprint arXiv:1806.00582*.

[11] Mahavaishnavi, V., Prithviraj, R. and Saminathan, R. (2024). Digital divides and cyber security challenges: Bridging the socioeconomic gap in India. *National Seminar on Securing the Digital Frontier: Navigating Cyberspace Challenges in National Security.*

[12] Smith, V., Chiang, C. K., Sanjabi, M. and Talwalkar, A. S. (2017). Federated multi-task learning. *Advances in Neural Information Processing Systems*, 30.

[13] Papernot, N., Abadi, M., Erlingsson, U., Goodfellow, I. and Talwar, K. (2016). Semi-supervised knowledge transfer for deep learning from private training data. *arXiv preprint arXiv:1610.05755*.

[14] Konečný, J., McMahan, H. B., Ramage, D. and Richtárik, P. (2016). Federated optimization: Distributed machine learning for on-device intelligence. *arXiv preprint arXiv:1610.02527*.

[15] Pillutla, K., Sham M. Kakade and Zaid Harchaoui. (2022). Robust aggregation for federated learning. *IEEE Transactions on Signal Processing*, 70: 1142–1154.

[16] Choudhury, O. G., Gokulalas-Divanis, A., Salonidis, T., Sylla, I., Park, X., Hsu, G. et al. (2019). Differential privacy-enabled federated learning for sensitive health data. *arXiv preprint arXiv:1910.02578.*
[17] Bagdasaryan, E., Veit, A., Hua, Y., Estrin, D. and Shmatikov, V. (2020, June). How to backdoor federated learning. In *International Conference on Artificial Intelligence and Statistics* (pp. 2938–2948). PMLR.
[18] Zhou, C., Tian, H., Zhang, H., Zhang, J., Dong, M. and Jia, J. (2021, May). TEA-fed: Time-efficient asynchronous federated learning for edge computing. In *Proceedings of the 18th ACM International Conference on Computing Frontiers* (pp. 30–37).
[19] Yu, S. and Cui, L. (2022). Secure multi-party computation in federated learning. In *Security and Privacy in Federated Learning* (pp. 89–98). Singapore: Springer Nature Singapore.
[20] Zhang, C., Xie, Y., Bai, H., Yu, B., Li, W. and Gao, Y. (2021). A survey on federated learning. *Knowledge-Based Systems*, 216: 106775.
[21] Mohri, M., Sivek, G. and Suresh, A. T. (2019, May). Agnostic federated learning. In *International Conference on Machine Learning* (pp. 4615–4625). PMLR.
[22] Li, C., Li, G. and Varshney, P. K. (2021). Communication-efficient federated learning based on compressed sensing. *IEEE Internet of Things Journal*, 8(20): 15531–15541.
[23] Arivazhagan, M. G., Aggarwal, V., Singh, A. K. and Choudhary, S. (2019). Federated learning with personalization layers. *arXiv preprint arXiv:1912.00818.*
[24] Melis, L., Song, C., De Cristofaro, E. and Shmatikov, V. (2019, May). Exploiting unintended feature leakage in collaborative learning. In *2019 IEEE Symposium on Security and Privacy (SP)* (pp. 691–706). IEEE.
[25] Blanchard, P., Mhamdi, E. M. E., Guerraoui, R. and Stainer, J. (2017). Byzantine-tolerant machine learning. *arXiv preprint arXiv:1703.02757.*
[26] Xia, F. and Cheng, W. (2024). A survey on privacy-preserving federated learning against poisoning attacks. *Cluster Computing*, 27(10): 13565–13582.
[27] Boulila, W., Khlifi, M. K., Ammar, A., Koubaa, A., Benjdira, B. and Farah, I. R. (2022). A hybrid privacy-preserving deep learning approach for object classification in very high-resolution satellite images. *Remote Sensing*, 14(18): 4631.
[28] Rieke, N., Hancox, J., Li, W., Milletari, F., Roth, H. R., Albarqouni, S. et al. (2020). The future of digital health with federated learning. *NPJ Digital Medicine*, 3(1): 119.
[29] Kang, J., Xiong, Z., Niyato, D., Xie, S. and Zhang, J. (2019). Incentive mechanism for reliable federated learning: A joint optimization approach to combining reputation and contract theory. *IEEE Internet of Things Journal*, 6(6): 10700–10714.
[30] Kaur, S., Kaur, U. and Kumari, A. (2024, December). Decentralized blockchain-empowered federated learning for secure and scalable solutions for electronic health record. In *2024 Eighth International Conference on Parallel, Distributed and Grid Computing (PDGC)* (pp. 528–534). IEEE.
[31] Regulation, P. (2018). General data protection regulation. *Intouch*, 25: 1–5.
[32] Silveira, A. J. A. (2009). The international standards on combating money laundering: A brazilian perspective. *Paper, The George Washington University, Washington.*
[33] Barocas, S., Hardt, M. and Narayanan, A. (2023). *Fairness and Machine Learning: Limitations and Opportunities*. MIT Press.
[34] Zeleke, S. N. and Bochicchio, M. (2024). Towards Explainable Federated Learning in Healthcare: A Study on Heart Arrhythmia Detection.

Index

N

P

R

S

T

About the Editors

Dr. Suvarna Sharma is an accomplished academician, researcher, and author in the field of computer science and artificial intelligence. She currently serves as an assistant professor at MIT World Peace University, Pune, India. She earned her Ph.D. from Maulana Azad National Institute of Technology (MANIT), Bhopal, with doctoral research focused on improving web crawler coverage using intelligent seed selection techniques. She has over a decade of experience spanning academia, research, and software development, having held academic positions at reputed institutions including Chitkara University and MANIT, Bhopal, and having worked as a software developer at the Defence Research and Development Establishment (DRDE), Gwalior. Her research interests encompass web mining, machine learning, deep learning, blockchain technology, IoT, healthcare analytics, digital twins, federated learning, and intelligent systems. She has published extensively in leading IEEE conferences and Scopus- and Springer-indexed journals, and has contributed numerous book chapters with international publishers such as Springer, Wiley, CRC Press, and IGI Global. Dr. Sharma is the recipient of a Best Paper Award at an IEEE international conference and holds multiple patents in blockchain-based trust mechanisms and smart system designs. Actively engaged in academic service, Dr. Sharma serves as a reviewer for international conferences and journals and is a member of professional computing societies. Her work reflects a strong commitment to interdisciplinary research, innovation, and the advancement of emerging technologies through education and scholarly contribution.

Jeetendra Kumar holds a Ph.D. degree in computer science from GLA University Mathura. Currently, he has been working as an assistant professor in the Department of Computer Science and Application at Atal Bihari Vajpayee University, Bilaspur, Chhattisgarh, India for the last 13 years. He holds an M.Sc. and a Master of Technology (M.Tech.) degree in computer science. He has published various research articles in reputed journals and conferences, including topics such as sentiment analysis, fall detection using machine learning techniques, IoT applications, automatic question generation, etc. He has also contributed book chapters on topics related to neuroscience, smartphone applications, and fog computing in healthcare. He has edited one book with CRC Press (Taylor

& Francis). Dr. Kumar has completed two research projects sponsored by the State Planning Commission, Chhattisgarh, Commonwealth Media Centre for Asia (CEMCA), New Delhi, and Atal Bihari Vajpayee University, Bilaspur. He is also a member of prestigious academic societies such as IEEE, the Indian Science Congress, the International Association of Engineers (IAENG), the International Computer Science and Engineering Society (ICSES), and the International Association of Academicians (IAASSE).

Rashmi Gupta holds a Ph.D. degree in computer applications from the NIT, Raipur. Currently, she serves as an assistant professor in the Department of Computer Science and Application at Atal Bihari Vajpayee University, Bilaspur, Chhattisgarh. She has published more than 25 research papers, conference papers, and book chapters, and has been awarded grants by AICTE to organize the ATAL Faculty Development Program and by the Science and Engineering Research Board (DST) for conducting high-end workshops and internships. Demonstrating her commitment to mentorship, Dr. Gupta has guided over 30 PG and 20 UG students in their research-related major projects. She has edited two books with CRC Press (Taylor & Francis). With over 15 years of teaching experience, her research interests encompass natural language processing, EEG signal processing, and human activity recognition. She is also a member of prestigious academic societies such as IEEE, the Indian Science Congress, the International Association of Engineers (IAENG), the International Computer Science and Engineering Society (ICSES), and the International Association of Academicians (IAASSE).

Valentina E. Balas is currently a full professor in the Department of Automatics and Applied Software at the Faculty of Engineering, Aurel Vlaicu University of Arad, Romania. She holds a Ph.D. Cum Laude in applied electronics and telecommunications from Polytechnic University of Timisoara. Dr. Balas is author of more than 350 research papers in refereed journals and international conferences. Her research interests are in intelligent systems, fuzzy control, soft computing, smart sensors, information fusion, modelling, and simulation. She is the Editor-in-Chief to the International Journal of Advanced Intelligence Paradigms (IJAIP) and to the International Journal of Computational Systems Engineering (IJCSysE). She is a member in the editorial boards of several national and international journals and is an evaluator expert for national–international projects and Ph.D. theses. Dr. Balas is the Director of Intelligent Systems Research Centre in Aurel Vlaicu University of Arad and the Director of the Department of International Relations, Programs and Projects in the same university. She served as General Chair of the International Workshop on Soft Computing and Applications (SOFA) in nine editions organized in the period of 2005–2020 held in Romania and Hungary. Dr. Balas participated in many international conferences as an organizer, Honorary Chair, Session Chair, a member in Steering, Advisory or International Program Committees, and a keynote speaker. Recently, she was working on a national project with EU funding support—BioCell-NanoART (Novel Bio-inspired Cellular Nano-Architectures – For Digital Integrated Circuits), and 3M Euro from National Authority for Scientific Research and Innovation. She is a member of European Society for Fuzzy Logic and Technology (EUSFLAT), a member of Society for Industrial and Applied Mathematics (SIAM), a senior member of IEEE, a member in Technical Committee – Fuzzy Systems (IEEE Computational Intelligence Society), Chair of the Task Force 14 in Technical Committee – Emergent Technologies (IEEE CIS), and a member in Technical Committee – Soft Computing (IEEE SMCS). Dr. Balas was Vice President (responsible with awards) of IFSA (International Fuzzy Systems Association Council, 2013–2015), is a joint secretary of the Governing Council of Forum for Interdisciplinary Mathematics (FIM), a multidisciplinary academic body, India, and recipient of the "Tudor Tanasescu" Prize from the Romanian Academy for contributions in the field of soft computing methods, in 2019.

Dr. Gaurav Dhiman is a highly accomplished academician and researcher with an impressive track record of excellence in computer science. He holds a postdoctoral degree from Federal University of Ceara (Brazil), a PhD in computer engineering from Thapar Institute of Engineering & Technology, Patiala, and has also completed his master's degree in computer applications from the same institute. Currently, he is serving as an assistant professor in the School of Sciences and Emerging Technologies, Jagat Guru Nanak Dev Punjab State Open University, Patiala. His research has been recognized at the highest level, as he has been named among one of the world's top 1% highly cited researchers by Clarivate Analytics. He is also listed among world's top 2% scientists by Elsevier and Stanford University, USA. He is the senior member of IEEE. He has also received accolades for his outstanding reviewer work from Knowledge-Based Systems (Elsevier). He has authored over 300 peer-reviewed research papers, all of which are indexed in SCI-SCIE, and 15 international books. He is currently serving as a guest editor for more than 40 special issues in various peer-reviewed journals. He is the Editor-in-Chief of the ICCK Transactions on Machine Intelligence and ICCK Transactions on Large Language Models. He is an associate editor of IEEE Transactions on Industrial Informatics, IEEE Transactions on Consumer Electronics, IEEE Transactions on Computational Social Systems, IET Software (Wiley), Expert Systems (Wiley), IEEE Systems, Man, and Cybernetics Magazine, Spatial Information Research (Springer), and many more. He is also an academic editor of Computational and Mathematical Methods in Medicine (Hindawi), Scientific Programming (Hindawi), Mobile Information Systems (Hindawi), and Review Editor of Frontiers in Energy Research (Fuel Cells), Frontiers in High-Performance Computing (Parallel and Distributed Software), Frontiers in Artificial Intelligence (Pattern Recognition), and more. His research interests span a wide range of topics including generative artificial intelligence, large language models, Internet of Things, machine learning, deep learning, single-, multi-, and many-objective optimization (bio-inspired, evolutionary, and quantum), soft computing (type-1 and type-2 fuzzy sets), power systems, and change detection using remotely sensed high-resolution satellite data. He has published his research in various reputed journals, including IEEE, Elsevier, Springer, Wiley, Taylor and Francis, among others.